DIVIDED LOYALTIES: EAST GERMAN WRITERS AND THE POLITICS OF GERMAN DIVISION 1945–1953

DIVIDED LOYALTIES:
EAST GERMAN WRITERS
AND THE POLITICS OF
GERMAN DIVISION
1945–1953

PETER DAVIES

MANEY PUBLISHING
for the
MODERN HUMANITIES RESEARCH ASSOCIATION
and the
INSTITUTE OF GERMANIC STUDIES
UNIVERSITY OF LONDON SCHOOL OF ADVANCED STUDY
2000

Maney Publishing
for the
Modern Humanities Research Association
and the
Institute of Germanic Studies
University of London School of Advanced Study

HONORARY TREASURER, MHRA
KING'S COLLEGE LONDON, STRAND
LONDON WC2R 2LS
ENGLAND

ISBN 1 902653 21 1
ISSN (Bithell Series of Dissertations) 0266–7932

Produced in England by
MANEY PUBLISHING
HUDSON ROAD   LEEDS LS9 7DL   UK

CONTENTS

PREFACE

This work is the slightly revised version of a PhD thesis accepted by the University of Manchester in 1997.

I would like to thank my supervisors in Manchester, Dr. Stephen Parker and Professor John Elsworth, for their invaluable criticism, support and encouragement throughout the period of researching and writing this thesis. Thanks are also due to David Heath and the staff at the Sprachenzentrum of the Universität Erlangen-Nürnberg for their understanding and patience, and to the staff and students in the Departments of German and Russian at the University of Manchester, for their constructive comments and criticisms.

I am also indebted to the Editors of this series for accepting the dissertation for publication, as well as to Professor Ron Speirs for his recommendation.

NOTE ON TRANSLATION

For sources in Russian, I have referred to published English translations wherever possible. Where no English version was available, the translation is my own.

CHAPTER ONE

THE INVERSE PERSONALITY CULT

The Deutsche Akademie der Künste, founded on 12 March 1950, seemed bound up with contradictions from the very beginning. Many of its members believed passionately in the possibility of using the Academy to promote the unity of German culture, in line with the SED's declared 'Bündnispolitik'. These hopes came into conflict with the aggressive intentions of SED cadres, whose campaign to extend their influence in the Academy has been well documented.[1] At first glance, it might seem that those artists and intellectuals who held out against the division of German culture were swimming hopelessly against the tide of history, that all that was left for them was 'der Versuch, den Schaden zu begrenzen'.[2] Certainly, the Academy's failure to attract support in West Germany, and the increasing virulence of the attacks on 'formalist' art within the Academy itself, indicate that, by mid-1952, those making their bid for power at the price of irrevocable division were in the ascendancy.

The transformation of the SED's rhetoric of unity from the relatively inclusive concept of the 'antifaschistisch-demokratische Umwälzung', designed to attract democratically-minded people of all parties, to the idea of a German national culture which excluded all non-communists, has been exhaustively documented by David Pike.[3] Otto Grotewohl's inaugural speech at the Academy's foundation is a fine example of this rhetorical juggling: the emphasis is very much on 'Einheit und Souveränität der deutschen Nation', while at the same time what is expected of the artist is 'Parteinahme für das Volk'.[4] The dilemma in which committed artists found themselves is clear: the government, which they needed

---

[1] See *Zwischen Diskussion und Disziplin: Dokumente zur Geschichte der Akademie der Künste (Ost), 1945/1950 bis 1993*, ed. by Ulrich Dietzel and Gudrun Geißler (Berlin: Stiftung Archiv der Akademie der Künste, 1997) and *Die Regierung ruft die Künstler*, ed. by Petra Uhlmann and Sabine Wolf (Berlin: Akademie der Künste, 1993).

[2] Uhlmann and Wolf, p. 23.

[3] David Pike, *The Politics of Culture in Soviet-Occupied Germany 1945–1949* (Stanford: Stanford University Press, 1992).

[4] Cit. Uhlmann and Wolf, p. 125.

to fulfil their hopes of a unified German culture with an honest approach to the legacy of Nazism, seemed to be moving in the opposite direction.

However, Grotewohl's choice of words indicates that the time was not yet ripe for the creation of a body under the complete administrative control of the SED, although this was clearly the intention of the hard-line 'Kulturfunktionäre' in the Party from the start, the Academy was to provide 'die noch fehlende ideologische Führung der Künste'.[5] As I shall show in the course of this study, research into GDR cultural history has tended to take for granted that the rhetoric of unity was merely a smokescreen behind which the SED grouping around Johannes R. Becher and Alexander Abusch could gradually advance their cause. Becher's considerable efforts in the immediate post-war years to promote German cultural unity are seen as expedient rhetoric. This view is problematic inasmuch as it fails to take into account the very real turnaround in the Academy's affairs in June 1953, and relies on an interpretation of Stalin's foreign policy concerns which has come under serious challenge, both by German historians and by historians of the Soviet Union.

The key issue here is the seriousness with which we treat Stalin's declarations on German unity, particularly the offers contained in the notorious diplomatic notes of March and April 1952. Opinions have been divided on whether this represents a genuine missed opportunity, although without access to the most important Soviet archives, historians have had to rely on a certain amount of speculation. Inevitably, those interpretations which relied on the established view of Stalin as omnipotent dictator with megalomaniac designs on Western Europe formed an orthodoxy, and any challenge to that orthodoxy seemed naive, 'die schöpferische Strapazierung der historisch-politischen Phantasie'.[6] However, the 'common-sense' view of Stalin's rule has been subject to considerable revision for some years, and an assessment of the implications of this important debate for GDR cultural history will form a substantial part of this study. I will also show how this challenge is supported by the availability of

---

[5] Cit. Uhlmann and Wolf, p. 64.

[6] Hermann Graml, 'Die Legende von der verpaßten Gelegenheit', *Vierteljahrshefte für Zeitgeschichte*, 29 (1981), 307–41 (309).

primary sources from former SED archives and how these sources have changed the tone of the debates on German division.

Taking these developments into account, this study will take issue with the view which sees the administrative take-over of the Academy as inevitable, as the final expression of Stalin's will, transmitted through a monolithic chain of command reaching from Moscow through the SMAD (Sowjetische Militär-Administration in Deutschland) to a unified and purposeful SED. As we shall see, this view relies on an almost metaphysical image of Stalin, which inhibits a full understanding of '17 June' and its consequences for the development of GDR cultural policy.

Any intentionalist view of a 'totalitarian' society must be based on the ability of the rulers to transmit their commands efficiently down a hierarchical system designed especially for this purpose. Evidence of conflicts of interest and inefficiencies, which might at first glance invalidate the 'pure' version of this theory, can be accommodated into its framework by reference to, for example, Stalin's mastery of factional politics and his ability to play off his subordinates against each other. In this view, Stalin's rise to power is seen as the inevitable progress of a master tactician, with each step on the road having been carefully calculated in advance. This highly personalised interpretation of Soviet politics (excluding the wider functioning of society) has been under concerted challenge for many years, and it is remarkable that such a vigorous debate has made so little impression on historical writing about German division, which is even today largely preoccupied with the analysis of high-level diplomatic activity. Similarly, the take-over of GDR cultural institutions by aggressive SED cadres is viewed, with hindsight, as premediated and inevitable and a calculated part of overall Soviet strategy. The purpose of the following chapters of this study will be to turn this analysis on its head, arguing that inconsistencies in SED cultural policy cannot simply be explained away as tactical variants, being the product of deeper divisions in Soviet policy-making.

This raises the central question of the personal influence of Stalin on foreign policy and its implementation in Germany. That this question remains controversial is indicative of the continued importance of the *figure* of 'Stalin' as a symbolic presence, as the embodiment of certain principles which defined the limits of the orthodoxy in historical writing on the GDR. The task which confronts us here is to illustrate the function of this image of Stalin by demonstrating how our perception of the beginnings of the Cold War is radically shifted by a closer inspection of the Soviet hierarchies of command. Chapters Two and Three of this study will examine the current state of historical debate on German division, focussing especially on conflicting views of Stalin's personal role, and on the struggle for power between 'moderates' and 'hard-liners' in the KPD/SED; particular reference will be made to Rolf Badstübner and Wilfried Loth's edition of the notes taken by Wilhelm Pieck during meetings with Stalin and with other high-ranking Soviet officials.[7]

Reactions to Badstübner and Loth's analysis, which states, in short, that Stalin was somewhat unwilling to see the establishment of the GDR as a separate state, reliant on Soviet patronage, have, in some cases, verged on the hysterical:

Autoren, die auf die Diskrepanz zwischen westlichen Erwartungen und sowjetischer Praxis aufmerksam machten, bekamen gelegentlich zu hören, sie betrieben 'ambitioniertes Verfälschen' mit 'totaliär[er] Intention'.[8]

Even serious academic discussion of this thesis has occasionally taken on a more aggressive tone, demonstrating that there is more at stake here than at first meets the eye; note, for example, the sense of irritable condescension in the title of Gerhard Wettig's challenge to the work of Wilfried Loth.[9] This is representative of an unease which Slavists have already experienced:

The mental revolution in the former USSR has created difficulties for Western Slavists, who for a long time have seen themselves as high priests, privileged guardians of some arcane, though essentially static, mystery.[10]

Attacks on attempts to reassess the history of German division are evidence of this unease, betraying an unwillingness to examine what is taken for granted in

---

[7] Rolf Badstübner and Wilfried Loth, *Wilhelm Pieck: Aufzeichnungen zur Deutschlandpolitik 1945–1953* (Berlin: Akademie Verlag, 1994).

[8] Wilfried Loth, 'Die Historiker und die deutsche Frage', *Historisches Jahrbuch*, 122 (1992), 336–82 (369).

[9] Gerhard Wettig, 'Stalin: Patriot und Demokrat für Deutschland?', *Deutschland Archiv*, 28 (1995), 743–48.

[10] Rosalind Marsh, *History and Literature in Contemporary Russia* (London: Macmillan, 1995), p. 3.

the notion of 'Stalinism': 'Die gesamtdeutsche Alternative implizierte eine Infrage-stellung der unterdessen erreichten demokratischen Stabilisierung im Rahmen der Westintegration.' [11]

Perceptions of the issues involved in German division will owe as much to an internalised acceptance of the integration of the Federal Republic into transatlantic cultural and security structures and to the concomitant monolithic view of Soviet politics, as to impartial analysis of the evidence. Consequently, a view of Stalin emerges which depends to a great extent on the regime's own projection of the leader as the man in overall control of his country and of events in Europe. It is, in fact, the mirror image of the personality cult. Much modern Russian writing on Stalin has taken up this theme, concentrating on 'psychological' analyses of the Leader, rather than on broader socio-political contexts. [12] If, however, as Gábor Rittersporn suggests, it is necessary to make a 'distinction [...] between the main trend of Soviet history in the 1930s and Stalinism', [13] because the development of Soviet politics and social forces often conflicted with Stalin's personal intentions, then 'Stalinism' comes to mean little more than 'what Stalin was up to at any given time'. Use of the term 'Stalinism' in writing on German division, whether to describe an ideology, a system, or a political practice, tends to contain unanalysed, metaphysical elements which locate the writer in the symbolic system of Cold War discourse. However, as will be shown in Chapter Three, there are signs that the end of the Cold War is bringing about, all too slowly, significant changes in this discourse, necessitating an uncomfortable reassessment of the significance of the GDR in the development of German history.

STALIN AS NECESSARY CARICATURE

Any commentator wishing to take issue with a highly personalised view of a dictatorship requires complex arguments about power and authority, the internal dynamics of organisations and societies, and fundamental economic and

[11] Loth, 'Die Historiker und die deutsche Frage', p. 369.
[12] See, for example, Edvard Radzinsky, *Stalin* (London: Hodder and Stoughton, 1996).
[13] Gábor Rittersporn, 'Rethinking Stalinism', *Russian History*, 11 (1984), 343–61 (361).

structural issues. These arguments are opposed by what has become the common-sense view, namely that a dictator dictates. However, the work of researchers such as Gábor Rittersporn shows that this was far from the case, even within the Soviet Union itself: 'Cadres' implementation of policies according to their own interests amounted to a systematic and institutionalized obstruction of the prevailing line.'[14]

This analysis of the 1930s, a period often conceptualised as 'High Stalinism', that is, the historical moment at which Stalin's personal power is assumed to be at its height, finds strong echoes in Badstübner and Loth's documentation of the SED's failure to implement Stalin's German policy. Rittersporn's criticism of interpretations which 'equate the outcome of complicated socio-political processes with [Stalin's] supposed intentions' is salutary.[15]

The appeal to common sense can be seen in the responses to the thesis of Badstübner and Loth. Certain things are taken for granted: '[Loths] Einschätzung steht in diametralem Widerspruch zu allem, was über den sowjetischen Führer sonst bekannt ist.'[16] However, the amount which is *known* with any certainty about Stalin is still relatively small, his intentions are only 'vaguely known',[17] but Pieck's notes give us at least some idea of what he wanted. Nevertheless, the inverse personality cult allows historians to feel that they understand Stalin well enough to explain his behaviour, and the argument is crudely caricatured. No historian, least of all Loth, has described Stalin as entirely 'in eklatanter Weise führungs- und kontrollschwach' or as 'einen vertrottelten Boß'.[18]

This attitude seems to expose a need to preserve Stalin as the all-powerful figure of Cold War nightmares, which is itself a calculated caricature enabling any deeper examination of responsibility or freedom of action to be left aside. This caricature is always present when attempts are made to understand the Soviet system in terms of Stalin's personality, and it is this unanalytical element which performs the structuring function in the discourse of the Cold War. The disgust felt at Stalinism and at the crimes of the regime defines the discourse of

---

[14] Rittersporn, p. 347.
[15] Rittersporn, p. 343.
[16] Wettig, 'Stalin: Patriot und Demokrat', p. 743.
[17] Rittersporn, p. 361.
[18] Wettig, 'Stalin: Patriot und Demokrat', p. 744.

the analysis. Arch Getty provides an instructive analogy: 'Cancer researchers [...] cannot afford to let their possible repulsion for their subject become the vehicle for their research.'[19] Similarly, flaws in the work of many historians of the GDR will only be addressed when researchers lose the habit of 'rewriting history in the dialectical manner',[20] that is, overturning one set of received truths with another, and of personalising events in twentieth-century history in a way which would seem strikingly old-fashioned to historians of other periods.

The intentionalist model of Stalin's rule has certain useful aspects when not presented in such a simplified way, it is probably true, though even this is disputed, that Stalin exhibited 'an extraordinary degree of personal dominance, in any matters to which he desired to give his attention'.[21] Of course, dominance over subordinates is by no means the same as the ability to force things to go his way throughout the whole hierarchy of command, riven as it was with conflict, inefficiency, and sometimes downright disobedience. Thus, few researchers would now agree entirely with the statement that Stalin's 'besondere Stärke' lay in his ability, 'seinen Willen zunehmend auf totale Weise zur Geltung zu bringen'.[22]

The flaw in this argument is one which besets all models of authoritarian societies which depend on the 'will' of the leader. For Stalin's will to be brought to bear so completely, one must assume an all-embracing and smoothly functioning Party and State apparatus, but the obvious inefficiency of many of the mechanisms of Soviet rule leaves this in grave doubt. Researchers influenced by the 'totalitarian' paradigm often contradict themselves in their gleeful descriptions of these inefficiencies, their 'Umständlichkeit, Ausführlichkeit und Langsamkeit'.[23] This is hardly an appropriate instrument for the implementation of Stalin's will in Germany. The peaceful coexistence of contradictory views is another sign that anti-Stalinism has become the medium for historical interpretation.

---

[19] J. Arch Getty, 'The Politics of Stalinism', in *The Stalin Phenomenon*, ed. by Alec Nove (London: Weidenfeld and Nicolson, 1993), pp. 100–51 (p. 108).

[20] Sheila Fitzpatrick, 'Constructing Stalinism: Changing Western and Soviet Perspectives', in Nove, pp. 75–99 (p. 95).

[21] Alec Nove, 'Stalin and Stalinism: Some Introductory Thoughts', in Nove, pp. 1–38 (p. 35).

[22] Wettig, 'Stalin: Patriot und Demokrat', p. 744.

[23] Wettig, 'Stalin: Patriot und Demokrat', p. 746, on the Soviet Foreign Ministry.

Wettig also claims that Soviet and SED functionaries, face-to-face with the revered Stalin, were not capable, 'etwas völlig anderes nach oben zu berichten, als was feststehender allerhöchster Weisheit entsprach',[24] a point supported by Nove, who further states that Stalin's ability to dominate 'had to rely on information, proposals and suggestions from subordinates'.[25] Wettig suggests that adulation of Stalin meant that subordinates dismissed any information which might contradict his wisdom, while Nove points at the possible existence of conflicting agendas. In either case, since power in any meaningful sense depends not only on efficient obedience but also on accurate information, this picture of Stalin, in a cocoon of ignorance created by his own ideological limitations and personality cult, cedes points to Wettig's opponents. We are left with an absurd description of Stalinism as characterised by '*both* efficiency and inefficiency'.[26] Stalin has immense authority, but power, let alone 'total power', is more elusive; this distinction is central to my discussion in the second part of this study of the relationship of ideology with power in GDR cultural life.

The first part of this study is concerned with establishing a broad political and historical context, which is often lacking in analyses of GDR cultural life. An understanding of this context, and of the issues raised in contemporary debates on the nature of 'Stalinism' and on the bitter power struggles within the SED leading up to June 1953, is essential if we are to make sense of the actions and opinions of key figures in the GDR intellectual community, such as Johannes R. Becher, Bertolt Brecht and Peter Huchel. In the second part, the focus of the analysis will narrow, concentrating first on the nature of intellectual complicity in the Marxist-Leninist system, and then showing how certain intellectuals were able, within the institutional context of the Deutsche Akademie der Künste, to create spaces for resistance to the imposition of power structures which accelerated the division of German culture. Drawing on this analysis, the study will conclude with a series of individual cases, in order to demonstrate the ways in which members of the Academy were able to exploit its ambiguous

---

[24] Wettig, 'Stalin: Patriot und Demokrat', p. 748.
[25] Nove, p. 35.
[26] Henry Reichman, 'Reconsidering Stalinism', *Theory and Society*, 17 (1988), 57–90 (57).

institutional position to protect themselves, to a certain extent, against attacks from hard-liners within the SED.

CHAPTER TWO

SOVIET GERMAN POLICY AND THE STRUGGLE FOR STALIN'S SUCCESSION

Soviet policy towards the GDR was always a function of the latter's ambiguous position within the complex interplay of forces in Europe. The problem which faced the Soviet leadership was that attempts to use the GDR as a tool in European policy cut both ways. The role of the *Arbeiter- und Bauernstaat* as ultra-loyal industrial powerhouse and Eastern Bloc flagship clashed with the periodic necessity for a more open approach to West Germany. In other words, the demands of *Blockpolitik* and the temptations of *Westpolitik* pulled in fundamentally incompatible directions.

Another factor needs to be added to this nexus of forces: if Soviet policy had to tread a precarious tightrope between a situation where 'the brutality of Soviet control over Eastern Europe [could] detract from Soviet influence over Western Europe', and its opposite pole, where 'the search for influence over Western Europe through détente [could] bring instability to Eastern Europe',[1] then we can recognise a space where national governments, particularly in the GDR, were able to exert a certain amount of influence. This influence was generally brought to bear in stalling manoeuvres when relations between the FRG and the Soviet Union threatened to become too cordial. Even a moderate thaw in East-West relations was a potential threat to the GDR, simply because of the questions liable to be raised about the legitimacy of SED rule. The precariousness of the GDR was an uncomfortable reminder of the instability of the post-war settlement, characterised as it was by an astoundingly complex flux of forces which are obscured, rather than elucidated, by the model of the two monolithic opposing blocs. In a sense, the Berlin Wall was an attempt to give a physical expression to this model, the concrete embodiment of a political

---

[1] Pierre Hassner, 'Soviet Policy in Western Europe', in *Soviet Policy in Eastern Europe*, ed. by Sarah Meiklejohn Terry (New Haven: Yale University Press, 1984), pp. 290–97 (p. 294).

construction which obsessed both sides in the conflict, but which grossly oversimplified the situation on the ground.

One of these sources of ambiguity is the issue of cultural policy, notoriously nebulous in its attempt to define something which has a tendency to demonstrate the artificiality of borders. The bulk of this study is concerned with an examination of GDR cultural policy in the context of the contradictions in Soviet foreign policy, and with its role in the shifting discourse of German division. I intend to show how the practice of German culture, with particular reference to the Deutsche Akademie der Künste in the period leading up to 17 June 1953, resists the imposition of black-and-white judgements which reflect an internal-isation of the bipolar model of post-war Europe.

However, in order to provide a coherent context for the acrimonious debates surrounding the Deutsche Akademie der Künste and the 17 June 1953, it is necessary to examine the complex interaction of the major policy-makers in Moscow. With a fuller understanding of the conflicts which underlie Soviet foreign policy formation, it is possible to trace fundamental contradictions and confrontations down the complex hierarchies of command, allowing us to shed light on the mysterious twists and turns in SED cultural policy.

An analysis of this process, which takes into account both the questioning of the absolute authority of Stalin and the wealth of new evidence emerging from SED archives,[2] will inevitably involve a re-examination of orthodoxies, the principal one of which is the interpretation of Stalin's supposed intentions for Germany. Many analyses have relied on Milovan Djilas' famous 'Conversations' as clinching proof of Stalin's deliberate policy of integrating

---

[2] See, in particular, Norman Naimark, *The Russians in Germany. A History of the Soviet Zone of Occupation, 1945–1949* (Cambridge/MA: Belknap Press, 1995). See also Dietrich Staritz, 'Die SED, Stalin, und der "Aufbau des Sozialismus" in der DDR. Aus den Akten des Zentralen Parteiarchivs', *Deutschland Archiv*, 24 (1991), 686–700, and by the same author, 'The SED, Stalin and the German Question: Interests and Decision-Making in the Light of New Sources', *German History*, 10 (1992), 274–89. For a contrasting view of the same evidence, see Gerhard Wettig, 'Stalin and German Reunification: Archival Evidence on Soviet Foreign Policy in Spring 1952', *The Historical Journal*, 37 (1994), 411–19, and by the same author, 'Stalin: Patriot und Demokrat für Deutschland?' *Deutschland Archiv*, 28 (1995), 743–48. Further documentation providing some evidence of KPD freedom of action can be found in Peter Erler, Horst Laude and Manfred Wilke (eds), *'Nach Hitler kommen wir' Dokumente zur Programmatik der Moskauer KPD-Führung 1944/5 für Nachkriegsdeutschland* (Berlin: Akademie Verlag, 1994).

Soviet-occupied Germany into the Eastern Bloc,[3] while others have been based on a model which has Stalin standing above the various factional disputes.[4] Thus, 'he alone [...] could afford to deal realistically with "concrete factors"'.[5]

A careful analysis of the circumstances surrounding the division of Germany shows that, in this case at least, Stalin was too intimately involved with the factional disputes in the Politburo to be able to push through his own policy. The idea of Stalin floating above the manoeuvrings of his subordinates presupposes several things:

i) that Stalin could act and exert influence independently in international affairs;
ii) that he orchestrated the factional rivalries, and that he had a firm grasp on their eventual outcome;
iii) that he alone could rise above factional interests to consider foreign policy dispassionately; and
iv) that he, and he alone, established channels of direct communication with the leadership in the GDR (in a similar vein to his increasing tendency to resort to his personal secretariat in 1952, in an attempt to circumvent the Politburo, whose influence was to be seriously curtailed at the Nineteenth Party Congress).[6]

In many ways, the factors involved in the formation of Soviet policy are of more significance for developments in Germany than are the stated policies themselves, in the sense that policy pronouncements are the rhetorical statement

---

[3] See Milovan Djilas, *Conversations with Stalin* (London: Rupert Hart-Davis, 1962), p. 139: 'Stalin stressed [in Spring 1947] that Germany would remain divided: "The West will make Western Germany their own, and we shall turn Eastern Germany into our own state."'

[4] For example, Alan Bullock, *Hitler and Stalin: Parallel Lives* (London: HarperCollins, 1991), p. 1034. For similar treatments of the figure of Stalin, see Dmitri Volkogonov, *Triumf i Tragediya: I. V. Stalin, politicheskii portret*, (Moscow: Agenstvo pechati Novosti, 1989), and Edvard Radzinsky, *Stalin* (London: Hodder and Stoughton, 1996). The nature of the biographical project means that history is often personalised in a way which emphasises the overriding importance of Stalin's will. Radzinsky in particular refers to Stalin's German policy as 'playing with democracy' in a way which implies that he was in absolute command of events. Even if one feels that Stalin exercised absolute power within the Soviet Union, it is important not to transfer this assumption unquestioned into foreign policy matters.

[5] Gavriel Ra'anan, *International Policy Formation in the USSR: Factional 'Debates' during the Zhdanov-shchina*, (Hamden/Conn.: Archon, 1985), p. 116.

[6] See Werner Hahn, *Post-war Soviet Politics: The Fall of Zhdanov and the Defeat of Moderation, 1946–1953* (Ithaca, NY: Cornell University Press, 1982), p. 145.

of the temporary victory of a group or coalition in the leadership, or of a precarious balance of forces. It is the *processes* which matter, since Soviet and SED attitudes to the division of Germany, and thus to cultural policy, are determined to a large extent by the interaction of rival fiefdoms, which spill over into the European arena. For this reason, the following analysis will attempt to take apart and re-examine the above mentioned components of the 'pyramid' which has Stalin at its apex.

The following qualifications will emerge in the course of this analysis:

i) Stalin undoubtedly guarded foreign policy jealously from his subordinates,[7] but in reality he relied on the support of particular factions in order to be able to push through his ideas. His German policy was made in opposition to the Zhdanovite line, which explains the contradictions and prevarications in Soviet attitudes to Germany.

ii) Stalin understood himself in the same way as the outside world saw him, as the apex of a pyramid of command, skilfully manipulating his subordinates in order to minimise the threat to himself. In actual fact, this was the case only to a certain extent,[8] and we must be careful to guard against 'concluding from the mere fact of [purges of high party officials] that Stalin's murderous machinations were at work'.[9] The analysis which emerges from Loth and Badstübner's work shows that Stalin's German policy was thwarted by the incessant demands of political infighting.

iii) Following from this, we can conclude that the positions of Beria and Malenkov on German policy were formed as a result of their roles in Soviet economic and political life, and are therefore not the result of some European 'vision'. Their opposition to the factions around Zhdanov, and later Khrushchev,

---

[7] See Khrushchev's account in *Khrushchev Remembers* (London: Sphere, 1971), tr. by Strobe Talbot, p. 326. Khrushchev describes Stalin's snarling rejection of advice. This indicates not, as Khrushchev disingenuously implies, that Stalin was able to maintain foreign policy as his own preserve, but Khrushchev's covetousness towards this kind of influence. In fact, Stalin's subordinates, especially Zhdanov, were busy exerting their own personal influence on foreign affairs, and this is doubtless the cause of the Leader's jealous rages.

[8] For a useful comparison, see Gábor Rittersporn's treatment of the Great Purges: *Stalinist Simplifications and Soviet Complications: Social Tensions and Political Conflicts in the USSR, 1933–1953* (Reading: Harwood, 1991). Rittersporn develops a model whereby campaigns which start in the leadership soon run out of control on the ground, and have to be reined in.

[9] Rittersporn, *Stalinist Simplifications*, p. 11.

explains the urgency of debates over policy. However, it would be wrong to suggest that the German policy of Stalin himself is totally dependent on this infighting; Stalin's continuing German policy shows a certain independence of thought, if not necessarily of action, in his analysis of the Soviet Union's long-term interests as they appeared in the late Forties and early Fifties. Naturally, this analysis is conducted within a set of ideological preconceptions which limit and define its terms, and so one must be careful with words like 'vision', which imply a detachment from day-to-day politics and ideology, and which carry echoes of the personality cult.

iv) Stalin had regular contact with the SED leadership, both in person and through the offices of the SMAD, and so it would seem that he could bring direct influence to bear on them. However, a close analysis of the contradictory actions of the SMAD and SED, with particular reference to the SED's declared *Bündnispolitik* and cultural policy, reveals that the conflicts of interest extend further down the chains of command than has previously been assumed. The idea of Stalin's direct influence on a unified SED leadership is illusory: there are conflicting interests within the SMAD and SED owing allegiance to, or sharing common goals with, other patrons, notably Beria and Zhdanov. This conflict can be traced through the various hierarchies of command to a point where they inform the debates surrounding and within the *Deutsche Akademie der Künste*. It will become clear that it was not so much the fact of direct communication between Stalin and the SED leadership which led to the demise of the all-German policy, as the carefully-fostered illusion of Walter Ulbricht as Stalin's 'represent-ative on earth'. This illusion is particularly important in the field of cultural policy, as it contributed to the isolation and eventual defeat of those politicians and intellectuals who were working for the unity of German culture.

The imagined immediacy of the connection between the SED leadership and Stalin has had further consequences in German historical writing, in that this illusion remains as a structuring given, an element largely taken for granted in a system of interpretation, in the work of those writers who have relied on the traditional view of Stalin's intentions towards the GDR. The following discussion will set the context for an examination of the all-German policy and misinterpretations of it by dealing with the problematic areas mentioned above, and by providing an overview of domestic Soviet political developments. In the course of this analysis, it will become clear that Stalin's handling of his German policy was, due to a combination of circumstance, opposition and personal limitations, far from 'masterly'.[10]

INTERNAL TENSIONS AND CONFLICTS IN THE POST-WAR SOVIET UNION

As the Soviet Union emerged from the Second World War, a new political constellation emerged with it. The demands of war had shifted the emphasis of social relations from an ideology of triumphalist proletarianism to the imposition of disciplined hierarchies and the creation of a competent technical intelligentsia. In fact, the 'virtual civil war'[11] in the Party-State had come to an end in 1939, with measures to create a privileged managerial class and 'the definitive elimination of any real possibility for subordinates to control the activities of their hierarchical superiors'.[12] New forms of social solidarity emerged during the war, and the regime needed to find new ways of imposing its authority without a return to the disastrous mass terror of the 1930s.

As we shall see, the *zhdanovshchina* (the post-war purges of Soviet cultural life), although vicious, did not spread beyond a certain well-defined section of the intelligentsia, as it was largely a matter of Zhdanov's attempt to reassert the primacy of his ideological *apparat*. Since it was not the all-embracing clampdown which is generally envisaged under the term 'Zhdanovism', purely coercive measures cannot explain the success of the reimposition of control.

Vera Dunham analyses post-war developments in terms of a tacit deal with the *meshchanstvo* (loosely translatable as 'middle-classes', with added associations of philistinism and acquisitiveness) in which the regime allowed a certain freedom to the materialistic aspirations of managers, technicians and their

---

[10] Bullock, p. 1030.

[11] Rittersporn, *Stalinist Simplifications*, p. 321.

[12] Rittersporn, *Stalinist Simplifications*, p. 320.

families.[13] In short, in a seemingly paradoxical attempt to disrupt the social bonds forged during the war, the government tried to create the private citizen. This movement marked the completion of the transformation of the Bolshevik Party from a revolutionary movement into a conservative ruling elite.

In Dunham's view, this policy produced a reversal in the age-old tension between the Russian intelligentsia, whose self-definition is directed outwards in a concern with social action, and the *meshchanstvo*, which 'does not fret except about private matters'.[14] The ascetic values of the intelligentsia had been uppermost in the literary culture of the Thirties, and the regime now had to find ways of producing a profound cultural change while seeming not to contradict the rhetorical orthodoxy which 'remained committed to combating the very principle of individual acquisitiveness'.[15] In the end, the economic situation and accelerated defence spending at the onset of the Cold War precluded any significant development of consumer-based industries, and it was in novels and plays, rather than in actual material objects, that these materialistic aspirations found their expression.

In our context, however, it is the regime's deliberate exploitation of the tension between intelligentsia and *meshchanstvo* which has the greatest resonance:

The intelligentsia [...] is capable of remembering its past. At times, it is inclined to do so openly, causing friction with the rulers. In this respect, *meshchanstvo* is happily blind. It knows no past. It sprouts anew at each juncture of social stabilization. Eminently visible, it does not plot. It has nothing to conceal. It is, therefore, manageable.[16]

This is reflected in a change in the social climate in the Soviet Union: the war had given rise to a situation where the enemy was an easily identifiable Other, rather than the hidden denouncer, family member or workmate, whose potential

---

[13] Vera Dunham, *In Stalin's Time: Middleclass Values in Soviet Fiction* (Durham: Duke University Press, 1990).

[14] Dunham, p. 20.

[15] Dunham, p. 40.

[16] Dunham, p. 20.

presence was felt in those aspects of life with which the citizen identified.[17] This re-formed self-consciousness brought a new sense of security in the private sphere, a comforting restrictiveness with an 'awareness of borders and distances'.[18] This provided fertile ground for the growth of a new chauvinism.

At the high point of Zhdanov's ideological campaign, Soviet culture is adjudged to have reached a plateau of *moral* superiority, entitling it to be exported as an example to the rest of the world: '[Soviet culture] possesses the right to instruct others in the new human morality.'[19] This assumption of the right to *sovietise* the cultures of the countries occupied by the Red Army has perhaps not been given the attention it deserves, because it has always been taken for granted as a 'Stalinist' tactic. If, however, we consider GDR cultural life in the light of this struggle between memory and forgetting, between outlooks conceptualised here as belonging to the 'intelligentsia' and the '*meshchanstvo*', the 'significant ambiguities' which arose in the post-war Soviet Union where 'the marxist-leninist-stalinist dogma was blending with the larger national purpose',[20] are multiplied in the imposition of control in Germany. In the case of the GDR, the ambiguities in Soviet cultural policy deepen significantly, as an examination of the consequences of factional in-fighting in the Soviet Communist Party shows. As will be shown below, the 'Zhdanovite' approach to the Soviet Zone in Germany was not by any means identical with Stalin's approach, nor with the aspirations of a significant group in the ranks of the SED.[21]

In order to legitimise its rule, the SED needed to adapt for its own purposes the Soviet tactic of demonising a common enemy, and yet to include, under the terms of the *Bündnispolitik*, the broadest possible spectrum of left-leaning sympathisers. As the 'integrationist' tendency began to gain the upper hand in

---

[17] See John and Carol Garrard, *Inside the Soviet Writers' Union* (London: Tauris, 1990), pp. 61ff., and Evgeni Dobrenko, 'Sumerki kul'tury: o natsional'nom samoznanii kul'tury pozdnego stalinizma', *Druzhba Narodov*, 2 (1991), 249–71.

[18] Dobrenko, p. 250. Unless otherwise stated, all translations from the Russian are my own.

[19] Zhdanov, in *Sokrashchennaya obobshchennaya stenogramma dokladov t. Zhdanova na sobranii partiinogo aktiva i na sobranii pisatelei v Leningrade*, August 1946, cit. Dobrenko, p. 251.

[20] Dunham, p. 7.

[21] This line, associated with Walter Ulbricht, gained strength in Germany even after Zhdanov's death and the purge of his supporters.For the period after Zhdanov's death, I will use the term 'integrationist' to refer to the tendency within the SED which hoped to preserve its position by ensuring the integration of the GDR into the Soviet Bloc.

the late Forties, the rhetorical definition of the enemy shifted from the vestiges and legacy of Nazism in the whole of Germany to a simplified politics of opposition to the West. The creation of rhetorical boundaries was absolutely essential for the SED's retention of power and influence, since it would have been doomed to electoral failure in any all-German elections. That this development clashed with Stalin's plans for Germany seemed unlikely to those Germans who opposed division, and we should not underestimate the psychological difficulties which the progressive abandonment of the *Bündnispolitik* caused for individuals concerned to make an honest confrontation with Nazism and a principled criticism of both capitalism and Soviet power.

The SED's policy of creating an 'intelligentsia',[22] a flattering but alien concept imported into German culture, as a privileged social stratum deliberately recalls the Soviet strategy of encouraging a blindness to the past, so that an independent, critical stance is exchanged for a series of privileges and the promise of social effectiveness. The sense of solidarity which opponents of Nazism had developed during the years of struggle was very different from the solidarity which the SED needed to create in its demonisation of the West, the former questioning and uncertain, with a sense of loss and responsibility, searching not for 'eine Versöhnung unvereinbarer Gegensätze', but for 'einen modus vivendi der Gegen-sätze',[23] the latter wedded to the Marxist-Leninist rhetoric ingrained since the 'bolshevisation' of the KPD in the 1920s. It is unfortunate for Stalin's conception of the post-war settlement that the uncompromising instinct for power which had been drummed into unprincipled KPD functionaries such as Walter Ulbricht proved counterproductive in the unforeseen circumstances of 1945. This is further evidence of the need to question established assumptions about 'Stalinism'; in this case, Stalin's flexibility over the German Question is thwarted by the dogmatism of functionaries trained in his name.

---

[22] See John Torpey, *Intellectuals, Socialism and Dissent. The East German Opposition* (Minneapolis: University of Minnesota Press, 1995).

[23] Alfred Kantorowicz, on his journal *Ost und West*, in Gerhard Hay, Hartmut Rambaldo and Joachim Storck, *Als der Krieg zu Ende war. Literarisch-politische Publizistik 1945–1950* (Stuttgart: Metzler, 1973), p.510.

The kind of solidarity and sense of responsibility felt by left-leaning intellectuals was dangerous, since it implied both a critical attitude to power and an open-minded willingness to approach politics and culture in an all-German, indeed pan-European, dimension. The threat which this posed for those within the SED who took the 'integrationist' line, represented chiefly by Walter Ulbricht, was not a product of some 'Stalinist' paranoia about culture, but had acute political relevance in view of Stalin's desire to jettison the Soviet Zone. It is therefore of vital importance to recognise that the viability of the GDR and the hold on power of those who wanted to accelerate integration into the Soviet sphere rested on an attempt to create an antagonism to the West *qualitatively* different from the democratic and socialist aspirations of many left-leaning artists and political figures. It is a mistake made by many Western commentators to assume that it is all a matter of degree, and that there was no space for independent action or thought.

STALIN'S HEIRS APPARENT

The ambiguities and contradictions in the implementation of the all-German policy seem so inexplicable when viewed without a broader perspective that many commentators have denied that they were contradictions at all. Instead, they are seen as tactical variants of Soviet policy towards Germany, thus allowing all developments to be simplified and traced back to their putative source: Stalin. Once again, an undifferentiated picture of 'Stalin' gives a distorted view of the period. A closer look at the struggle for power in the Politburo of the Soviet Communist Party can provide a much clearer picture of the significance of cultural policy development in the Soviet Zone/GDR, subjecting the established model to a radical re-examination.

Of course, this raises important questions of command and causality, and one must be careful to avoid simply reallocating 'the blame' for German division, with the obvious danger of substituting one opaque, taken-for-granted element for another. Perhaps the interaction of the various factors can be best described as a causal network, where the conflicts of factions within the Soviet Party stand in a complex reciprocal relationship with the changing social conditions in the post-war Soviet Union. These processes and conflicts now interact with the forces at work in Germany, where the chaotic situation after the capitulation seems to allow for any number of different outcomes. The key concepts of freedom of action and political/artistic responsibility can help to bring some kind of clarity to our interpretation. The focus of this study is therefore shifted from allotting blame, which implies the exaggeration of an individual's capacity to influence events, to identifying areas of potential freedom of action and issues of complicity and resistance in the defeat of the all-German cultural policy and the eventual, incomplete victory of the 'Zhdanovite' or 'integrationist' line.

This line originated in the jockeying for position between rival ministries and the fundamental change in the always strained relationship between the party and government *apparat* brought about by the demands of war. The emergence of a new class of technical managers favoured the economic ministries over the ideological apparatus, boosting Malenkov at the expense of his arch-rival Zhdanov. This rivalry provided the fundamental dynamic of policy formation in these years, as older Politburo members, such as Voroshilov, Andreyev and Mikoyan, were increasingly excluded from decision-making.

In late 1944, Malenkov had been placed in charge of the Committee for the Rehabilitation of the Economy of Liberated Areas.[24] The committee was set up by the Council of People's Commissars to oversee the extraction of reparations from the Soviet Zone through the dismantling of industrial capacity.[25] This made Malenkov a natural ally of Beria, whom Stalin had placed in charge of the Soviet nuclear programme[26] and whose NKVD 'economic enterprises' stood to benefit, and of Kaganovich, head of the Ministry of Construction.[27] In the rush to build a nuclear device, Beria relied on the exploitation of German uranium mines, and

---

[24] Amy Knight, *Beria: Stalin's First Lieutenant* (Princeton: Princeton University Press, 1993), p. 143. Also Susan J. Linz (ed.), *The Impact of World War II on the Soviet Union* (Totowa: Rowman & Allanheld, 1985), particularly the chapter by Robert M. Slusser, 'Soviet Policy and the Division of Germany, 1941–1945', pp. 107–25.

[25] Caroline Kennedy-Pipe, *Stalin's Cold War. Soviet Strategies in Europe, 1943–1956* (Manchester: Manchester University Press, 1995), p. 95.

[26] Knight, p. 138. See the chapter, 'The Soviet Use of German Science', in Naimark, pp. 205–50, and David Holloway, *Stalin and the Bomb: The Soviet Union and Atomic Energy, 1939–1956* (New Haven: Yale University Press, 1994), pp. 109–12, for an account of Beria's involvement.

[27] Kennedy-Pipe, p. 96.

it was therefore in his interest to avoid having to deal with an independent, or even nominally independent, Communist government. The survival of Beria and Malenkov had come to depend at least partially on their ability to assert a German policy which favoured their respective economic interests. It seems likely that the complex foreign policy calculations which obsessed Stalin meant little to them: indeed, Amy Knight demonstrates that Beria's programme after Stalin's death 'aimed at undermining the Stalinist system',[28] which would have led to dangerous instability both within the Soviet Union and among its European satellites.

It was considerations such as these which would motivate the enemies of Beria and Malenkov, and which provided the impetus for the *zhdanovshchina*. Mishandling of the dismantling programme in Germany resulted in 'chaos and wastage',[29] and was subject to a devastating campaign of orchestrated criticism by Zhdanov, which led to Malenkov's removal from the Party Secretariat in May 1946, a devastating blow for a man regarded as a cadre specialist.[30] Zhdanov, as the rising star of the Politburo, was able to place his own protégés in influential positions in Germany, and transfer responsibility for reparations from the economic ministries to his sphere of influence in the SMAD, effectively ending dismantling of German industry[31] and hastening the establishment of independent East German statehood. This contributed to a set of conditions in which those pressing for unification, for whatever reason, were swimming against the tide.

Zhdanov's agenda, and the success or failure of his campaigns, have been the subject of much debate; the ambiguity of his positions and motivation is confusing until one recognises that the *zhdanovshchina* was merely a 'function of political manoeuvring'.[32] The ideological crackdown which followed Zhdanov's short-lived triumph affected only the arts, the media and the party-state *apparat*, leaving the sciences, economics, philosophy and wider social institutions largely unaffected. It was a highly pragmatic campaign, intended to

---

[28] Knight, p. 9.
[29] Kennedy-Pipe, p. 97.
[30] Hahn, p. 12.
[31] Knight, p. 144.
[32] Hahn, p. 10.

consolidate Zhdanov's position in a highly visible way, facilitating a thorough purge of the Central Committee apparatus in 1946.

It was Zhdanov who announced the new hard-line Soviet foreign policy at the conference of the Cominform in 1947. This was the famous 'two camps' speech, which seemed to cement the division of Europe into Soviet and Western spheres of influence. The importance of the 'two camps' thesis for East German politics lies, however, in the ambiguity of Zhdanov's statements, which describe political and ideological constellations, rather than simply geographical divisions:

A new constellation of political forces has emerged [...] two general directions stand out in post-war international politics [...] the imperialistic and antidemocratic camp on one side, and the antiimperialistic and democratic camp on the other.[33]

The gradual abandonment of the SED's declared all-German policy marks the reinterpretation of the thesis in the Soviet Zone from an expression of ideological conflict into an expression of geographical division. Words such as 'direction' (*napravleniye*) encapsulate precisely this ambiguity, which allowed less dogmatic intellectuals in the Eastern part of Germany to be manoeuvred into positions of weakness in their confrontation with the 'integrationist' line.

Werner Hahn asserts that Zhdanov favoured consumer spending over defence industries, and that the militant foreign policy announced in September 1947, was forced on him by opponents who were using accusations of ideological laxness to undermine him:

Even though he announced the two camps thesis, Zhdanov may have suffered for his earlier enthusiasm for détente and consumerism during this period when Stalin swung to hostility toward the West and placed renewed stress on defense [...] [Zhdanov's] September 1947 Cominform speech may have been more a reflection of the Soviet leadership's position than of Zhdanov's own preferences.[34]

---

[33] Speech to the 1947 conference in *The Cominform. Minutes of the Three Conferences, 1947/1948/1949*, ed. by Giuliano Procacci (Milan: Fondazione Giangiacomo Feltrinelli, 1994), pp. 224f.. See also W. O. McCagg Jr., 'Domestic Politics and Soviet Foreign Policy at the Cominform Conference in 1947', *Slavic and Soviet Series*, vol. 2, no. 1, Spring 1977, pp. 3–31.

[34] Hahn., p. 25.

The situation, especially with regard to the role of Zhdanov, is unclear, and there is certainly still room for interpretations in which Stalin's line in foreign affairs is 'more cautious and less ebullient'[35] than Zhdanov's. A full account of the Politburo manoeuvrings in the years up to Stalin's death would fill a volume in its own right;[36] for our purposes, it is important to show how foreign policy was made in the context of conflicting European fiefdoms, largely fuelled by intense resentment towards Zhdanov as the assumed 'heir apparent'in early 1947.[37] This has a profound effect on our understanding of German division, as it enables us to see how the 'integrationist' line was able to establish itself in Germany and survive beyond Zhdanov's death (31 August 1948). A further degree of complex-ity is added to our view of cultural policy in the GDR, as we are no longer able to use the word 'Zhdanovism' as a simple conceptualisation of the imposition of Socialist Realism in the GDR. Use of the term implies, i) that Zhdanov ordered the ideological crackdown, ii) that positions of extreme ideological dogmatism should always be associated with his name, iii) that there is a direct correlation between the post-war ideological crackdown in the USSR and the imposition of Socialist Realism in the GDR, and iv) that this was a consistently implemented policy of the Soviet government, that is, that 'Stalin apparently backed Zhdanov's policy'.[38] That this model of direct, consistent Soviet influence on GDR cultural policy is false will become even clearer with further exploration of the various hierarchies of command. The concept of 'Zhdanovism', when used in the German context, performs a similar simplifying function to 'Stalinism', allowing models of Soviet influence to be constructed which are in fact not suited to the complexities and ambiguities of the situation.

Many of the members of the Politburo cultivated protégés to represent their interests within local Communist governments; for example, Beria's relationship

[35] Ra'anan, p. 116.

[36] For further reference, see also Leonard Schapiro, *The Communist Party of the Soviet Union* (London: Methuen, 1970); Robert Conquest, *Power and Politics in the USSR: The Study of Soviet Dynastics* (London: Macmillan, 1961); Victor Baras, 'Beria's Fall and Ulbricht's Survival', *Soviet Studies*, 27 (1975), 381–95; Moshe Lewin, 'Byurokratiya i stalinizm', *Voprosy Istorii*, 3 (1995), 16–28; Yurii N. Zhukov, 'Bor'ba za vlast' v rukovodstve SSSR v 1945–1952 godakh', *Voprosy Istorii*, 1 (1995), 23–39; and A. M. Filitov, *Germanskii vopros: ot raskola k ob''edineniyu* (Moscow: Mezhdunarodnye otnosheniya, 1993), for an interesting view of the German Question from the perspective of post-Soviet historical reassessment.

[37] Hahn, p. 60.

[38] Knight, p. 145.

with the GDR security police was to contribute to the attempts to overthrow Walter Ulbricht in the Summer of 1953. Zhdanov's vast ambition led him to far grander schemes than his rivals, arousing Stalin's suspicious nature. Stalin sheltered Zhdanov's opponents during the latter's ascendancy,[39] but it is hard to avoid the impression that the Leader was not in total control of his heir.

Zhdanov overreached himself by going further than simple patronage and influence; instead, he wanted to create a European fiefdom, 'a German communist leadership which, once in control, would be obligated to him [...] and would have the local resourses to avoid the necessity of recourse to (possibly hostile factions in) Moscow'.[40] There is some evidence that he cultivated officers in the SMAD, notably Colonel Tyul'panov, the head of the Information Administration who exerted an influence on the 'integrationist' tendency in the KPD/SED.[41] This could only work in favour of SED hard-liners like Walter Ulbricht.

With this in mind, and with our current understanding of Stalin's plans for Germany, it is necessary to modify considerably Hahn's assertion that the militant foreign policy was not favoured by Zhdanov: the forcible integration of the GDR into the Soviet Bloc seems to be the only conceivable way of protecting his own factional interests there. This power game, combined with the rapid escalation of Cold War tensions, ensured that the SED was entrenched in power. However, the fact that their hold on power was guaranteed to a large

---

[39] In particular, Beria was able to ensure that enough uranium was taken from Germany to sustain the nuclear programme: Knight, p. 144, and Norman Naimark, *The Russians in Germany: A History of the Soviet Zone of Occupation 1945–1949* (Cambridge, Mass. and London: Belknap Press of Harvard University, 1995) pp. 207–14.

[40] Ra'anan, p. 94.

[41] The role of Tyul'panov, and the nature of his informal activities in cultivating a particular policy direction within the SED, have been a key issue in recent debates, focussing on the wealth of new information which is emerging from Soviet and GDR archives. For an analysis of the work and structure of the SMAD, see Jan Foitzik, 'Sowjetische Militäradministration in Deutschland (SMAD)', in Martin Broszat and Hermann Weber (eds), *SBZ-Handbuch* (Munich: R. Oldenbourg, 1993), pp. 7–69. While acknowledging that Tyul'panov was a charming exception to the rank-and-file Soviet functionaries, Foitzik has found no evidence for his particular importance: 'Dennoch war seine Bedeutung in der SMAD-Hierarchie geringer als vielfach angenommen' (p. 23). However, Norman Naimark asserts that Tyul'panov's role was considerably more significant than this, and that he played the role of an informal political fixer: 'With Tyul'panov in the zone, Stalin kept his options open' (Naimark, p. 352). See also the documentation in Norman Naimark, Bernd Bonwetsch and Gennadii Bordyugov (eds), *SVAG: Upravlenie propagandy (informatsii) i S. I. Tyul'panov, 1945–1949: Sbornik dokumentov* (Moscow: Rossiya Molodaya, 1994). Tyul'panov's role will be discussed in greater detail Chapter Three of this study.

extent by the state of factional disputes in Moscow which were reflected in the power struggles within the SED itself, demonstrates that the SED's position, and particularly the dominance within the party of the 'integrationist' line, was not as secure as it might at first seem.

THE FALL OF ZHDANOV

On 14 August 1946, Zhdanov had just reached the apex of his power. The decree concerning the journals *Leningrad* and *Zvezda* was to unleash the purge which fatally upset the precarious Politburo balance with Malenkov and his supporters, so that by early 1947 Zhdanov seemed unassailable. However, this was his last major action which represented a political gain; though the evidence is ambiguous, as we have seen, it is clear that Zhdanov was losing political ground by the time he came to declare the Soviet Union's hardening Cold War line in September 1947.

East-West confrontation had come to seem inevitable, although it seems difficult to portray Stalin's German policy in these years as in any way consistent. It is only possible to detect consistency, or masterful forward planning, in these years if one ignores the obvious contradiction between Stalin's hard line in 1947/48 and the evidence of his desire to jettison the Soviet Zone in Germany. A complex combination of political processes, along with the exposure of the severe limitation of Stalin's ability to exert a *personal* influence on events in Germany, were forcing the fulfilment of his long-term goals further into the future. Thus, it is perfectly possible for the collective Politburo hard line to be simultaneously a means of isolating Zhdanov,[42] an expression of the worsening international situation, and a tool which Stalin hoped would gain him leverage in his drive for a united Germany. This seeming paradox, that the long-term aim of the Berlin blockade was the unification of Germany, is resolved if one rejects the over-simplified models of linearity and causality which have bedevilled writing on the origins of the Cold War, and remembers that the

---

[42] Hahn, p. 20. Malenkov and Beria constantly stress the dangers of the international situation, largely because their economic and political interests rest on the defence industries.

people on whom Stalin had to rely in Germany were the very ones whose political survival depended on the failure of his plans. Similarly, it is important not to be fooled by the impeccable united front which the Soviet leadership presented to the world, nor to underestimate the peculiar 'group neurosis' of the Politburo,[43] where policy-making was inseparable from the feverish atmosphere of suspicion, fear and mutual dependence.

Beneath the surface, the resentments created by Zhdanov's high-handedness were coalescing into a new alliance. As Zhdanov's rivalry with Malenkov centred on the Central Committee *apparat*,[44] it was natural that the old ideological clique which had been displaced during 1946/47 should gravitate to Malenkov's camp.[45] The issues on which they sought to undermine Zhdanov were his ideological laxness in internal affairs and his cultivation of Yugoslavia as a personal fiefdom.

The three 'Great Debates', in Philosophy, Biology and Economics, provided an opportunity for hard-line isolationists to undermine a more moderate establish-ment, which, although beholden to Zhdanov for protection, showed far greater openness to the outside world and a willingness to share ideas with Western colleagues. A good example is Zhdanov's sheltering of the biologist Kedrov against the advances of Lysenkoist pseudo-science. These debates continued until early 1949, when the 'moderates' were finally defeated in the wake of Zhdanov's death and the Cosmopolitanism campaign, although the arguments had become increasingly one-sided once Stalin's harder line had begun to break up Zhdanov's power base in mid-1947.[46]

As far as foreign policy is concerned, it was the split with Yugoslavia which precipitated Zhdanov's fall. The Soviet representative in Belgrade, Yudin, seems to have done what he could to aggravate the Yugoslav crisis as part of a concerted campaign to discredit Zhdanov, whose failing health and endangered position in Moscow weakened his influence in the Balkans.[47] Since he was in overall charge of Cominform affairs, Zhdanov took full responsibility for the

[43] Knight, p. 8.
[44] Hahn, pp. 34f.
[45] Hahn, p. 26.
[46] Hahn, p. 68.
[47] Knight, p. 150, Hahn, p. 26. For a fuller account of the split with Yugoslavia, see Leonid Gibianskii, 'The Beginning of the Soviet-Yugoslav Conflict and the Cominform', in Procacci, pp. 465–81.

final break with Tito in July 1948, adding weight to the charges of internationalism which had damaged him since mid-1947. This marked the point of his final defeat, and he died a month later.

The crackdown which followed the Yugoslav crisis had repercussions throughout the Soviet sphere, but, as will become clear in the next chapter, the campaign in Germany was by no means as successful in producing ideological conformity as has often been assumed. The demands of the international situation meant that at least the appearance of an all-German stance had to be maintained, but an examination of cultural policy and artistic activity shows that the all-German policy had far deeper roots in government and cultural organisations in the Soviet Zone than the word 'appearance' might suggest. Stalin's hand was being forced on German policy by an enormously complex set of factors, some of which seem to contradict each other: increasing Cold War tensions, compounded by foreign policy positions originating less from strategic considerations than from the manoeuvrings of Zhdanov and his rivals; the appalling miscalculation over the Berlin Blockade; and, finally, Stalin's reliance on the SED leadership, many of whom saw that their interest lay in forcing German division, and who were thus inclined to pursue purges more forcefully and push the hard-line rhetoric further than Stalin desired.

FROM COSMOPOLITANISM TO THE DEATH OF STALIN

The initiation of the Cosmopolitanism campaign in late 1948 was a development of the charges of internationalism which had been levelled at Zhdanov. The campaign was directed at breaking the influence of the Zhdanovite faction in party and government, and its success was marked by the victory of hard-liners in the Great Debates and the purging of Zhdanovite protégés in the SMAD. However, Zhdanov's patronage had been so pervasive in the party and state apparatus, that it took until late 1950 before the purge was complete: Beria and Abakumov, head of the MVD (Interior Ministry) had, with some difficulty, fabricated an elaborate conspiracy, the 'Leningrad Case', with which they finally broke the back of the Zhdanov faction. In the wake of this, Stalin immediately, and inevitably, began conspiring against Malenkov and Beria.

Malenkov had been reappointed to the Central Committee Secretariat in July 1948 as part of the continuing campaign to undermine Zhdanov, and the Politburo manoeuvring began again. This period has been characterised as the 'post-Zhdanov *zhdanovshchina*' because of the extent and ferocity of the purge,[48] but once again the SED leadership in Germany managed to escape relatively unscathed. Those in the leadership who supported the 'integrationist' line were able to use the Cosmopolitanism campaign as a further means of consolidating their position by pressing for the sovietisation of German culture. For Stalin, the requirements of internal politics constantly undermined his ability to pursue his desired German policy.

In the political realignment which followed the new purge, the most important factor was the return from Kiev in December 1949 of Khrushchev, where he had been Ukrainian First Secretary since 1938. With his Politburo post and his new appointment to the Central Committee Secretariat, Khrushchev was clearly intended by Stalin to provide a check on Malenkov, who was the main beneficiary of the 'Leningrad Case'. Disputes between Khrushchev, Malenkov and Beria broke out almost immediately, especially over agriculture, in which Khrushchev saw himself as a specialist.[49] His hard-line foreign policy, which was to win out in the Politburo only after the arrest of Beria, attracted Zhdanov's surviving protégés, who harboured bitter grievances against those who had toppled their patron. This camp opposed a softer line which Beria and Malenkov had begun to develop in the light of the unpopularity of the purges and the adverse effect on international opinion of their anti-Semitic nature.[50]

According to Amy Knight, Beria himself had always been 'sympathetic' to the cause of the Soviet Jews, and of other national minorities threatened by the post-war centralising drive and the 'russification' of Soviet culture promulgated under the *zhdanovshchina*, and he had managed to protect Jewish party

---

[48] Hahn, p. 114, Schapiro, p. 514.

[49] Khrushchev was criticised in the press for his crackpot schemes, but he stuck to his guns and the criticism does not seem to have damaged him. See Schapiro, p. 520.

[50] Hahn, p. 143.

colleagues during the worst months of the Cosmopolitanism campaign.[51] He was perhaps the most skilful Politburo exponent of the art of political expediency, and was certainly more talented than his associate Malenkov. However, his tendency to drift towards a softer line on domestic and foreign policy, with an extraordinary and inexplicable tangle of motives, ultimately left him vulnerable to attack.

Khrushchev spent the months leading up to the Nineteenth Congress (5–15 October 1952) conspiring to undermine Beria, whose assiduous cultivation of Stalin's paranoia began to rebound on him. Again, the requirements of internal politicking led Stalin to rely on a faction utterly opposed to his long-term plans for Germany. The arrest, on 27 November 1951, of Rudolf Slánský, Beria's protégé in Czechoslovakia, provoked another round of consolidation in the People's Democracies, further entrenching divisions with the West and strengthening the 'integrationist' line in the GDR.

A further serious threat to Beria was the Mingrelian purge, initiated in April 1952 by S. D. Ignatiev, Abakumov's successor at the MVD. The various post-war purges had been highly selective, serving measurable political ends without being allowed to spread out of control as they had in the Thirties, and the purge of Beria's power base in his tiny homeland must have sent a clear signal that he was in deep trouble. There were signs that Stalin was preparing a major purge in 1953, and Beria was sure to fall victim of it.

The preparations for the Nineteenth Congress showed that Stalin, ageing and unwell as he was, was trying to reassert a degree of *personal* control in political life. That he felt that this effort was necessary at all is yet another indication that his personal influence was delimited in significant ways by the various factional configurations through and against which he had to work. The twin aims of securing his position and pursuing specific policies clashed at vital moments in the process of German division; what is remarkable is the doggedness with which Stalin pressed for his German policy in the face of these difficulties. The important distinction which needs to be made here is between *authority* and *power*: Stalin had immense authority, but power, defined as the ability to cause

---

[51] Knight, p. 147. Beria himself belonged to the Mingrelian minority, a small ethnic group within the Georgian Soviet Socialist Republic.

things to happen within and beyond a political structure, is more elusive. It depends on a) accurate information, b) efficient transmission of command through structures which do not tend to dissipate or redirect directives from above, and c) the absence of competing interests among subordinates or significant economic or social forces with their own momentum. The further a system of rule moves from this ideal model, the less one can speak of absolute power at the top.

These statements may seem commonplace, but it is remarkable how many histories of German division have relied on a view which assumes, against the weight of evidence, that Stalin had a free hand in integrating the GDR into the Soviet sphere. We should be wary of generalising about 'Stalinism' from the particular problems which the regime faced in dealing with the beginnings of the Cold War in Europe, but it is important not to fall into the trap of seeing Germany purely as an exception to the Stalinist rule (although Stalin may well have seen it this way). However, it is clear that the results of an investigation into Stalin's German policy fall loosely within what has been termed the 'revisionist' line in Soviet Studies, and is rather less sympathetic to rival models.

The planned overhaul of party structures, through which Stalin hoped to reassert his control, was to be extraordinarily radical in scope. In fact, Stalin had already begun to act increasingly though his own personal secretariat, in order to bypass the rest of the leadership.[52] Without substantial constitutional change, this could hope to be little more than a temporary measure. To this end, Stalin ensured that the Congress would run to his agenda through the high-profile publication of his tract, 'Economic Problems of Socialism in the USSR',[53] two days beforehand. Stalin's intervention settled once and for all the Economists' Debate on the side of the militant opponents of the moderate economist Evgenii Varga.

In late 1946, Varga had published a book[54] in which he argued that post-war capitalism was not in a state of imminent crisis, that certain European economies could achieve reforms of a socialist nature without revolution, and that a new

---

[52] Hahn, p. 145.

[53] *Ekonomicheskie problemy sotsializma v SSSR*, published in *Pravda*, 3–4 October 1952. I. V. Stalin, *Sochineniya*, 3 vols (Stanford: Stanford University Press, 1967), III, pp. 188–245.

[54] *Izmeneniya v kapitalisticheskoi ekonomike v itoge vtoroi mirovoi voiny* (Moscow: Gospolitizdat, 1946).

war was not inevitable. The Economists' controversy, although largely determined by the exigencies of factional politics, 'contained some elements of a genuine search for the correct scientific solution to urgent practical problems',[55] and thus had profound implications for the Soviet attitude to relations with the West. Stalin's final repudiation of Varga's view demonstrates that his hopes for a new European settlement, based on his diplomatic efforts of March and April 1952, had been dashed.

The ideological campaign which accompanied the publication ensured that everyone was busy preparing a suitable response rather than promoting their own interests, and so the sweeping changes which Stalin put forward seem to have come as a complete surprise. In this case, Stalin managed to exploit his unique authority in order to consolidate personal power. Both Politburo and Orgburo were abolished and replaced by a new, expanded Presidium, consisting of 25 members and 11 candidates, effectively swamping the 10 members of the old Politburo (minus Andreyev, who lost his place) by younger newcomers. The Central Committee was also expanded,[56] but there was considerable continuity of membership: over 60% of the old membership found their way into the new Committee. The results were thus rather equivocal: on the one hand, Stalin wanted to break or limit the power of the older, more experienced leaders, whom he mistrusted, and whose well-established systems of patronage frustrated him, by importing a younger generation who would be easier to manage. From another perspective, it seemed to put a seal on the constitutional regularisation of the party's affairs, creating a stable ruling elite, and emphasising Soviet nationalism.

Stalin's brief address (the main Congress report having been entrusted to Malenkov, a singular honour)[57] concentrated on the international situation. He spoke of the need for peace, but couched his attacks on the 'bourgeois' countries in extreme terms which left no doubt of his renewed militancy, thus convincing observers that the 'Stalin notes' on German reunification of a few months earlier

---

[55] Schapiro, p. 537. For a useful discussion of the importance of the Economists' Debate for Soviet policy towards Germany, see Wilfried Loth, *Stalins ungeliebtes Kind: Warum Moskau die DDR nicht wollte* (Berlin: Rowohlt, 1994), pp. 107–15.

[56] To 236 members, nearly twice the size of the Committee elected in 1939. See Schapiro, pp. 523–7.

[57] Khrushchev won second-place honours by being permitted to present the report on the new party rules.

had been nothing but a bluff.[58] This foreign policy aspect of the Congress will be discussed in more detail in the next chapter.

The tendency of the Soviet leadership was always to centralise decision-making, so a 25-member Presidium was considered too cumbersome, and Stalin selected a Bureau of nine: himself, Malenkov, Beria, Khrushchev, Voroshilov, Kaganovich, Bulganin, and two technocrats, Saburov and Pervukhin. The winners in the restructuring were Malenkov and Khrushchev: there was a balance among the new Presidium members between technocrats (Malenkov's men) and Khrushchev protégés, including Brezhnev and the rehabilitated Kosygin. Beria was an obvious loser, and it is reasonable to assume that Stalin was preparing for the elimination of some of the most senior members of the Politburo, and for a purge of the apparatus in order to make way for 'a new generation of party members who owed everything to his patronage',[59] as he had in 1937–8.

According to Khrushchev, the new Presidium never actually met, and party work continued for a while much as before, with an inner circle of Malenkov, Beria, Bulganin and himself.[60] This state of affairs lasted for three months, until the 'discovery' of the 'Doctors' Plot'. A group of high-ranking doctors (seven out of the nine named being Jewish) were implicated in the death of Zhdanov, and, ominously for Beria, the security services were reproached for 'lack of vigilance'. This could easily have led to accusations of treason, and the Mingrelian purge begins to look like a 'dress-rehearsal' for an attack on Beria himself.[61] Stalin's death, on 5 March 1953, came in the nick of time.

'COLLECTIVE LEADERSHIP' AND THE FALL OF BERIA

In the early 1950s, the relationship between local party officials and industrial managers had begun to show signs of strain, originating in the basic inefficiency of the system. Coinciding with the increasing emphasis on nationalism,

---

[58] Stalin, vol. 3, pp. 310–15. See also Loth, *Stalins ungeliebtes Kind*, pp. 191f.

[59] Schapiro, p. 549.

[60] Khrushchev, p. 248.

[61] Schapiro, p. 549.

particularly in its expression at the Nineteenth Congress, official pronouncements stressed organisation at the expense of ideology.[62] The party began to turn up the heat on middle-range officials, urging them to be more flexible and conciliatory. Condemnations of corrupt officials began to appear before Stalin's death, signalling one of the party's periodic bouts of soul-searching. What exactly was the role of the party in a post-revolutionary society?

The relative neglect of the party and its functions after the Great Purges indicate its problematic status as a likely cause of economic inefficiency in a period of rapid modernisation. In the Fifties, it was becoming clear that the pace of reconstruction was unsatisfactory, and continuing material deprivation began to trigger the resurgence of resentments and conflicts which had been shelved during the war. In this light, the spirit of party revivalism given encouragement by the rapid rise of Khrushchev and his challenge to the ascendancy of Malenkov after the Nineteenth Congress can be seen as another attempt to reassert the ideological over the governmental/industrial apparatus. In the long run, this revival was to go further through the hierarchies than the *zhdanovshchina*, and culminate in the monumental projects of the Khrushchev era.

The economic stakes were high in the political contest following Stalin's death, and this factor played a vital role in determining the outcome of policy decisions in 1953. Beria's proposed programme of reforms aimed at the elimination of economic inefficiency, and the cancellation of many of the huge construction projects which appealed to Stalin. This inevitably brought about conflict with Khrushchev, who favoured grand schemes such as his 'agro-towns' and the ideological revival necessary to set them in motion.[63]

Initially, though, the regime maintained its mask of unity. For a week following Stalin's death, it seemed as though a new personality cult was to be built up around Malenkov, but this was only a temporary measure, designed to ensure stability.[64] The organisational changes in the leadership produced a

---

[62] See the discussion in Dunham, pp. 150ff.

[63] See Knight, pp. 184ff.

[64] Many in the West believed that Malenkov was destined to become the new dictator: see Martin Ebon, *Malenkov: A Biographical Study of Stalin's Successor* (London: Macmillan, 1953), a warning tract hurriedly cobbled together in the wake of Stalin's death, and overtaken by events within a few weeks.

'division of power [which] represented a common desire among the party leaders to prevent the re-emergence of a new dictator'.[65] This desire for a form of collective leadership resulted in changes to party and government structures which gathered power firmly in the hands of the clique of Stalin's successors. A five-man Presidium was created for the Council of Ministers, consisting of Malenkov (Chairman), Beria, Molotov, Bulganin and Kaganovich. Beria became Minister of the Interior, thus combining MGB and MVD functions under his leadership, and dismissing his rival Ignat'ev from his post; Beria's position was strengthened considerably, giving him authority over the security apparatus, the police, a large military force and significant economic interests.[66]

The party leadership was also streamlined: the new Bureau of the Presidium of the Central Committee was abolished, and the Presidium itself reduced to 10 members.[67] Malenkov relinquished his post in the Secretariat, in order to avoid the concentration of the posts of senior party secretary and head of government apparatus in the hands of one man. Khrushchev was now head of the Secretariat, and the scene was set for an epic struggle between these two men, which lasted until 1957. At stake would be the issue of whether party or government apparatus would be the driving force in Soviet society.

The announcement that the 'Doctors' Plot' had been a hoax marked a certain change in climate, as the leadership tentatively distanced itself from Stalin. Beria, who had the most to lose as the man associated with the most brutal aspects of Stalin's rule, wanted 'to change his own public image from that of policeman to liberal statesman [...] Reform followed reform in dizzying succession'.[68] Beria clearly went further than the rest of the leadership would have liked. Amy Knight has shown that Beria was behind the move to discredit the 'Doctors' Plot', and that, at a meeting of Central Committee members, he even went so far as to implicate Stalin himself in the fabrication of the

---

[65] Schapiro, p. 559, where a comprehensive account of the leadership changes can be found.

[66] Knight, p. 184.

[67] Schapiro, p. 558.

[68] Knight, p. 184. The rumours which leaked out about Beria's reform programme were greeted with disbelief. This was Dmitri Shostakovich's reaction: 'How can you believe such deliberate lies, lies that have been put into circulation by *that* department! *Beriya*, who personally cut up corpses and flushed them down the toilet, now wants people to believe that he has grown wings. And you are inclined to believe it!' See Elizabeth Wilson, *Shostakovich: A Life Remembered* (London: Faber and Faber, 1994), p. 261.

conspiracy.[69] Beria's MVD was also behind a massive amnesty of prisoners,[70] and his desperation to dissociate himself from Stalin led him to embark on a programme of panicky destalinisation which threatened to destabilise the fabric of the Soviet state itself.

Perhaps the most significant aspect of Beria's programme was his approach to the rights of the non-Russian minorities. This 'attempt to gain credibility by destalinisation required some recognition of national rights',[71] but this strategy was extraordinarily risky in view of the explosive tensions which could be unleashed in any relaxation of the forcible domination of minorities by the Great Russian majority. This decentralising drive, and Beria's now total dominance over the security apparatus, were a significant threat to his opponents, and the conflict with Khrushchev deepened when Beria began interfering in Ukrainian nationality politics.

There were signs that the government apparatus was beginning to win out at the expense of party structures, and Khrushchev's survival depended on his ability to reassert the primacy of the party and of ideological matters. Beria's reforming zeal provided the opportunity for Khrushchev to drive a wedge between Malenkov and Beria, and so the months between March and June 1953 were characterised by an intense struggle between decentralising and centralising forces. Although the outside world knew little or nothing about these battles until Beria's arrest was announced on 10 July, two weeks after the event, the stability of the entire Soviet Bloc hung in the balance.

The vast economic and social forces in the Soviet Union, which determined the shape and strategies of the power struggle in the leadership, thus came to have an immediate bearing on the GDR's viability as an independent entity. The survival of the 'integrationist' line and the leadership of Walter Ulbricht depended on Khrushchev's success in re-establishing the primacy of centralised party control. Whereas Stalin had always been more circumspect in his German policy, eventually allowing the practical demands of the escalating Cold War and his reliance on the SED as his representatives to force his hand, Beria was

---

[69] Knight, pp. 185ff.

[70] 1,202,000, according to R. W. Davies, 'Forced Labour under Stalin: The Archive Revelations', *New Left Review*, no. 214 (1995), p. 78.

[71] Knight, p. 190.

literally fighting for survival, and he allowed no such considerations to distract him.

The unrest in Berlin in mid-June 1953 was one of the pretexts for Beria's arrest. Others included his supposed attempt to usurp the powers of the party Presidium through his security apparatus, and the amnesties. It is an indication of the importance of destalinisation as a political tactic, that these large-scale amnesty proposals were cancelled after Beria's arrest, and then resumed by Khrushchev in 1954 when destalinisation became the vital tool in his own bid for power. It is notable, however, that Khrushchev could afford to bide his time and ensure a policy of *controlled* destalinisation in order to guarantee the continued stability of the Soviet state.

The criminal case which Khrushchev concocted against Beria was weak, and he was aware of the risk he was taking, but the German issue caused many neutrals to side against Beria. Still, the problem remained of how to arrest and charge the man to whom the Interior Ministry, the secret police and the regular police force owed their allegiance. Khrushchev relied on the continuing resentment against Beria in the armed forces, which stemmed from the surveillance role of the NKVD during the war, and the adverse effect which this had had on Soviet military performance. More immediately, the army command was dismayed by Beria's German policy, his gradual dismantling of military control in Berlin, and his replacement of military staff with civilians under his own influence. The final straw was his indecisiveness in putting down the June uprising, which provided the immediate spur for the arrest on 26 June.[72]

The regime moved quickly to break up Beria's security monopoly: the MVD was stripped of its economic interests and the newly-created KGB (Committee for State Security) made fully accountable to the Council of Ministers, ensuring that the security services could never become the dangerous state-within-a-state which they had been under Beria. Khrushchev was appointed First Secretary of

---

[72] Khrushchev's account (Khrushchev, pp. 287–307) is the most famous. See also Robert Conquest, *Power and Policy in the USSR: The Study of Soviet Dynastics* (London: Macmillan, 1961), for the official reports of the trial of Beria, and Knight, pp. 194–217, for an evaluation of the various accounts and an attempt to reconstruct Khrushchev's clever manipulation of Malenkov, Molotov, and the other leaders. It is still not entirely clear who was aware of the plot, except that Malenkov, Molotov and Bulganin were persuaded to participate fully, and certain others, such as Voroshilov, may have been informed at the last minute.

the CPSU in September 1953, and the 'experiment in oligarchy'[73] lasted only until he had eliminated all opposition and reasserted the dominance of the party over the government machinery.

[73] Schapiro, p. 560.

CHAPTER THREE

'STALINS UNGELIEBTES KIND'[1]

The notes taken by Wilhelm Pieck during consultations with Stalin and senior Soviet officials in the USSR and SBZ/GDR lay unseen for many years, in the Central Party Archive of the SED. The first indication that such consultations had taken place comes in a Pieck biography of 1975.[2] However, it was only in 1990 that the Institut für Geschichte der Arbeiterbewegung opened its archive (now incorporated into the Bundesarchiv) to researchers, and the publication of portions of Pieck's notes became possible.[3]

The appearance in 1994 of the complete edition of the notes, edited by Rolf Badstübner and Wilfried Loth, shed fresh light on the ongoing controversy over Stalin's intentions for Germany.[4] Essentially, it provided a new impetus to attempts to apply a serious critique to what had, in the West, become the orthodox view of German division, a critique which had previously lacked the necessary hard evidence. As we have seen, it has been possible to discern incongruities which undermine interpretations based on a monolithic view of 'Stalinism' and SED rule. Lack of access to the relevant archives has meant that the debate has often been conducted on an ideological level, based on 'gut feelings' and instinctive attitudes towards the integration of the FRG into Western structures; the tendency on both sides to make categorical statements

---

[1] Wilfried Loth, *Stalins ungeliebtes Kind: Warum Moskau die DDR nicht wollte* (Berlin: Rowohlt, 1994).

[2] Heinz Voßke and Gerhard Nitzsche, *Wilhelm Pieck: Biographischer Abriß* (Berlin: Dietz, 1975): cf. p. 305. Voßke and Nitzsche mention trips in January/February 1947, March and December 1948, and September 1949, 'zur Erörterung grundlegender Fragen der internationalen Lage und der Politik der SED.' The most explicit reference to Stalin's foreign policy is as follows: 'Am 31. Januar 1947 wurde die Delegation der SED [Grotewohl, Fechner, Ulbricht, Oelßner and Pieck] in einer Beratung mit J. W. Stalin ausführlich über die Deutschlandpolitik der imperialistischen Westmächte sowie über die Außenpolitik der UdSSR zur strikten Einhaltung der grundlegenden Bestimmungen des Potsdamer Abkommens informiert.' No source is indicated by the authors.

[3] See Wilfriede Otto, 'Sowjetische Deutschlandnote 1952. Bisher unveröffentlichte handschriftliche Notizen Wilhelm Piecks', *Beiträge zur Geschichte der Arbeiterbewegung*, 33 (1991), 374–89; Dietrich Staritz, 'Die SED, Stalin und die Gründung der DDR', *Aus Politik und Zeitgeschichte*, B 5/91, 25.1.1991, 3–16; D. S., 'Die SED, Stalin und der "Aufbau des Sozialismus" in der DDR. Aus den Akten des Zentralen Parteiarchivs', *Deutschland Archiv*, 24 (1991), 686–700; and D. S., 'The SED, Stalin and the German question: Interests and Decision–Making in the Light of New Sources', *German History*, 10 (1992), 274–89.

[4] Rolf Badstübner and Wilfried Loth, op cit.

without appropriate evidence did nothing to ease the febrile atmosphere of Cold War politics.

Although many have disagreed with Badstübner and Loth's analysis, the conclusions which they draw provide the most satisfactory explanation for the initial support for, and prolonged survival of, the 'all-German' orientation in cultural policy and its expression in institutions such as the Kulturbund, the Deutsche Akademie der Künste, and the journal Sinn und Form:

Mit präziser Quellenkritik und methodisch kontrollierter Einordnung der deutschland-politischen Praxis der Sowjetunion in den Zusammenhang der Ost-West-Beziehungen bei Kriegsende ließ sich wohl zeigen, daß Stalin einen gesamtdeutschen, auf Kompromisse mit den westlichen Besatzungsmächten hin ausgelegten Ansatz verfolgte, der in zunehmenden Widerspruch zu systemimmanenten Abschottungstendenzen geriet.[5]

Loth and Badstübner point out that Stalin's personal style of government 'läßt es auch als wenig wahrscheinlich erscheinen, daß parallele Aufzeichnungen von gleicher Dichte entstanden sind'.[6] Certainly, Pieck was an avid note-taker, even during the dangerous years of exile in the Soviet Union, and it is to this habit that we owe such insights as we have.[7]

Pieck and Ulbricht survived the most vicious purges of 1936–1938 by proving themselves the most loyal servants of the regime, and by making every effort, 'die "nationale" Politik der deutschen Kommunisten jedem Winkelzug der Stalinschen Politik anzupassen'.[8] Thus, it was natural that Stalin would come to rely on them for the implementation of his policies in Germany, especially if he became aware that other interests in the Soviet *apparat* were putting a different emphasis on his policies: the SED leaders 'nahmen in der informellen Machtstruktur im Prinzip den gleichen Rang wie die SMAD–Spitzen ein'.[9] The tensions between this position and the SED's role as representative of an

---

[5] Badstübner and Loth, p. 14.

[6] Badstübner and Loth, p. 16.

[7] See *'Nach Hitler kommen wir'. Dokumente zur Programmatik der Moskauer KPD–Führung 1944/45 für Nachkriegsdeutschland*, ed. by Peter Erler, Horst Laude and Manfred Wilke (Berlin: Akademie Verlag, 1994), p. 18.

[8] Badstübner and Loth, p. 18.

[9] Badstübner and Loth, p. 22.

occupied power account for the peculiar problems and opportunities which presented themselves to the leadership in this period.

Pieck's notes indicate the extraordinarily detailed nature of Stalin's instructions, indicating his desire to exert a close personal influence on developments. Badstübner and Loth define two limiting factors in Stalin's ability to translate his authority into power:

> Zum einen war [Stalin] infolge der Fülle der Entscheidungen, die er sich vorbehalten hatte, ständig überfordert, und blieben folglich viele Entscheidungen ohne steuernden Zugriff. Das galt um so mehr, als seine Gesundheit in den Nachkriegsjahren doch schon ziemlich angegriffen war, und er sich wiederholt zu längeren Kuraufenthalten ans Schwarze Meer begab. Zum anderen war er über die Situation im Ausland und auch im besetzten Deutschland notorisch schlecht informiert, aufgrund seiner ideologischen Scheuklappen, aber auch, weil ihm die verschiedenen Informanten aus nur zu verständlichen Gründen nach dem Mund redeten und die eingehenden Informationen keineswegs der Kritik einer kollegialen Diskussion unterzogen wurden.[10]

Pieck's notes give no indication about the extent to which individuals may have exploited their (by no means insignificant) room for manoeuvre. Previous commentators have on occasion assumed the existence of a 'GDR faction' actively opposed to Stalin's policy,[11] but Badstübner and Loth are more cautious, arguing that Stalin's instructions were 'unterschiedlich interpretierbar [...] Daraus konnten sich in der Praxis unterschiedliche Handlungsweisen ergeben, darunter auch solche, die miteinander in Konkurrenz traten und den Intentionen Stalins zuwiderliefen'.[12] Whether this caution tallies precisely with the picture painted by Loth in *Stalins ungeliebtes Kind* of the activities of Ulbricht and Tyul'panov remains to be seen. In any case, it seems advisable not to use terms such as 'faction', but instead to talk about an 'integrationist' line which gradually asserted itself in the conjunction of the self–interest of various parties.

Stalin's primary consideration in forming his German policy was security, specifically, the need to prevent a renewed attack on the Soviet Union. The

---

[10] Badstübner and Loth, p. 21.

[11] See Bernd Bonwetsch, 'Deutschlandpolitische Alternative der Sowjetunion 1945–1955', *Deutsche Studien*, 24 (1986), 320–40.

[12] Badstübner and Loth, p. 22.

economic dominance of the United States at the end of the war roused 'geradezu apokalyptische Ängste' about any emerging alliance of German and American capital and military capacity.[13] To this end, the Soviet Zone in Germany was 'ein Faustpfand, das ein Mitspracherecht bei der künftigen Gestaltung Deutschlands wahrscheinlicher machte; eine eigene Perspektive wurde für sie nicht entwickelt'.[14]

Thus, KPD dominance in the Eastern zone had to be secured quickly in the months following the surrender, in order for Stalin to be able to exert the kind of leverage necessary to achieve his aims. This is the first of the problematic areas around which this study of GDR cultural policy is centred: the contradictory situation in which policy was made, which meant that the 'all–German' concept relied for its implementation on people whose grip on power depended on its failure. The second area of investigation is the massive discrepancy of intentions between Stalin's plans for a united Germany and the hopes for German cultural unity expressed by many GDR artists and intellectuals of the period. Stalin's reparations policy reflected the immense damage which had been done to the Soviet national economy, and the need to ensure access to the industrial capacity of the Ruhr and the Rhineland. Bearing in mind the rancour which the reparations issue caused among the manoeuvring factions in Moscow, we can begin to situate desires for German cultural unity within the extraordinarily complex interplay of motives, political agendas and economic forces which were shaping Germany.

Soviet calculations about reparations and security issues are reflected in the *Gründungsaufruf* of the KPD Central Committee,[15] where the word 'Sozialismus' does not appear (in contrast to the more radical–sounding SPD manifesto of 15 June). Instead, the emphasis is on the 'Aufrichtung eines antifaschistischen, demokratischen Regimes, einer parlamentarisch–demokratischen Republik mit allen demokratischen Rechten und Freiheiten für

---

[13] Loth, *Stalins ungeliebtes Kind*, p. 16.
[14] Loth, *Stalins ungeliebtes Kind*, p. 22.
[15] Published in *Deutsche Volkszeitung*, no. 1, 13.6.1945, cit. Gerd Dietrich, *Politik und Kultur in der SBZ 1945–1949*, (Bern: Peter Lang, 1993), pp. 20f.

das Volk'.[16] This attitude had been drummed into the KPD leaders in Moscow, and the *Aufruf* had already been prepared there by Ackermann in consultation with Georgi Dimitrov;[17] revolutionary aims 'rückten damit in eine ungewisse Zukunft'.[18] Loth argues, on the basis of Pieck's notes and the security needs of the USSR, that the appeals for a 'bürger[lich]–demokr[atische] Regierung'[19] are genuine:

Wenn man auf die Zusammenarbeit mit den Westmächten angewiesen war—und das war nach Lage der Dinge Voraussetzung eines einigermaßen erträglichen Friedens—dann war eine solche Demokratie eine gute Basis. Bei einigermaßen nüchterner Betrachtung der Verhältnisse im besetzten Deutschland konnte es gar kein anderes Programm geben.[20]

The programme of the KPD contained the seeds of future trouble, as it specifically opposed all native German attempts to construct an autonomous socialism, which was to be rooted out as a 'schädliche Tendenz'.[21] The attempts to impose democracy 'from above'—Soviet–trained officers could not have worked any other way—for example, by the licensing of political parties according to a pre-conceived scheme, played into the hands of those in the KPD/SPD leadership whose priorities were the consolidation of power. However, this tendency to give *institutional* expression to intended political outcomes could cut both ways: once the 'all-German' orientation was written into the statutes of the KPD, and later the SED, it had an institutional basis from which to resist, with varying degrees of success, the encroachment of 'integrationist' rhetoric. It is in the cultural sphere, and specifically in cultural institutions, that this resistance was most successful, lasting well beyond the announcement of the 'Aufbau des Sozialismus' at the Second SED Conference in 1952.

[16] Dietrich, p. 20. Note that the potential for rhetorical shifts in the meaning of the words is already present, particularly through the gradual encroachment of the Leninist definition of democracy and a more radically politicised use of the word 'Volk'.

[17] Loth, *Stalins ungeliebtes Kind*, p. 24.

[18] Loth, *Stalins ungeliebtes Kind*, p. 25.

[19] Briefing with Stalin, Molotov and Zhdanov, 4.6.1945: Badstübner and Loth, p. 51.

[20] Loth, *Stalins ungeliebtes Kind*, p. 25.

[21] Loth, *Stalins ungeliebtes Kind*, p. 23.

The obstacles and opportunities which confronted the 'integrationists' were mirrored in the situation of those who supported the 'all-German' line. The imposition of democratic structures from above contained within it the potential for dictatorship while at the same time creating spaces for resistance within the structures themselves.

SOCIALIST UNITY AND STALIN'S AUTHORITY

We have already examined some of the background to the KPD/SPD merger, but it is worth returning to the question of the discrepancy between Stalin's intentions and the eventual outcome, since it gives us some idea of the extent of the room for manoeuvre enjoyed by the various parties. Many German communists still viewed members of the SPD as traitors, and persisted in demanding working-class unity only on their own terms. Ulbricht was particularly insistent in this regard, seeing his project as ensuring 'die Kohärenz der KPD'.[22] It was only when communist parties began experiencing defeats in Hungary and Austria, in November 1945, that the KPD leaders realised that their only hope of avoiding marginalisation was to make 'bemerkenswerte ideologische Zugeständnisse' to the SPD.[23]

Loth's assessment of the reasons for the merger puts a slightly different emphasis on the interpretation which emerged in my discussion of Zhdanov's policy in the previous chapter. While at first they seem to clash in many respects, the two interpretations can be reconciled by considering them as views from the respective Soviet and German perspectives. Loth considers that the conditions under which KPD/SPD unity was forced represent significant concessions from the KPD leadership, and this is certainly true if one considers that the communist *Führungsanspruch* had to be abandoned. The problem, in Loth's view, was that the SMAD officers were simply unaware of the possibility that their tendency to resort to heavy-handed administrative measures against hesitant Social Demo-

---

[22] Loth, *Stalins ungeliebtes Kind*, p. 47.

[23] It is at this point at which Zhukov makes his offer to Grotewohl to have Ulbricht removed from the leadership for his continued insistence on the communist *Führungsanspruch*. Grotewohl's failure to act on this offer marks the loss of a significant opportunity to assert a more independent line.

crats, 'nicht gerade die Einheit Deutschlands sicherte, sondern im Gegenteil seine Spaltung vorantrieb'.[24]

Even with a combination of Stalin's ill-informed isolation, and the rigorously-schooled mentality of the Soviet officers, it would be somewhat surprising if nobody at all had been aware of the extreme unlikelihood of pushing through KPD/SPD unity in the Western zones. Yet this seems to be the conclusion that Loth draws, having noted Stalin's initial hesitation on the unity issue. His motives for changing his mind are not clear, except that he 'die Gefahr einer Ost-West-Spaltung Deutschlands verdrängte und das Vereinigungsprojekt [that is, the formation of the SED] weiterhin als zentrales Element seiner gesamtdeutschen Strategie begriff'.[25]

This fundamental error in Stalin's calculations marks a crucial moment in the development of the 'all-German' orientation. Loth comments that 'die Vereinigung der beiden Arbeiterparteien nur im Rahmen einer gesamtdeutschen Strategie sinnvoll [war]'.[26] Failure to persuade Schumacher and the SPD in the Western zones to participate in the unification process ensured that the merger hastened rather than hindered German division. The initial reluctance of Ulbricht, whose identification with the Zhdanov-inspired 'integrationist' line is apparent very early, may be explainable in the light of Stalin's hopes that working-class unity would promote German unity. Once it became clear that the SPD in the Western zones was not interested, then the usefulness of a merger in the Soviet Zone for the purposes of the 'integrationists' was obvious. Bearing this in mind, we can go some way to resolving the apparent discrepancy between the ideological concessions made to the SPD and the enthusiasm with which the 'integrationist' Tyul'panov pushed for the merger.

At this moment, the parameters are set for the conflicts to come over the 'all-German' orientation. On the one hand, a campaign of rhetoric initiated by Stalin which strove to present the merger of KPD and SPD as a step towards German unity underwent a shift of meaning; against Stalin's wishes, the rhetoric of German unity was becoming part of the discourse of German division, both in

---

[24] Loth, *Stalins ungeliebtes Kind*, p. 51.
[25] Loth, *Stalins ungeliebtes Kind*, p. 53.
[26] Loth, *Stalins ungeliebtes Kind*, p. 53.

the eyes of suspicious observers in the West and as part of the 'integrationist' strategy. Thus, the concepts of unity and democracy came to be synonymous with integration into the Soviet sphere and sovietisation of society. From this point onwards, those who genuinely wanted to work for reunification had to speak within discursive boundaries set by the 'integrationists' and use concepts and categories whose meanings they were not fully able to control.

On the other hand, the 'all-German' orientation was now firmly written into the SED's statutes, in other words, given a form of institutional expression to which, along with the Potsdam Treaty, proponents of German political and/or cultural unity could refer. This factor, combined with Stalin's continued efforts to force unity, meant that alternative ideas could combine to exert a powerful influence, an influence so disruptive that it nearly led to the fall of the regime in 1953.

The ambiguity, which was implicit in the battle for control of the rhetoric of German unity from the very start, had profound consequences for cultural policy. Functionaries in the various cultural institutions, such as Alexander Abusch, were able to exploit this problematic rhetoric in order to manoeuvre more idealistic artists and intellectuals towards positions of compromise with the 'integrationist' line. However, this tactic was a double-edged sword, as attempts to impose absolute standards of meaning on these nebulous concepts, in other words, to create a monosemic cultural discourse, legitimising SED rule, foundered on the very ambiguities which it sought to exploit. This was a particular difficulty, (a) because the regime itself, let alone the obstreperous artistic community, was hardly as united as the leadership claimed, and (b) because the 'integrationist' line in cultural policy (that is, the drive for 'sovietisation') sought to derive its legitimacy from a source, Stalin, who was fundamentally opposed to its project.

'FEHLEN DER SELBSTKRITIK'[27] RHETORIC AND IDEOLOGY IN THE RUN-UP TO THE SECOND CONFERENCE OF THE SED

Norman Naimark has identified 'two kinds of responses [among the SED leaders] to the challenges presented by the cold war', which indicate the presence of conflicting schools of thought within the SED and within the 'Soviet ranks [which] were no more unified on this question than were the German'.[28] The issue in question, the failure of the Moscow Conference in March/April 1947 to produce an agreement on a central German administration,[29] divided the SED leadership into those (including Ulbricht, Pieck and Dahlem) who wanted to concentrate on the economy and administration of the Soviet Zone, and for whom German unity was a secondary question, and figures like Ackermann, Becher, Max Fechner and Otto Meier, who had serious doubts about political developments.[30] The significance which a particular historian attaches to these differences will depend on how much credence is given to Loth's argument about Stalin's intentions with regard to Germany. There are doubts surrounding what Stalin actually meant by 'bourgeois-democratic government', which are founded on legitimate concerns about the heavy-handedness of the SMAD's attempts to impose democratic structures from above. However, the survival of an all-German orientation within GDR cultural institutions, and the inability of the 'integrationists' within the SED fully to push through their programme in these institutions, support the idea that Stalin's persistence in keeping unity on

[27] Report by Tyul'panov on 11.7.1947, Badstübner and Loth, p. 129.

[28] Naimark pp. 302f.

[29] See Loth, pp. 83–88. Loth contrasts the Soviet 'Interesse an einem erfolgreichen Abschluß' with the obstructive negotiating stance of Bevin and Bidault, who regarded the result as 'erfolgreiches Scheitern' in the context of the newly-declared 'Truman Doctrine' (Truman, speech to Congress, 12 March 1947). See Martina Kessel, *Westeuropa und die deutsche Teilung. Englische und französische Deutschlandpolitik auf den Außenminister-konferenzen von 1945 bis 1947* (Munich: R. Oldenbourg, 1989), pp. 241–46. Kessel argues that Bevin made sure that the Soviet willingness to compromise was not seriously tested. See also Elisabeth Kraus, *Ministerien für ganz Deutschland? Der alliierte Kontrollrat und die Frage gesamtdeutscher Zentralverwaltungen* (Munich: R. Oldenbourg, 1990), p. 308, where she argues that the Soviets shot themselves in the foot out of fear of an Allied majority in any central administration, by insisting that the individual zonal authorities should be able to overrule central decisions.

[30] Although Fechner and Meier were ex-SPD, it would be too simple to ascribe concern about the impending division of Germany to remnants of SPD thinking. Many KPD members shared these concerns, which were, after all, embedded in the *Gründungsaufruf* of the KPD and the statutes of the SED.

the agenda was a reflection of his reluctance to sanction the full integration of the GDR into the Soviet sphere.

The failure of the Moscow Conference, and the 'fiasco' of the London Foreign Ministers' Conference in December 1947, where the obvious unwillingness of the Allies to negotiate away their intention to create a West German state led Stalin to express his 'düstere Vision'[31]in the presence of Milovan Djilas, reflects the Soviet underestimation of the importance of the creation of the Bizone in December 1946. Any form of economic union between the Eastern and Western zones was becoming increasingly unlikely; however, it is important to guard against identifying any particular event as a point of no return in a way which would contribute to a view which sees subsequent developments as inevitable. Instead of raising a particular event to the status of a determiner, giving actors on the diplomatic scene a causal potency reflecting their own self-perception, we should think of developments in the Soviet Zone as forming part of the same complex network of interactions which characterised political life in the Soviet Union (as outlined in the previous chapter). In this context, the various interpretations of the all-German line, with their differing motivations, are caught in a situation where integration of the Soviet Zone into the 'Soviet Bloc' is rapidly becoming the path of least resistance. Attempts to exert influence to reverse or divert this develop-ment become ever more problematic, and it is the great strength of Loth's work that it identifies the series of opportunities which were missed through a combination of opportunism, short-sightedness and chance.

The pluralistic atmosphere of late 1945 and 1946, which encouraged the expression of all-German ideals, was reflected in the rapid growth of the SED.[32] Even accounting for the fact that some of these new members must have joined for opportunistic reasons, this still represents a significant endorsement for the 'im Kern nicht mehr leninistische Programm' of the SED. Despite widespread resentment against the heavy-handed, often oppressive, measures of the SMAD, many people set to work with an 'Elan, der von dem Willen zur Neugestaltung

---

[31] Loth, *Stalins ungeliebtes Kind*, p. 99; Kessel, p. 293.

[32] 1.3 million members in the autumn of 1946, rising to 1.8 million a year later: cit. Naimark, p. 294.

ausing'.[33] It is noticeable, however, that this atmosphere is most pronounced within the SED leadership and in the cultural sphere, where intellectuals were largely cushioned against the worst effects of the arbitrariness of, say, Soviet actions in the dismantling of industrial capacity.

Within the SED, the all-German line was, for the moment, in the ascendancy. It is of course impossible to know which SED leaders supported Ackermann's 'German Road' thesis from conviction, and which from expediency, but it seemed to offer a way of asserting a measure of independence from the Soviet authorities.[34] In the case of Pieck and Dahlem, as indicated above, the 'German Road' may well have seemed the most convenient way of consolidating SED control or of promoting more efficient administration, with the implications for German unity taking a back seat, whereas the other leaders shared varying degrees of faith in more pluralistic politics and a desire to assert a line independent of 'Moscow'.

Ulbricht, who was positioning himself as the most loyal servant of the Soviets was, according to Gniffke, effectively shunned in this period, although his patience would be rewarded with time.[35] By emphasising his usefulness to the SMAD, Ulbricht came to be 'used to pass on ideological directives and to discipline particular SED members'.[36] The unpopularity which this brought him was compensated for by his absolute identification with the occupation authorities, so that it was natural to assume that he represented 'Moscow's' line. According to Naimark, Ulbricht's 'protector' in the SMAD, and his contact with the Soviet Communist Party, was Lieutenant-Colonel P. F. Nazarov,

---

[33] Loth, *Stalins ungeliebtes Kind*, p. 73

[34] The Social Democrat Central Committee Secretary 'S. F.' claims that, among the former KPD members, Paul Merker, Wilhelm Zaisser, Franz Dahlem and Wilhelm Pieck, as well as ex-SPD members such as Otto Grotewohl (who was known as 'der Zauderer') and Erich Gniffke, supported Ackermann. 'S. F.' also maintains that Soviet officers, including 'dieser Oberst Tjulpanow', never agreed with the 'German Road': 'Und es hat mich immer gewundert, daß Anton Ackermann, er war ja ein intelligenter Mensch, [...] der, das Schicksal Titos vor Augen, eigentlich nicht für sich selbst die Konsequenzen gezogen hat und sich gesagt hat, das kannst du nicht machen.' See Beatrix W. Bouvier and Horst-Peter Schulz (eds), *'...die SPD aber aufgehört hat, zu existieren.' Sozial-demokraten unter sowjetischer Besatzung* (Bonn: J. H. W. Dietz Nachf., 1991), p. 64.

[35] Gniffke, pp. 181f. It is interesting to note the unfavourable impression which Ulbricht produced in those around him. Naimark (p. 43) records the unhappiness of many communists with Ulbricht's 'fetish for administration', and quotes (p. 332) Tyul'panov's opinion that he was 'excessively sharp with his comrades'. On the other hand, Tyul'panov admired Ulbricht's conspiratorial skills ('Stenogramma soveshchaniya v Upravlenii Propagandy SVAG', September 17–18, 1946, cit. Naimark, p. 332).

[36] Naimark, p. 288.

Tyul'panov's deputy in the Propaganda Administration; it was connections such as these which Ulbricht exploited to pursue his 'integrationist' goals. Ulbricht's line and Tyul'panov's ideological campaign helped to push the SED away from its all-German commitments, and Ulbricht's position as 'contact man'[37] with the Soviets ensured that he could use the aura of prestige which this created to present himself as the interpreter of Stalin's policy. In this sense, Stalin's desire to create a form of democratic system in Germany acceptable to the Allies, in order to achieve the goals of his *Deutschlandpolitik*, foundered on his inability to trust subordinates who were not fully-trained 'Stalinist' *apparatchiks*.

An examination of the range of differing stances within the SED leadership produces a differentiated view of the SED's 'dependence' on the Soviets. Figures such as Ackermann, Wolfgang Leonhard, and Becher, for whom the 'German Road' meant more than just a slogan, still suffered from habits of mind ingrained in Soviet exile, and so the terms in which they formed and expressed their ideas were inevitably saturated with the categories of Marxism-Leninism. Ex-SPD members, such as Gniffke and Grotewohl, inevitably brought with them an entirely different set of ideological preconceptions, which led to their progressive marginalisation within SED structures. Grotewohl himself 'probably had the most complex relationship with the Soviets', who 'courted' and 'shamelessly flattered' him because of his vital role in securing his party's acquiescence in the merger, while at the same time never letting him forget that with his SPD background 'he could never quite match up to the Soviets' understanding of German affairs'.[38] The bullying attitude of the SMAD officers, particularly Tyul'panov with his 'barrage of ideological lessons',[39] goes some way to explaining Grotewohl's vacillation and the growing predominance of a form of Marxist-Leninist rhetorical discourse, with which anyone desiring to make an effective intervention in the public sphere had to conform.

An analysis of the rhetoric of the period leading up to the 17 June 1953, and particularly of the ambiguities in cultural policy, which does not take into account the functioning of this discourse in the relationship of people to power

[37] Naimark, p. 287.
[38] Naimark, p. 288.
[39] Naimark, p. 284.

and in the formation and development of political categories, will tend to interpret attempts at meaningful, independent action as either irrelevant or cynical. This un-differentiated view, which characterised much Western writing on German division until very recently, is to some extent to be explained by the general unavailability of archival sources in the GDR, but also stems from a failure to engage with the broader view of the functioning of Soviet politics and society which has emerged in the last two decades. Its persistence in parts of the academic community (to say nothing of post-Cold War politics) is a manifestation of that peculiar process by which attitudes which were ingrained during the Cold War have resisted introspection since the collapse of the Soviet Bloc. The various positions occupied by historians in this debate can be seen as developments of the controversies over issues such as Stalin's *Notenkampagne* of 1952, which have occupied commentators throughout the last four decades.[40]

---

[40] A volume by the Göttinger Arbeitskreis, *Die Deutschlandfrage von der staatlichen Teilung Deutschlands bis zum Tode Stalins* (Berlin: Duncker & Humblot, 1994), provides a good overview of the most recent arguments against the conclusions drawn by Wilfried Loth. Loth's work, which has been referred to in this study, places him squarely in the camp of those who had to rely on a feeling that something was amiss with the orthodox Western view of Stalin's European policy, a feeling based necessarily on evidence which seemed unconvincing to many; see, for example, Rolf Steininger, *Eine vertane Chance: Die Stalin-Note vom 10. März 1952 und die Wiedervereinigung* (Berlin: J. H. W. Dietz Nachf., 1986). Since the opening up of the archives of the former Soviet Union and GDR, historians whose work places them within this tradition can refer to a body of evidence at least sufficient to rebut charges of political naivety. What I have identified as the 'orthodox' view of Stalin in the Western historiography of the GDR seems, with reference to debates among historians of 'Stalinism', to be in itself as much a product of speculation as anything in the work of Steininger or Loth. A more nuanced analysis is beginning to emerge, for example in the work of Norman Naimark, but his account of the SMAD is still forced to rely on speculation when it comes to Stalin's intentions (see, for example, p. 352, where Naimark makes a leap of faith concerning an identity of interests between Stalin and Tyul'panov). In the previous chapter, the ideological implications of the use of the word 'Stalinism' were discussed; in a similar way, many historians refer to 'Moscow' as the ultimate source of policy or decision–making, a rather journalistic usage which conveys a feeling of Nineteenth-Century Great Power politics and the historiographical *Primat der Außenpolitik*. Naimark is occasionally guilty of this, reflecting the tone of many studies whose parameters were set before 1989. In the field of cultural policy, the conclusions drawn in the most comprehensive recent study—David Pike, *The Politics of Culture in Soviet-Occupied Germany, 1945-1949* (Stanford: Stanford University Press, 1992)—are distorted by this speculative style, reflecting an unwillingness to engage in the opportunity for re-evaluation presented by the end of the Cold War. Other analyses, attempting to broaden the methodological approaches to GDR cultural policy, are also emerging: see, for instance, David Bathrick's interesting Foucault-inspired study of the functioning of power and resistance in GDR literary discourse, *The Powers of Speech. The Politics of Culture in the GDR* (Lincoln: University of Nebraska Press, 1996), John Torpey's sketchier attempt to apply a form of Gramscian analysis to the intellectual community, *Intellectuals, Socialism and Dissent. The East German Opposition and its Legacy* (Minneapolis: University of Minnesota Press, 1995), and Albert O. Hirschman, 'Exit, Voice, and the Fate of the German Democratic Republic. An Essay in Conceptual History', *World Politics*, 45 (1993), 173-202. For an example of the rich rewards which this kind of work *can* bring, see Stephen Kotkin's brilliant application of Foucault's analysis of the functioning of 'power at the micro-level' in Magnitogorsk during the Stalin era, *Magnetic Mountain. Stalinism as a Civilization* (Berkeley: University of California Press, 1995).

If we are to deal with these issues, which ultimately boil down to questions of political responsibility and the problem of distinguishing resistance from complicity, then we need to distance ourselves from a view which sees Marxist-Leninist rhetoric *simply* as a means of control 'from above', rather than as a dynamic discursive system in which the individual's self-understanding is formed in a continuing dialectical relationship with centres of power which reserve for themselves the right to define meanings, categories and boundaries. The apparatus of power was employed literally to change the meanings of words: the specific case referred to here is the unrelenting ideological campaign of SMAD officers such as Tyul'panov, which, interacting with other competing or complementary influences, produced a self-fulfilling prophecy by which East-West conflict and the division of Germany came to *seem* inevitable. The consequences of this for individuals within the SED leadership were profound:

i) Anyone who wished to make a political intervention was obliged to work within the parameters of Marxism-Leninism, or else be branded a 'renegade', with all the threat of physical coercion which this implied. Thus, a conscious effort was needed to 'dress up' ideas in acceptable clothing.

ii) However, the self-understanding of the SED leaders was formed in their upbringing within the all-pervasive categories of Marxism-Leninism, so the language in which they expressed concepts such as 'democracy', and which delimited the meanings which they could ascribe to it, was instantly unacceptable to Western politicians (and voters).

SED leaders such as Ackermann and, especially, Johannes R. Becher are caught in this tension between the desire to work within the system to which they have committed themselves, and to exploit Marxist rhetoric in order to further their own passionately-held beliefs,[41] and their vulnerability to manipulation of the language and the meanings in which these beliefs are formed.

---

[41] See Gniffke, p. 192, who reports a speech made by Ackermann at a meeting of SED leaders on 17 July 1946, in which he declares: 'Wir müssen zurück zum Ur-Marxismus, der kein Dogma sein wollte, sondern nur *eine Anleitung zum Handeln*' [my emphasis].

The insights which this kind of investigation can bring allow us to view the function of rhetoric in a more meaningful light than is possible if it is seen simply as a means of control. Situating the shifting discourse of German division within a broader framework of the functioning of power within the Soviet Zone avoids interpretations which rely on a purely utilitarian view of this rhetoric, and which consequently devote their energy to identifying what was happening 'behind' the rhetoric, to uncovering what was 'concealed'.

When Colonel Tyul'panov warns the SED leadership against 'Unterschätzung der Ideologie als Herrschaftsmittel',[42] he recognises the importance of ideology in a way which is ignored in the methodology of many Western historians. This recognition of the constitutive role of Marxist-Leninist ideology in the self-understanding of the SED leaders demolishes the idea that understanding the rhetoric of the SMAD is simply a question of distinguishing 'truth' from 'falsehood', and undermines the critical position from which the complexity of compromised figures within the leadership can be dismissed out of hand and the very basis of their actions discredited. The ambiguity of Marxism-Leninism, which was also its strength in this peculiarly German context, lies in the tension between its claims to scientific objectivity and its self-conscious application as instrument of power; for German intellectuals who had opposed Nazism, the options for opposition to the sovietisation of Eastern Germany were severely limited, as a stance based on capitalism, or the kind of nationalist opposition which developed in Russia and other states in the Soviet Union or Eastern Bloc, could not be countenanced. Instead, they were obliged to conduct their interventions from within a discourse whose centres of power excluded them, and the definition of whose meanings, categories and boundaries was out of their hands.[43]

The identification of Marxism-Leninism with the objective, scientific truth has more in common with the procedures of many of its Western critics than they would care to admit: it is, so the argument goes, simply a matter of

---

[42] Report of 10.7.1947 on the SED's work in the first half of 1947, Badstübner and Loth, p. 128.

[43] I hesitate to use the word 'obliged' in this sentence, as it does not adequately describe an interaction of coercion and free choice which is both external—the boundaries of public action and expression and the threat of retaliation if they are violated—and internalised. The chooser exerts free will, but the choice is made from within ideology, so the terms of the choice, which seem to be self-evident to the chooser, are pre-determined.

stripping away the lies in order to expose the reality of the system underneath. This has the effect of 'rewriting history in the dialectical manner', that is, of replacing one set of received truths with another.[44] Both *apparatchik* and Western critic share a faith in the ability of language to give a truthful account of a historical situation, so that if the rhetorical acrobatics of Marxism-Leninism are not 'the truth', then they must be 'lies'. At the centre of this symbolic system is the figure of Stalin as the undifferentiated embodiment of an evil which transcends history, and which obviates the necessity of examining issues of individual responsibility and of complicity and resistance to power.

As we have seen, this view of Stalin can no longer be sustained, and interpretations which contain elements deriving from Cold War political ortho-doxies are beginning to fade in serious academic debate. Thus, by overcoming their adversary, which was, after all, only the mirror image, the propagandistic obverse on which they relied for their legitimacy, Western triumphalist visions brought about their own dissolution in favour of the more nuanced understanding which has had to struggle against orthodoxies in both halves of the divided Germany. Rolf Badstübner, in an article exploring the consequences of the fall of the Berlin Wall for East German historiography, describes an opportunity to explore GDR history 'in einer radikal veränderten Sicht, von einem Ergebnis der Geschichte her, das eine beträchtliche Umwertung von Werten einschließt'.[45] This critique of previous practice is part of the historicisation of the claims to truth made by the conflicting ideological systems, a point made by Slavoj Žižek in his analysis of 'the two modes of cynical ideology' (that is, consumerism and 'really existing socialism'):

Perhaps the key feature of the symbolic economy of the late 'real Socialism' was [...] the almost paranoiac *belief in the power of the Word*; the state and the ruling party reacted with utmost nervousness and panic at the slightest public criticism, as if some vague critical hints in an obscure poem published in a low-circulation literary journal, or an essay in an academic philosophical journal, possessed the potential capacity to trigger the explosion of the entire socialist system [...] ['Real Socialism'] bears witness to the legacy of the Enlightenment (the

[44] Sheila Fitzpatrick, 'Constructing Stalinism: Changing Western and Soviet Perspectives', in *The Stalin Phen-omenon*, ed. by Alec Nove (London: Weidenfeld and Nicolson, 1993), p. 95.

[45] Rolf Badstübner, 'Die Abkehr vom "besonderen deutschen Weg"', in *Brüche—Krisen—Wendepunkte: Neu-befragung von DDR-Geschichte*, ed. by Jochen Černý (Leipzig: Urania-Verlag, 1990), pp. 14–27 (p. 15).

belief in the social efficacy of rational argument) that survived in it. This, perhaps, was why it was possible to undermine 'real Socialism' by means of peaceful civil society movements that operated at the level of the Word: belief in the power of the Word was the system's Achilles heel.[46]

Thus, the demise of 'Real Socialism' threatens a form of Western historical and cultural discourse which based its opposition to 'Communism' on this 'belief in the power of the Word'.

Analysis of GDR political and cultural life is now able to take into account the progress of current investigations into conflicts of interest within Soviet and SED *Deutschlandpolitik*, the breaking down of the monolithic view of 'Stalinism' and of Stalin as omnipotent dictator with an almost mystical ability to impose his will on events,[47] and the important theoretical considerations which arise when the claims to truth of certain forms of historical and cultural criticism are seen in their proper historical context. Bearing this in mind, we are now able to offer a more satisfactory account of the development of SED policy and the movement towards German division than interpretations which stress the *purely* utilitarian nature of Marxist-Leninist rhetorical discourse as an integrative ideology demonstrating the monolithic consistency of Soviet and SED policy.

In the most comprehensive recent attempt to analyse the development of SMAD and SED rhetoric (in the context of cultural policy) David Pike bases his assumptions about the 'German Road' and the actions of figures such as Becher on a highly mechanistic understanding of the functioning of rhetorical discourse. He is right to see the changing emphases in the rhetoric of German unity as a means of control, but language cannot function purely as an instrument, as

---

[46] Slavoj Žižek, 'The Spectre of Ideology', in *Mapping Ideology* (London: Verso, 1994), ed. by Slavoj Žižek, pp. 18f. Emphasis in original. The argument put forward here is central to any understanding of GDR cultural policy, and I will return to it in the following chapters. It seems to me that the reason why the literary culture of the GDR, with its ambiguous coexistence of complicity and resistance, still has the ability to provoke and disturb in a unified Germany lies precisely in this point: its stubborn refusal to conform satisfactorily to the categories in which many West German critics and politicians conceived it, implicitly calls into question certain values and concepts of truth which crystallised during the Cold War.

[47] See, for instance, Robert Conquest's discussion of willpower in politics in *20/20. A view of the Century: Controlling,* BBC Radio 4, October 1995 (Producer: Susanne Levy): 'Well, the more one reads about Stalin, and of course about Hitler, the more one gets the feeling that there is something about willpower in politics [...] the ability to impose your will which Lenin had as well, which when you read it, it doesn't feel rational.'

Zweck-Sprache, whatever the intentions of the speaker. The confines of the discourse in which the Stalinist *apparatchik* has been trained must contribute to defining the limitations of his/her thinking, and this should be taken into account in any attempt to fathom the intentions behind a particular rhetorical device. To see Becher and Ackermann, to name two of the most important examples, as simply masters of expedient rhetoric is to miss layers of meaning and vital questions of political—and artistic—responsibility, as well as to leave un-questioned assumptions which, as we have seen, have been seriously challenged in recent writing on Soviet history.

Ackermann's 'German Road' thesis is intimately bound up with the questions of intellectual responsibility which are the subject of my study. In a sense, it is the key issue. If his position was a tactical counterpoint to that of Ulbricht, if, in Pike's words, 'each approach was a tactical variant of Soviet policy toward Germany in general',[48] designed as a 'carrot and stick' policy for the intellectual community, then it *is* possible to dismiss all aspirations for German unity, and all historical studies which look for possible alternative outcomes, as fanciful nonsense.

If an analysis of the rhetoric is based on this rather superficial reading, then it is possible to assume that the twists and turns of policy are simply 'tampering with theoretical rationalizations',[49] but often these rationalisations are symptom-atic of deeper power struggles, so that debates on German policy in the Politburo of the Soviet Communist Party 'constituted a means to an end, rather than being at the core of the issue itself'.[50] This phenomenon has been amply analysed in the field of Soviet Studies, as the discussion in the previous chapter has shown, but it is a concept which, until recently, has made only a limited impression on writing about GDR history, much of which shows a marked reluctance to engage with the imposing myth of Stalin. The holes in our knowledge about the chains of command between the various conflicting interests in Moscow, SMAD and SED are filled with speculation; for example, the SED's harder-line approach in

---

[48] Pike, *The Politics of Culture*, p. 44.
[49] Pike, *The Politics of Culture*, p. 34.
[50] Ra'anan, p. 159.

Autumn 1947 is 'a rigid political line *presumably* encouraged by Stalin'.[51] It is to be hoped that an analysis which takes into account both the end of the monolithic model of Soviet rule, and a more satisfactory approach to the problem of Marxist-Leninist rhetoric, will provide a more nuanced understanding of the survival within the SED of ideas and aspirations taking their inspiration from the 'German Road' thesis.

It is true that Ackermann's presentation of his ideas, and their expression in the *Grundsätze und Ziele* of the SED (which he co-edited with Helmut Lehmann), are encumbered with the baggage of Marxism-Leninism, but this is inevitable given his background and training, with its stress on the historical inevitability of Socialism. His association with the SMAD officers opposed to the group connected with Zhdanov indicates that his ideas are representative of a current of opinion encouraged in the KPD/SED in order to assist in a purely political struggle within the Soviet camp. The disparity between the aspirations expressed by the 'German Road' thesis and the plundering intentions of Beria and Malenkov is shocking, but there is a clear common interest in negotiations over German unity.

In the light of my discussion of Marxist-Leninist rhetoric, we can begin to move towards an understanding of why those in the SED leadership who were inclined towards an all-German line were, finally, incapable of exploiting the considerable room for manoeuvre which was open to them.[52] The period in question, the run-up to the 2nd SED Congress (20–24 September 1947), was to prove crucial in setting the parameters for this room for manoeuvre, as the contradictions within Soviet German policy began to crystallise as Stalin was forced onto the defensive over the Marshall Plan. The ideological campaign conducted by Tyul'panov in this period, which seems to contain so many contradictory elements, begins to make more sense now that we have attempted

---

[51] Pike, *The Politics of Culture*, p. 375. My emphasis.

[52] The further development of Ackermann's career shows that he had been involved in real struggles within the SED: his involvement with and support for Rudolf Herrnstadt and Wilhelm Zaisser in their attempt to unseat Ulbricht in June 1953 led to his expulsion from the Central Committee. Despite his political rehabilitation in July 1956, he never regained the high office or influence which he had enjoyed. He committed suicide in 1973, aged 67.

to examine the function of this rhetoric in the particular circumstances of post-war Germany.

As we have seen, any hopes that the Moscow Foreign Ministers' Conference would produce movement towards German unity were dashed on seemingly irreconcilable differences between the Soviets and the Allies. However, an examination of the positions of the SED delegation and Stalin during the formers' visit to Moscow (30 January to 7 February 1947) in preparation for the con-ference shows that Stalin exhibited a far greater readiness to compromise on the issue of the form of a united Germany than did the SED. As will become clear, this throws a new light on the campaign for ideological conformity which preceded the SED's September Congress.

The SED delegation consisted of Pieck, Grotewohl, Ulbricht, Fechner and Fred Oelßner in his capacity as interpreter.[53] The bulk of the programme was taken up with courtesy visits and cultural occasions, possessing all the 'ritualistic qualities'[54] which were intended to enhance the prestige of the leadership. Clearly, visits such as this did not increase the 'prestige' of the SED leaders amongst the bulk of the population, or indeed with all of the rank-and-file membership, but they instead gave a ritualistic expression to the idea of the SED as the 'Russians' party'; this could only work to the benefit of those within the party who favoured integration of the GDR into the Soviet sphere.

The discussion with Stalin and other Soviet leaders on 31 January began with a report read by Grotewohl in which he set out the SED's opposition to the Allies' insistence on a federal form of government for a united Germany. This opposition had support from the Soviet side, ostensibly because federalism would lead to a 'Schwächung D[eutschlands]'.[55] We have already seen that the Soviet opposition to a federal structure at the Moscow Conference was based on a fear, to a great extent justified, that this would ensure Allied dominance over any central administration. This is the first issue over which the divergence between Stalin and the SED becomes clear:

---

[53] Pieck's notes from the Moscow trip are in Badstübner and Loth, pp. 110–126. Complementing Pieck's notes is a Soviet stenographic version of the meeting with Stalin on 31 January, published by Rolf Badstübner in *Utopie: Kreativ,* 7 (1991), 105–7.

[54] Naimark, p. 298.

[55] Badstübner and Loth, p. 112.

Die sowjetische Seite war offensichtlich zu weitergehenden Kompromissen in Richtung auf das von den Westmächten stark favorisierte föderalistische Prinzip in bezug auf Deutschland bereit bis hin zur möglichen provisorischen deutschen Regierungsbildung aus den Länderregierungen und einem Zweikammersystem.[56]

The harder-line approach articulated by the SED leadership concentrated exclusively on central representation and the primacy of the *Blockparteien* and mass organisations. In March 1947, Grotewohl expressed his opposition to the bicameral system suggested by Molotov at the Moscow Conference,[57] and this intransigence 'on the ground', where the SED was anyway 'taking a terrible propaganda beating',[58] was bound to prove more decisive than Stalin's vaguely-defined readiness to compromise, hedged about as it was by fearful caveats about Western domination and by the internal factional conflicts which were finding their expression in the Economists' Debate. As Loth has shown, Stalin retained this willingness to compromise at least until the 19th Congress of the Soviet Communist Party. This conclusion is supported by the survival of an all-German line within the SED leadership, and particularly within GDR cultural institutions, even after Ackermann was forced to retract the 'German Road' thesis in September 1948.

The disparity between Stalin's willingness to compromise and the intransigence of the most influential line in the SED leadership, which was closer to the line which Zhdanov was developing at this time, brings us to the other issue over which differences between Stalin and the SED are beginning to crystallise. At issue is Stalin's belief that he *can* bring about a unified Germany, and his lack of genuine understanding of the situation on the ground in the Soviet Zone. For example, Grotewohl's report at the meeting on 31 January evidently contained the assertion that a referendum would achieve a majority in favour of German unity of 30 million of the 50 million eligible to vote. Pieck's notes record Stalin's comment: 'Ob bei Volksabstimmung über Einheit D[eutschlands] nicht noch/ größere Mehrheit als 30 Mill. von 50 Mill.'[59]

---

[56] Badstübner and Loth, p. 124, footnote 6.
[57] *10. Tagung des Parteivorstandes*, 26/27.3.1947, cit. Badstübner and Loth, p. 124, footnote 6.
[58] Naimark, p. 301.
[59] Badstübner and Loth, p. 111.

Stalin is seemingly unaware that his vision of German unity, identified with the SED and with the imposition of a system by an unaccountable Soviet executive, is simply unacceptable to the overwhelming majority of voters in the Western zones; the ideology of revolution which informs Soviet political culture not only leaves its leaders unable to conceive of finding solutions which are not imposed directly from above, but also blinds them to aspects of their history which do not fit this pattern. As Moshe Lewin has said, the Soviet state has 'a history itself that is not all made by itself and not entirely to its own taste'.[60] The suppression of any analysis which might show that fundamentally uncontrollable social processes had contributed to, or even determined, Soviet history, doubtless combined with a fear that things could go terrifyingly out of hand without strict controls (as, in fact, happened in the 1930s), meant that Stalin was constrained in his German policy both by circumstances (Cold War tensions and Politburo in-fighting) and by his own position within the prevailing ideology.[61]

Many of the suggestions made by Stalin and Molotov illustrate their conceptual inadequacy, particularly their interest in combating the influence of the SPD. The SED's opposition to the suggestion that the SPD could be licensed in the Soviet Zone in exchange for the legalisation of the SED in the West, is understandable, as the suggestion shows an astonishing lack of understanding of

---

[60] Moshe Lewin, *The Making of the Soviet System: Essays in the Social History of Interwar Russia* (London: Methuen, 1985), p. 8.

[61] His privileged position within the discourse of Marxism-Leninism, which allowed him an influence on the definition of meanings and boundaries within this discourse, allowed Stalin to develop a somewhat more independent vision for his German policy, and a certain amount of leeway in exploiting ideology as a tool. Loth, while dismantling the view of Stalin as all-powerful, but blinkered, ideologue (surely, anyway, a contradiction in terms), underestimates the ideological constraints on Stalin's ability to form policy independently: '[Stalins] Sozialismus-Begriff war relativ offen und orientierte sich an dem, was er im Interesse des Sowjetstaates für notwendig hielt. Die realpolitischen Notwendigkeiten, die er bei Kriegsende sah, bestimmten nicht nur sein Programm, sondern griffen auch auf seine Vorstellungen von der Zukunft des Sozialismus über' (Loth, p. 34). This picture of rational calculation of interests is not quite consistent with the manner in which Stalin conducts his campaign, although it must certainly have appeared rational to him. What is fascinating about the struggle for ideological supremacy in the Soviet Zone is that it is conducted from within the parameters of a specific ideological discourse, with each actor attempting, with never more than partial success, to exploit ideology as a tool. Stalin's ability to create definitions within the discourse of Marxism-Leninism was necessarily limited by, for example, the legacy of Lenin, the enormous socio-political developments in the Soviet Union (let alone Central Europe in 1945) which forced the regime to redefine its ideology if it was to continue to appear in control, and by the need to personify the regime's failings in figures such as Trotsky, Tito and Schumacher. Thus, Stalin could not be the final arbiter of 'historical truth', as he has been portrayed in Western political discourse ('Big Brother'); the vital symbolic role which the figure of Stalin played in Marxism-Leninism could thus work against his programme in Germany, where he was removed from the everyday interactions of people with ideology and power.

the SED's potential support in both West and East. Objections on the part of the SED leaders are brushed aside,[62] and the Soviets instead indulge their demonisation of Schumacher as the major opponent of German unity, imagining that the SPD in the West can be split.[63] Such ideas must have worried the SED leadership, with their superior understanding of conditions on the ground, as their political hegemony, and quite likely their influence on politics in a unified Germany, would have been under threat. It seems unlikely that Stalin would have been concerned about the electoral fate of Ulbricht, Pieck and Grotewohl if his programme for Germany had succeeded, so the political survival of the SED leaders depended on the Soviets' inability to trust anyone who did not constantly protest their loyalty. Paradoxically, the louder the declarations of loyalty in the SED, the less likely it became that Stalin would achieve his aims in Germany.

As it was, the SED did not have to worry about the licensing of the SPD in the Soviet Zone, as Kurt Schumacher refused to apply for a licence. However, the problem remained that the achievement of German unity was fundamentally incompatible with the maintenance of SED hegemony, and so the SED leadership was no doubt pleased to hear Molotov state, in his summing up at the end of the 31 January meeting, that a unified government might have to be formed in the SBZ if a central German administration proved unachievable.[64]

The 31 January meeting was the most important as far as policy was concerned, but if we apply the type of analysis developed in the course of this study to the remaining events in the itinerary, then seemingly minor details, when placed in the context of the drive for conformity, yield a fuller understanding of the contradictions in the SED's position. On 4 February, a meeting was arranged with Suslov, in order to give the SED leaders a more detailed insight into the organisation and structure of the Soviet Communist Party. It is not clear why this was deemed necessary for functionaries such as Pieck and Ulbricht, with their long experience of Soviet affairs; Naimark asserts

---

[62] Comment on Grotewohl's report: '*Zulassung der SPD* in sowj. Besatzungszone,/ ob SED Angst hat vor SPD/ man muß sie politisch schlagen.' Badstübner and Loth, p. 112.

[63] 'Ob linke Elemente in der SPD—mit denen Einheitsfront-Komitees/—Ausschüsse gegen Reaktion im Westen' Badstübner and Loth, p. 112.

[64] Naimark, p. 300.

that the meeting was held 'at the request of the Germans',[65] so it may well have been for the benefit of Fechner and Grotewohl, as an exercise in ideological loyalty. What is significant in this context is the internalisation of instinctive expressions of loyalty, and perhaps more important, the unconscious acceptance of the institutional authority of the Soviet model, which hinders the flexible approach to policymaking which would have been necessary for the achievement of German unity.

The disastrous effect of this ideological campaign on hopes of achieving German unity makes itself felt in the smallest details: Pieck's notes record Suslov's insistence on the Bolshevik virtues of 'Disziplin', 'Einheit', 'Reinheit der Parteireihen' and 'Aktivität jedes Parteimitgliedes'. However, he also makes statements which, in the context of Stalin's developing line in the run-up to the Moscow Conference, can be read as warnings to the SED. The Soviet party is to be 'keine Schablone', and there are certain conditions which must be met before a Communist party can become the 'Regierungspartei': 'unter Bedingungen der sozialistischen Gesellschaft, wo Klassengegner liquidiert u. Prod. Mittel/ in Händen der Werktätigen.'[66]

Here we see very clearly the divergence between the official Soviet line and the interests of the 'integrationists' within the SED. The instinct to adopt Soviet models, or at least to refer to Soviet models as a legitimising device in establishing power, is constantly being reinforced by the ritualised trappings of the visit to Moscow, and by, in this case, Suslov's detailed and no doubt tediously self-important account of the party structure. This self-importance, the assumption of the right to rule, is an integral characteristic of functionaries like Ulbricht, and the threat to this *Führungsanspruch* implicit in nuanced warnings about Communist rule being impossible without the correct economic conditions, would not have been lost on him.

The increasingly virulent propaganda battles in the first half of 1947, combined with the oppressive nature of SMAD control, should not blind us to the fact that 'Stalin and his lieutenants seriously considered an "all-German" formula for solving both their problems in Central Europe and the SED's

---

[65] Naimark, p. 301.
[66] Badstübner and Loth, p. 114.

problems in the zone'.[67] The issue in question is what motivated this 'all-German' line and how long it continued to be a factor in Soviet deliberations; if we continue to use formulae such as 'Stalin and his lieutenants', then it seems to me that we are unlikely to be able to achieve a fuller understanding, in the sense that elements of the monolithic model of Soviet politics will tend to distort interpretation. It is only by following developments in the GDR and Soviet Union through to June 1953 that we are able to understand the survival, seemingly against all odds, of the 'all-German' orientation within GDR institutions.

The 'German Road' thesis was coming under increasing pressure by the middle of 1947; until this point, it was of a piece with the policy of separate roads to socialism associated with politicians like Władysław Gomułka and Georgi Dimitrov. The special situation with regard to the continuing negotiations with the Allies over Germany meant that the SED was not invited to the inaugural conference of the Cominform (22–27 September) where the idea of separate roads to socialism was finally put to rest. The suspicions of the opponents of the 'German road' thesis, such as Pieck and Ulbricht, were encouraged by Tyul'panov in the run-up to the Second SED Congress: Naimark notes that Tyul'panov complained about 'residual nationalism and chauvinism' in Ackermann's ideas.[68] At a time when Stalin was pressing for negotiations over German unity, Tyul'panov's actions demonstrate a remarkable independence, placing him firmly in the 'integrationist' camp. Along with Ulbricht, he seems to be trying to create 'facts on the ground' which make the physical unification of the two Germanies increasingly difficult.

The cadres policy pursued by Ulbricht is a case in point: the Soviet administrators were noted for their 'interference, inconsistency, and the ingrained habit of blaming others (in this case the Germans) for their own failings'.[69] Ulbricht's policy was to develop the reliability and competence of German administrators, who would then be able to assume responsibility in the Soviet Zone and give the Germans a measure of control over their own affairs.

[67] Naimark, p. 301.
[68] Naimark, p. 303.
[69] Naimark, p. 46.

His success in this is another reflection of the duality within Soviet policy: the training and employment of German administrators was fully consistent with the policy of independent German political development, but Ulbricht's hold over the appointment of cadres made sovietisation more, rather than less, likely. This is the paradoxical situation in which those who opposed sovietisation were caught: assertion of a line independent of 'Stalinism' made the independent development of Germany less likely.

The Personnel Policy Department of the SED was modelled closely on the Cadres Department of the Soviet Central Committee, allowing the creation of a more hierarchical administrative structure, which facilitated the removal of opponents while also contributing to increased efficiency.[70] Clearly, the constant emphasis on Soviet models clashed with the aims of Stalin's foreign policy, giving the green light to Ulbricht's efforts to ensure that German unity was impossible.[71] The great achievement of the 'integrationists' in the ideological sphere was to present sovietisation and Soviet models as the norm, as the symbolic foundation (in the monolithic figure of Stalin) of Marxist discourse, so that attempts to establish different meanings for concepts such as 'democracy', or even 'Marxism' (for example, Ackermann's 'Ur-Marxismus') came to seem deviant. Those who defended these alternative positions had also to struggle against the norms which governed the ideological system in which they formed their views.

The drive for ideological conformity gained pace in the Summer of 1947, in the wake of the declaration of the Marshall Plan (5 June 1947). Stalin actually came close to accepting the Plan: 'Stalin hatte sich mit der Absage an den Marshall-Plan offensichtlich schwergetan.'[72] Similarly, the Soviet response to

---

[70] Even so, it took until the end of 1947 to remove Dr Ferdinand Friedensburg, whom Ulbricht deeply mistrusted. As co-founder of the CDU in the Soviet Zone, First Deputy Mayor of Greater Berlin, Deputy Chairman of the Gesellschaft zum Studium der Kultur der Sowjetunion Berlin, and member of the Präsidialrat of the Kulturbund, Friedensburg enjoyed considerable support within the SMAD. He fled to the West in late 1947 when the pressure on him became unbearable. The departure of important figures such as Friedensburg meant that there was little or no opposition to 'sovietisation' amongst politicians in the SBZ which did not originate from within the discourse of Marxism-Leninism.

[71] The emphasis of SED cadres policy changed in 1947, when Franz Dahlem took over the Personnel Policy Department; Dahlem 'tried to balance the competence of the individual with their party attributes' (Naimark, p. 47). This policy lasted until early 1949.

[72] Loth, *Stalins ungeliebtes Kind*, p. 92. The Soviets prevaricated for some weeks before rejecting the Plan. See Alexander O. Tschubarjan, 'Auf dem Weg nach Europa—aus Moskauer Sicht', in *Der Lange Weg nach*

the Munich Conference of Chief Ministers (5–8 June 1947) was far from consistent,[73] but it is notable that a majority in the SED Central Secretariat[74] voted in favour of participation, overruling Ulbricht, who was positioning himself as the represent-ative of Soviet wishes. The failure of the conference, on the issue of central German administration as opposed to federalism, can only have worked to Ulbricht's advantage.[75]

The willingness to compromise and negotiate exhibited by Stalin bore little resemblance to the hard line peddled by Ulbricht; the Soviets' obsession with counteracting the supposedly pernicious influence of Schumacher, in order to achieve conformity within the SED, detracted from the party's usefulness as a tool in Stalin's German policy.[76] This basic contradiction in SMAD policy is illustrated in remarks made by Tyul'panov in an extraordinarily critical report on the SED's work in the first half of 1947.[77] The first point of importance is the Soviet insistence that the Moscow Conference had been a success; this official optimism indicates a certain desperation on the part of the Soviet leadership. This optimism about the possibility of unification runs side-by-side with critical comments on the ideological work of the party, and attacks on Schumacher. There seems to be no indication that Tyul'panov is at all aware of the incongruity of the views expressed in this document, although it would have been clear to anyone who stood to gain from German division that the ideological criticisms made here could only increase the influence of the

Europa, ed. by Wolfgang J. Mommsen (Berlin: Peter Lang, 1992), pp. 267–302. Documents from the Soviet Foreign Ministry show that the Soviet government seriously considered participation in the European reconstruction plan, and that the debate in Moscow was divided, along the lines set in the Economists' Debate, between those who favoured participation and negotiation, and hard-liners who believed in the imminent crisis of capitalism (Tschubarjan, p. 288). The final straw was the obstructive behaviour of Bevin and Bidault at the Paris Conference (25 June–2 July).

[73] The official SMAD line changed from cautious approval of sending representatives from the SBZ, to outright rejection; presumably this prevarication centred around the fear that the conference might encourage federalist tendencies. See Loth, *Stalins ungeliebtes Kind*, p. 90.

[74] Including Gniffke, Fechner, Ackermann, Paul Merker and Elli Schmidt, according to Gniffke, pp. 236–41.

[75] On the Munich Conference, see Rolf Steininger, 'Zur Geschichte der Münchener Ministerpräsidentenkonferenz 1947', *Vierteljahrshefte für Zeitgeschichte*, 23 (1975), 375–453; and R. S., '"Dieser Vorfall bedeutet die Spaltung Deutschlands." Neue Dokumente zur Münchener Ministerpräsidentenkonferenz im Juni 1947', *Geschichte im Westen*, 7 (1992), 213–30.

[76] The assertion made by Badstübner and Loth, that 'die politische Ausrichtung der SED gegen die "Schumacher SPD" von Seiten der SMAD wenn nicht initiiert, so doch besonders vehement und unnachgiebig gefordert und betrieben wurde' (Badstübner and Loth, p. 130), seems incontrovertible.

[77] 'Bericht über innerparteiliche Lage im letzten Halbjahr', 11.7.1947, Badstübner and Loth, pp. 127–30.

'integrationist' line. Tyul'panov's criticisms of 'Schwächen in der ideolog. Arbeit', of 'Widersprüche u. Schwank-ungen / in den Leitungen', and of 'Sektierertum' sit uneasily at the very least with explicit references to past KPD failures, which stemmed from 'Unterschätzung des demokr. Parlamentarismus'.

Even this sharp criticism of past KPD practice, reaching back deliberately to the extensive self-criticism which led to the Popular Front policy, is ambiguous: the tactic of reassessing the past in order to change the ideological perspective on the present brings with it an indeterminacy in the meaning of concepts used in the rhetoric which distinctly favours those with the power to influence meanings, as well as physical circumstances, on the ground. Tyul'panov's criticism continues:

Fehlen einer richtigen u. Konkreten Analyse / der Vergangenheit / Frage der Ideologie ohne Verbindung zu den / Klassen / u. Trennung von den materiellen Verhältnissen / Hitler-Ideologie nicht als Klassenideologie der / Großkap. u. Großgrundbes.

This renewed emphasis on the traditional Marxist-Leninist theory of fascism has clear implications both for relations with Western Germany and for attempts at *Vergangenheitsbewältigung* in the Soviet Zone. The SED leadership is being primed to accept as natural a militant ideology, with the Soviet Union as paradigm, which is presented as the best way to guarantee German unity.[78] Those who perceived the contradiction were better placed to assert their line in the Soviet Zone. Tyul'panov has left himself some room for manoeuvre by characterising fascism as the ideology of the great landowners, rather than of the bourgeoisie as such; this distinction, meaningless in practical terms and from the point of view of anyone not trained within Marxist-Leninist discursive practice, meant that Tyul'panov had the correct ideological justification for keeping a door open for the CDU.[79]

---

[78] Tyul'panov regrets 'Mangel in der Übermittlung einer richtigen / Vorstellung / über ökon. u. pol. System der SU'.

[79] Tyul'panov gave assurances to Jakob Kaiser, head of the CDU in the Soviet Zone, in August 1947: 'Wir wissen, daß die CDU die stärkste Partei ist und wahrscheinlich auch in einer künftigen deutschen Regierung einen sehr starken Einfluß haben wird, stärker als die SED. Wir wollen mit der CDU wirklich arbeiten, nicht nur spielen' (cit. Loth, *Stalins ungeliebtes Kind*, p. 104). Kaiser and his deputy Ernst Lemmer were removed from their posts by the SMAD on 19 December 1947 for refusing to participate in the First German People's Congress. See also Rolf Badstübner, 'Die sowjetische Deutschlandpolitik im Lichte neuer Quellen', in Wilfried

The official Soviet line on federalism remained more flexible than that of the SED, exhibiting a still optimistic negotiating position: 'Einheit Deutschlands / gut gestellt—aber doch—ob Föderalismus besser / als Spaltung in zwei Teile'.[80] The consequences of a federal system for the survival of the SED as a political force would have been disastrous, and the seeming readiness of the Soviets to sacrifice the SED in the interests of securing German unity helps to explain the careful advances made by SMAD officers to the leaders of the other parties in the Soviet Zone. The dualistic nature of Tyul'panov's position, as set out in this report, is reflected in the officially upbeat tone: what Rolf Badstübner describes as 'einen doch recht oberflächlichen Optimismus'.[81] These somewhat strained aspirations contrast starkly with the effectiveness of the ideological campaign which undermined them, and which characterised any attempt at independence of thought as 'bourgeois nationalism'.[82]

Further critical assessments of SED policy and preparation followed,[83] whose ideological thrust continued to undermine the credibility of the all-German programme, while contributing to a set of conditions in which division seemed inevitable:

Weil [die Sowjet-Administratoren und die SED-Führer] aber nicht wußten und auch kaum wissen konnten, was sie taten, konnten sie auch die Gegenwehr der demokratischen Kräfte gegen ihre vermeintlichen Hegemonieansprüche nur als Angriff auf die demokratische Ordnung schlechthin wahrnehmen. Der Zwang zum Rückgriff auf Repression und Agitation wurde folglich immer stärker empfunden, und die daraus resultierende Praxis heizte die Furcht der Demokraten nur noch weiter an. Gleichzeitig wuchs der Einfluß derjenigen, die, bewußt oder unbewußt, tatsächlich auf Hegemonie aus waren.[84]

Loth (ed.), *Die deutsche Frage in der Nachkriegszeit* (Berlin: Akademie Verlag, 1994), pp. 115–33 (pp. 121–22), for details of the approaches made to LDP Chairman Wilhelm Külz.

[80] Badstübner and Loth, p. 128.

[81] 'Je größer das Geschrei, desto näher die Verständigung', Tyul'panov is heard to say to Kaiser in August 1947, cit. Badstübner, 'Die sowjetische Deutschlandpolitik', p. 122.

[82] Becher is mentioned by name in Tyul'panov's report, for his inaugural speech at the Kulturbund.

[83] See, in particular, the extensive criticism of preparations for the Second SED Congress, reproduced in Badstübner and Loth, pp. 131–34, which documents the dissatisfaction of many members with the demonisation of Schumacher, with its implications for the marginalisation of former Social Democrats within the SED, and a state of widespread apathy and disunity.

[84] Loth, *Stalins ungeliebtes Kind*, p. 105.

The key phrase here is 'bewußt oder unbewußt': the effect of the contradiction at the heart of Soviet policy is to hand effective power, power in this case being defined as the ability to exert a conscious influence on the parameters of debate and the limits of political possibilities, to those who better understood the existential implications for the SED of questions of national unity. Thus, Pieck's ringing declarations at the Second SED Congress, attempting to identify the party with a new socialist international,[85] met with Soviet disapproval for the radicalism of their phrasing, but in the light of the abrupt change in the tenor of Soviet rhetoric with the founding of the Cominform, Pieck's words simply contributed to the perception of the SED as the 'Russians' Party'. The duality in Soviet policy is amply demonstrated by the decision not to invite the SED to the inaugural conference of the Cominform, held in Szklarska Poręba from 22–27 September 1947, or even to inform them of its occurrence.[86] All that the SED leadership could do, once the founding of the Cominform had been proclaimed on 5 October, was to cobble together an expression of support.[87] Pieck's declarations had been 'excessively presumptuous'[88] because they had overstepped the boundaries of the carefully-constructed shift in rhetoric towards an 'integrationist' stance within domestic policy, by making an intervention on the international stage which flagrantly contradicted Stalin's stance on Germany.

The tenor of the Second SED Congress itself was to present the SED as a Soviet-style party, a development noted by Tyul'panov with 'considerable satisfaction'. The limit of Stalin's reach is demonstrated by the incompatibility of the ideological identification of the SED with the Soviet Communist Party, using the typical formal trappings of similar Soviet gatherings, with the achievement of a German policy which demanded that the SED remain outside the Cominform. Naimark notes the 'nervousness and insecurity'[89] of the SED leadership at the Congress, who were faced with growing economic problems at

---

[85] Speech at 2nd Congress, *Protokoll der Verhandlungen des II. Parteitages der Sozialistischen Einheitspartei Deutschlands, 20–24 September 1947 in der Deutschen Staatsoper zu Berlin* (Berlin: Dietz, 1947).

[86] See *The Cominform. Minutes of the Three Conferences, 1947/1948/1949*, ed. by Giuliano Procacci (Milan: Fondazione Giangiacomo Feltrinelli, 1994), pp. 3–461.

[87] Cit. Naimark, pp. 305f.

[88] Naimark, p. 305.

[89] Naimark, p. 305.

home and the economic and propaganda threat of the Marshall Plan in the West. The symbolic reassurance in identification with the Soviet Union offered a degree of certainty in stark contrast with the threatening complexity of the world outside; for those not directly engaged in the deliberate shift of the SED's ideological stance, identification with a symbolically-constructed Soviet Union (and the figure of 'Stalin') offered a tempting retreat into certainty in the face of ambiguity and opportunity, guilt and responsibility. This is why the ideological build-up to the Second Congress is of such importance for an understanding of GDR cultural policy in the following years: it is at this stage that the ideological context is set for that peculiar combination of resistance and complicity which characterised the response of GDR intellectuals to the regime, and which seems baffling without the appropriate critical tools.

THE END OF THE 'GERMAN ROAD'?

The reason that Zhdanov's shallow polemics at the Cominform conference succeeded in disguising the obvious defensiveness of the Soviet position, faced with the realisation that they were lagging behind the West in economic and military strength, lies in the unwillingness of Western leaders to test the seriousness of Stalin's intentions, and in the exploitation of the ambiguities in the 'two camps' thesis by the 'integrationists' within the SED in order to counter their own specific reasons for defensiveness.[90] The bunker mentality which drove both sides towards division in the late 1940s has affected historical writing ever since, with a widespread willingness to take Soviet rhetoric at face value, rather than testing its claims. Certainly, Zhdanov himself may have intended his 'two camps' speech as an expression of sentiments more in keeping with the 'integrationist' line, but Malenkov took the trouble soon afterwards to clear up the ambiguity, stating that the 'two camps' were intended politically, rather than geographically.[91]

---

[90] Note the Soviet attempts 'to put a damper on Pieck's effusive readiness to march into the socialist future.' Naimark, pp. 307–8.

[91] Malenkov emphasises the idea (expressed in Zhdanov's speech, cited in Chapter Two of this study) that the 'two camps' express 'two opposing directions in international politics', in 'Za prochnyi mir, za narodnuyu

Malenkov's comments were made at the time of the Foreign Ministers' Conference in London (25 November–15 December 1947), where Molotov's attempt to place a unified German government on the agenda were rejected as manoeuvres designed to undermine the Marshall Plan.[92] Zhdanov's absurd rhetoric had played its part in the failure of the London Conference, and the tone of SMAD pronouncements began to harden considerably. Once again, Tyul'panov was at the forefront of the ideological campaign, noting in December 1947 (while Molotov was trying to achieve precisely the opposite result in London!) that the SED needed to take a firm stance on the 'necessity of establishing the dictatorship of the proletariat in Germany'.[93] The only concession to the 'German Road' is the idea that the 'dictatorship' can take different forms in different countries; Tyul'panov had left himself sufficient room for further rhetoric able to attract those who favoured unity, and whose training in Marxism-Leninism had formed their world-view around these minute rhetorical distinctions.

While the campaign for SED conformity was being stepped up, the rhetoric of German unity was transferred to the Volkskongreßbewegung (first meeting 6–7 December in Berlin)[94] which was hurriedly improvised as a way of bypassing the official representatives of the *Blockparteien* (including Jakob Kaiser, who was dismissed over his refusal to participate in the Congress) once it had become clear that the leaders of the Western parties had no interest in all-German negotiations.

In his statements at the Second SED Congress, proposing negotiations with the Western parties, Otto Grotewohl reflected Stalin's blindness to the realities of the political situation in the West: 'Die Aufrechterhaltung der Forderung nach der deutschen Einheit macht die Durchführung des Marshall-Plans unmöglich.'[95]

---

demokratiyu!', *Pravda*, 1.12.1947.

[92] Kessel, p. 293.

[93] Cit. Naimark, p. 309.

[94] See Klaus Bender, *Deutschland einig Vaterland? Die Volkskongressbewegung für deutsche Einheit und einen gerechten Frieden in der Deutschlandpolitik der Sozialistischen Einheitspartei Deutschlands* (Frankfurt a.M.: Peter Lang, 1992), pp. 130–47. 18 of the 2215 participants were elected as a delegation to the London Foreign Ministers' Conference, where they hoped to bring a resolution of the Congress to the assembled foreign ministers. However, they were refused entry into the UK, because the British government felt, correctly, that the Congress was unrepresentative of German opinion.

[95] Otto Grotewohl, *Im Kampf um Deutschland. Reden und Aufsätze*, 2 vols (Berlin: Dietz, 1948), II, p. 243.

The weakness of Stalin's position lies in this very misjudgement, and in his reliance on the SED as his only available instrument in German politics; the conflicting interests of Stalin and the hard-line section of the SED leadership show that Grotewohl's pleas for negotiations on German unity are not to be taken at face value, as, for example, Rolf Badstübner assumes:

Und nachdem alle Versuche [at the London Conference] gescheitert waren, auf die eine oder andere Weise gesamtdeutsche Verständigungen zustandezubringen, blieb für die SED nur noch der Versuch, mittels einer 'Volksbewegung', 'von unten', die Einheit Deutschlands herbeizuführen.[96]

However, Grotewohl's position is not completely unequivocal on the issue of sovietisation, as is shown in the Soviet reports of Pieck and Grotewohl's visit to Moscow from 25 March to 1 April. Grotewohl was 'markedly unenthusiastic' about Pieck's plan for the introduction of compulsory courses in 'scientific socialism' in schools and universities. At a meeting on March 29, Suslov also expressed grave doubts about this plan, citing Soviet experience in the creation of an intelligentsia from the working class which did not involve 'trying to teach Marxism-Leninism to unwilling class enemies'.[97]

The report made by Wilhelm Pieck to Stalin and other Politburo members on 26 March 1948 demonstrates the ideological optimism which was expected when discussing Stalin's initiatives.[98] Pieck begins with a catalogue of the SED's problems, concentrating on the 'Hetze' in the West against the Soviet Union and SED. He admits that the Western powers are enjoying 'gewisse Erfolge mit dieser Hetze', causing 'Verwirrung in den Massen', who fear 'totalitäre Bestrebungen usw'. Pieck's comments are remarkably open, reflecting the SED leadership's growing fear that they are losing the battle, and,

---

[96] Badstübner, 'Die sowjetische Deutschlandpolitik', p. 123.

[97] Naimark, pp. 307f.

[98] Badstübner and Loth, pp. 190–202. For a discussion of Stalin's own optimism about the success of his initiatives, and its gradual erosion in the context of the Economists' Debate, see Loth, *Stalins ungeliebtes Kind*, pp. 107–15. Loth seems to assume that the debate was influenced purely by the developing international situation, rather than also being a function of social and political processes within the Soviet Union itself. Stalin's ability to make autonomous foreign policy decisions was influenced by many factors.

significantly, that the Soviet Union is not fully behind them.[99] Despite this
catalogue of woes, Pieck strikes a sudden, jarring note of optimism:

Trotzdem gewinnt die SED / an (*pol.*) Vertrauen durch ihre Arbeit / durch ihre konsequente
Politik—/ durch ihren Kampf gegen die Reaktion / Beweis—die Volkskongreßbewegung /
durch ihren Kampf für die / Einheit D. u. gerechten Frieden / gegen den Marshallplan u.
Weststaat.

As we have seen with the SED's pleas to Stalin before the Second Congress,
one had to be careful when deciding what to mention in front of Stalin, although
whether this was a deliberate ploy on the part of the SED, or a result of the cult
of personality which meant that they were simply unable, 'etwas völlig anderes
nach oben zu berichten, als was feststehender allerhöchster Weisheit entsprach',
is unclear.[100] It is possible, given the tensions in the ideological system within
which the issues of German division were being defined, that both factors were
at work. In any case, where this jarring optimism occurs, as with Tyul'panov,
we can be sure that deeper issues are at stake, that is, the necessary illusions at
the heart of the ideological system (in this case connected to the concept of
historical inevitability and the role of the figure of Stalin constructed at the heart
of the system). The superficiality of this optimism disguises significant
evasions, whether conscious or unconscious, in Pieck's report. His attempts to
pin the blame for escalating tension on hostile propaganda clearly avoids
addressing the actions of the SMAD and SED. However, this is not all that is at

---

[99] See also the draft of a letter to Stalin agreed with Sokolovski on 28 August 1947, in which the SED leaders
beg for help in advance of the Second Congress (Badstübner and Loth, pp. 149–151). The text of the letter
recognises that the desperate economic situation is turning the population against the SED, ensuring 'daß keine
Aussicht auf Verwirklichung der Einheit Deutschlands besteht.' Since it was difficult to bring up the subject of
Soviet reparations policy when dismantling of industrial capacity was so obviously supported by much of the
Soviet leadership, the authors of the letter try another tack: 'Demgegenüber versucht die Reaktion alles, die
Massen mit der Behauptung gegen die Sowjetunion und gegen die sowjetische Besatzungsmacht aufzuhetzen,
daß die Entnahme von Reparationen aus der laufenden Produktion und die Demontagen dazu beitragen, die Lage
des Volkes immer mehr zu verschlechtern.' Whether the letter was sent in this form is unknown, but the SED
leadership did send Stalin minutes of the 13th Plenum of the party leadership, during which several speakers
openly criticised the failure of the Soviets to keep promises about ending dismantling. As Badstübner and Loth
comment: 'Da die SED-Führung die Demontagefrage unter den gegebenen Bedingungen der SMAD-Zensur nicht
offen aufwerfen konnten oder das gegenüber Stalin auch nicht wollte, verfolgte sie auf die Weise, das Protokoll
der 13. Tagung des Parteivorstandes beizulegen, eine geschickte Taktik.' (Badstübner and Loth, p. 159) Given
the importance of the reparations issue in Soviet internal politics, such tactics could only work in favour of the
'integrationist' line.
[100] Gerhard Wettig, 'Stalin—Patriot und Demokrat', p. 748.

stake: also left unexplained is the central issue of the way in which the progressive identification of the SED leadership with an ideologically-constructed Soviet Union is in itself contributing to German division. The inability to analyse this situation represents the limit of Stalin's influence in German politics.

The tightening of the SED's ideological stance against opposition from both Left and Right during 1948 seemed to set the seal on the party's identification with Soviet power, a process made explicit by the intention to transform it into a 'Partei neuen Typus'[101] and Ackermann's retraction of his 'German Road' thesis on 16 September 1948. The struggle against those who opposed closer identification with the Soviet Union using a 'falsified Marxism-Leninism'[102] had enormous success in ridding the party of many independently-minded critics, including Erich Gniffke, who fled to the West in October 1948, fearing arrest. One of the unforeseen results of this policy was the creation of a more privileged space for the intelligentsia through a crackdown on 'extremist' elements who objected to the extra material benefits enjoyed by specialists and intellectuals.

Understanding of this process is often clouded with notions of inevitability and of a monolithic unity of purpose between the SED leadership and the Soviet Politburo: the tense contest of strength over the Berlin Blockade,[103] the creation of the Deutsche Wirtschaftskommission (DWK) on 14 June 1947 in response to the setting up, at the end of May 1947, of an economic council for the Bizone, both of which seemed to foreshadow independent administrations or parliaments, and the outbreak of the Yugoslav crisis, seemed to offer no way back to the Potsdam Treaty. That the situation with regard to Soviet foreign policy was more complex than it seemed on the surface, particularly with regard to Yugoslavia, will have become clear from my discussion in the previous chapter. The Soviet instinct to centralise control began to manifest itself in the

---

[101] First mentioned in a resolution of the meeting of the party leadership on 30 June 1948. For a fuller account of the campaign against internal opposition, see the section 'The Party of the New Type' in Naimark, pp. 308–16.

[102] Lieutenant Colonel Blestkin to Tyul'panov, 10 February 1948, cit. Naimark, p. 309.

[103] The 'Mini-Blockade' lasted from 27 March–5 April 1948, while Pieck and Grotewohl were in Moscow, and the blockade proper was in place 24 June 1948–12 May 1949. See Loth, *Stalins ungeliebtes Kind*, pp. 115–128, and Rolf Steininger, 'Wie die Teilung Deutschlands verhindert werden sollte. Der Robertson-Plan aus dem Jahre 1948', in *Militärgeschichtliche Mitteilungen*, 33 (1983), 49–89.

campaign against Zhdanov's influence, and in the round of consolidation within the Soviet Bloc.[104] However, the complexities of the German situation called for different tactics, and the adequacy of Stalin's approach to this problem has been the subject of considerable debate.

The essence of the question lies in whether Soviet policy represented a consistent line, with tactics tailored to suit changing circumstances, or whether we are dealing with a more complex interplay of competing forces. More recent studies, drawing on material made available after the collapse of the Soviet union, also disagree, although there has been a certain convergence from the polarised positions which used to characterise the debate. At one extreme, it is assumed that Ulbricht and Tyul'panov are simply 'Kreaturen' of Stalin, fulfilling his will in Germany.[105] Naimark sees Stalin's instructions to the SED leaders at the meeting in Moscow on 18 December 1948 as tactical suggestions that 'the SED not be so blunt about its Leninist programme for German society', while going about its task of eliminating internal opposition and modelling the party along Soviet lines.[106] An alternative response is to see Soviet policy in 1948 as a 'dual strategy' which was 'directed at persuading the West to agree to a demilitarised regime for Germany whilst simultaneously securing communist rule for the Eastern zone'.[107] This view, which attempts to take into account the obvious ambiguities in Soviet policy, still relies on the idea of Stalin as ultimate author of these contrasting strategies: if the 'all-German' line fails, then at least the Soviet Zone will be fully under his control.

More willing to accept the seriousness of Stalin's intentions in pushing for German unity is Rolf Badstübner who, basing his arguments on Pieck's notes, states that the SED intended to form an East German state, but were surprised at the 'all-German' line taken by Stalin at the 18 December meeting.[108] Pieck's

---

[104] For an interesting examination of one of the principal instruments in this ideological campaign, albeit itself a *glasnost'*- era attempt to rehabilitate certain aspects of Leninism, see N. N. Maslov, 'Short Course of the History of the All-Russian Communist Party (Bolshevik)—An Encyclopedia of Stalin's Personality Cult', *Soviet Studies in History*, vol. 28, no. 3, Winter 1989/90, 41–66.

[105] Wettig, 'Stalin—Patriot und Demokrat', p. 744.

[106] Naimark, pp. 312–14.

[107] Kennedy-Pipe, p. 144.

[108] Badstübner, 'Die sowjetische Deutschlandpolitik', p. 125. Pieck's notes on the meeting are reproduced in Badstübner and Loth, pp. 259–63. Badstübner cites a series of meetings with senior SMAD officers in Autumn 1948, from which Pieck took clear indications that the SED should prepare to steer the SBZ towards 'People's

notes do indeed show that Stalin wanted to slow down the pace of SED consolidation in the Soviet Zone (the communists 'stehen nicht vor der Macht') in order to keep the German question open, and that he demanded a change of course, which was duly announced at the First SED Conference.[109] This change of course manifested itself in a range of measures, particularly in an easing in industrial policy, and the withdrawal of the official *Führungsanspruch* which had disrupted the work of the Bloc parties; however, these were only 'taktische Operationen' which were intended simply to disguise the continuing sovietisation of the party. Certainly, but Badstübner assumes a uniformity within the SED leadership which an analysis of the evidence shows not to have been the case: 'Nur in den eigenen Propagandasichtweisen befangene Blindheit konnte glauben, daß die Ostzone solcherart eine Anziehungskraft auf den Westen auszuüben vermochte.'[110] This picture of an SED leadership blundering unwittingly into the creation of an East German state relies on the assumption that leaders like Pieck and Ulbricht would have been prepared to sacrifice power for the sake of democracy, an idea which is scarcely credible. Also, we have already seen that there were considerable differences within the leadership about the pace of sovietisation, and we should not ignore the fact that Ulbricht conducted a concerted campaign in order to impose his own line within the SED, a line which used the identification of the SED with Soviet models as a way of ensuring personal dominance within the party, and the party's dominance in the Eastern part of Germany.

Democracy' status: 'Doch es war offensichtlich nicht nach Karlshorst gedrungen, daß Stalin in einer Besprechung mit den drei Botschaftern der Westmächte am 2. August 1948 voll auf das Offenhalten der deutschen Frage gesetzt, auf ein zeitweiliges Sistieren der Londoner Beschlüsse und auf neue Verhandlungen gedrängt hatte.' (Badstübner, pp. 124f.) Although Badstübner appears on occasion, as in this case, too willing to take Stalin at his word in this diplomatic manoeuvring, the gradual reassertion of Stalin's line against Zhdanovite influence after Zhdanov's death, may explain the discrepancies between Stalin's statements and the SMAD briefings.

[109] See *Protokoll der Parteikonferenz der Sozialistischen Einheitspartei Deutschlands, 25–28.1.1949* (Berlin: Dietz, 1949), p. 356, where Grotewohl announces, 'daß kein noch so schönes Ostdeutschland [...] die Aufgabe erfüllen kann, die ein einheitliches, fortschrittliches, friedliebendes und demokratisches Deutschland in ganz Europa erfüllen kann'. Also, in March 1949, Grotewohl for the first time acknowledges that an east German state 'eine Belastung des südöstlichen Staatenblocks darstellt.' (cit. Badstübner, p. 126.)

[110] Badstübner, 'Die sowjetische Deutschlandpolitik', p. 127. Badstübner often uses the words 'sowjetisch' and 'stalinistisch' interchangeably, perpetuating the identification of Soviet state and society with the figure of Stalin.

As we shall see, in the final balance, the events of 17 June 1953 demonstrate the precariousness of this dominance in its reliance on a thoroughly ambivalent Soviet Union, and any interpretation which sees SED and Soviet *Deutschland-politik* (whatever opinion one has about its aims) as the result of a concerted campaign on the part of Stalin, SMAD and SED cannot explain this precariousness or the survival of an 'all-German' line in GDR institutions.

ULBRICHT SIEZES POWER

From mid-1947, the 'integrationist' line began to gain ground within the SMAD and the SED leadership, represented by functionaries, 'die mit der Vorstellung von der Vollendung der bürgerlichen Revolution schon immer besonders wenig anzufangen wußten'.[111] The struggle for German unity is identified with the elimination of 'reactionary' elements and the establishment of a monopoly on power, and the concept of democracy is stripped of its threatening ambiguities and becomes synonymous with Soviet power, rather than with vaguely-defined notions of socialism or 'Ur-Marxismus'. For our own purposes, the most important aspect in this power struggle is the ability of those who have no illusions about the ideological environment in which they move, to put their stamp on the rhetoric of German unity.

For example, in the Summer of 1948, SMAD officers began to concern themselves with the issue of nationalism, or rather a new 'nationale[n] "Einfärbung" des Kampfes um die Einheit Deutschlands'.[112] The calls for a 'wahren Nationalismus', introducing a 'neue Argumentation' which will attract 'Ehem. Nazi—/Ehem. Militär', culminates in the licensing of the National-demokratische Partei Deutschlands and the Demokratische Bauernpartei, with a view to influencing 'Wahlen im Westen'.[113] Great names in German cultural history (Lessing, Beethoven, Goethe, Wagner, Humboldt) are to be drawn into a 'Manifest' to guard against the 'Gefahr' of 'Kosmopolitismus'.

---

[111] Loth, *Stalins ungeliebtes Kind*, p. 129.

[112] Badstübner and Loth, p. 233.

[113] Briefing with Semenov, 10.6.1948, Badstübner and Loth, p. 233.

This national emphasis is close to the stance of Becher in his concern to rescue the best aspects of German culture from the legacy of Nazism. However, the national idea is undergoing a semantic shift, in the same way as the 'two camps' theory rapidly crystallised into a geographical expression. The German national idea, which attracted many intellectuals, shifted into an expression of East German nationalism, as opposed to the 'bourgeois nationalism' of which Becher is accused, forcing its adherents into positions of compromise with the move to division. Note, in this context, a briefing between Semenov, Pieck and Ulbricht in mid-August 1948, in the course of which Grotewohl is sharply criticised, in his absence, for 'Objektivismus'.[114] Any hopes that the German national idea could be used to promote openness or dialogue with the West, along with the necessary re-evaluation of the past, are gradually being eroded.

An examination of the role of Walter Ulbricht in the consolidation of SED power shows that he shared few or none of the illusions about German unity which held back certain other SED politicians, such as Becher, or, to a lesser extent, Grotewohl. In his drive for power and his belief in the imperatives of the class struggle, Ulbricht received support from Tyul'panov, whose rhetoric always seemed to pre-empt political developments. On 8 May 1948, Tyul'panov had delivered a speech declaring that there had been a 'Veränderung in der politischen und [...] in der staatlichen Situation der Sowjetzone', and that the SED 'faktisch an der Macht steht'.[115] We also find here the 'two camps' theory expressed decisively in its geographical sense: 'Die Sozialistische Einheitspartei befindet sich an der Grenze zweier Welten, dort, wo die Welt des Kapitalismus auf die Welt des Sozialismus trifft.' The SED must therefore become a truly Leninist party by creating 'ein festes, diszipliniertes Parteiaktiv' which will overcome 'die Furcht vor entscheidenden Maßnahmen'. That this clashes substantially with Stalin's own programme is clear, and Semenov expressed to Grotewohl his doubts about this new direction, stating 'daß einige von

---

[114] Badstübner and Loth, p. 236. Grotewohl had stated that any new constitution for a united Germany had to be developed independently of the influence of the occupying powers: '[Das Verfassungswerk] muß sich völlig unabhängig nach deutschen Gesichtspunkten orientieren [...] [auf] einer für ganz Deutschland tragbaren mittleren Linie, der Einigung sowohl der linkesten wie der rechtesten Auffassungen unter fortschrittlichen und demokratischen Prinzipien' (Speech at Fourth Congress of the Volksrat, *Deutschlands Stimme*, 8.8.1948, cit. Badstübner and Loth, p. 237).

[115] Badstübner and Loth, pp. 216–27.

Tulpanow und Ulbricht eingeleitete Maßnahmen über das Ziel der Moskauer Politik hinausgehen und die derzeitige an sich schon schwierige Lage noch komplizieren können'.[116] Certainly, 'der klassenkämpferische Amoklauf Ulbrichts und Tulpanows'[117] has no precursor in the March/April 1948 meeting with Stalin; it seems therefore that, although Stalin attempted at the 18 December meeting to slow down the development of the SBZ into a People's Democracy, he had to make certain concessions to developments in Germany which had occurred when he was unable to turn his entire attention to the matter. Stalin could only deal 'sporadisch' with German policy, and so an 'integrationist' line could prevail 'trotz des Mangels an Delegation von Verantwortung, der seinen Regierungsstil kennzeichnete'.[118]

In the light of my discussion of the ideological issues involved with this shift in policy, and with Stalin's authority, it seems to me to be more appropriate to say that the 'integrationist' line prevailed *because of* Stalin's style of rule and the type of system which drew its legitimacy from him, rather than *in spite of* it. Anybody who had had his or her understanding of the world formed in the context of Marxism-Leninism 'war [...] für Tulpanows Anstöße empfänglich'.[119] The internalised authority of the figure of Stalin meant that Ulbricht's strategy of positioning himself as 'Stalin's man' eventually paid off. The energy and self-confidence exhibited by Ulbricht and Tyul'panov ensured that Grotewohl capitulated decisively to the 'integrationist' line at the meeting of the party leadership on 29/30 June 1948, where the Two-Year Plan was declared.[120]

---

[116] Gniffke, p. 223.

[117] Loth, *Stalins ungeliebtes Kind*, p. 135.

[118] Loth, *Stalins ungeliebtes Kind*, p. 136. Pieck developed Tyul'panov's ideas in a speech to the party leadership on 12.5.1948, on occasion citing his words directly (cit. Badstübner and Loth, p. 227). Dahlem and Oelßner speak of a 'Wende' in SED policy (cit. Loth, p. 137). Stalin's abrupt criticisms at the 18 December meeting must have come as a shock.

[119] Loth, *Stalins ungeliebtes Kind*, p. 136, on Sokolovski. Even those SMAD functionaries who had certain doubts about the direction of policy in the Soviet Zone were vulnerable to this kind of ideological strategy, as it functioned largely on an unconscious level.

[120] Grotewohl had been declaring his discomfort with the 'Ostorientierung' for some time, particularly at the meeting of the party leadership on 20 March 1948, where he warned against creating institutions (such as the Two-Year Plan), 'die ein späteres Zusammenkommen der getrennten Teile Deutschlands unter Umständen ausschließen'. (cit. Loth, *Stalins ungeliebtes Kind*, p. 137) See also Gniffke, pp. 298–313 for Grotewohl's private doubts.

Grotewohl and Pieck had evidently come to the conclusion that Stalin was behind Ulbricht's actions, although there was no direct reason to believe this.

The Yugoslav crisis (the Yugoslav Communist Party had been expelled from the Cominform on 28 June) provided the opportunity for Ulbricht to push for the sovietisation of the party, to declare its transformation into the 'Partei neuen Typus', which entailed a general purge of former social democrats (who had in any case fallen silent after Grotewohl's capitulation), and to centralise the police under party control. Ackermann's self-criticism followed in September 1948,[121] even though Pieck protested that the 'German Road' had once been 'Parteilinie'.[122] Extraordinarily, and with an unconscious irony which pervades the whole issue of the 'all-German' orientation, Pieck objected: 'Gegen diese Formulierung [the 'German Road'] ist auch niemals von der WKP(B) [Soviet Communist Party] Einspruch erhoben worden'.[123] Nevertheless, Ulbricht insisted on a self-criticism, against the objections of Pieck and Grotewohl.

Ulbricht's programme seemed certain to lead to German division, and Semenov, who often seemed to favour those seeking an 'all-German' solution, possibly because of his connections with Beria, made several attempts to decelerate the process of division.[124] As we have seen, at the 18 December meeting with Stalin, the SED leaders were not entirely honest about the recently-declared 'sozialistischer Aufbau', but even so the events of this period show that Ulbricht's position was not as secure as it appeared.

A concerted campaign against Tyul'panov was being conducted from Moscow, presumably in connection with the Cosmopolitanism campaign and the post-Zhdanov purge.[125] Even so, the international situation was such that German division had come to seem inevitable, although in this context even a

---

[121] Anton Ackermann, 'Über den einzig möglichen Weg zum Sozialismus', *Neues Deutschland*, 24.9.1948.

[122] Cf. Gniffke, pp. 340f.

[123] Meeting of party leadership 15–16 September 1948, cit. Loth, *Stalins ungeliebtes Kind*, p. 141.

[124] Cf. the 10.6.1948 meeting, mentioned above, and a briefing on 26.6.1948 (Badstübner and Loth, p. 234), where he replies to the question, 'ob Regierung in Ostzone' with the words 'vorläufig / Wirtsch. Kommiss'. Also at this meeting, the leaders discussed the question of Heinrich Mann's possible return to Germany: 'Heinrich Mann schlechte Lage in New York / krank, ohne Wohnung / Honorare in Valuta übermitteln / ob nach SU, dann nach Deutschl'. The symbolic value of Heinrich Mann for the 'all-German' orientation in Becher's conception of the Deutsche Akademie der Künste, and the importance of his return as a political gesture, are indicated in high-level discussions like this.

[125] See Naimark, pp. 346–52.

word like 'seem' is loaded with ideological baggage: the standpoint of the historian will generally determine whether division appeared inevitable. While not going as far as Rolf Badstübner in his rather sweeping statement that 'die DDR im Selbstverständnis ihrer Gründer und noch mehr ihrer sowjetischen Befürworter tatsächlich als Provisorium, als Mittel zum Zweck und als Staat auf Zeit [entstand]',[126] I agree that Stalin's (and Beria's) desire to force German unity, in all its 'Widersprüchlichkeit und Polyvalenz', is present in Soviet *Deutschlandpolitik* 'als immer wieder deutlich werdender roter Faden'.[127]

FAITS ACCOMPLIS

The failure of the Paris Foreign Ministers' Conference (23 May–2 June 1949) came as little surprise to anybody, and the proclamation of the Nationale Front des demokratischen Deutschlands (4 October 1949) looked like nothing more than another tool in the SED's campaign to break the 'bourgeois' parties (culminating in January 1950 with the purge of the CDU and LDPD),[128] although it is possible that Stalin was still under the impression that the 'masses' in West Germany were generally opposed to division and Marshall Aid.[129]

This may help to explain Stalin's criticisms of the SED leadership when Pieck, Grotewohl, Ulbricht and Oelßner visited Moscow in the first week of May 1950, in order to discuss the Five-Year Plan.[130] On their return, the Politburo of the SED passed an internal 'Beschluß über die Verstärkung des Kampfes in Westberlin und Westdeutschland' (2.6.1950), which stated:

---

[126] Badstübner, 'Die sowjetische Deutschlandpolitik', p. 127.

[127] Badstübner, p. 109.

[128] See Siegfried Suckut, 'Die Entscheidung zur Gründung der DDR', in *Vierteljahrshefte für Zeitgeschichte*, 39, 1991, 125–75, for documents relating to the end of resistance on the part of the CDU and LDPD, and their acceptance (on 5.10.1949) of the postponement of elections, and relating to the subsequent purges.

[129] Coinciding with the lifting of the Blockade, Semenov was summoned to Moscow to receive instructions on forming the *Nationale Front* which should go 'Schritt weiter [...] als Volkskongreß'. Report by Grotewohl of Semenov's speech to the SED Politbureau, 23 May 1949, cit. Loth, *Stalins ungeliebtes Kind*, p. 153.

[130] See Badstübner and Loth, pp. 343–48. Pieck's deteriorating health meant that he was unable to take notes as usual, but the self-critical tone of the subsequent SED resolutions gives a good idea of the tenor of Stalin's criticisms.

Das Politbüro der SED stellt selbstkritisch fest, daß die Politik und die praktische Arbeit der SED ungenügend auf die Lösung der gesamtdeutschen Aufgaben orientiert ist ... [In Anbetracht der Tatsache,] daß die Hauptaufgabe in der Entwicklung einer gesamtdeutschen Politik besteht, dürfen sich die führenden Organe der Partei nicht auf die Aufgaben in der DDR beschränken.[131]

Even so, the SED leadership continued to create 'facts on the ground', such as the establishment of the Ministerium für Staatssicherheit (8 February 1950), which made Stalin's criticisms seem like so much empty rhetoric. However, the 'all-German' orientation was still official policy, and any direct attack on institutions which were founded explicitly to promote this conception, such as the Deutsche Akademie der Künste (24 March 1950), would be an unacceptable encroachment onto Stalin's authority in foreign policy matters, as opposed to his ability to do more than respond to developments on the ground.

Thus, the suggestion of the Prague Foreign Ministers' Conference (20–21 October 1950) that a new compromise be made with the Bonn regime[132] was 'für Ulbricht gewiß keine sehr angenehme Aussicht'.[133] The proposals for the creation of a 'Gesamtdeutscher Konstituierender Rat' came as a response to the decisions reached in New York in mid-September that the FRG be admitted to Western security structures, and the proposals' far-reaching nature would have put into question the integrity of both German states. The threat to hard-liners in the SED was clear, and there are signs that Ulbricht was forced onto the back foot;[134] a more moderate line, still containing strong traces of 'German Road' ideas, was being elaborated by Rudolf Herrnstadt.[135]

The Prague proposals were so radical that Western diplomats doubted their sincerity, although they reflect Stalin's line perfectly: he was driven by fear of

---

[131] Cit. Badstübner and Loth, p. 343.

[132] The text can be found in *Neues Deutschland*, 22.10.1950.

[133] Loth, *Stalins ungeliebtes Kind*, p. 172.

[134] In August 1950, Ulbricht had demanded that Adenauer be 'vor ein Volksgericht gestellt', but by the time of the Central Committee meeting of 26–27 October, he was forced to speak against any intention, 'die Forderung des Sturzes der Bonner Regierung in den Vordergrund zu stellen' (cit. Loth, *Stalins ungeliebtes Kind*, p. 172).

[135] 'Manche von uns würden [...] guttun, sich von der undialektischen Vorstellung freizumachen, das kommende einheitliche, demokratische Deutschland würde einfach eine vergrößerte Kopie der gegenwärtigen Deutschen Demokratischen Republik sein' (Central Committee meeting, 26–27 October 1950, cit. Loth, *Stalins ungeliebtes Kind*, p. 173).

war, and of a rearmed FRG.[136] It is this fear, rather than any concern over reparations, which seems to be driving Stalin's policy now, as his offers become less cautious, and thus easier for Adenauer to reject.[137]

STALIN'S NOTES, THE SECOND CONFERENCE OF THE SED AND THE QUESTION OF EAST GERMAN NATIONAL IDENTITY

Periodic bouts of soul-searching on the question of 'national identity' are a regular feature of the German political culture; it is not so much the conclusions reached (if any) during these 'identity crises' which are important (at least, not for an outsider) but the fact that they occur at all, and the shifting context of the debate. Inevitably, historical writing on the causes and effects of German division is coloured by these issues. The focus of much of this debate on the sincerity or otherwise of Stalin's 'Notenkampagne' in March/April 1952 has been remarkably narrow, giving the misleading impression that vital questions of national identity can be settled if the actions of one side or another are vindicated.

The oversimplifying attention of much of the press has helped to create an orthodoxy in which historians who believe that Stalin saw his best interests in pressing for negotiations on German unity, have had to move in a somewhat more difficult environment than their colleagues, who have enjoyed refuting 'die Legende von der verpaßten Chance'.[138] It is, unfortunately, beyond the

---

[136] Stalin's obsessive fear of a new war, which must have seemed less likely to anyone with a closer acquaintance with the situation in Germany, is passed on through the SMAD to the SED leadership: Chuikov informs Pieck that the proposed referendum against remilitarisation is intended to prevent war: 'Pläne Adenauers zum Scheitern, nur so Krieg verhindern' (4 April 1951, Badstübner and Loth, p. 363).

[137] For example, shortly after the appeal of the Volkskammer to the Bundestag (15.9.1951, renewed 10.10. 1951) for negotiations to prepare for free all-German elections, Semenov (who always seems prepared to go a step further than his colleagues) put forward the suggestion that the elections could be held according to the Weimar electoral law. This would have been an unheard-of concession for German communists, who blamed the Weimar constitution for the victory of Hitler. In the same briefing (1 November 1951) Semenov states that the UN (presumably with reference to Soviet objections to UN supervision of elections) is 'nicht hoffnungslos strittige Frage' (Badstübner and Loth, p. 377).

[138] For example, a single phrase: 'Perspektive—es wird 2 Deutschlands geben' (Briefing with Stalin, Molotov and Zhdanov, 4.6.1945, Badstübner and Loth, p. 50) was taken up from a publication by Dietrich Staritz ('Die SED, Stalin, und die Gründung der DDR. Aus den Akten des Zentralen Parteiarchivs', *Aus Politik und Zeitgeschichte*, B 5/91, 25 January 1991) and used to demonstrate that the division of Germany was Stalin's policy from 1945 (see *Die Welt*,

scope of this study to trace the development of this debate, which has at times been perceived by its participants as 'eine Fortsetzung des Kalten Krieges mit anderen Mitteln';[139] in other words, as the attempted exercise of power over historians from the former GDR, who found themselves confronted with the need, 'das Scheitern des von ihnen einst Gefeierten auf eine Weise zu erklären, die dem realen Desaster entsprach, ihre Identität aber nicht allzusehr verletzte'.[140] The issue on which this conflict has turned has been the extent of German responsibility for division, and the position of the GDR historians changed markedly after the 'Wende'. In the GDR, it had been taken for granted that the state, naturally in accordance with the laws of history, had been the work of German communists. In 1989/90, during that peculiar cross-over period when work was still appearing which had been completed during the last months of the GDR's existence, this thesis was abandoned.[141] It was replaced by its opposite, namely the idea that Stalin had foisted the process of division onto the Germans.[142]

Thus, in the process of abandoning the falsifications of GDR historiography, the ideas are stood on their heads instead of going through a period of genuine

17.4.1991, 'Stalins Befehl fand sich mit List versteckt in einem Schuhkarton', and *Der Spiegel*, no. 16/1991, which claimed that the 'Expertenstreit' was 'beendet'). Rolf Badstübner published the text (Rolf Badstübner, 'Beratungen bei J. W. Stalin. Neue Dokumente. Dokumente aus den Jahren 1945–1948', *Utopie: Kreativ*, 7 (1991), 99–101) but it has taken some years until researchers have been able to put Pieck's notes in their proper context. Badstübner and Loth comment: 'Die "2 Deutschlands" sind nicht als eine Zielsetzung der sowjetischen Politik zu interpretieren, sondern als eine mögliche Entwicklung, der die KPD jedoch mit allen Mitteln entgegenwirken sollte' (Badstübner and Loth, p. 52).

[139] Jochen Laufer, 'Die UdSSR, die SED und die deutsche Frage', *Deutschland Archiv*, 26 (1993), 1201–04 (1204).

[140] Dietrich Staritz, 'Die SED, Stalin und der "Aufbau des Sozialismus" in der DDR', *Deutschland Archiv*, 24 (1995), 686–700 (686).

[141] In early 1990, Rolf Badstübner took issue with 'Verfälschungen des Werdens und Wachsens der DDR', that is, against claims that it was a process of 'Revolution von oben' or 'Sowjetisierung': Rolf Badstübner, *Friedenssicherung und deutsche Frage. Vom Untergang des "Reiches" bis zur deutschen Zweistaatlichkeit (1945 bis 1949)*, (Aufbau: Berlin, 1990) p. 11. At the same time, writers were calling for 'Erneuerung' or 'Neubefragung' of GDR history (see, for example, Heinz Heitzer, 'Für eine radikale Erneuerung der Geschichtsschreibung über die DDR', *Zeitschrift für Geschichtswissenschaft*, 38 (1990) 498–501).

[142] See, for example, Rolf Stöckigt, 'Direktiven aus Moskau. Sowjetische Einflußnahme auf die DDR-Politik 1952–53, in Černý, pp. 81–8. The debate was often carried out in the newspapers, indicating the unusual urgency of the situation, and this led to some overstatements which have left their mark. See Rolf Stöckigt, 'Ein forcierter stalinistischer Kurs führte 1953 in die Krise', *Berliner Zeitung*, 8.3.1990, where he states that the SKK imposed policy on the SED in 'Memoranden [...] gegen deren Inhalt es kaum eine Einspruchsmöglichkeit gab', or Rolf Stöckigt, 'Der 17. Juni 1953: Neue Erkenntnisse aus bisher geheimgehaltenen Dokumenten. Eine historische Chance wurde vertan', *Neues Deutschland*, 16/17.6.1990, in which he states that the 'Aufbau des Sozialismus' was imposed on the SED; Stalin's supposed policy is then contrasted with the 'missed opportunity' presented by new discoveries about Beria's imposition of the New Course. A very different view of the SKK and of the Second Conference of the SED will emerge in the course of this analysis.

reassessment, and paradoxically, two opposing camps of historians (and politicians) find themselves using the monolithic figure of Stalin to absolve their own, opposing, predecessors from responsibility for German division. Where this symbolic Stalin appears in German historical or political discourse, without being subjected to sustained critical analysis, it signals the presence of a subtext which concerns issues of responsibility and/or legitimisation; there are moments in German history at which attempts are made to deny German involvement in German affairs, and the debate over the 'inevitability' of division is one of them.

Now that something of the requisite sense of proportion has returned to the issue, and signs of the breaking down of entrenched positions can be noticed, we can begin to move beyond a narrow focus on 'missed opportunities' (which, since unconscious motivations mingle with reasoned argument, seems greatly over-determined) to an understanding of how notions of German nationhood affected ideological and political developments in the GDR leading up to June 1953.

The preference of the Soviet regime for high-level conferences, an environment where the opponent was easily defined and could be imagined to represent certain clear interests, was the result of the leadership's dramatic isolation from contact with anything outside itself, their neurotic mutual dependence. The question of German division was riven with ambiguities, and Stalin's fearful attitude towards the Germans led him to try to promote his cause through diplomacy, which gave him and his opponents an impression of personal power. This emphasis on diplomacy is prevalent in historical writing as well, and for similar reasons: the material is easier to shape and to personalise. As we have seen, Norman Naimark has, in a departure from this practice, traced the extent to which practicalities in Germany, and the administrative zeal of Walter Ulbricht, led the SMAD to delegate bureaucratic functions to the SED, and yet the feeling that the victors of 1945 were still disposing of Germany's fate must have been felt as a profound humiliation.

Although the SMAD had been disbanded in 1949, the Control Commission (SKK) remained the organ of Soviet authority in the GDR, and the SED regime was still left in the uncomfortable position of having to determine the future

shape of the country without possessing the sovereignty which would guarantee
it a future. However, the replacement of many of the SMAD's military staff in
the more civilian-orientated SKK, along with the disappearance of Tyul'panov
from influence in Germany, led to a somewhat different emphasis in the work
of the SKK. Semenov in particular, whose possible connections with Beria have
already been raised in this study, seemed prepared to place greater emphasis on
the 'all-German' strategy.[143] The SKK became a centre where East Germans
unhappy with the SED's *Deutschlandpolitik* could meet West Germans critical
of their own regime: 'diese sowjetischen Gremien [wurden] nicht nur zu
"Klagemauern", sondern auch zu einer Art gesamtdeutscher Institution'.[144]

The need to assert an East German identity based on a sense of sovereignty
became all the more urgent for the SED; this desire is visible both in the
'integrationists' who saw it primarily as a way of consolidating the party's
monopoly on power, and in those for whom the achievement of German unity
was still a valid (though increasingly long-term) aim. Once again, this peculiar
common ground meant that the rhetoric of German nationhood began to work
in favour of those who were willing to use it as a tool for securing power. The
worrying ambiguities which faced any communist who began to consider the
problems associated with reunification were not resolvable within the Marxist-
Leninist system of thought, and this necessitated a retreat into the certainties of
division.

Grotewohl's report to Wilhelm Pieck on 23 October 1950 about the Prague
Foreign Ministers' Conference reflects the increasing self-confidence of the
regime, or rather, its need to assert its own legitimacy. The SED's presence at
the Conference represents an achievement which allows Germany 'wirklich am
Tisch der Völker zu sitzen und alle jene moralisch-politischen Minderwertig-

---

[143] In October 1951, Semenov had passed on a message to Ernst Lemmer, perhaps considered a potential ally in the
West, stating, 'die sowjetische Politik wolle sich jetzt ohne Rücksicht auf die SED ernstlich um die Wiedervereinigung
bemühen, sofern Gesamtdeutschland neutralisiert werde; Moskau sei bereit, für ein neutralisiertes Deutschland einen
hohen Preis zu zahlen' (Report by Lemmer to the Berlin representative of the US High Commission on 29 October
1951, cit. Hermann Graml, 'Die Legende von der verpaßten Gelegenheit', *Vierteljahrshefte für Zeitgeschichte*, 29
(1981), 307–41). The involvement of Grotewohl in this secret exchange of messages is indicative of his hesitancy
concerning an all-out drive for division.

[144] Michael Lemke, 'Die DDR und die deutsche Frage 1949–1955', in Loth, *Die deutsche Frage in der Nachkriegszeit*, p. 142.

keitsgefühle, die wir [...] immer mit uns herumtragen mußten, langsam immer mehr ablegen zu können'.[145]

This shrugging off of the issue of German guilt was made easy by the demonisation of the West, in the person of Adenauer, allowing the real threat to the SED's grip on power, that is, Soviet diplomatic efforts, to be evaded by 'talking up' the threat from the West. Thus, 'national unity' came to be inseparable from absurd rhetoric about toppling Adenauer; whoever used the language of unity without being fully aware that the meanings of the words had shifted so radically was also contributing to the end of the 'all-German' aspiration.

The most extreme rhetoric came from Ulbricht: in his view, intra-governmental talks should only take place once Adenauer and Schumacher had been shown the door in an all-German referendum.[146] Such appeals to the popular will were more congenial for Ulbricht than the Soviet strategy of pursuing negotiations through the elected representatives of the Federal Republic, and they naturally had the effect of further jeopardising the chances that negotiations could actually occur. Whatever Ulbricht hoped to achieve with calls for this referendum, the Soviet assessment of the situation in the Federal Republic was sobering: 'Bewegung für Volksbefragung im Westen noch schwach.'[147]

The dangers for the SED were all too apparent, but Soviet freedom for manoeuvre was also limited to the extent that Stalin now relied on the internal consolidation and external legitimacy of the GDR regime as his only possible tool in Germany. The question of reunification therefore involves more than a contest between East and West: another major focus is the struggle, unacknowledged but nevertheless real, between differing interests in the Soviet and GDR regimes: 'Die Initiative in der nationalen Frage zu behalten, bot die einzige Chance, ihren Sprengstoff zu entschärfen.'[148] This struggle was fought for the upper hand in determining the form of negotiations for German unity; since all were obliged to hold a united Germany up as their stated aim, the

---

[145] Cit. Lemke, p. 139.
[146] Plan presented in Neues Deutschland, 16.6.1951.
[147] Briefing with Chuikov at Pieck's house, 11.5.1951, 'Walter verreist'. Badstübner and Loth, p. 365.
[148] Laufer, p. 1203.

initiative had to be fought for in ritualised rhetorical exchanges, whose apparent target, the Federal Republic, is often a pretext, if an unconscious one. The obligation for Ulbricht to conduct his campaign using the language of German unity was not only a source of strength, as we saw above, but meant that institutions and individuals which held to an 'all-German' line had a context for a kind of compromised survival (compromised because, as we have seen, insistence on using the language of German unity in the GDR also contributed to division). This vicious circle enclosed every communist intellectual and politician who still clung to an aspiration for unity, providing a context both for resistance and for complicity with the regime.

All shades of opinion within the SED leadership were concerned about the possible imposition of Western electoral structures, even those who were prepared to put greater emphasis on unity than were the 'integrationists' considered that the Federal Republic exhibited fascistic tendencies,[149] but the key question for the 'integrationist' tendency was to find the correct moment when Stalin's authority could be turned against him. In late 1950, the Korean War was raising anxieties about international conflict, and so the emphasis of SED propaganda was on opposing West German rearmament, and on condemning the FRG as an American creation. The dominant line in the Politburo was expressed in October 1950 by Rudolf Herrnstadt, who recommended, 'unser Feuer im wesentlichen auf den amerikanischen Aggressor zu konzentrieren und die deutschen Handlanger nur insoweit namentlich anzugreifen, als wir sicher sein können, daß unsere Angriffe die Zustimmung auch der breiten verständigungswilligen Massen Westdeutschlands finden'. Ulbricht agreed that it would be wrong, 'in der jetzigen Etappe die Forderung des Sturzes der Bonner Regierung in den Vordergrund zu stellen'.[150] It was not long before Ulbricht and Pieck began to introduce anti-Adenauer slogans while suggesting that the time was not ripe for an all-out campaign,[151] and by 1952, the German national question was linked explicitly with Adenauer's overthrow: in a speech to the FDJ on 29 May 1952, Ulbricht described Adenauer's

---

[149] 'Freiheit für die Kriegshetzer, [...] Freiheit für die Monopole und Bankherren, aber zugleich [...] System der Unterdrückung'. Anton Ackermann in the Central Committee, 24.8.1950 (cit. Lemke, p. 145).

[150] Central Committee Plenum, 26–27.10.1950, cit. Lemke, p. 149.

[151] Central Committee, 17–19.1.1951, cit. Lemke, p. 149.

overthrow as 'eine ausgesprochene innere Angelegenheit des deutschen Volkes'.[152]

This rhetorical twist ensured that support for the camp of peace was conditional on the overthrow of Adenauer, and the struggle for German unity was essentially a matter of unquestioning support for the SED's monopoly on power. That large numbers of GDR intellectuals could talk themselves into believing this demonstrates the emotional power of this argument for communist antifascists, who were seeking positive approaches to German history, while trying, with a certain amount of success, to resist the portrayal of German history as simply the prehistory of the SED.[153]

It seems that the bulk of the leadership never managed to resolve the contradiction between their view of themselves as German patriots and true inheritors of the traditions of German Marxism (and thus the rightful government of Germany, not least due to their role in opposing Nazism), and the fact that the *Deutschlandpolitik* expounded by Pieck and Ulbricht drove in the direction of division. This contradiction could, of course, be resolved dialectically, so the goal of unity was able to be maintained 'im Analysezeitraum'.[154] If German history was an inevitable progression towards unity (1871, 1933 and 1945 could certainly be squeezed into this dialectical scheme), then the SED must be the agent of that progression; thus, support for unity entailed support for division.

With certain exceptions, notably Herrnstadt's October 1950 speech in the Central Committee, quoted above, the SED leadership was silent on the issue of the Soviet insistence that they might have to contemplate relinquishing power. All members of the SED leadership felt that the party had a moral right to speak for Germany as a whole, especially since the Federal Republic was seen as a rebirth of fascism. Their actions exhibited 'missionärisches Selbstbewußtsein und elitäre Überheblichkeit'[155] (a characteristic also of many intellectuals,

---

[152] Cit. Lemke, p. 150.

[153] This question, with Ulbricht's dismissal of approaches which saw German history as 'eine einzige Misere', is the key element in the struggle over the 'all-German' orientation of the Deutsche Akademie der Künste, particularly in the controversy over Hanns Eisler's *Faustus*.

[154] Lemke, p. 151.

[155] Lemke, p. 154.

whose concern to impose their vision on German culture led easily to collusion with power).

The SED's attempts to export their *Deutschlandpolitik* to the West were wholly unsuccessful. The 'Friedensbewegung' of late 1950, with its seductive but deceptive echoes of the 'Nationale Front' strategy, suffered not only from the disdain of the public, but also from the SED's ingrained suspicion of the 'bourgeois' parties.[156] The extraordinary demonisation of Schumacher can be seen in the light of the leadership's realisation that the 'Friedensbewegung' could make no progress without the SPD; the clumsiness of their attacks on Schumacher, which undermined their cause considerably, can be traced back to the deeply-felt antagonism towards the 'traitors' whom the communists considered responsible for the victory of the Nazis in 1933.

The difficulty which the SED experienced in presenting a national concept to the outside world which did not seem to rely on Soviet models has led researchers to assume that there were no significant conflicts of interest; However, those that existed were fought out in the minutiae of day-to-day policymaking. Stalin had for the most part to react to events on the international stage and to *faits accomplis* in the internal politics of the GDR which made negotiations on reunification less and less likely. As for the SED, they had access to an extraordinary amount of detailed, accurate information about developments in the FRG, which they either ignored or disdained,[157] and so, without a long-term view, dominance was achieved through the details of *Tagespolitik*.

Although the 'integrationists' enjoyed a certain amount of freedom of action in 1950/51, Stalin began to assert his authority again in late 1951, with his influence on Grotewohl's appeal in the Volkskammer on 15 September 1951.[158] The emphasis was on free elections, although supervision by the UN was still

---

[156] The commission set up to oversee the peace movement is authorised, 'die gesamte Arbeit der Friedensbewegung in Berlin, in der DDR und Westdeutschland von der Partei aus zu leiten, zu kontrollieren und dem Politbüro rechtzeitig Vorschläge zu unterbreiten.' Politburo resolution of 8.8.1950, cit. Lemke, p. 156.

[157] Cf. Lemke, p. 160.

[158] The appeal was the product of long consultations with Semenov and Chuikov, with Stalin having the last word. See Gerhard Wettig, 'Die Deutschland-Note vom 10. März 1952 auf der Basis der diplomatischen Akten des russischen Außenministeriums', *Deutschland Archiv*, 26 (1993), 786–805. The text of Grotewohl's Volkskammer speech, where he presented an appeal for 'gemeinsame gesamtdeutsche Beratung der Vertreter Ost- und Westdeutschlands' can be found in *Europa Archiv*, 6 (1951), p. 4398.

ruled out. Instead, Pieck wrote an open letter to the President of the Federal Republic, Theodor Heuss,[159] proposing that elections should be supervised by a commission comprising representatives of both German states and of the four occupying powers. On 9 January 1952, as a response to the Bonn electoral law of 30 October, the Volkskammer passed a draft electoral law which took Weimar 'als Grundlage'. The law did, however, envisage the participation of 'Massenorganisationen' in the election, and failed to specify who was to decide which parties qualified as 'democratic'.[160] The Bundestag's (predictable) rejection of this unacceptable proposal led to the flurry of diplomatic activity around the March and April notes, in which Stalin again made substantial concessions.[161]

As far as the Soviets were concerned, the risks were minimal, and the prevention of German integration into the European Defence Community was worth the sacrifice. Stalin's view of the EDC was complex: he did not see it as an immediate threat to the Soviet Union, but 'als einen komplexen Machtmechanismus, als eine neue Kraft, den "Imperialismus" in Europa zu erhalten',[162] and thus as an entity with which he could pursue his favoured bloc politics. As far as Stalin was concerned, trading unity for neutrality was a suitable evasion of risk, while leaving open the possibility of later influence:

---

[159] *Neues Deutschland*, 4.11.1951. Pieck had discussed the letter in a meeting with Semenov on 1.11.1951, when Semenov had also mentioned the possibility of conducting elections according to the Weimar constitution (Badstübner and Loth, pp. 376f.).

[160] Draft in *Neues Deutschland*, 3.1.1952.

[161] The text of the notes of 10 March and 9 April is in *Europa Archiv*, 7 (1952), pp. 4805 and 4866–68. A complete analysis of the debate over the sincerity or otherwise of Stalin's intentions is beyond the scope of this study. In addition to works already cited in this study, see Wilfried Loth, 'Die Historiker und die deutsche Frage', *Historisches Jahrbuch*, 122 (1992), 336–82; W.L., 'Stalin, die deutsche Frage und die DDR', *Deutschland Archiv*, 28 (1995), 290–98; and W.L., 'Kritik ohne Grundlagen. Erwiderung auf Gerhard Wettig', *Deutschland Archiv*, 28 (1995), 749–50; Dietrich Staritz, 'Zwischen Ostintegration und nationaler Verpflichtung. Zur Ost- und Deutschlandpolitik der SED 1948 bis 1952', in Ludolf Herbst (ed.), *Westdeutschland 1945–1955. Unterwerfung, Kontrolle, Integration* (Munich: R. Oldenbourg, 1986), pp. 279–89; Rolf Steininger, *Eine vertane Chance: Die Stalin-Note vom 10. März 1952 und die Wiedervereinigung* (Berlin: J.H.W.Dietz Nachf., 1986); Gerhard Wettig, 'Übereinstimmung und Auseinandersetzung über die sowjetische Deutschland-Politik im Frühjahr 1952', *Deutschland Archiv*, 26 (1993), 1205–10; G.W., 'Stalin—Patriot und Demokrat für Deutschland?', *Deutschland Archiv*, 28 (1995), 743–48; and G.W., 'Allzu schnell abgewehrte Kritik. Erwiderung auf Wilfried Loth', *Deutschland Archiv*, 28 (1995), 973.

[162] Lemke, p. 162. See also his discussion (p. 163) of some of the possible motivations for Stalin's policy of playing off Central against Western Europe, which he finds in 'Crimean War Syndrome': the perpetual fear of Russian and Soviet leaders that Western European governments intend to undermine Russia by mobilising states on its border.

'Da es in [Stalins] Sicht keinen Sozialismus in der DDR gab, konnte es auch nicht darum gehen, ihn wieder preiszugeben.'[163]

A direct order from Stalin could not be countermanded (in other words, Stalin, by paying continual attention to the problem, had managed to bring his authority to bear in a way which served his purposes, rather than having it usurped by the 'integrationists') and so the various strands of opinion within the SED leadership began to come out into the open. We have already seen how Grotewohl was quick to come out on the side of Semenov's proposal to Ernst Lemmer, while others felt that free elections would anyway lead to the fall of the Adenauer government. Wilhelm Zaisser, who was to come to grief in the wake of 17 June 1953, is said to have declared in April or May 1952, that 'wir [die SED] bei einer gemeinsamen Wahl damit rechnen müssen, daß wir nicht mehr die Mehrheit des Volkes hinter uns haben'.[164] We need to treat this statement with care, as it reflects the substance of the accusations against Zaisser in July 1953. However, in the context of other statements made by the leaders in this period, such as Ulbricht's declaration in January 1952 to the Central Committee Secretariat that the SED might have to give up the 'Herrschaft des Kommunismus', at least temporarily,[165] Zaisser's statement, or something like it, seems credible.[166]

Although the 'integrationist' line was thrown onto the defensive for the moment, Ulbricht kept up a steady stream of rhetoric against 'Kriegs-brandstifter' in Bonn and Washington.[167] Whether Ulbricht actually believed that the cause of unity was best served by strengthening the GDR (a perfectly reasonable belief within contemporary ideological terms) is never likely to be known. However, since he had set himself up as 'Stalin's man', any change in Soviet policy after the Western rejection of the notes was bound to work in his favour. The SED *apparat*, now largely purged of former SPD members, was bound to think in terms of class conflict, seeing power as their reward for their

[163] Loth, *Stalins ungeliebtes Kind*, p. 182.

[164] Cit. Lemke, p. 164.

[165] Cit. Loth, *Stalins ungeliebtes Kind*, p. 183.

[166] See Helmut Müller-Enbergs, *Der Fall Rudolf Herrnstadt. Tauwetterpolitik vor dem 17. Juni* (Berlin: LinksDruck Verlag, 1991), pp. 286–308, for an account of the construction of the case against Herrnstadt and Zaisser on 26 July 1953.

[167] *Neues Deutschland*, 12.3.1952, commentary on the Soviet note.

opposition to Nazism (whether each particular individual had been entirely consistent in antifascist resistance was neither here nor there: assistance in easing the party's cadre difficulties represented a route to rapid forgiveness). There was no question of any SED members criticising Stalin's line, but they interpreted it according to their own requirements; it would have taken courage and a sustained effort of will, not to mention an ability to discard entrenched ideological habits, to oppose the gathering momentum of division.

The Western rejection of Stalin's notes represents a turning point in the SED's self-confidence in the national question. By this I mean that it shattered any remaining feelings that a form of 'Nationale Front' strategy would succeed in bringing the West German public to its feet in protest. The complexity of the international situation forced itself on minds which were used to thinking in clear categories, and the certainties expressed in the 'Aufbau' resolution were an attempt to compensate by entrenching German national feeling firmly in the GDR. In this period, institutions which were based on expressions of the 'all-German' aspiration came under consistent attack because a willingness to experiment with ideas of German nationhood which exposed the artificiality of the inner-German border, and by extension the optimistic view of German history promulgated by the SED, could not be tolerated. It was, quite simply, an affront.

Stalin's attitude, which had up till now provided some legitimacy for an 'all-German' line, changed rapidly after the rejection of the first note. It has been claimed that the SED's declaration of the 'Aufbau des Sozialismus' at the Second Party Conference had no precedent in the SED's discussions with Stalin, and that it was presented to him as a *fait accompli* to which he had no choice but to agree.[168] However, the situation is rather more complex, and Lemke expresses it cautiously: 'Die Ablehnung der Märznote der UdSSR und der Beschluß über den Aufbau des Sozialismus in der DDR standen offensichtlich in einem ursächlichen Zusammenhang.'[169] It is possible to tease

---

[168] See Rolf Badstübner, 'Die sowjetische Deutschlandpolitik', p. 130. Badstübner is often guilty of oversimplifying his analysis of the interrelationship between Stalin and SED, seemingly in order to place the entire blame for division on power-hungry elites in both German governments. For a more satisfactory account of the run-up to the Conference, see Staritz, 'Die SED, Stalin, und der "Aufbau des Sozialismus" in der DDR', 686–700; and Loth, pp. 185–92.

[169] Lemke, p. 168.

out some of these correspondences, which can give us some idea of the growing self-confidence of the national line peddled by the triumphant 'integrationists'.

The notes taken by Wilhelm Pieck during the SED leadership's visit to Moscow, 29 March to 10 April 1952, show very clearly the change in the Soviet leader's attitude.[170] The feeling that Pieck was deliberately misleading Stalin is hard to avoid when, in his list of questions for Stalin, he can make the following statement: 'Der Vorschlag der Sowjetregierung hat eine große Bewegung der Massen ausgelöst'. Can he have believed this? He did go on to suggest that the SED saw free elections as an opportunity to conduct a 'Massenkampf zum Sturz der Adenauer-Regierung',[171] so perhaps he did believe it. Stalin himself demonstrates his sudden awareness that his German policy has failed: 'bisher alle Vorschläge abgelehnt', by ordering the rapid remilitarisation of the GDR: 'Nicht Miliz, sondern ausgebildete Armee. Alles ohne Geschrei, / aber beharrlich', and land reform: 'Schaffung von Produktiv-Genossenschaften im Dorfe'. He does, however, make the caveat that this should all be carried out tactfully: 'Niemand zwingen. / Nicht schreien Kolchosen—Sozialismus. / Tatsachen schaffen. Im Anfang die Tat. /—Weg zum Sozialismus—staatl[iche] Prod[uktion] ist sozialistische.'[172] It is clear that this does not amount to carte blanche for the forcible sovietisation of the GDR, but the SED leadership took away with them an important endorsement of their legitimacy.

As soon as Pieck, Ulbricht and Grotewohl returned from Moscow, they set about creating 'Tatsachen'; a Politburo resolution of 11 April declared the break-up of the old *Länder* and their replacement by fourteen *Bezirke*.[173] Although nothing like this had been discussed in Moscow, the SKK approved the move.[174] The Soviet authorities were now reacting to developments in Germany, and the diplomatic activity around Stalin's second note made little difference to the new atmosphere in the GDR. The preparations for the Second

---

[170] See Badstübner and Loth, pp. 382–99.

[171] Badstübner and Loth, p. 383.

[172] Stalin, in the 'Schlußbesprechung' on 7.4.1952, Badstübner and Loth, pp. 396–97. Stalin does not approach the question of how to remilitarise the GDR 'ohne Geschrei'. It should be noted here that the instructions for stealth given by Stalin here are qualitatively different from his earlier warnings to the SED not to proceed with sovietisation: he is now only concerned with securing a balance of power in Europe.

[173] Loth, p. 187.

[174] Briefing with Chuikov, 7.5.1952, Badstübner and Loth, p. 403.

Conference continued to consolidate Ulbricht's dominance, as he appropriated Stalin's authority in order to push the Soviet leader's plans as far as he could. The Soviet government's increasingly pessimistic assessment of the international situation in the run-up to the Nineteenth Congress of the Soviet Communist Party no doubt contributed to the willingness to sanction the boldness of the changes in the GDR.

However, the Soviets had given no indication that the SED should declare an immediate upswing in socialist construction, although Stalin's statements in Moscow in April had been ambiguous on the subject. Dietrich Staritz has established that the final slogan for the conference developed slowly and in secrecy, and the Politburo wrote to Stalin on 2 July (that is, only one week before the conference) asking for his approval.[175] The letter plays on Stalin's obsessions, claiming that the GDR is ready for the 'Übergang zum Sozialismus', and that such a development is necessary to persuade workers in both German states, 'daß man bei uns besser leben kann als in Westdeutschland [...] Das ist von großer Bedeutung für die Sicherung der Deutschen Demokratischen Republik gegen feindliche Sabotage und Diversions- maßnahmen und für die Organisierung der bewaffneten Streitkräfte der Deutschen Demokratischen Republik'.

Stalin's reply arrived on 8 July, in time for the Central Committee meeting on the eve of the conference.[176] Ulbricht read out the resolution declaring the 'Aufbau des Sozialismus', which had not been presented for discussion, presumably because Stalin's endorsement was seen to be sufficient. Ulbricht's excuse ('Es war uns nicht möglich, den Text vorher zu vervielfältigen') is not entirely convincing.

The fact that the Soviets did not send a delegation to the conference, and that Stalin's congratulatory telegram does not mention socialism, has provoked much speculation, with echoes of the Kremlinological debates about the semantics of official pronouncements. Wilfriede Otto claimed in 1991 that this

---

[175] Staritz, 'Die SED, Stalin und der "Aufbau des Sozialismus" in der DDR', pp. 698–99.

[176] See Staritz, 'Die SED, Stalin und der "Aufbau des Sozialismus" in der DDR', p. 700. The protocol of the meeting records Becher's hope that the construction of socialism will help in the 'Hebung des Kulturniveaus', which is lagging behind the West.

provided one more piece of evidence for the SED's disloyalty to Stalin.[177] Dietrich Staritz takes an article in the *Tägliche Rundschau* of 12.7.1952, for a sign of Stalin's approval, although the expression of support for the 'Aufbau' resolution is not in his actual words;[178] in an earlier analysis, Staritz had shown that an informant to the SPD's *Ostbüro* claimed that the SKK had criticised the conference's resolutions.[179]

Whatever the case may be, the conference marked the triumph of the 'integrationist' line, and Ulbricht and Pieck indulged in much rhetoric about the 'Sturz des Bonner Vassallen-Regimes'.[180] Stalin was largely preoccupied with preparations for the Nineteenth Congress and with his conspiracy theories, and so the establishment of security was his primary concern in Germany; whether we can assert, with Loth, 'daß [Stalin] durch sein Interesse an einem militärischen Gleichgewicht in Europa zu einem Gefangenen Ulbrichts geworden war', is another matter.[181] This would be to assume that German unity was a pet project for the Soviet leader, and that he was unable to be flexible in his assessment of the best interests of the Soviet Union; Stalin's flexibility in foreign policy matters is surely at the heart of Loth's thesis.

The flaw in Stalin's ability to translate his authority into the power to shape events in Germany was his inability to trust any subordinate who did not express absolute allegiance to him. In other words, a genuine commitment to democracy was beyond him, although he needed to offer the guarantee of free elections in Germany if he was to have any hope of preventing the integration of the Federal Republic into the EDC. Therefore, it would be wrong to assume

---

[177] See Wilfriede Otto, 'Sowjetische Deutschland-Note 1952. Stalin und die DDR. Bisher unveröffentlichte handschriftliche Notizen Wilhelm Piecks', *Beiträge zur Geschichte der Arbeiterbewegung*, 33 (1991), 374–89.

[178] 'J. W. Stalin hatte die Gründung der friedliebenden Deutschen Demokratischen Republik einen "Wendepunkt der Geschichte Europas" genannt. Sein Wort gilt angesichts des planmäßigen Aufbaus des Sozialismus in der DDR noch mehr'. Cit. Staritz, 'Die SED, Stalin und der "Aufbau des Sozialismus" in der DDR', p. 700. Staritz calls this approval 'auf Stalinsche Art'.

[179] Dietrich Staritz, *Geschichte der DDR* (Frankfurt a. M.: Neue Historische Bibliothek, 1985), pp. 75f.

[180] Resolution of the conference, *Protokoll der Verhandlungen der II. Parteikonferenz der Sozialistischen Einheitspartei Deutschlands, 9.–12. Juli 1952* (Berlin: Dietz, 1952), p. 490.

[181] Loth, *Stalins ungeliebtes Kind*, p. 190. There is a tendency in Loth's work to see Ulbricht as the unique instigator of the developing 'integrationist' line, perhaps as a figure to demonise in place of Stalin. For example, a phrase which appears in Gerhard Wettig's earlier piece, 'Die sowjetische Deutschland-Politik am Vorabend des 17. Juni', in Ilse Spittmann and Karl Wilhelm Fricke (eds), *17. Juni 1953. Arbeiteraufstand in der DDR*, 2nd. edn. (Cologne: Edition Deutschland Archiv, 1988), p. 58 ('Die Führung um Ulbricht wies die Berichte [über die Stimmung der Bevölkerung] als tendenziös-parteifeindliche Elaborate zurück') appears in Loth, p. 196, as: 'Ulbricht wies die Warnungen als tendentiös-parteifeindliche Elaborate zurück'. In neither case does the author provide a concrete reference.

that Stalin was simply intent on domination in Europe as a whole: his conception was more flexible than this would imply, concentrating on the protection of the Soviet Union's borders. If absolute dominance was his policy in the rest of Eastern Europe, his German policy, which represents something of an exception, makes perfect sense in this light.

THE NEW COURSE AND THE 17 JUNE 1953

The developments in the GDR and Soviet Union in the months between the declaration of the 'Aufbau des Sozialismus' and June 1953 have been extensively documented,[182] and much of the debate has focused on the intentions of Beria in the period after Stalin's death, and academic opinion in recent years has had to take into account evidence suggesting that Beria was serious in his German policy. However, the atmosphere of crisis set in earlier.[183]

The SED leadership's campaigns in late 1952, such as the imposition of highly unpopular austerity measures and the renewed attacks on independent artistic activity, did not go uncriticised. According to Heinz Lippmann, the deputy head of the FDJ at the time, the SKK commissioned investigations in Autumn 1952 into the attitudes and opinions of various social groups and organisations, the results of which were alarming for the SED.[184] Rolf Stöckigt has shown that the Central Committee of the SED devoted time between February and March 1953 to analysing the situation in the country, and

---

[182] For the most comprehensive accounts, see Arnulf Baring, *Der 17. Juni 1953* (Cologne: Kiepenhauer & Witsch, 1966); Karl-Wilhelm Fricke, 'Der Arbeiteraufstand—Vorgeschichte, Verlauf, Folgen', in Spittmann and Fricke (eds), pp. 5–22.

[183] Contrast Gerhard Wettig, 'Die sowjetische Deutschland-Politik am Vorabend des 17. Juni', with his more recent contributions: 'Zum Stand der Forschung über Berijas Deutschland-Politik im Frühjahr 1953', *Deutschland Archiv*, 26 (1993), 674–82, and 'Nochmals: Berijas Deutschland-Politik', *Deutschland Archiv*, 26 (1993), 1089–93. An early, and largely unsubstantiated, expression of the view that Beria and Malenkov found common cause with Herrnstadt and Zaisser, can be found in Richard Löwenthal's Foreword to Arnulf Baring, *op. cit.* See also the contrasting views expressed in Wilfriede Otto, 'Sowjetische Deutschlandpolitik 1952/53. Forschungs- und Wahrheitsprobleme', *Deutschland Archiv*, 26 (1993), 948–54; and Jochen Laufer, 'Die UdSSR, die SED und die deutsche Frage', *Deutschland Archiv*, 26 (1993), 1201–04. Russian research on the subject has been limited since 1991, but see A. M. Filitov, *Germanskii vopros: ot raskola k soedineniyu* (Moscow: Mezhdunarodnye otnosheniya, 1993); and Lew Besymenski, '1953—Berija will die DDR beseitigen', *Die Zeit*, 15 October 1993, pp. 81–83.

[184] Heinz Lippmann, 'Der 17. Juni im Zentralkomitee der SED', *Aus Politik und Zeitgeschichte*, 13.6.1956, p. 374.

discovered widespread hostility to the government.[185] The SKK took these findings very seriously, and Semenov visited Moscow in April for urgent discussion with the Soviet leadership.[186]

Ulbricht's response was to tighten the apparatus of repression and to conduct purges within the party; over 150,000 members or candidate members were expelled from the party in the wake of the Slánský trial of December 1952.[187] Rudolf Herrnstadt began to feel his position threatened when *Neues Deutschland* published approving articles on the discovery of the 'Doctors' Plot' in January 1953.[188] Ulbricht ignored all signs of opposition to his policies, simply stepping up campaigns against 'Saboteure' and 'Hetzer'; however, his appeals to the Soviet government for help are a sign that he acknowledged the problem.[189]

In February, Ulbricht wrote to Stalin requesting urgent credits, but his letter went unanswered in the Soviet leader's final illness. Similarly, Grotewohl's urgent requests to Beria and Malenkov at Stalin's funeral for financial assistance were turned down, and a further begging letter to Moscow in early April provoked a sharp response, demanding that the SED regime slow down its economic programme.[190] Instead, the SED passed the two austerity measures which tipped the country into social conflict: on 9 April, the Council of Ministers passed a resolution withdrawing ration coupons from approximately two million people, and on 14 May, the Central Committee decreed the raising of work norms by ten per cent. At the same meeting, Ulbricht engineered the expulsion of Franz Dahlem from the Central Committee, as part of a purge designed to turn the repercussions of the Slánský trial away from himself.[191]

[185] Rolf Stöckigt, 'Ein forcierter stalinistischer Kurs führte 1953 in die Krise', *Berliner Zeitung*, 8.3.1990.

[186] Lippmann, 'Der 17. Juni im Zentralkomitee der SED', p. 363.

[187] Loth, *Stalins ungeliebtes Kind*, p. 195.

[188] *Neues Deutschland*, 14.1.1953. See also Müller-Enbergs, p. 164.

[189] For a full account of these meetings with Soviet leaders, see also Loth, *Stalins ungeliebtes Kind*, pp. 196–209, and Gerhard Wettig, 'Neue Erkenntnisse über Berijas Deutschland-Politik', *Deutschland Archiv*, 26 (1993), 1412–13.

[190] Baring, p. 37. Pressure was kept up on the GDR regime by visits from senior figures in the Soviet hierarchy, such as the deputy head of the Soviet Planning Commission, Nikitin, who declared: 'Die Sowjetführung plane einen neuen Kurs, der auf die Verbesserung des Lebensstandards der Bevölkerung abziele.' Fritz Schenk, *Im Vorzimmer der Diktatur: Zwölf Jahre Pankow* (Cologne: Kiepenhauer & Witsch, 1962), p. 185.

[191] Erich Honecker states that Ulbricht had been in danger: 'Es bestand die Gefahr, daß, wie die anderen General-sekretäre, auch Walter Ulbricht in diesen Prozeß einbezogen werden sollte. Wir haben das zum Glück abgewehrt' Reinhold Andert and Wolfgang Herzberg, *Der Sturz. Erich Honecker im Kreuzverhör* (Berlin: Aufbau, 1990), p. 232.

As the events of 17 June proved, the SED hard-liners' grip on power was less than secure, so these measures, and the increasing persecution which accompanied them, need to be seen as a sign of an awareness that the regime's lack of legitimacy, and the equivocal attitude of the Soviet leadership, represented a real threat. The beginnings of a personality cult around Walter Ulbricht, to be initiated by a special commission under Lotte Ulbricht and Fred Oelßner set up to prepare celebrations for his 60th birthday on 30 June, attest to this insecurity.

Beria's desperate campaign to save his life after Stalin's death, and its implications for the GDR were discussed in Chapter Two of this study. According to Pavel Sudoplatov, at that time a senior officer in the MGB, Beria was playing an elaborate double game, seemingly also with the agreement of Malenkov.[192] As well as playing a prominent role in the Politburo discussions on the 'New Course' in Germany, Beria attempted to make clandestine contact with senior figures in Bonn and Washington in order to trade German unity for substantial financial help to ease the severe economic crisis in the Soviet Union. He envisaged a coalition government in Germany, with the participation of the four occupying powers; in return for this, the Germans would continue reparations payments to the Soviet Union, and Western backers would support, to the tune of 10 billion dollars, a massive reconstruction programme for the parts of the Soviet Union which had been devastated during the war. When informed by Foreign Ministry officials that even an SPD government in the FRG would reject such a plan, Beria refused to believe it.[193] In the words of Gerhard Wettig, 'Es wäre bezeichnend für die Figur Berija, wenn er tatsächlich auf ein so unseriöses Vorgehen gesetzt hätte'.[194]

Whatever the chances of success for Beria's plan, it seems that the other members of the Politburo were kept completely in the dark about it, as it would surely have formed a major part of the accusations of treason against Beria in

---

[192] Cf. Besymenski, *op. cit.*

[193] Vladislav M. Zubok, *Soviet Intelligence and the Cold War: The 'Small' Committee for Information*, CWIHP Working Paper no. 4, December 1992, cit. Loth, *Stalins ungeliebtes Kind*, p. 199.

[194] Gerhard Wettig, 'Neue Erkenntnisse', p. 1412.

July.[195] Similarly, clandestine attempts by Beria and Malenkov to facilitate a reconciliation with Tito were kept from the rest of the leadership.[196] A certain amount of mystery still surrounds the involvement of members of the SED leadership in Beria's plans: Besymenski asserts that Ernst Wollweber knew about them, but his activities remained undetected, so that he avoided the accusations of treachery which affected Herrnstadt and Zaisser. It may be that Herrnstadt and Zaisser were unaware of Beria's high-level conspiracy, but instead supported the imposition of the 'New Course' whose impetus came from Beria's campaign to distance himself from Stalin.[197] It is, after all, all too easy to assume the existence of extraordinary conspiracies in circumstances where the evidence is so sparse.

The resolution which was to enforce the 'New Course' was passed by the Soviet Council of Ministers on 27 May;[198] the 'Aufbau des Sozialismus', and 'die bis zu dieser Zeit durchgeführte Propaganda' are declared 'unrichtig'. Any signs of dissension in the Soviet leadership were covered up when Ulbricht, Grotewohl and Oelßner visited Moscow to receive the new instructions (2–4.6.1953).[199] Semenov told the SED Politburo on 6 June that the SED should become 'ein magnetisches Feld [...] für Westd[eutschland], Frankreich, Italien',

---

[195] See Viktor Knoll and Lothar Kölm (eds), *Der Fall Beria: Protokoll einer Abrechnung. Das Plenum des ZK der KPdSU Juli 1953, Stenographischer Bericht* (Berlin: Aufbau, 1993). The accusations that Beria wanted, '18 Millionen Deutsche der Herrschaft der amerikanischen Imperialisten zu übergeben' (Khrushchev, cit. Knoll and Kölm, p. 66), which have always appeared to be simply part of the fabricated case against him, now appear in a different light, although Khrushchev was unaware of Beria's plan. According to Molotov, the Politburo debates centred around the issue of whether a 'bourgeois' Germany could be peaceful, and that Malenkov and Beria were eventually defeated because of fears of renewed German aggression: 'Esli GDR ne poidet po puti sotsializma, eto budet staraya Germaniya.' [A GDR without socialism would be the same old Germany] (*Sto sorok besed s Molotovym. Iz dnevnika F. Chueva* (Moscow: Terra, 1991), p. 336).

[196] Cf. Besymenski, *op. cit.*

[197] Cf. Filitov, p. 155. See also R. Herrnstadt, *Das Herrnstadt-Dokument. Das Poliburo der SED und die Geschichte des 17. Juni 1953*, ed. by N. Stulz-Herrnstadt (Reinbek: Rowohlt, 1990). The document written by Rudolf Herrnstadt in 1956 ('Zur Angelegenheit Zaisser/Herrnstadt', pp. 55ff.) gives an extraordinarily detailed insight into the Central Committee discussions.

[198] 'Maßnahmen zur Gesundung der politischen Lage in der Deutschen Demokratischen Republik', cit. in Rolf Stöckigt, 'Ein Dokument von großer historischer Bedeutung vom Mai 1953', *Beiträge zur Geschichte der Arbeiterbewegung*, 32 (1990), 648–50. As has been pointed out several times since, Stöckigt's version contains an important typing error: point 6 of the resolution should read, '[...] der Kampf für die Vereinigung Deutschlands [...]' instead of 'Verteidigung'.

[199] Most accounts comment on Beria's supercilious behaviour, remarking that he seemed to enjoy humiliating his German counterparts: see Oelßner's report to the SED Politbüro on 6 June, in Herrnstadt, pp. 58–59. Khrushchev, no impartial observer, claims that Beria screamed at the Germans to such an extent that it became 'peinlich' (*Der Fall Berija*, p. 67). Note also Molotov's statement, 'So viele Fehler, darum so korrigieren, daß ganz Deutschland es sieht'(cit. Loth, p. 203).

and that what was required was 'keine Reformen, sondern Wendung'.[200] That the national legitimacy of the GDR was at stake was clear to all: if the propaganda which had accompanied the 'Aufbau' campaign had been entirely mistaken, then the question of German national identity was thrown wide open once again. The struggle over the rhetoric of German division had taken a turn against the 'integrationists'.

This becomes clearer when reading the material connected with the important Politburo meeting of 6 June. Ulbricht was clearly on the defensive, accused of 'Diktatur'[201] and of 'souveräne[r] Überlegenheit'.[202] The suspicion that Ulbricht had carved out an exclusive niche for himself is strengthened by Friedrich Ebert's complaint that Ulbricht had access to sources of information denied to the other leaders.[203] Oelßner called for 'Vereinsfreiheit', 'Auflockerung' in the 'Pressewesen' and 'Lockerung der Diktatur',[204] and there is a general round of self-criticism.[205] However, a few days later, a speech by Grotewohl on the occasion of the 'Tag des Lehrers' made it clear that the 'integrationist' line, with all that it implied for the national self-consciousness of the GDR (in effect, the ideological self-consciousness of the SED leadership), was not going to be abandoned without a fight.

Grotewohl spoke out against 'faschistische Kräfte im Westen unseres Vater-landes', declaring that education should be conducted 'im Geiste unserer großen nationalen Traditionen und für den friedlichen Weg zur Herstellung der Einheit unseres Vaterlandes', and that the teacher's task was, 'Patrioten zu erziehen, die ihrer Heimat, ihrem Volke und der Regierung treu sind,

---

[200] Notes made by Otto Grotewohl, in Elke Scherstjanoi, '"Wollen wir den Sozialismus?" Dokumente aus der Sitzung des Politbüros des ZK der SED am 6. Juni 1953', *Beiträge zur Geschichte der Arbeiterbewegung*, 33 (1991), 658–680 (670).

[201] Herrnstadt, p. 64. See also Zaisser's description of Ulbricht's leadership style: 'Charaktereigenschaften— unnatürlich empfindlich, grob— Drang z[um] Kommandieren [...] Von oben bis unten zuviel kommandiert. Das Gefühl für Parteidemokratie ist verlorengegangen' (Scherstjanoi, pp. 669–70).

[202] Friedrich Ebert, 'Diskussionsrede', in Scherstjanoi, p. 674.

[203] Scherstjanoi., p. 679. Ebert also complains about the way in which Grotewohl, Pieck and Ulbricht exploit their connections with the Soviets in order to impose their own line on policy: 'Die berichtenden Genossen erwecken hier sicher nicht ohne Absicht den Eindruck, daß es sich bei den Empfehlungen und Wünschen unserer Freunde einfach um Weisungen handle, die sie in dieser oder jener Form verwirklicht zu sehen wünschen'. In particular, he comments that this tactic was used against 'Bedenken, die besonders häufig und energisch von Anton Ackermann vertreten wurden'. (Scherstjanoi, p. 676)

[204] Zaisser, cit. Scherstjanoi, p. 669.

[205] Ulbricht: 'Ich habe Verantwortung zu tragen und werde meine Arbeit ändern' (*ibid.*).

Menschen, die bereit sind zur Freundschaft mit der Sowjetunion, den
Volksdemokratien und mit allen für Frieden und Fortschritt kämpfenden
Menschen'.[206] In terms of the struggle for control of the rhetoric of national
unity, Grotewohl is speaking in terms which fit with the renewed emphasis on
unity demanded by the Soviets, but, like Ulbricht in the years since 1945,
Grotewohl is exploiting the authority of his connections with the Soviet Union
in order to promote a cause fundamentally at odds with the Soviet Politburo's
declared policy. Anyone who accepted the truth of Marxism-Leninism would
have to agree that the highest expression of German nationhood lay in its
fulfilment in the triumph of Marxism, so accepting the troubling ambiguities
exposed by the Soviet demands would have meant, essentially, questioning the
whole basis of one's beliefs. How many of the SED leaders would have been
genuinely able to abandon the faith which had sustained them in opposition to
Nazism, must remain in doubt.

The Soviets, however, were entirely serious, and, when Ulbricht returned to
his autocratic manner, Semenov and Ivan Il'ichev, head of the Soviet
Diplomatic Mission to the GDR Government, began to talk openly about
replacing him. Herrnstadt reports that Il'ichev suggested that Herrnstadt,
Zaisser and 'ein paar Genossen aus dem Politbüro' should talk to Ulbricht about
a change of leadership style, 'und wenn er nicht verstehen will—dann berichten
Sie uns, und wir werden tätig werden'.[207] Other sources indicate that Semenov
may have intended to replace the SED's monopoly on power with a more
'bourgeois' government, possibly headed by Joseph Wirth.[208]

The events of 17 June nearly led to Ulbricht's downfall. Just how narrow was
his escape can be seen from the predominance of Herrnstadt's views in internal
SED debate and in the press in the days leading up to the 17th ('Alle fallen über
Ulbricht her. Er wird wohl unterliegen', reports Erich Honecker after a stormy

---

[206] Speech on 12 June, in Otto Grotewohl, *Im Kampf um die einige Deutsche Demokratische Republik*, 2nd
edn., 3 vols (Berlin: Dietz, 1959), III, pp. 335–36.

[207] Herrnstadt, pp. 78–79. Herrnstadt did not act on this suggestion, but instead decided to take the matter up
with Ulbricht himself. He found himself, 'wie oft, wieder von ihm begeistert, von seiner Elastizität, der
Schnelligkeit seines Denkens, und vor allem davon, daß er letzten Endes, wie mir schien, guten Willens war.'
Müller-Enbergs makes the perceptive comment: 'Der Intellektuelle Rudolf Herrnstadt ließ sich von Ulbricht
blenden' Müller-Enbergs, p. 194.

[208] Hermann Osten, 'Die Deutschlandpolitik der Sowjetunion in den Jahren 1952/53', *Osteuropa*, 14 (1964),
3–18 (6).

Politburo meeting on 16 June[209]) and from the absolute support given to these views by Semenov. However, it was not until 26 June that the Organisations-kommission of the Central Committee, meeting to prepare for the Central Committee meeting scheduled for the next day, proposed a resolution which would strip Ulbricht of the personal power which he had amassed.[210]

The first indications that Ulbricht would weather the crisis came in an article in *Pravda* on 27 June, in which Beria's name did not appear in a list of dignitaries attending a performance at the Bolshoi Theatre. Ulbricht could take comfort from the fact that the security of the GDR was guaranteed through its importance in the accusations against Beria, and his fightback began from this point. By the time of the Politburo meeting of 18 July, Ulbricht had managed to make a connection between Zaisser and Herrnstadt and the disgraced Beria, and those who had opposed him initially began to withdraw their accusations.[211] Semenov withheld further support from Herrnstadt, presumably hoping to avoid entanglement in the case against Beria; in his recently-published memoirs, Semenov takes particular care to distance himself from Beria's incompetence and the meddling of the NKVD in German affairs.[212]

The failure of the opposition group to push through their programme and to depose Ulbricht can be traced back to their inconsistency in the face of a genuine opportunity, a lack of organisation probably due to the general shock at the suddenness of the outburst of public anger, and to sheer bad timing. Whether there actually was another 'missed opportunity' for German unity is, in the final analysis, not the most important lesson to be drawn from these events; for the vital question of German nationhood in the self-consciousness of the GDR political and intellectual community, the key issue is the way in

---

[209] Heinz Lippmann, *Honecker: Porträt eines Nachfolgers* (Cologne: Verlag Wissenschaft und Politik, 1971), p. 161.

[210] The text of the resolution can be found in Wilfriede Otto, 'Dokumente zur Auseinandersetzung in der SED 1953', *Beiträge zur Geschichte der Arbeiterbewegung*, 32 (1990), 655–72.

[211] On 7 July, Ackermann had expressed years of frustration: 'Lange Zeit habe ich geschwiegen, aus Disziplin, aus Hoffnung, aus Angst. Heute liegt das alles hinter mir'. Herrnstadt, p. 128. Ackermann was forced into self-criticism on 22 July. Herrnstadt may have embellished his memoir somewhat (the text was written only three years after the event), but the impression of a collective release of tension in the leadership is irresistible. See also Loth, *Stalins ungeliebtes Kind*, pp. 209–16 for a fuller account of the debates.

[212] See Wladimir S.Semjonow, *Von Stalin bis Gorbatschow. Ein halbes Jahrhundert in diplomatischer Mission 1939-1991* (Berlin: Nicolaischer Verlagsbuchhandlung, 1995), particularly pp. 287ff.

which, for a few days, the tables were turned against an 'integrationist' line which depended for its grip on power on the imposition of artificial barriers, both physical and linguistic.

CHAPTER FOUR

'DAS WORT WIRD ZUR VOKABEL'[1]:

THE QUESTION OF INTELLECTUAL RESPONSIBILITY

In the preceding chapters, I have attempted a critical examination of some of the models which have been applied to the issues surrounding German division, and have introduced some new approaches which take into account the most recent scholarship on the subject. Without entirely abandoning a chronological narrative, this study will now to focus more specifically on the implications of the historical debates for an understanding of cultural life in the Soviet Zone/GDR. As we have seen, much, if not most, of the historical writing about the founding of the GDR has been preoccupied with a complex of themes arising from the question of whether there was a 'missed opportunity' for reunification at various times up to mid-1953. Although the polarisation which characterised this debate is beginning to break down, the obvious emotional appeal of the subject continues to influence attempts to find new approaches. However, as an analysis of the ideological, discursive and broader political context of German division shows, interpretations which rely on divining the supposed intentions of the various individuals (principally, in this case, Stalin, Ulbricht, Tyul'panov and Becher) cannot do justice to the functioning of power under the particular conditions of Soviet occupation.[2] Even an interpretation such as Loth's, which seems to me to provide the most satisfactory model for the political background to the development of SED cultural policy, relies on a

---

[1] From Johannes R. Becher, 'Der Turm von Babel', *Gesammelte Werke*, ed. by Johannes-R.-Becher-Archiv der Akademie der Künste zu Berlin, 18 vols (Berlin and Weimar: Aufbau, 1966-1981), VI, p. 40. (This edition is here-after referred to as *GW*) The poem is an expression of Becher's desire to recover a 'lost' authenticity, supposedly to be found in the literary language of German Classicism.

[2] For recent research examining the functioning of power in the SBZ/GDR, using a variety of archival sources and methodological approaches, see Mary Fulbrook, *Anatomy of a Dictatorship. Inside the GDR 1949-1989* (Oxford: Oxford University Press, 1995); Hartmut Kaelbe, Jürgen Kocka and Hartmut Zwahr (eds), *Sozial-geschichte der DDR* (Stuttgart: Klett-Cotta, 1994); Jürgen Kocka (ed.), *Historische DDR-Forschung: Aufsätze und Studien* (Berlin: Akademie Verlag, 1993); and Sigrid Meuschel, *Legitimation und Parteiherrschaft* (Frankfurt a. M.: Suhrkamp, 1992).

clear distinction between rhetoric or ideology (the two terms often being used interchangeably) and a political 'reality', a complex of power struggles and administrative measures, which can be separated from this linguistic dimension. However, the nature of power relations within the SED depended to a great extent on control over changing meanings and the boundaries of discourse within the framework of Marxism-Leninism, and it is for this reason that the study of cultural policy can give us a profound insight into the operation of these power relations in the Soviet Zone/GDR. Now that the broader political context has been established, the following sections will examine the foundations and functioning of the ideological system in which many communist intellectuals were caught, concentrating particularly on the important figure of J. R. Becher; in this way, we can begin to explain the sometimes limited success of attempts to exert administrative control over various cultural institutions, including the Deutsche Akademie der Künste.

'TWO LINES' OR 'TWO CAMPS'?

At the beginning of Chapter Two of this study, I made some criticisms of a bipolar model, which takes too literally the 'two camps' theory presented by Zhdanov at the founding conference of the Cominform, and which fails to do justice to the extraordinary interplay of influences, whether economic, political or cultural which characterised post-war Europe. This section will apply this critique to the corresponding models which have been applied to cultural life in the Soviet Zone, and which have exerted a profound influence on the polarisation of debate.

The contrasting approaches to the historical problem of Stalin's plans for Germany have tended, as we have seen, to fall into two camps themselves, which seemed irrevocably polarised in the atmosphere of the Cold War, where the study of post-war European history often resembled a branch of political science; the need to make historical developments comprehensible to politicians led to the overemphasis on politics and diplomacy, which in its turn was reassuring to those who needed to feel that their actions had an effect on a national or international stage. It would be an overstatement to deny the importance of the figure or image of the high-profile 'statesman' in a period characterised by conflicts over notions of sovereignty, but I have already examined the negative consequences for historical understanding of the assumption that Stalin had the ability to exert a practical, day-to-day influence on the vital minutiae of East German politics. We should be careful not to confuse Stalin's authority with his power.

The previous chapters dealt at some length with the model of the inevitable take-over of Eastern Germany by a unified SED/SMAD leadership, under the ultimate control of Stalin; the corresponding view of East German cultural life, with particular reference to the attempts by an aggressive SED group to take over the running of the Deutsche Akademie der Künste, will be examined below. I have already referred to the problems associated with the use of the term 'Zhdanovism' to refer to the administrative imposition of Socialist Realism in the Soviet Zone: although it may be accurate to assume that Socialist Realism served the purposes of the developing 'integrationist' line in the zone, any direct equation with the circumstances within the Soviet Union must prove misleading. As we have seen, the campaign generally known as the *zhdanovshchina* was instigated as part of Zhdanov's bid to assert his ideological apparatus over the dominion of Malenkov and others in industry and government, and the ideological campaign of Tyul'panov and others in the Soviet Zone on the issues of reparations and KPD/SPD unity in particular served a factional purpose rather than reflecting Stalin's German policy. In this light, 'Zhdanovism' is already beginning to lose its unanalytical, almost metaphysical association with a monolithic campaign of cultural control. However, if we move on to consider the Cosmopolitanism campaign which followed Zhdanov's death, it becomes obvious that we can make no direct correlation between the effects of the campaign in the Soviet Union and its repercussions in the Soviet Zone. Whereas the Cosmopolitanism campaign was designed at the outset to purge the Soviet Central Committee apparatus of Zhdanov's supporters, the consequence of its introduction in Germany was to further consolidate the dominance of an 'integrationist' line within the SED, whose position was made more secure by the worsening international situation.

The conscious introduction of Soviet models, as part of the ideological campaign to undermine the 'German Road to Socialism', was retained as part of the armoury of SED politicians such as Ulbricht even after the removal of Tyul'panov from influence in the Soviet Zone, and so the Cosmopolitanism campaign in the SBZ/GDR came to serve a purpose quite different from its Soviet original. Stalin's reliance on the SED as his only possible means of influence in German politics, and his inability to conceive of any solution to German division which was not imposed from above, meant that the progressive modelling of the SED on what were referred to as 'Leninist' principles, in order to ensure the party's absolute loyalty, in fact tended to work against the German policy which Stalin and Molotov were trying to pursue.

In other words, use of the term 'Zhdanovism', as with 'Stalinism', obscures rather than illuminates the complex and contradictory issues surrounding cultural policy in the Soviet Zone. Its employment as a blanket term for the administrative imposition of certain aesthetic norms relies on the acceptance of an understanding of Soviet politics, culture and society which is very close to the rhetorical self-definition of the Soviet regime itself, with the all-powerful Stalin watching over every aspect of life, and which cannot account for the survival, and repeated self-assertion in GDR cultural institutions, of a line which questioned and undermined the division of German culture.

A model which brings us closer to an understanding of the survival of this seemingly anomalous 'all-German' line asserts that there were 'two lines' in cultural policy in the Soviet Zone, corresponding to conflicting tendencies in Soviet and SED policy and reflected in struggles for power within the Politbureaus of the SED and Soviet Communist Party. This approach, which draws on the work of those historians who consider that there *was* a 'missed opportunity' for German reunification, finds in an examination of cultural politics a 'demokratische "Linie"' within the bureaucracy, as well as within the artistic community itself, which, 'bis 1950', was present as a 'trag- und konsensfähige Alternative zu einer administrativ reglementierenden Politik'.[3]

---

[3] Gerd Dietrich, 'Zwei Linien in der Kulturpolitik? Diskussionen in der SED-Führung 1947/48', in Černý, pp. 44–51. Dietrich also asserts elsewhere, though without much hard evidence, that (unspecified) SMAD cultural officers 'versuchten [...], außerhalb des Zugriffs sowjetischer Gesetze, auf einem fremden Territorium eine umsichtige, großzügige, tolerante und demokratische Kulturpolitik zu entwickeln' Gerd Dietrich, *Politik und*

The preceding chapters have examined the evidence pertaining to this model, and the arguments for and against, and, through an analysis of the functioning of the ideological system in which political and cultural debates took place, some of its deficiencies have been indicated. I intend now to explore these criticisms with a view to proposing a more satisfactory model for understanding the role of the intellectual or politically-minded artist within this ideological system.

Gerd Dietrich's 'two lines' argument is particularly interesting for its insistence that there were conflicts of interest within the cultural *apparat* of both SED and SMAD, in other words, that there were spaces for differing interpretations of ambiguous official policy pronouncements at the level of the individual, and generally invisible, functionary.[4] Unfortunately, Dietrich's 1993 book does not take up the challenge offered by this idea, which could have led to a detailed exploration of the functioning of power, ideology, meaning, resistance and complicity within the hierarchies themselves. Power is still defined as a force which proceeds from the top downwards, so that conflicts within the leadership are seen as the primary factor in determining the various ambiguities in the day-to-day practicalities of policy implementation. Although this model gives a more satisfactory account of the contradictions in cultural policy and its implementation than a view which sees these contradictions as simply tactical variants of a single policy, it is rather schematic, and would benefit from a more consistent analysis of the effect of the ideological and administrative system on the individual within it.[5] I intend to develop these ideas further, in order to arrive at a more effective account of the position of the

---

Kultur in der Sowjetischen Besatzungszone Deutschlands 1945–1949 (Bern: Peter Lang, 1993), p. 14. This highly speculative statement demonstrates the difficulty experienced by critics who are unwilling to pass over obvious discrepancies in Soviet policy, but whose methods and models crystallised in the ongoing debate over the 'missed opportunity'.

[4] 'Es lag viel an der Kenntnis und Erfahrungen der einzelnen Kulturarbeiter, wie weit sie sich den wachsenden dogmatischen Einflüssen entziehen konnten' (Dietrich, 'Zwei Linien', p. 50). This is also a salutary reminder of the danger of a schematic opposition of 'culture' and 'bureaucracy'.

[5] I refer here to the work of Michel Foucault, some of whose techniques for the analysis of power can be fruitfully applied to Communist societies, in particular his insistence that it is the structure of a hierarchy which produces the effects of power, rather than its 'head': 'Although it is true that its pyramidal organization gives it a 'head', it is the apparatus as a whole that produces 'power' and distributes individuals in this permanent and continuous field' Michel Foucault, *Discipline and Punish. The Birth of the Prison* (Harmondsworth: Penguin, 1991), p. 177.

work and actions of the intellectual community within this system, and to use this analysis to begin to develop a more useful model for assessing the vital issues of complicity and resistance.

What had been referred to here as the 'two lines' argument is as much a product of the polarisation of debate during the Cold War years as the Kremlinological interpretations which relied on the ideologically-constructed figure of an all-powerful Stalin. The argument, along with the various 'missed opportunity' theses, was formulated in opposition to the dominant 'totalitarian' theory, with its sometimes wild extrapolations from émigré accounts.[6] However, just as the preoccupation with the idea of a 'missed opportunity' led to undue emphasis on the theory that one or other faction or individual was effectively 'in control', debates over the existence of a more conciliatory 'line' in cultural politics have too often relied on an opposition of 'rhetoric' and 'reality' which depends on an instrumental view of the functioning of rhetorical discourse. In other words, it sees rhetoric simply as a means of 'disguising' a political reality which can be unearthed by researchers whose own language is untainted by Leninist ideology. Similarly, analyses of cultural issues, whether they take seriously the existence of an 'all-German' aspiration or not, often rely on the rather schematic opposition of 'culture' and 'politics', which simply recapitulates the error of many of the East German intellectual community, who, in the words of Michael Rohrwasser in his analysis of Alfred Kantorowicz's *Spanisches Kriegstagebuch*, 'Zuflucht zum WIR der Schriftsteller [fanden]'. This convenient fantasy, 'die ordentliche Scheidung zwischen diesem WIR und dem IHR der Funktionäre, zwischen "Geist" und "Macht"',[7] relies on a faith in the power and potential truthfulness of the Word; this faith links both East German intellectuals who found themselves drawn into compromising with the regime, and those critics who condemn them for their compromise while constructing the largely artificial figure of the 'dissident writer as heretic'. In Rohrwasser's words, this distinction between 'Geist' and

---

[6] See, for example, R. W. Davies' careful criticism of Robert Conquest's extraordinary figures for deaths under Stalin: R. W. Davies, 'Forced Labour under Stalin: The Archive Revelations', *New Left Review*, 214 (1995), 62–80. It is emblematic that much post-glasnost' Russian historical scholarship, as well as the popular press, has unquestioningly accepted Conquest's figures, first set out in his book, *The Great Terror: Stalin's Purge of the Thirties* (London: Macmillan, 1968).

[7] Rohrwasser, p. 121.

'Macht' 'verlangt ein Fragezeichen'.[8] As we shall see, this assertion of common ground between two seemingly implacably opposed positions is not as paradoxical as it might at first appear.

The analysis, in Chapter Three of this study, of issues arising from the shifts in the meanings of concepts connected with German unity and antifascism, demonstrates the difficulties in attempting to arrive at 'true' definitions for these abstractions which are not dependent on cultural or political contexts. The vulnerability of left-leaning intellectuals, as well as certain political figures, to administrative control, lay in their attachment to an extrapolitical truth in these concepts, which could be preserved in 'good' German traditions; while they clung to these comforting abstractions, the meaning of the words in which they expressed them changed, leaving them open both to manipulation by those within the SED who had fewer illusions, and to the charge of ideological doublespeak. Thus, it would be difficult to maintain that the most important representatives of the intellectual community were, in some ill-defined way, 'blind' to the direction of policy in the Soviet Zone, as, for example, Robert Havemann claims, in a characteristic moment of self-exculpation through self-accusation: 'Erfüllt von unserem Sendungsbewußtsein hielten wir uns für die einzigen historisch Berufenen. Wir wurden zu Stalinisten, ohne es überhaupt zu wissen.'[9]

The attempt to cling to what is imagined to be the true meaning of socialism is characteristic both of the 'renegade' and of the intellectual who remains within the system. The animosity of mutual accusations of 'treachery' or 'capitulation' are an acknowledgement of this similarity. The type of ideological analysis undertaken in this study questions the idea of 'blindness' which, whatever one may mean by it, seems unhelpful. We also need to modify considerably an opposing view, formulated by Manès Sperber in his essay on Ernst Fischer: 'Sie wußten, was sie taten, anders gesagt: sie wußten ganz genau,

---

[8] Rohrwasser, p. 121..

[9] Robert Havemann, *Fragen antworten Fragen. Aus der Biographie eines deutschen Marxisten* (Munich: R. Piper & Co., 1970), p. 65. Note the sophistication of the argument, that this 'blindness' can be explained as a symptom of an attachment to the true meaning of socialism, and the sublimation of doubts, ambiguities and the problems connected with this faith in essential meanings, in the figure of Stalin. The importance of this figure as the focal point of conflicting ideological systems, a more-than-human symbol of absolute good, rationality and power, or of absolute evil, irrationality and dominance, cannot be overestimated.

was zu wissen sie entschieden ablehnten.'[10] Sperber's concept of 'praktikable Unwissenheit' gives us some idea of the mental energies which went into the reconciliation of personal ideals with increasingly dictatorial practice, and may be fully applicable in particular cases, such as that of Bertolt Brecht, who 'durch seine Selbstberufung als (Macht-)Politiker am Schweigen und an einer totalitären Propaganda partizipiert [hat]',[11] but it focusses too closely on individuals' undivided freedom to make choices, and does not consider their position within the prevailing ideological system which determines the parameters of these choices.

However, it is with the help of this kind of investigation that we can begin to move beyond a rather sterile debate characterised on one side by analyses conducted 'im Stil der staatsanwaltlichen Anklageerhebung',[12] and on the other by attempts at psychological exculpation.[13] Both arguments focus too exclusively on the character or psychology of the individual for the purpose of denunciation or defence, and neglect the broader functioning of the ideological system. In order to reach a fuller understanding of the place of the individual within this system, in this case the member of the 'artistic intelligentsia', who already occupies a unique position in Marxism-Leninism, we need to begin by examining the claims to extra-ideological authenticity made for literature in the context of the reconstruction of the Soviet Zone after 1945. In this way, we can shed light on the paradoxical common ground between the attitudes of the artist-functionary and of the artist-critic armed with the language of 'dissidence'.

---

[10] Manès Sperber, 'Stufen der praktikablen Unwissenheit', *Essays zur täglichen Weltgeschichte* (Vienna: Europa Verlag, 1981), p. 717.

[11] Rohrwasser, p. 166. See Case Study no. 2, in Chapter Six of this study.

[12] Rohrwasser, p. 321. Rohrwasser is referring to David Pike, *Lukács und Brecht* (Tübingen: Max Niemeyer, 1986). See also Jens Hacker, *Deutsche Irrtümer: Schönfärber und Helfershelfer der SED-Diktatur im Westen* (Frankfurt a. M.: Ullstein, 1992).

[13] As, for example, Heiner Müller on Brecht: 'Und wegen der Fixierung auf Hitler hat [Brecht] das Problem Stalin verdrängt, und das war ganz legitim in der Zeit, in der er gelebt hat, und das wurde für ihn zunehmend ein Problem in der DDR [...] er hat nie mit beiden Augen auf diese neue Wirklichkeit geguckt, das konnte er nicht, das konnte man von ihm auch nicht verlangen, das hätte er nicht ausgehalten' Heiner Müller, *Ich bin ein Neger. Dis-kussion mit Heiner Müller* (Darmstadt: Verlag der Georg Büchner Buchhandlung, 1986), p. 24. The defensiveness of Müller's tone, particularly in the use of the word 'legitim', which evokes a courtroom, says more about the accusatory nature of debate about the GDR than it does about Brecht.

'VOLLENDUNG TRÄUMEND'[14]: A SUPERFICIAL PROFUNDITY

The sonnet 'Vollendung träumend' is an interesting example of Johannes R. Becher's later style, a style for which he made the following claim: 'Allmählich ist es mir gelungen, *einen* Gedanken durchzuführen, ihn nach allen Seiten hin zu beleuchten und auf diese Weise ein einheitliches Gedicht zu schaffen.'[15] The poem represents a journey from darkness into light, a justification of the visionary artist who may not live to see the fulfilment of his dream, but who knows it will come. The unspoken thought is that the artist's certainty about the future rests in his grasp of the inevitable logic of history; Becher would not lower himself to mention this in a poem in which his profoundest longings are expressed, but lines such as 'die Zeiten / Erfüllen sich' point to the phases of Marxist historical theory, infused with the transfigurative quality which attracted so many refugees from the Expressionist movement to the Marxist claim to the unity of theory and praxis. The poem hovers in an ambiguous space between personal expression and public declaration — the positioning of the lyrical voice within the 'wir' of the dreamers pulls in both directions — and the religiosity of the language is an attempt to depict history as a spiritual progression towards 'Vollendung'. This is a rather crude example of the various attempts to 'return to Hegel' which, at various moments since Lukács' *Geschichte und Klassenbewußtsein*, had been an important aspect of German Marxist intellectuals' self-assertion against overly deterministic interpretations of dialectical materialism. Indeed, the vulnerability of many writers to administrative control lay in the position of Socialist Realism within the ideological system of Marxism-Leninism: the vigorous denunciation and suppression of rampant proletarianism in art gave intellectuals a sense of their own importance, and seemed to offer them the social role which they had always imagined should belong to them.

   Becher defines his own role thus:

---

[14] 'Vollendung träumend' (1947), Johannes R. Becher, *GW*, v, p. 678.

[15] Letter to Mia Bittel, 20 March 1946, in Johannes R. Becher, *Briefe 1909–1958*, ed. by Rolf Harder (Berlin: Aufbau, 1993), pp. 286–87 (p. 286).

Unsere Weltanschauung stellt zu große Anforderungen an den Einzelnen, der sie sozusagen erst aus den klassischen Werken mühsam auf das Gegenwärtige übertragen muß. Das können aber nur ganz wenige, und leider setzen die wenigen sich nicht hin, um ihre Fähigkeiten den anderen in einer gründlichen, umfassenden Art zu vermitteln.[16]

Similarly, the poem radiates this sense of mission, and of intellectual isolation; an inverse Cassandra, whose prophecies of triumph are ignored. However, there is a further ambiguity here, a tension between poet as observer and dreamer, and intellectual as educator, which has often been concealed in the word 'Dichter'. In 'Vollendung träumend', Becher makes it clear that social change (conflated here with spiritual development) relies on 'des Menschen Schöpferkraft', reflecting the humanism of the early Marx, and of Lukács, as opposed to an austere determinism, which would render the intellectual superfluous. Note here also Becher's characteristic conflation, in the word 'Schöpferkraft', of the creative potential of the Proletariat as a historical actor in Marxist theory, with the creativity of the artist. The 'dreamers' of the poem are, however, observers and prophets, who '*ahnten* [...] des Menschen Schöpferkraft' and '*sahen* [...] die Zeiten / Erfüllen sich'. The neat wordplay of 'keine Zeit versäumend' establishes both the urgency of their task and a continuity of progressive 'dreamers' fulfilling this task in every historical epoch. However, this view of the 'Dichter' contrasts with the image conjured up by Becher in his letter to Mia Bittel, and quoted above: the intellectual as educator is an idea which has a long pedigree, but it also corresponds to the Leninist view of the Communist Party *intelligentsia* leading the people in its wake. Becher's political career is marked by the tension between the need to perform the practical work of education and propaganda and the desire to observe, comment, and dream.

What these conflicting sides in Becher have in common is a tendency to simplification, to search for the purity of expression which will distil the essence of an idea, whether elucidating Marxism or dreaming of German cultural unity. In Becher's case, this results in a rhetoric of abstractions which permits flight from the troubling ambiguity of a world in which he found

---

[16] Letter to Mia Bittel, 20 March 1946, p. 287.

himself justifying ever more dictatorial methods.[17] Similarly, the breaking up of the form of the sonnet, giving an impression of inevitability to the movement of the thought, contradicts Becher's aim '[den Gedanken] nach allen Seiten hin zu beleuchten', and instead resolves all conflicts in a rhythmic gesture.

Becher's own vulnerability to the material and intellectual blandishments offered to him in the Soviet Zone speaks through every line of his work; the abstractions through which he expresses his thoughts and the desire for an authenticity in language, which he sees in the language of German Classicism, leave him open to the ideological manipulation of the meanings of the concepts closest to his heart. Attempts to penetrate to the 'genuine' meanings and values of German cultural traditions demonstrate a failure to recognise that words do not possess this authentic core of meaning, but are shot through with ambiguities which threaten Becher's control over the implications of his own language. An inability to engage with these ambiguities, and to turn them to his own advantage, as did Brecht and, in a very different way, Peter Huchel in his editorship of *Sinn und Form*, are at the root of Becher's intellectual capitulation.

A PROBLEMATIC LEGACY

To begin to analyse in this way the relationship between a particular, and in certain ways representative, individual and the system of ideological control in which his thoughts and actions are embedded can help us to undermine the schematic opposition of 'Geist' and 'Macht' which bedevils discussion of the role of the intellectual in communist societies, and to expose the common ground between what I have called the 'monolithic' and the 'two lines' models, and between the intellectual-functionaries and their critics.[18] Similarly, an account which notes the existence of a system of power which functions to a

---

[17] Cf. J. R. Becher, 'Selbstzensur', *Sinn und Form*, 39 (1988), 543–51, for his late attempted confession of loss of faith.

[18] A glance at the number of books about the place of the artist-intellectual in communist societies whose titles involve the juxtaposition of 'culture' and 'politics', shows that the polarisation of these concepts is still pervasive, and may account for some of the bitterness which characterises the debate.

certain extent independently of those at its head, can help explain the partial failure of many of the attempts by 'integrationists' in the SED to impose their authority on cultural production. We will return to this argument below.

An important formative influence on the attitudes of many German communist intellectuals was the idealistic atmosphere of the so-called 'Rote Künstlerkolonie', built by the Bühnengenossenschaft and the Schutzverband Deutscher Schrift-steller for their members in Berlin-Wilmersdorf. The ragbag collection of artists and their followers who gathered in this block in the late twenties and early thirties, including Becher, Ernst Bloch, Erich Engel, Peter Huchel, Alfred Kantorowicz, and Arthur Koestler, enjoyed greater freedom of expression than was usual in other KPD organisations.[19] Significantly, this was also a place where socialists and intellectuals of all parties or of none met, talked and co-operated in the years up to 1933. Although a definitive history of the 'Künstlerkolonie' has yet to be written, what is perhaps more important for our purposes is the image which many of these artists took away with them, of an open community of intellectuals ('Funktionäre, politische Geschäftemacher, Denunzianten, Spitzel waren nicht unter denen zu finden', declares Alfred Kantorowicz with hindsight intensified by his later bitterness[20]) which provided an ideal for the self-understanding of intellectuals in a future socialist society. Axel Eggebrecht notes, 'daß unser "Roter Block" ein Beispiel gab, wie das braune Unheil möglicherweise hätte abgewendet werden können',[21] with the implication that the functionaries are to blame for the failure of the KPD in the face of Nazism. It is notable in the comments of Kantorowicz and Eggebrecht, among others, that the 'Künstler-kolonie' ideal forms a reference point through which future experiences can be interpreted: Socialism *can* and *should* be like this, and if it is not, then the 'Funktionäre' are to blame.[22]

Kantorowicz's disgust at Becher's assumption of the functionary's role in 1945 ('fand einen bösartigen Parteigeheimrat'[23]) can be read in this light; his

---

[19] The KPD cell formed by Kantorowicz contained a small number of those who lived at the 'Kolonie', including Karola Pietrowska and Gustav Regler.

[20] Alfred Kantorowicz, *Deutsches Tagebuch*, 2 vols (Munich: Kindler, 1959), I, p. 26.

[21] Axel Eggebrecht, *Der halbe Weg. Zwischenbilanz einer Epoche* (Reinbek: Rowohlt, 1975), pp. 258–59.

[22] See, for example Arthur Koestler, *Frühe Empörung* (Vienna: Molden, 1970), p. 327, and Hans Sahl, *Memoiren eines Moralisten. Erinnerungen* (Zurich: Amman, 1983), p. 200.

[23] Kantorowicz, p. 257.

experiences with KPD officers during the Spanish Civil War had entrenched the perception of the polarisation of 'Geist' and 'Macht'. The ruthless separation of the two concepts, which can only be accomplished in the inward-directed rhetoric of abstractions described above in the case of Becher, serves to suppress the writer's own ambivalence about the role of the intellectual, whether he or she stays within the system or, finally, leaves. In Rohrwasser's words, 'Kantorowicz versucht das Doppelgesicht des Renegaten als Täter und Opfer zu verdrängen'.[24] Self-disgust is evaded by calling on the image of the intellectual as heretic or dissident, and of the extra-ideological authority of the dissident's language. In this sense, the 'renegade' shares an ideological common ground with the communist intellectual who tries to preserve a space for an intellectual elite, for 'Geist', within the GDR itself, and with the Western critic who occupies a platform for judgement which he/she assumes to lie outside ideology. In all these cases, the claim of a retreat from ideology is the ideological act *par excellence*.

The preservation of the 'Künstlerkolonie' idea during the long years of Nazi rule had several consequences. The experience of Nazi cultural barbarity led to a fetishisation of language, an overloading of the capacity of the written word to carry moral force. This belief in the 'verwandelnde Kraft des Wortes'[25] stems from a defensive, but incomplete, retreat from the transformative urgency of Expressionism (which, for all its patricidal claims, was simply an intensification of the classical German belief in the transcendental authority of poetic language), and owes, via Lukács, much to the didactic claims of Nineteenth-century Realism. The perceived defeat of German culture led to a turning-inward of this moral function of language, away from the idea of transformation towards the *preservation* of cultural values which are somehow embodied in the uncorrupted Word.

Becher tended to simplification through the aesthetic resolution of con-tradictions (although he saw this as a distillation of the essence of a thought). This particular formal device, being common to 'Classicism', Nineteenth-Century 'Realism' and Socialist Realism, is more than just an aesthetic

---

[24] Rohrwasser, p. 125.
[25] Becher, letter to Benno Reifenberg, 12.11.1947: *Briefe*, p. 350.

problem: as we have seen with Becher, and with Kantorowicz, the self-justifying rhetoric of abstractions permeates both the artistic and political thought of many GDR intellectuals who had worked in opposition to Nazism. The shifting boundaries between the genres of Realism constitute one of those areas of ambiguity where battles are fought over the ideological control of literature: it is precisely the insistence of authors that they are defending a 'truer' realism, that is, one whose language embodies the supposed humanist cultural values of the past, which makes them vulnerable to the claims of Communism to represent the culmination of these values and to compromises with the encroachment of administrative control. In the same way, insistence on the validity of the 'all-German' line left many intellectuals susceptible to manipulation by those who exerted greater control over the terms of discourse. Thus, complicity and resistance are closely intertwined, an uncomfortable idea which has too often been an unspoken presence in much of the embittered debate about the legacy of the GDR. For both the 'renegade', like Kantorowicz, and the ambivalent functionary, like Becher, the terms and limits of their resistance are set by the unexamined series of polarities, such as 'Geist'–'Macht', democracy–fascism, truth–lies, or by abstractions like the idea of a true German national culture, which dominate their world-view. Kantorowicz is thus able to deny his own complicity by assuming the mantle of 'dissident', and Becher is able to justify to himself his recourse to repressive measures. However, as was made clear in the previous chapter, it is my thesis that the importance and ambiguity of these abstract ideals within the ideological and institutional context of Soviet-zone politics (and particularly within the Deutsche Akademie der Künste) both facilitated administrative control over the intellectual community and provided a context for genuine resistance. In the later sections of this study, I will analyse the development of cultural policy and the position of the Academy in the context of the theoretical framework outlined in this chapter.

'DAS EINZIGE UND LETZTE SCHLUPFLOCH FÜR DEN GEDANKEN'[26]

The full story of the experiences of the exiled German communists in the Soviet Union is just beginning to emerge,[27] and it is not possible within the confines of this study to make more than a few general remarks about the effects which the murder of so many loyal antifascists had on those who remained alive. Naturally, the arguments about this period have focused on the behaviour of individuals, with the protagonists divided into the conventional camps of moral denunciation and guilty defensiveness; a more satisfying account would locate the individual in the context of the issues of the functioning of power in Soviet society which have been touched on in previous chapters. David Pike's account perpetuates the absolute identification of the KPD leadership with a rather abstract Soviet government personified in the figure of Stalin as the embodiment of an omnipotent totalitarian principle. It is particularly notable how Ulbricht seems to appear bearing directives from the regions where 'power' resides. It may have seemed like that to those involved, but the feeling that absolute authority was vested in the mythical figure of Stalin was, in itself, part of the apparatus of power. It is as well for us as commentators writing after the end of the Cold War to rid ourselves of some of these ideological preconceptions until we can draw on more satisfactory accounts of the functioning of power in the Soviet Union.[28]

Some of the strategies employed by surviving exiles to justify their action or inaction in the GDR have already been commented on; the attitudes of extreme defensiveness forced on those KPD members who spent any time in the Soviet Union had a lasting effect on the cultural sensibilities of people like Becher, ensuring that the idea of literary culture as the carrier of a moral tradition and of

---

[26] Alexei Kondratovich, 'Das letzte Jahr. Twardowski und "Nowy Mir", *Sinn und Form*, 42 (1991), 649–63 (653).

[27] See Carola Tischler, *Flucht in die Verfolgung: Deutsche Emigranten im sowjetischen Exil 1933 bis 1945* (Münster: LIT, 1996), and David Pike, *German Writers in Soviet Exile 1933–1945* (Chapel Hill: University of N. Carolina Press, 1982).

[28] Ulbricht had already positioned himself as the ultra-loyal functionary, but we should not overlook the evidence of the surprising freedom which senior KPD cadres enjoyed in the development of their programme for post-war Germany, collected in Peter Erler, Horst Laude and Manfred Wilke (eds), *'Nach Hitler kommen wir' Dokumente zur Programmatik der Moskauer KPD-Führung 1944/45 für Nachkriegsdeutschland* (Berlin: Akademie Verlag, 1994).

a core of uncorrupted truth, became firmly entrenched, and was carried over
into German politics. There is a tension here between this instinctive retreat into
the comforting security of a literary and intellectual elite, and the conviction of
the social usefulness of literature, a tension which Becher typically tries to
resolve in an aesthetic manner, in his absolute insistence on high literary
quality. This stance, in which we can find the roots of the Academy idea and
Becher's commitment to, and decisive influence on, the character of *Sinn und
Form*, goes some way to explaining his highly ambivalent attitude to the
administrative imposition of Socialist Realism. In discussing the development
of the Academy idea in the context of my analysis of the rhetorical development
of the 'all-German' line, this study will expand on this ambivalence, as it is
central to a conception of complicity and resistance which will allow us to
move away from the inquisitional nature of much recent debate.

A significant role in this debate is played by the concept of literary
dissidence, that is, the idea that genuine literature contains truths which are
necessarily subversive of power structures or ideological systems. When
applied to former Eastern Bloc societies, this idea takes on an enormous
emotional charge, focused on a series of high-profile individuals, for example,
Václav Havel, Wolf Biermann, or the archetypal dissident Aleksander
Solzhenitsyn, who take on a representative role which may or may not have any
genuine basis in the life or work.[29]

For example, Václav Havel's intense literary preoccupation with questions
of language and cliché ('The cliché organises life; it expropriates people's
identity; it becomes ruler, defence lawyer, judge, and the law'[30]) gives us an
insight into the psychological ambiguities of ideology and power which is
generally excluded from the austere moral universe of Solzhenitsyn, with its
focus on truth-telling and judgement. In this way, Havel's iconic status in the
West has been achieved somewhat at the expense of his work, with its profound
mistrust of heroes and of categorical absolutes, whereas the forcefulness of the
critique contained in Solzhenitsyn's work, and the exacting standard of personal

---

[29] It is important to point out here that my discussion concerns the significance of the concept, or category,
of 'dissidence' in the study of GDR literary culture, rather than an analysis of the lives of the individuals
mentioned in the text.

[30] Václav Havel, *Disturbing the Peace* (New York: Vintage, 1991), p. 193.

integrity which underlies it, is central to his reception in the West. The dissolution of some of the certainties of Cold War discourses, along with the continuing deconstruction of the metaphysically absolute image of 'Stalin' and 'Stalinism', allows us for the first time to conduct a genuinely critical re-evaluation of the concept of dissidence.

The literary dissident as truth-teller has performed an important function in the various ideological systems of the Cold War. Literary language has been made to carry an improbable burden of truth, leading to an emphasis on allegorical interpretation, 'looking behind' the surface of a work of fiction, in order to expose the truths concealed underneath. Of course, an ability to break the code was a measure of the cleverness of the critic: a form of literary Kremlinology.

The implication of this kind of analysis, of a piece with the analysis of the behaviour of individuals, which takes as a benchmark an idealised figure of absolute moral integrity, such as Solzhenitsyn, is that the critic feels entitled to pass judgement on a work of literature in terms of whether its language is 'tainted' by Socialist Realism. This taint is then transformed into a moral failing on the part of the author: strenuous codes of integrity are required for ex-GDR authors which would be unthinkable in a democracy. What remains unsaid is that the absolute standard of truth in language is as much a product of the ideological confrontation with 'Stalinism' as is Socialist Realism. Russell Reising identifies 'Stalinism' as the last great undeconstructed absolute, speculating that the resistance of the idea of Stalinism to the deconstructive practice of modern theory, despite the challenge which it has come under from historians, lies in its usefulness as an imagined reference point of absolute linguistic totalitarianism (deconstruction rejecting all metanarrative as totalitarian) against which post-structuralist practice can assert itself:

Stalin and Stalinism are figured as a complex historical origin, almost literally as a given and irrefragable truth, by a community of literary thinkers that otherwise questions all such designations of a historical origin as functions of representational practice, not referential accuracy or truth. How has it come to pass that Stalin and Stalinism have escaped the same deconstructive interrogation that current literary theory applies to any and all references to history?[31]

Although Reising somewhat overstates his case, it is undeniable that reference to 'Stalinism' as an absolute, detached from the historical questions, allows the critic to celebrate ambiguity and irony in literature while demanding truth and integrity from GDR writers. It is this belief in the extra-ideological authority of language which links a functionary like Becher, a 'renegade' like Kantorowicz, and their Western critics, making all three susceptible to fatal misjudgements of the nature of power in the GDR.

There have been attempts to open up the debate to an appreciation of the problem of ideology and power in GDR cultural politics, but they have remained marginal through the necessity of avoiding overly categorical statements without a satisfactory model for the question of intellectual and artistic responsibility. One such attempt bears directly on the subject of this study: In 1991, *Sinn und Form* published a selection of documents as part of their ongoing policy of examining the archives of the Deutsche Akademie der Künste.[32] This issue, which dealt specifically with the motivation for the founding of the Academy and some of the efforts in the course of its history to push back the limits imposed on freedom of expression, also included an extract from the diary of Alexei Kondratovich, a colleague of the poet Alexander Tvardovsky on the editorial board of the literary journal *Noviy Mir*.[33] Tvardovsky was an important figure in the literary life of the 'Thaw', and the journal had published, amongst other works, Solzhenitsyn's *Odin den' Ivana Denisovicha*. Tvardovsky's policy was cautious, gradually establishing space for himself by publishing according to Party directive, and by joining in the chorus of condemnation of Pasternak's *Doctor Zhivago*, while trying to expand the boundaries of the permissible.[34]

---

[31] Russell J. Reising, 'Lionel Trilling, *The Liberal Imagination*, and the Emergence of the Cultural Discourse of Anti-Stalinism', *boundary 2*, 20 (1993), 94–124 (123). Emphasis in original.

[32] 'Aus der Akademie der Künste zu Berlin', *Sinn und Form*, 42 (1991), 664–73.

[33] Alexei Kondratovich, *op cit*.

[34] See John and Carol Garrard, *Inside the Soviet Writers' Union* (London: I. B. Tauris & Co., 1990), pp. 156–57.

The excerpt from Kondratovich's diary covers the events leading up to the expulsion of Solzhenitsyn from the Soviet Writers' Union, on 4 November 1969. Solzhenitsyn had sent his famous open letter to the Fourth Congress of the Union in May 1967,[35] and Tvardovsky had been involved in attempts to bring about a conciliation between the two sides: Solzhenitsyn, as a name well-known in the outside world, ran less of a risk than others, such as Tvardovsky and his colleagues. The attempt had failed, as Solzhenitsyn refused to recant, and the process leading up to his expulsion was set in motion. The diary records Solzhenitsyn's uncompromising behaviour, and the effect it had on the morale of the editors of *Noviy Mir*, who began to feel that they were to be dragged down with him, as the 1967 Writers' Congress had begun to discuss, ominously, 'the need for the Union to take a much larger part in Soviet literary life'.[36] Indeed, Tvardovsky was forced to resign in 1970, and died of cancer the following year. In Kondratovich's words: 'A. T. sagte sich, daß Solshenizyn weder auf "Nowy Mir" noch auf ihn Rücksicht nimmt, weil wir für ihn auch bloß "Partei-bürokraten" sind.'[37] The question of 'dissidence', as it is applied to the discussion of GDR cultural politics, is fraught with disturbing ambiguities and issues of power and compromise, which expose the inadequacy of the categorical moral and literary judgements which have marred much of the debate.

[35] The text can be found in Aleksandr Solzhenitsyn, *Sobranie sochinenii*, 18 vols (Paris: YMCA Press, 1988), VI, pp. 7–13. There is an English version, with commentary, in John B. Dunlop, Richard Haugh and Alexis Klimoff (eds), *Aleksandr Solzhenitsyn, Critical Essays and Documentary Materials* (Belmont, MA: Nordland, 1973), pp. 463–71. Official Soviet documents relating to Solzhenitsyn's case, including transcripts of Central Committee meetings and reports of the Soviet Writers' Union, have been collected in Michael Scammell (ed.), *The Solzhenitsyn Files* (Chicago: edition q, 1995). For materials relating to Solzhenitsyn's expulsion from the Union, see pp. 41–89. Note, in passing, the book's rather melodramatic subtitle: 'Secret Soviet Documents Reveal One Man's Fight Against the Monolith.' Despite the usefulness of the documentation, the editor's single-minded concentration on 'the story' somewhat obscures the wider context.

[36] Garrard, p. 81.

[37] Kondratovich, p. 661.

'UNSERER KLASSIK IST NIEMALS EINE KLASSISCHE POLITIK GEFOLGT'[38]: RHETORICAL SOLUTIONS TO PRACTICAL PROBLEMS

We have already seen how the years of exile in the Soviet Union had produced a particular attitude to the use-value of culture, which came to predominate in the Soviet Zone for two apparently contradictory reasons. Firstly, because it was more amenable to the 'all-German' policy pursued by Stalin for his own strategic purposes, and by sections of the KPD/SED with the peculiar mixture of conviction and expediency which characterised the functioning of the ideological system described in the previous chapter; and secondly, because it was more susceptible to the kind of ideological control practised by the 'integrationists' than a stance based on revolutionary artistic proletarianism. The kind of analysis required to uncover this contradiction was in effect impossible before the collapse of the Soviet Union, although, as has been indicated, there have been many attempts to assert a nuanced understanding against a more rigid orthodoxy. It is only by questioning entrenched attitudes to the opposition of 'Geist' and 'Macht' that we can begin to penetrate to the heart of the matter.

The reconciliation of a belief that a realm of spiritual values can be preserved in literary language and the theory that literary language can be used in order to produce beneficial practical effects in political life is possible only within the ideological rhetoric of abstractions which has been examined in the case of Becher. In the following sections, the thesis will be put forward that the idea of the Deutsche Akademie der Künste both as a defensive institution for the 'intelligentsia' and as a means for achieving a unified German culture (or of preserving its remnants) in the increasingly hostile atmosphere of the GDR developed out of the increasing difficulty of providing a rhetorical camouflage for this contradiction in cultural policy. The conflict between Stalin's German policy and the attempts of the 'integrationists' within the SED to secure their own hold on power provided the context both for the Academy's survival and

---

[38] J. R. Becher, 'Auferstehen!' Speech to the first meeting of the Kulturbund, 3 July 1945, in *GW*, xvi, pp. 454–62.

for the threat to its all-German foundation. Similarly, the language in which Becher formed his conceptions of the relation of culture and politics, and the location of that language in the ideological system analysed here, embody the contradiction in the thinking of many Soviet Zone intellectuals and SED politicians. This contra-diction was both the source of their vulnerability and of their ability to resist coercion.

The peculiar attitude to language, identified here as primarily defensive in nature, which gave rise to the eventual creation of the Academy, is basically incompatible with the kind of Marxist thinking which Becher was hoping to apply in the Soviet Zone. It is also inherently 'gesamtdeutsch', drawing on aspects of the German intellectual tradition, in which 'die deutsche Nation [...] ganz sprachlich-kultureller Natur [war]'.[39] Thus, the 'all-German' basis of the Acad-emy, and of Becher's other projects, such as *Sinn und Form*, can be seen not only as an expression of idealism (or naivety) in the wake of the defeat of Nazism, but as the natural outcome of this instinctive retreat from the 'cultural barbarism' of both halves of the divided Germany into the comforting embrace of an intellectual elite. The survival of this idea in its institutional form seems to me to provide one more piece of evidence for the existence of a serious, if inconsistently pursued, 'all-German' policy option within the Soviet government and the SMAD; conversely, an understanding of this option, and of the conflicts and campaigns documented in this study, is vital for an analysis of the functioning of the ideo-logical system within which the Academy did its work.

The highly-charged rhetoric of many intellectuals in the first months after the end of the War reflects a general hope that the triumph of a form of Marxist theory could finally overcome the dichotomy of 'Geist' and 'Macht' in the promised unity of theory and praxis:

Aus diesem unheilvollen Widerspruch zwischen Geist und Macht müssen wir heraus, der uns zum schwersten Verhängnis unserer Geschichte geworden ist und der letzten Endes auch jedes freie Geistesschaffen vernichtet hat.[40]

---

[39] Hagen Schulze, *Staat und Nation in der Europäischen Geschichte* (Munich: C. H. Beck, 1995), p. 147.
[40] Becher, 'Auferstehen!', p. 461.

This theoretical unity is a vital issue in the question of intellectual responsibility, as it was perceived by intellectuals in the Soviet Zone, and is indicative of the task which the most committed among them set themselves. Peter Huchel, in his speech at the celebrations of the first 'Tag des freien Buches' on 10 May 1947, offers the same view of the years of Nazi rule as the time of the most disastrous split between 'Geist' and 'Macht':

Es lag daran, daß unsere besten Dichter — und ich meine jetzt die wieder, die ideologisch keineswegs mit den Nazis paktierten — auch dann noch ins Gebirge der dichterischen Schau stiegen und auf den höchsten Eisfirnen, losgelöst von jeder Realität, in metaphysischer Einsamkeit mit dem Unendlichen Zwiesprache hielten, als am Fuße des Gebirges schon längst Städte und Dörfer in Flammen aufgingen und Menschen erschlagen wurden. Es war eine Flucht aus der Verantwortung [...] [Der Schriftsteller] darf vor der Drohung eines neuen imperialistischen Krieges nicht kapitulieren, er muß für den Frieden kämpfen.[41]

This expected synthesis of 'Geist' and 'Macht' within the new socialist society was naturally particularly attractive to the trained dialectician, especially if National Socialism could be portrayed as the most extreme contradiction between thesis and antithesis, leading inevitably to the final synthesis, where intellectuals would be able to fulfil their rightful mission. However, as we have seen, the tendency to perceive the relation between culture and politics in such a dichotomous way, as either inevitably antagonistic to each other or in a dialectical relation, leads to a fundamental misunderstanding of the functioning of power relations. In the case of the Soviet Zone/GDR, culture and politics are usually imagined as two separate spheres which interfere with each other, with politics 'contaminating' culture, for example, or culture helping to undermine power. Manfred Jäger, in the first edition of his useful analysis of GDR cultural politics, describes their interrelation thus:

Kultur und Politik [...] stehen in einer Wechselbeziehung und durchdringen einander, so daß einseitige schematische Konstruktionen unzulässig sind, weil sie öffentlich verkündete Programme als Stimulantien oder Hemmnisse leicht überschätzen.[42]

---

[41] Peter Huchel, 'Rede zum "Tag des Freien Buches"', 10 May 1947, in *Gesammelte Werke*, 2 vols (Frankfurt a. M.: Suhrkamp, 1984), II, p. 264.
[42] Manfred Jäger, *Kultur und Politik in der DDR* (Cologne: Edition Deutschland Archiv, 1982), p. ii. Further references to Jäger's book will be taken from the 1995 edition.

Jäger's analysis explicitly rejects any exclusive focus on individuals at the expense of structural issues, the changing interests of the *apparat*, and the demands of the reading public; however, the question of defining 'culture' and 'politics' is still left untouched, because the more sophisticated one's analysis, the more problematic these definitions become. Therefore, rather than taking for granted the construction of 'Geist' and 'Macht' as two entities whose interrelation can then be scrutinised, it seems to me to be more useful in the study of cultural policy in the Soviet Zone to ask questions about the reasons for the predominance of this view of culture in debates over the division of Germany, and its effect on the relation of the individual to power in this particular system. In this context, the linking factor in the self-understanding of intellectuals like Becher, Huchel and Kantorowicz, for all their differences, is the 'all-German' aspiration. The extreme polarity implied by the 'Geist-Macht' opposition contains within it strong echoes of the view that the aspiration for German unity was contained in the literary language. Thus, the equation of literary quality, the truth-telling potential of the Word, and an 'all-German' stance was absolutely instinctive for artists such as Becher, and this attitude combined readily with the defensiveness of intellectuals who had survived, compromised, the experience of Soviet or Nazi dictatorship to enable a certain amount of resistance to the encroachment of administrative control. However, only those with an ideological predisposition to Marxism could claim that this attitude was able to provide a dialectical synthesis of 'Geist' and 'Macht' which would ensure the intellectuals' effectiveness among the 'masses', producing the kind of 'Wandlung' for which Becher hoped.[43]

The hyperbolic tone of much of this rhetoric reflects not only the catastrophic nature of the German defeat, but also the hope that the policies of the occupiers would find a place for antifascist intellectuals which reflected the

---

[43] Note that the Kulturbund was originally intended to provide the impetus for the spiritual transformation of the German people, as it were, *en masse*; it was to be 'eine geistige Instanz [...] die mit Rat und Tat einem neu erstehenden Deutschland zur Verfügung [steht]': *Manifest und Aussprachen gehalten bei der Gründungs- kundgebung des Kulturbundes zur demokratischen Erneuerung Deutschlands am 4. Juli 1945* (Berlin: Dietz, 1945), p. 8. Its status as a mass organisation tied closely to the programme of the KPD made this problematic, and the gradual erosion of its effectiveness in upholding the 'all-German' aspiration necessitated the founding of the Academy as a more defensive, and consequently more elitist, institution.

intellectuals' own self-understanding. Not least among these hopes was the desire to bring about German cultural unity, and at first it seemed as if the KPD programme, and the doctrine of the 'German Road to Socialism', were destined to fulfil these hopes. However, the rhetoric of cultural unity (which will be examined in greater detail in the next chapter) was affected in a similar way to the shifting meaning of the notion of German unity between 1945 and 1953, undermining the position of those who believed in an 'all-German' solution. The contradictions in the belief system of many Marxist intellectuals left them open to this same process of rhetorical redefinition backed up by the ever-present threat of coercion.

For example, Becher's gift for the aesthetic resolution of practical problems indicates a fastidious retreat from the dirty reality of administration, no doubt conditioned by his experience of, and complicity in, the viciousness of the Soviet purges of German communists. However, his increasing absence from the centres of decision-making meant that he neglected opportunities to influence the developing meanings of the words which he used, although his work with the Academy shows that he could influence events if he discovered the motivation within himself.

The difficulty with the all-German aspiration, as seen through the eyes of communist intellectuals in the Soviet Zone, was that Marxism was seen as the highest expression of a historical progression which therefore had the greatest claim (as the highest term in the dialectic) to be the unifying force in German culture. Unlike the austere dialectic of Brecht, Becher's Marxism is heavily influenced by those aspects of Soviet orthodoxy which seemed most conducive to his aims, namely, the leading role of the intelligentsia. In a process similar to that set out in my discussion of the effect of Tyul'panov's ideological pronounce-ments, the intersection of these beliefs with Soviet models ensured that resistance to the assertion of Stalin's authority became problematic; the process of accommodation is at least partially unconscious, as well as being driven by political expediency and cowardice, and so a study of the methods of rhetorical self-justification is particularly important.

I have already explored some of the ways in which ideas dominant among Marxist intellectuals at the time, derived in particular from Lukács, and with a defensive edge resulting from the dual experience of victimhood and complicity in the Soviet purges, gave rise to a particular view of the role of the intellectual. The special place assigned to the intellectual in this view is bound up both with the need to eliminate the 'false consciousness' of the proletariat and to preserve 'objective' values from Germany's intellectual tradition (a psychological, as well as political, necessity in the wake of Nazism). This is the reason for artists' vulnerability to compromise with the administrative imposition of Socialist Realism: it is part of a system which seems to protect intellectuals from a radical proletarianism which threatens to undermine the very reason for their existence. The position in which intellectuals are caught means that they can be taken to task both for lagging behind the superior consciousness of the proletariat and for failing to provide the necessary political leadership.

The contradiction between the task of preserving cultural values from the past and the recognition of the 'objective' consciousness of the proletariat can only be resolved using a form of spurious dialectic which is one of the characteristics of Marxism-Leninism. For example, Becher approaches the question of German unity in this way, regarding a united Germany as the highest term in the dialectic: 'Im Sinne einer Geistesverwandtschaft mit unseren Besten, im Sinne einer volksmäßigen Verbundenheit, in diesem Sinne muß Deutschland: Deutschland werden!'[44] This reflex to resolve practical problems by defining them so that they can be wished away in a rhetorical gesture distances Becher from his own responsibility for a situation in which one term in his equation, the 'Volk', is politically repressed. This linguistic misrepresentation of material reality in the spurious rationalising which Adorno calls 'abstraktive Vereinheitlichung',[45] enables Becher to separate his idealism in the question of German unity from his culpability. The courage to make some

---

[44] Becher, 'Auferstehen!', *GW*, pp. 461–62.

[45] Theodor W. Adorno, *Negative Dialektik*, in *Gesammelte Schriften*, 23 vols (Frankfurt a. M.: Suhrkamp, 1973), VI, p. 53. Adorno's critique of rationalism in the service of ideological systems and of Idealism is pertinent to the case of intellectuals in the Soviet Zone; particularly useful are his contributions to the analysis of ideology as constitutive of the identity of the individual in the misrepresentation of social and political relations and the erasure of difference and otherness: 'Im Idealismus [...] waltet bewußtlos die Ideologie, das Nichtich, l'autrui, schließlich alles an Natur Mahnende sei minderwertig, damit die Einheit des sich erhaltenden Gedankens getrost es verschlingen darf' (*Negative Dialektik*, p. 33).

kind of connection between the two is the basis of any assertion of moral responsibility.

This chapter has explored some of the ways in which the ideological struggle centres on the meanings of words, and proposed the idea that the theory of the inherence of a set of 'objective' values in the German literary tradition made the intellectual vulnerable to manipulation through an ideological system characterised not by pedantic insistence on fixed meanings, but by a remarkable semantic flexibility. The official self-definition of Marxism-Leninism at the time of Stalin, as the arbiter of absolute truth, is, of course, another question: the immutable position of the *figure* of Stalin, as the symbolic cornerstone of the system and the source of the system's authority, entailed this emphasis on absolutes. As a consequence, the legacy of the German literary and Idealistic tradition combined with the psychological dependence of many German antifascist intellectuals on a transcendental Stalin to make these intellectuals peculiarly vulnerable to manipulation through the invocation of Stalin's authority. The limitation of Stalin's actual ability to influence events in Germany on a day-to-day basis adds a further level of complication; the semantic flexibility of Marxism-Leninism could be exploited by power-brokers within the SED in order to use campaigns for German unity as a means of legitimising their own power.

CHAPTER FIVE

THE *DEUTSCHE AKADEMIE DER KÜNSTE* AND THE END OF GERMAN UNITY

This chapter will set the context of cultural policy in the Soviet Zone and GDR in the period up to the founding of the Deutsche Akademie der Künste on 24 March 1950. Instead of providing a step-by-step, chronological account, which has been the approach of many works produced since 1989, this study will proceed from a somewhat different angle, namely via an analysis of the origins of the Academy within the developing ideological system of the Soviet Zone, with particular reference to the key role played by Johannes R. Becher. The purpose of this analysis is to locate Becher and the Academy within this ideological system, in order to arrive at a fuller understanding of the issues of complicity and resistance set out in the previous chapter.

Some of the rhetorical strategies developed by Becher in this period will be examined in the context of developments in the Soviet Zone, in order to show how the Academy could come into being both as part of a renewed effort by the SED to impose some kind of order in cultural affairs, and as a (limited) haven from these inroads. We have already examined the importance of the rhetoric of German national unity for the self-understanding of the East German intellectual community, as well as some of the ways in which this self-understanding could be made to serve the purposes of the consolidation of the state and its integration into Soviet-led security and economic structures. Although this interpretation can accommodate an instrumental view of rhetorical discourse, which focuses, in the words of David Pike, on rhetoric as an 'outgrowth of furtive policy-making on a day-to-day basis',[1] it is clear that the kind of analysis with which we are concerned goes beyond this purely mechanistic conception.

The issues of *Vergangenheitsbewältigung,* and the interplay in the minds of exiles returning from Moscow between the assimilation of the legacy of Nazism

---

[1] David Pike, *The Politics of Culture*, p. 9.

and the repression of their complicity in the crimes of the Soviet dictatorship, are not dealt with satisfactorily by the simple assertion that the purpose of the rhetoric of 'antifascism-democracy' 'was to transform the non-Marxian or even anti-Marxist expedient of collective guilt into a Marxist-Leninist version of the will of the people'.[2] Again, it is not the accuracy of this kind of statement which is in dispute, but its *sufficiency*; a theory which presupposes an easily-definable separation of rhetoric and political practice, and which sees the purpose of analysis in discovering 'actual objectives' by 'comparing rhetoric with actual circumstances',[3] tends to suffer from several deficiencies: firstly, it assumes a monolithic unity of purpose between the Soviet regime (that is, 'Stalin'), SMAD and KPD/SED, which is belied by evidence both in the broader political context and by documentation of smaller struggles for control in institutions such as the Academy. Thus, the historian will overlook the extent to which his/her view of these 'actual circumstances' is also conditioned by a set of ideological pre-suppositions. This theoretical problem is further complicated by the fact that the various actors in the political and cultural life of the Soviet Zone and GDR were themselves working within a complex ideological system which conditioned their self-understanding and their response to the world.

Through an examination of the particluar case of J. R. Becher and the founding of the Academy, the thesis will be put forward in this chapter that the *idea* of the Academy emerged from an attitude to language and culture which had taken a new twist during years of exile; the failure of the *Kulturbund* and other organisations to produce the expected 'Wandlung' in the German nation led to an increasingly elitist conception of culture which had sufficient elements in common with Socialist Realism for a significant number of artists to succumb, wholly or in part, to the intellectual and material comforts offered by compromise with the dominant 'integrationist' line. This conception of culture meant that the Academy occupied a highly ambiguous institutional position within GDR society, as it provided space for the assertion of a strong 'all-German' line at odds with prevailing political trends.

[2] Pike, *The Politics of Culture*, p. 29.
[3] Pike, *The Politics of Culture*, p. 158.

'DIE BESEITIGUNG VON MISSVERSTÄNDNISSEN'[4]: A VISION OF INTELLECTUAL HARMONY

Gerd Dietrich has described with some sympathy the attitude of what we might loosely call the culture-consuming classes in 1945: 'Im tristen Alltag der Nachkriegszeit wurde 'Kultur' zu einem Akt derFeierstunde und der Erbauung.'[5] Productions of classics such as *Nathan der Weise* tended to confirm that the *Bildungsbürgertum* could rescue something of value from its own shattered self-image. However, there is a clear contradiction in this attitude between the idea that culture is somehow above politics, and the notion that it can play an active role in the promotion of moral values. Dietrich's use of the word 'Erbauung' here is well-judged, reflecting a belief in the power of the Word, when placed in a literary context, to intervene directly in the moral life of the nation without needing to resort to partisan politics. Such an ideology could only develop in a nation with a tradition of etatist politics, and, while Dietrich is at pains to point this out,[6] he still takes the distinction seriously: Becher and the Kulturbund are described as existing in a 'Spannungsfeld zwischen der wertfreien Pflege der Künste und Wissenschaften und ihrem engagierten erzieherischen Einsatz'.[7] While Dietrich provides a useful analysis of this tension, we need to go further back if we are to understand exactly why this tension was *perceived* in this way: in the light of the previous chapter's discussion of attitudes to the separation of 'Geist' and 'Macht', we can begin to examine the effects of this ideological system on Becher's cultural-political work.

The idea of German unity was of overriding importance for Becher, and he returns to it constantly in his speeches and poems. Given the intimate link between the German language and national unity, it is hardly surprising that Germany is unified time and time again in the poetry, particularly in Becher's pedantic use of sonnet form (which also has the advantage of a built-in

---

[4] Becher, letter to Alfred Andersch, 5 May 1948, *Briefe*, p. 375.
[5] Gerd Dietrich, *Politik und Kultur*, p. 9.
[6] Cf. Dietrich, *Politik und Kultur*, p. 10.
[7] Dietrich, *Politik und Kultur*, p. 31.

dialectical structure). Becher's rhetoric of abstractions embodies in a resurgent Germany the synthesis of perceived opposites between intellectual and society (suitably abstracted to the more easily manageable 'Geist' and 'Macht'), and between form and content. Becher's Germany is an entirely abstract entity with obvious parallels with its image in the work of writers to whose work Becher constantly returns, such as Hölderlin. This attitude has one seemingly paradoxical feature: it allows Becher to work to keep channels of communication open with West German writers while following a political programme which deepens political and economic division.

The Kulturbund embodies one aspect of Becher's programme for German renewal, the moral education of the masses, although in his rhetoric he also attempts to present it as a promoter of high culture:

Eine große Literatur entsteht dort, wo ein möglichst breites Interesse für Literatur bekundet wird und wo eine möglichst große Anzahl von Schriftstellern verschiedenen Charakters, verschieden in der Gattung ihrer Werke und ihres Wertes, an der Hervorbringung dieser Literatur mitarbeiten. Es ist nicht so, daß ein Gipfel wie Goethe in der Luft schwebt, er baut sich empor auf Vorgebirgen und Mittelgebirgen, und der verschiedensten Höhenunterschiede bedarf es, daß aufragende Höhen entstehen und Gipfelleistungen.[8]

The seeds of Becher's increasingly elitist separation of cultural matters (with their all-German aspiration) from the day-to-day politics of a mass organisation are already apparent in his *personal* conception of the Kulturbund's work, which differs in significant ways from the official KPD line. Becher's conception implies that mass participation in cultural life serves the purpose of preparing the social context for the production of great art. This democratic centralism of the mind is at odds with talk of a mass spiritual transformation and with the more pragmatic, though ill-defined, intentions of the KPD leadership.

The Kulturbund was required to act as an umbrella organisation for a multiplicity of different 'cultural' organisations, as well as to represent the interests of the 'intelligentsia', an artificial category which resisted definition:

---

[8] J. R. Becher, 'Erziehung zur Freiheit', 1946, *GW*, XVI, p. 637.

Gleich ob die Zielgruppe mit den Termini "Geistesschaffende", "Intelligenz" oder "Intellektuelle" umschrieben wurde, bedeutete dies für die organisatorische Praxis doch nur, daß es nicht
die Arbeiterschaft, Verwaltungsangestellte oder Bauern und Bäuerinnen waren.[9]

Was this a social grouping, in which case did it exclude factory workers who
took an interest in 'high' culture, or a more inclusive concept, which would
preclude its effectiveness as a defender of its target group's interests? A further
compli-cation was the requirement to act 'als ein Instrument der Erweckung
wahrhaft freiheitlichen Fühlens und Denkens, als ein Instrument der Erweckung
des Gewissens der Nation' in the elimination of fascism, and to participate in
'die Erziehung unseres deutschen Volkes im Geist der Wahrheit, im Geist eines
streitbaren Demokratismus'.[10] The Kulturbund 'mußte [...] Organisationsformen
entwickeln, die ihn in die Lage setzten, gestützt auf seine Verankerung in der
"Intelligenz",   in   die   ganze   Gesellschaft   auszustrahlen,   ohne
Zielgruppenkonflikte mit anderen Verbänden zu provozieren'.[11] The split
between the role of cultural organisations as defenders of the interests of the
'intelligentsia' and as promoters of positive cultural intervention is present from
the start, and is passed on, albeit in modified form, to the Academy.

Becher's preference for attempts to solve these problems in his rhetoric has
led commentators to pass superficial judgements on his problematic relationship
with power; if one accepts the existence within theSED of competing and
overlapping emphases in the question of German unity, it is no longer possible
to be satisfied with statements to the effect that 'Johannes R. Becher [...] was
best at couching doctrinal principles in language that appeared to be
ideologically non-committed'.[12] Of course, on one level this is true, and
Becher's belated attempts to exonerate himself rely on a similar separation of
rhetoric and practice. However, there is more to this question than might at first
meet the eye; as we have seen, the concept of *unity* underlies Becher's work in

---

[9] Magdalena Heider, *Politik – Kultur – Kulturbund: Zur Gründungs- und Frühgeschichte des Kulturbundes
zur demokratischen Erneuerung Deutschlands 1945–1954 in der SBZ/DDR* (Cologne: Bibliothek Wissenschaft
und Politik, 1993), p. 73.
[10] *Manifest des Kulturbunds zur demokratischen Erneuerung Deutschlands*, in Dietrich, *Politik und Kultur*,
pp. 216– 9 (p. 218).
[11] Heider, p. 73.
[12] Pike, *The Politics of Culture*, p. 75.

this period as an obsessively recurring theme.[13] This idea is extraordinarily overdetermined, and an examination of some of the possible reasons for this leads us towards an understanding of Becher's vulnerability. Ever since the tragic outcome of his youthful suicide attempt,[14] Becher's mental health had been delicate, and Willi Bredel had been assigned by Dimitrov to 'look after' Becher in Moscow. The bitterness and rivalry which this hadcreated had carried over into the Kulturbund, causing considerable organisational difficulties.[15] Becher never fully recovered from these experiences, and his obsessive preoccupation with unity as an abstract category in his work can be read at least in part as an expression of a longing for wholeness, transferred from inner life to political ambition. In this way, Becher makes his accommodation with, and is located within, the ideological system.

This becomes clearer if we consider the fetishisation of Goethe; the symbolic significance invested in this figure is not simply a function of the intense competition between East and West to claim Goethe for the cause, although, as we have seen, attitudes to language and to the works of German Classicism played an important role in convincing many intellectuals that they were working for German unity while their actions had the opposite effect. Rather, Goethe becomes the archetype of a personality at ease with itself, to which all Germans will aspire in the new society: 'Goethe: ein schönes

---

[13] That Becher thought of his literary and cultural-political work as a kind of grand artistic unity is clear from a letter to the editors of the journal *Deutschunterricht*, which had published dictation examples (*Deutschunterricht*, no. 9/1953) including a short text on Becher. Becher's comments and suggestions for improvements are self-serving, but he also exhibits his tendency to conflate literary forms with political persuasion: 'Johannes R. Becher [...] war auch bemüht, die Rede wieder zu einer literarischen Kunstform zu entwickeln.' (The word 'wieder' is interesting, indicating both an attempt to return to some supposed classical ideal of the moral purpose of literature, and an attempt to use this reference to indicate a certain distance from day-to-day politics: note the date.) Becher also tries to present himself primarily as an artist, rather than 'Auch-Schriftsteller' who wrote the National Anthem, and states that, in a report on his literary development, 'der Eintritt in die Kommunistische Partei Deutschlands nicht un-bedingt berichtet werden muß' (Becher, letter to the editors of *Deutschunterricht*, 5.9.1953, *Briefe*, pp. 461–62).

[14] On 17 April 1910, the teenage Becher had made a suicide pact with Franziska (Fanny) Fuß, eight years his senior, who was killed. Becher survived with severe injuries, and the affair came back to haunt him on more than one occasion. See his reply (*Briefe*, pp. 407–10) to an article in the *Frankfurter Rundschau* ('Großer Dichterfürst mit kleinem Mord', 16.9.1950) in which the story is used to attack him both politically and personally.

[15] See Heider, pp. 44–46.

ungetrenntes Ganzes [...] wer aber wünscht sich nicht als solches auch sein Volk, seine Heimat, sein Vaterland?'[16]

The role of the Kulturbund incorporates the attempt to unite a traditional 'bourgeois' ideology of the education of the individual towards a desired personal harmony and autonomy with the Marxist aspiration to social harmony through mass action. This has little to do with the tenets of Leninism, and is more akin to Ackermann's 'Ur-Marxismus' and to the 'German Road' thesis:

Unser Erziehungsideal ist ein humanistisches, das eine gleichermaßen an Körper, Geist und Seele ausgebildete, einheitliche, freiheitliche Persönlichkeit anstrebt, in welcher Verein-heitlichung die Verdinglichung des Menschen, die Entfremdung des Menschen mit sich selbst aufgehoben ist und nicht das Herz dem Verstand widerspricht und Fühlen und Denken miteinander uneins sind und nicht das innere Sehnen im äußeren Handeln als Gegenteil und als verzerrt erscheint.[17]

The rhapsodic tone should not lead us to overlook the mingling of personal and ideological concerns, which is so pronounced that it gives the impression that Becher has staked his mental health on the success of the Kulturbund's work. Further indications of what this actually means for the individual can be found in similar statements of the period. For example, Becher's tract, *Erziehung zur Freiheit*, which was largely written in exile, places a greater emphasis on the recognition of historical necessity than was usual while the emphasis was on the *Bündnispolitik*: 'Die Aufgabe des Menschen besteht darin, sich als Subjekt in Übereinstimmung zu bringen mit den objektiven Forderungen, die der Ge-schichtsverlauf einer Epoche, einer Zeit an uns stellt.' This task consists princi-pally in 'die Konstituierung des Menschen als einer gesellschaftlich-geschichtlich notwendigen Einheit'.[18] Becher's constant prevarication between discipline and independent action indicates the extent to which subjection to party discipline (conceptualised as acceptance of historical necessity) offered a refuge from the uncertainties, failures and compromises of practical work.

The assumed success of Goethe's non-partisan interventions in the moral life of the nation, without apparent recourse to bureaucracy, provided a model for

---

[16] Becher, 'Der Befreier', speech at the Goethe celebrations in Weimar, 28.8.1949, in *GW*, XVII, p. 262.
[17] Becher, 'Rede an München', 1946, *GW*, XVII, p. 19.
[18] Becher, *GW*, XVI, p. 523.

the political work of the Kulturbund which it could never live up to. Becher did make spasmodic attempts to exert his autonomy and to use the Kulturbund to intervene in campaigns for German unity. For example, Vladimir Semenov, head of the SMAD, records a meeting with Becher on 13 November 1946, at which Becher complained that he felt that he no longer enjoyed the trust of SMAD officers, and that he was being harrassed by a certain Major Patent. Becher criticises SMAD policy: '[Becher] considers it wrong that the SMAD is alienating certain loyal elements in the bourgeois parties and concentrating exclusively on the SED leadership.'[19] Becher also claims that the SMAD officers have a '[...] a false impression of those Germans working in the English or American zones'.[20] Semenov declares in his report that Becher is still under suspicion of 'bourgeois' influences, but that he is 'subjectively' on the right side, and should therefore be retained in his post in the Kulturbund.[21]

We have no indication of how frequently Becher attempted to exert his influence in similar ways, but these individual efforts could not halt the gradual narrowing of the remaining possibilities for political pluralism within the organisation. It should be noted at this point that this process of narrowing possibilities is less a case of the imposition of a preordained SED cultural programme, than a reflection of the changing emphases within the SED itself. The *Leitsätze* of the Kulturbund, far from being a 'concealed party cultural program',[22] were an overt reflection of the party's line in 1945, which, with all the ideological contradictions and pitfalls which I have outlined in the previous chapters, is based on principles sanctioned by Stalin. The changes in the Kulturbund reflected the growing influence of the 'integrationist' line within the SED and the increasing exclusion of non-SED members from positions of influence; however, the difficulties experienced by the SED in finding appropriate administrative forms for the Kulturbund reflected the problems

[19] Norman Naimark, Bernd Bonwetsch and Gennadii Bordyugov (eds), *SVAG: Upravlenie Propagandy (Informatsii) i S. I. Tyul'panov 1945–1949: Sbornik Dokumentov* (Moscow: Rossiya Molodaya, 1994), pp. 69–71 (p. 69).

[20] Naimark, Bonwetsch and Bordyugov, p. 70.

[21] Naimark, Bonwetsch and Bordyugov, p. 71. This intriguing hint, that certain Soviet officers were considering replacing Becher because he opposed the 'integrationist' line, is not supported by any other documentation. However, the indication of internal conflicts within the SMAD supports the analysis presented in Chapters Two and Three of this study.

[22] Pike, *The Politics of Culture*, p. 84.

encountered by the 'integrationists' in pushing for complete SED control when this was likely to produce a result, the irrevocable division of Germany, which contradicted the signals coming from Stalin, and by the supporters of an 'all-German' line who were caught within the contradictory influences of a system of power which left them vulnerable to manipulation by those who could call on Stalin's authority. The arenas left open for the struggle for influence, cadres policy and bureaucratic tinkering ('[die] Ad-hoc-Zuweisung neuer Aufgaben und Mitgliedergruppen'[23]) and the illusionless manipulation of rhetorical discourse, were a particular speciality of 'integrationists' like Ulbricht.

Becher's idealisation of Goethe leads us once again to the fundamental paradox on which this study is based: his attempts to use the Kulturbund to promote interventions in the political life of the 'nation' in the cause of German unity actually contributed to division by attracting accusations of the 'politicisation' of culture. The constant failure of these attempts, and Becher's weakness and tendency to self-aggrandisement and to prefer the trappings of power to the substance drove these hopes into a theoretical realm presided over by the figure of Goethe, 'als hätte Deutschland, bevor es seine Einheit politisch verwirklichte, sich im voraus nach der Sprachschöpfung Luthers nun auch in der Sprache Goethes ein Instrument seiner Einheit geschaffen'.[24]

Under careful examination, this attitude reveals the kind of internalised contradiction necessary for the acceptance of Marxism-Leninism: German unity is embodied and prefigured in the person of Goethe; committed intellectuals are needed to continue this work, and to prevent further abuses of German culture, therefore intellectuals need unprecedented access to power; Marxism-Leninism and the doctrines of Socialist Realism offer the intellectual social effectiveness and protection from marginalisation under capitalism and annihilation under rampant proletarianism; German national self-assertion, the 'true Germany', is best expressed through this synthesis of 'Geist' and 'Macht', so support for the GDR is a precondition of working for German unity. Goethe needs the GDR to fulfil his historical potential.[25]

---

[23] Heider, p. 109.

[24] Becher, 'Der Befreier', *GW*, XVII, p. 234.

[25] '[Tolstois und Puschkins] Geist ging in die Macht ein, die als Herrschende nunmehr erstand, und untrennbar von dieser Macht lebt ihr Geist, denn Lenin kam.' Becher, 'Der Befreier', *GW*, XVII, p. 239.

While Becher was preoccupied with these grand declarations, his lack of interest in administrative work caused friction with the party leadership, culminating in his objections to the Kulturbund's exclusion from the first Volkskongreß (6/7 December 1947) (just the kind of intervention which the Kulturbund had to make if it was to follow its original concept) and his threat to resign as Kulturbund President. His letter of resignation (8.12.1947) takes issue with complaints by Pieck that he had undertaken 'keinerlei politische Arbeit', and hints darkly about persecution and his position within the party:

Da ich nicht gewillt bin und außerdem durch meine besondere Begabung als Schriftsteller innerlich nicht in der Lage bin, den Forderungen nach einer politischen Arbeit, so wie sie offenbar der Genosse Wilhelm Pieck auffaßt, nachzukommen, muß ich es dem Zentral-vorstand [der SED] anheimstellen, seinerseits aus dieser Tatsache die Konsequenzen zu ziehen.[26]

The agreement to allow the Kulturbund to send a delegation to the Second Congress (17/18 March 1948) was enough to bring him back into the fold, just at the point when the Congress became irrevocably an instrument of German division.

We can gain some idea of how Becher proposed to maintain this stark distinction between political work and the role of the functionary by studying the part he played during the First Writers' Congress (4–8 October 1947). The Congress was the first and last such meeting on an 'all-German' basis, and much behind-the-scenes effort went into ensuring the appearance of unity. Becher played a major role in this stage-management, and his interventions after the eruption of recriminations following attacks on the Soviet delegation by the American journalist Melvin Lasky eventually brought the delegates to an agreed resolution.[27] Despite all the differences between the delegates, the principles of the Kulturbund had, possibly for the last time, been accepted on a collective basis. That such collective action became impossible after the

---

[26] In Carsten Gansel (ed.), *Der gespaltene Dichter. Johannes R. Becher. Gedichte, Briefe, Dokumente, 1945– 1958* (Berlin: Aufbau, 1991), pp. 42–43. See also Anneli Hartmann and Wolfram Eggeling, 'Zum "Verbot" des Kulturbunds in West-Berlin, 1946', *Deutschland Archiv*, 28 (1995), 1161–70.

[27] 'Bekenntnis zu Deutschland. Resolution des I. Deutschen Schriftstellerkongresses in Berlin 4.–8. Oktober 1947', in Dietrich, *Politik und Kultur*, pp. 285–86.

banning of the Kulturbund in the US and British sectors of Berlin on 1 November 1947, should not blind us to the fact that the 'all-German' concept could draw on a reservoir of good will from intellectuals in all parts of Germany; Becher's efforts to cultivate contacts in the West, particularly through the offices of the Academy, show how he managed to separate these efforts from the exercise of power.

From this point on, all declarations in favour of German unity which relied on a concept of mass action played into the hands of the 'integrationists'. Intellectuals like Becher were powerless to affect the shifts in the discourse of unity, because they could not dispense with the language and categories in which they conceived their opposition to Nazism. It seems to me that it is only with the help of an idealised figure like Goethe that Becher could still imagine that the 'politicisation' of culture could somehow prevent division: as with Stalin, contradictions are reconciled in a figure whose authority cannot be questioned. In this way, Becher could appeal with a sincerity intensified by threats, real and perceived, to his own position, to 'das Prinzip der "höheren Politik"',[28] declaring: 'Die Politik verschlingt die Literatur, wenn nicht die Literatur auf eine ihr eigentümliche und selbständige Art politisch wird',[29] while complaining in private, 'daß die Politiker unerfüllbare Ansprüche an den Dichter stellen und ihn als eine Art Funktionär betrachten, der auf dem Gebiet der Propaganda arbeitet'.[30] Becher finds himself in the position of working to keep doors open to the West while contributing significantly to their closing.

The separation of individual contacts from political practice parallels the retreat into a literary language which is supposed to preserve a realm of truth and objective moral values. It is characteristic of Becher, as his letters attest, that he can spend so much time on 'die Beseitigung von Mißverständnissen' on a personal level, particularly when it comes to 'mistaken' interpretations of his poetry. The implication is that if all is made plain in the purest (literary) language, there can be no cause for division or disagreement. He is still thinking dialectically, in terms of the resolution of differences according to

---

[28] Dietrich, *Politik und Kultur*, p. 100.
[29] Speech to the First Writers' Congress, Becher, *GW*, XVII, p. 170.
[30] Becher, *Der Aufstand im Menschen* (Berlin: Aufbau, 1983), p. 168.

'objektive Wertgesetze'.[31] In the final analysis, this does not amount to an acceptance of difference, however honourable his motives may have been; there is no room for ambiguity and contingency, because they threaten the integrity of his literary work, as political compromise and power-broking threaten the integrity of his self-image as an intellectual in the tradition of Goethe. In the previous chapter, it was noted that the tendency to fix meanings and rely on 'objective' standards left intellectuals open to manipulation through the ideological system of Marxism-Leninism; in this case, the increasingly unpleasant elitism of Becher's conception of culture, his insistence that artists should ignore, 'was subalterne Naturen in unsere Worte hineindeuten',[32] provides, paradoxically, the standard of literary quality which forms the context for resistance within the Academy.

BARRIERS TO UNDERSTANDING: THE TYRANNY OF THE CLICHÉ

This section will expand on the conclusion put forward at the end of Chapter Three, that the 'integrationist' line within the SED depended for its grip on power on the imposition of artificial barriers to which Marxist intellectuals had to defer if they were to preserve the coherence of their self-image as anti-fascists. In the context of the foundation of the Academy, several ways will be examined in which these barriers complement or contradict the purely physical, or political, barriers which were being erected in the late Forties (that is, the 'geographical' expression of the 'two camps' theory). Various types of exclusionary practice were developed which often flatly contradicted each other, and this accounts for the tensions and ambiguities of the Academy's position within the institutional structure of the Soviet Zone/GDR.

This will become clearer if we consider the following scheme: the deepening division between 'East' and 'West' was crossed by a number of other forms of exclusion. Thus, political elites were established, whose survival depended not

---

[31] 'Es wäre unsere Sache, dafür Sorge zu tragen, daß ein anständiger menschlicher Ton bei geistigen Ausein-andersetzungen gewahrt bleibt und daß eine Kritik sich entwickelt, die objektive Wertgesetze anerkennt und in nichts anderem ihr Maß hat' (Speech to the First Writers' Congress, Becher, *GW*, XVII, p. 177).

[32] Becher, *Briefe*, p. 282.

only on the maintenanceof the political division of Germany, but also on a further separation from potentially disruptive labour movements, whose demands had in some way to be defused. In the cultural sphere, the separation of elite from mass culture in the Soviet Zone was actively pursued by those who had most to lose from a resurgent proletarianism; this separation revealed a common interest with a political elite which also had much to fear from mass discontent. However, as we have seen, the preservationof an elite culture from German intellectual history depended absolutely on an all-German conception, that the literary language, with its claim to transcendent values, was inseparable from the idea of German cultural-political unity. Therefore, those in the intellectual community who depended for the legitimacy of their social position on the creation of a political elite, and thus on the institutionalisation of German division, also placed great value on the maintenance of links with fellow-artists in the West. Western artists' complaints of marginalisation find a disturbingly distorted echo in the belief of Marxist artists that a 'use' can be found for their work in the new society without compromising its integrity.[33] As in the case of Becher, concentration on the artistic integrity of one's work can become a way of evading or repressing issues of personal integrity and responsibility.

In the previous section, this last point was discussed with respect to the emphasis which Becher put on representative figures from German literary history; the importance of persuading the ailing Heinrich Mann to take up the post of Academy President is clearly in the same category. There is a tension between this ambivalent motivation and the evident desire of SED cadres to provide figureheads in order to conceal their activities, which enables figures like Becher to evade their responsibility for the worsening political climate. That this tension also provides a context for forms of resistance to the imposition of cultural norms, despite the extensive campaigns, gives us further insight into both the functioning of the ideological system and the tenuous nature of the SED's grip on power in this period.

The retreat from responsibility on the part of many intellectuals is characterised by the erection of a further set of barriers: the disturbing tendency

---

[33] 'Kunst dient nicht, indem sie dem Volke dient, sondern Kunst dient dem Volke, indem sie eine künstlerisch vollendete Gestalt annimmt', Becher, letter to Siegfried Bahne, 11.3.1949, *Briefe*, p. 388.

of words to change their meanings, as the catastrophe of 1945 recedes in the face of the day-to-day realities of construction andthe maintenance of power, can be repressed by fixing language in cliché, attempting to cling on to some 'objective' value or meaning which will see one through situations of persecution or complicity. In this light, we can compare the survival strategies of various important cultural figures, with whom this study of the Academy's work will mainly be concerned: Becher, with his fine-tuning of language, so that the search for 'objective' values ended in linguistic clichés whosemeanings ran out of his control; Brecht, with his self-conscious manipulation of language, mingling personal ends with equivocal principles, and his ironicdistancing from the inevitable compromises with power; Peter Huchel, whose strategy, in a telling contrast with Becher's, was based on irony, contingency and multiple viewpoints, a deliberate distancing from the physical business of politics while continuing to posit the relevance of literature to politics (note also that, as Huchel made little effort to reconcile the contradictions in his stance, he could avoid many of Becher's agonies and compromises); and Hanns Eisler, who attempted a principled defence of an independently-minded Marxist approach to history through his *Faustus* libretto. These strategies will be further discussed in Chapter Six.

DRAWING A LINE THROUGH THE PAST

Becher's absolute insistence on high literary quality (whether or not his own work lives up to this standard) is, as we have seen, a symptom with many causes; the readiness with which his identification of quality with simplicity, clarity, 'objectivity' and formal closure slips into cliché is an indication of unfinished business below the surface. The process of *Vergangenheitsbewältigung*, of which the Kulturbund was supposed to be the instrument, provides a convenient means for a returning exile to escape a confrontation with the consequences of complicity with the Soviet regime. The search for the 'other Germany', which is extrapolated from individuals' moral objections to Nazism into a grand personification of the German nation, is inextricably connected with the image of the Soviet Union. The question of German relations with the Soviet Union is a constant theme in Becher's speeches, and one can trace the increasing insistence on the authority of Soviet models in the context of the fate of the 'German Road' theory; however, as is usual with Becher, there is more to his statements than simple rhetorical virtuosity.

There is a subtext to Becher's statements on the Soviet Union which emerges in his writings on occasion, but which is by no means fully worked out; it is the idea that the Soviet state, personified in 'Stalin', actually embodies Germany's 'better nature', so that the German attack on the Soviet Union was in fact an act of civil war. Not only was Operation Barbarossa 'selbstmörderisch' for Germany in the sense that it was an immense strategic blunder, but it constituted an act of violence against itself:

Die deutsche Tragödie gipfelt darin, daß Millionen Deutscher, die im Krieg gegen die Sowjetunion gefallen sind, zugleich auch gefallen sind: gegen Deutschland. Im Glauben, für Deutschland zu sterben, haben diese Männer [...] sich gegen sich selbst zum Opfer gebracht.[34]

The ideological implications of these statements are clear enough; the attempt to create a delicate rhetorical balance for the sake of the KPD's *Bündnispolitik*. However, we have already seen how Becher would use references to murderous campaigns in the Soviet Union in order to justify his pleas for openness and unity. This image of the Soviet Union, which Becher knew to be false, is used to externalise, or objectify, his conscience: condemnation of Nazism can become a cliché, to be used as a polar opposite to the equally clichéd image of the Soviet Union. This characteristic dialectic of abstractions then obviates the necessity for serious self-examination of motives or attitudes.

The demonisation of Western institutions and ideas was, of course, the fundamental legitimising device of Marxism-Leninism, and SED functionaries were adept at the manipulation of this rhetoric and at the personification of social problems, policy failures or personal doubts as 'hostile elements', 'saboteurs', etc.; in other words, their *externalisation*. The mingling of German intellectual traditions with Marxist-Leninist elements meant that many German

---

[34] Becher, 'Erziehung zur Freiheit', *GW*, XVI, p. 606.

Marxist intellectuals could not readily come to terms with this imposition of a bipolar model and the consequent denial of intellectual freedom and creativity. The debates within the Academy attest to the various types of resistance strategy, some of which I have already commented on. However, the notion of the moral purpose of literature left many of them, particularly those who combined literary activity with political responsibilities, vulnerable to ideological compromise with the 'integrationists', and flight into the language of 'objective values' (identified with the German literary tradition) was a means of avoiding confrontation with uncomfortable realities.

Thus, Becher is able to say that 'Literature' resisted Nazism: '[...] unsere Literatur hat in ihren besten Vertretern, in ihrer eigentlichen schöpferischen Substanz, die härteste Prüfung deutscher Geschichte in Ehren bestanden.'[35] Armed with this confirmation that the values of German classicism have triumphed, he can begin to plead for the reinstatement of German culture into the community of nations.[36] Note, though that his rhetoric follows the same trajectory as the rhetoric of German national self-assertion, discussed in Chapter Three. The movement is from *inclusive* to *exclusive*, in the same way that, by the time of the Prague Foreign Ministers' Conference in 1950, the language of German re-surgence and *Vergangenheitsbewältigung* had become synonymous with integration into Soviet-dominated security structures.

An analysis of these rhetorical strategies reveals the exclusionary practices beneath the benign cliché, so that the language of inclusiveness comes to mean its opposite; the fake semantic closure of the cliché is another factor in the defensive rhetoric of abstractions in which Becher makes sense of cultural politics. The following examples will demonstrate the relevance of this encroaching exclusivity to the hopes placed in the Deutsche Akademie der Künste.

Aside from the agonising details of his relationship with his son, one of the most poignant aspects of Becher's correspondence is the exchange of letters with Hans Lorbeer (co-founder of the Bund Proletarisch-Revolutionärer

---

[35] 'Rede auf dem ersten deutschen Schriftstellerkongreß in Berlin' (7 October 1947), *GW*, XVII, pp. 167– 68
[36] Cf. also his plea for acceptance at the Copenhagen PEN Congress (31 May – 5 June 1948), in Becher, *GW*, XVII, pp. 202–6.

Schriftsteller), whose sentiments concerning the *Bündnispolitik* have been much quoted and have been used to represent the views of 'ordinary' KPD members.[37] The urgent question behind Lorbeer's pleas has the potential to threaten any system of thought which relies on the transcendent value of literary language, namely: Who decides what quality means?

Ich habe eben meine Prosa und meine Gedichte geschrieben. Daß sie 'rhetorische Tiraden' sind [Becher had criticised them in these terms] oder sonst ihre Gebrechen haben, wird mir merkwürdigerweise nur immer wieder von Dir gesagt. Ich weiß genau, hätte ich erst einmal Gelegenheit, an die Öffentlichkeit zu treten, so würde man mich anerkennen, dann würdest auch Du meine Arbeiten schätzen lernen. Da ich aber nicht zu sehen und zu hören bin, weil ich eben so schreibe, wie ich will und muß und nicht so, wie es den Herren Literatur-gewaltigen schmeckt, darf ich auch weiterhin nicht zu sehen und zu hören sein. Die Masse wird hier gar nicht gefragt: Wollt ihr das? Gefällt euch das?

An elite comprising 'hohe gebildete Bürger'[38] is being empowered to pass judgement on literary standards, to the exclusion of broader participation by other writers, whose resentment is palpable after years of struggle and sacrifice. These writers would eventually gravitate towards the journal of the Schriftsteller-verband, *Neue Deutsche Literatur*, which was founded in 1953 by Willi Bredel as a direct challenge to the elitism of *Sinn und Form*. It is a reflection of the extraordinary confusion in SED cultural policy that the exclusivity of the Academy, that is, its function as state-sponsored arbiter of quality, should have served to protect it to a certain extent from the imposition of Socialist Realist norms.

Other instances of this creeping exclusivity in Becher's thinking rise to the surface whenever his language hardens into cliché, indicating an attempt to cover over unresolved traumas or dilemmas with a claim to superior literary or

---

[37] 'Herr Fallada ist schon da, Herr Heinrich Mann, der der "demokratischen" Gummiknüppelpolizei im schönen Preußenlande damals so hochherzige Worte zu sagen wußte, Herr Hauptmann und wie sie alle heißen' Letter from Hans Lorbeer, January 1946, *Briefe an Johannes R. Becher* (Berlin: Aufbau, 1993), pp. 194–98 (p. 197). Cited in Dietrich, *Politik und Kultur*, p. 93; Heider, p. 37; Pike, *The Politics of Culture*, p. 187. Taken out of context, Lorbeer's words do not capture the tone of anxiety, critical respect and idealism hovering at the edge of disillusion which characterises the letter as a whole: 'Besser ist es, einen Johannes R. Becher zu besitzen, wie ich ihn als jungen Enthusiasten kannte!'

[38] Hans Lorbeer, letter to Becher, 7 June 1946, *Briefe an Johannes R. Becher*, pp. 253 and 254.

moral judgement. Phrases like 'objektive Maße und Werte'[39] occur as a
linguistic reflex, trying to give form to the troubling ambiguity of the world; in
this case, the reference to the model of Thomas Mann's exile journal *Maß und
Wert* indicates the emotional significance for Becher of such high-profile artists
as unifying figures and as channels of communication.[40] The literary values
which Becher espouses become ever more defensive, and his pleas for the
political involvement of the Kulturbund combine several of these reflexes: the
fading belief in the spiritual transformation of the German people, the belief
that 'mass movements' can somehow bring about German unity (we have
already seen how mass action for unity came to imply movement towards
division, and how this shift took many unsuspecting people with it) and the
need to protect his own position and influence. All of thesefactors are behind
his protests about 'Kunstvereinsmeierei' in the Kulturbund[41] and his sporadic
protests about SED cultural policy.

Several of Becher's turns of phrase allow us to trace these processes. The
phrase 'guter Wille' occurs frequently, as in phrases such as: 'Die Menschen
guten Willens sind es, welche die Welt in Gang halten', and: 'Der gute Wille
muß über alle Grenzen hinaus sich vereinigen und muß eine Macht werden'.[42]
Note the context of these remarks: the articles by Dymschitz which opened the
'Formalism'campaign[43] followed warning signals that artistic production was to
be directly involved in the Two-Year Plan.[44] The wording is still moderate,

---

[39] 'Auf andere Art so große Hoffnung', speech at the anniversary of the founding of the Kulturbund, 7 July
1946, *GW*, XVII, p. 47.

[40] The title *Maß und Wert*, with its associations with Mann and the preservation of high culture against Nazi
barbarism, was perfectly suited to Becher's needs, and he wanted to use it for the journal which eventually
became *Sinn und Form*. See Becher's letter to Mann requesting permission to use the title (24 April 1948, *Briefe*,
pp. 373– 74) and Mann's polite refusal (20 May 1948, *Briefe an Johannes R. Becher*, p. 345).

[41] 'Um die Erneuerung unserer Kultur', speech at a cultural conference in Schwerin, 24/25 August 1946,
GW, XVII, p. 59.

[42] 'Mahnende Botschaft', speech at the Kulturbund 'Friedenskundgebung', 24 October 1948, *GW*, XVII,
pp. 212 and 215.

[43] 'Über die formalistische Richtung in der deutschen Malerei', *Tägliche Rundschau*, 19 and 24 November
1948.

[44] See 'Aufruf einer Beratung von Kulturschaffenden der SED in Kleinmachnow 3. September 1948', in
Dietrich, *Politik und Kultur*, pp. 330–31. The term 'Formalism' does not appear in this document, but the
protocols of the meeting show that it was already on the agenda, as part of Ulbricht's consolidation of power
after the Yugoslav crisis. Ulbricht declares that the majority of SED artists are 'vom Formalismus beherrscht',
and that the party has 'das Recht, gegen expressionistische und andere Auffassungen Stellung zu nehmen'
(Protocol of Kleinmachnow meeting, 2 September 1948, cit. Heider, p. 91).

indicating continued doubts about coercion, but the turnaround in cultural policy continues which began at the First SED *Kulturtag* in May 1948, and which formed part of the ideological preparation for the First SED Conference in January 1949. It is clear, therefore, that Becher's conception of 'guter Wille' can mean many things: in this case, opposition to the banning of the Kulturbund is a precondition for possessing 'good will', and, although Becher could still count on substantial support from friends and colleagues in all parts of Germany, this concept is beginning to refer purely to public approval of the SED's policy. There is more involved in this rhetoric than simple verbal dexterity: the idea of 'guter Wille' can operate in two ways simultaneously, by excluding a majority of people who reject the SED, thus contributing to the dominance of the 'integrationist' line and the demise of the 'German Road', while at the same time salving Becher's conscience by appealing to high-profile artistic figures and to the values of 'Literature', thus keeping elite channels of communication open to the West. Clichés, wherever they appear, conceal a retreat from responsibility.

The fate of the *Bündnispolitik*, as a broad-based attempt to forge consensus, rather than a continuing critical exchange of views between individual artists, hangs from the changing emphasis in such clichés, which conceal the increasing dominance of an 'integrationist' line within the SED. Becher's statements on Gerhart Hauptmann are a case in point: Becher showed that he was aware of the problems connected with the *Bündnispolitik* when he attempted in 1947 to justify his approaches to Hauptmann; although there were 'bedauerliche[n] Schwächen in Gerhart Hauptmanns Charakter', he had been 'ein unbeugsamer Zeuge des Menschlichseins, obgleich er in mancher seiner Erklärungen und in seinem persönlichen Verhalten diesem inneren Gesetz seines Werkes zuwiderhandelt'.[45] 'Literature', so to speak, transcends the character of the writer. After the founding of the GDR, the tone has changed in line with the theory that formalistic tendencies in art betray personal weaknesses in the artist:

---

[45] Cit. Rolf Harder, 'Zum Anteil Johannes R.Becher an der Herausbildung einer Konzeption zur politisch-moralischen Vernichtung des Faschismus', *Weimarer Beiträge*, 31 (1983), 724–33 (730).

Die Größe des Kunstwerks ist bestimmt von der menschlichen Größe dessen, der es hervorbringt. Die Größe eines Kunstwerks, das ist die menschliche, die weltanschauliche Höhe, die einer Zeit erreichbar ist. Die menschliche Substanz ist es, die einem Kunstwerk seinen entscheidenden Wert verleiht und welche die Form prägt.[46]

In the light of my analysis of the relationship between Becher's psychology and ideas of cultural and national unity, the intense personal significance of this approach to literature in a divided Germany is clear enough. Becher's striving for purity of expression reflects a need for personal, or psychological, unity (an Enlightenment ideal brought into service as an unattainable goal for a troubled personality) as well as national unity, and so it would be easy to invert these unconscious gestures in order to condemn those whose work does not live up to these standards. If Nazism, as one of the extremes in Becher's bipolar world view, is the epitome of disunity and irrationality, then any slippage must be condemned.

By 1949, however, even this form of *Vergangenheitsbewältigung*, which amounted to a vain effort to achieve an essentially non-rational transcendence out of a trauma which defied such attempts to impose meaning, was officially dispensed with. The notorious *Kulturverordnung* of March 1949 had drawn artistic production directly into the Two-Year Plan, while granting the 'intelligentsia' considerable material benefits in return.[47] The new *Grund-aufgaben* for the Kulturbund signalled that the concept of the moral purpose of art had mutated into a more easily quantifiable theory of its usefulness and that the political responsibility of the artist had become synonymous with support for the GDR: 'Der Kulturbund zur demokratischen Erneuerung Deutschlands bekennt sich zur Deutschen Demokratischen Republik und zur Nationalen Front des demokratischen Deutschlands'. Its duty to work 'mit allen Deutschen und mit allen Organisationen in ganz Deutschland zusammen' is clearly conditional

---

[46] 'Befreiung. Deutsche Kultur und nationale Einheit', speech at the Second Conference of the Kulturbund, 24 November 1949, in *GW*, XVII, pp. 277–78.

[47] 'Die Erhaltung und die Entwicklung der deutschen Wissenschaft und Kultur, die weitere Verbesserung der Lage der Intelligenz und die Steigerung ihrer Rolle in der Produktion und im öffentlichen Leben. Verordnung der Deutschen Wirtschaftskommission, 31 March 1949', in Dietrich, *Politik und Kultur*, pp. 369–77.

on their sympathy towards the GDR. The Kulturbund's previous primary duty to eradicate the remnants of fascism is conspicuous by its absence.[48]

Becher's comments make it clear that a line is to be drawn through the past, rather than under it,consigning the trauma of Nazism, and consequently of Soviet terror, to the status of a structuring absence in the ideological discourse of the GDR: 'Wir haben uns, indem wir zu einer demokratischen Erneuerung Deutschlands aufgerufen haben, befreit von der Schmach und Schande unserer Vergangenheit.'[49] This categorical statement, with its dismissal of Nazism in an alliterative formula and the total identification with the new state, indicate that the idea of resurgent German nationhood is to serve to distract from historical traumas. The personal aspect of this attempt at repression becomes clear if we look more closely at Becher's language here. A poem published in 1945 in Becher's collection *Ausgewählte Dichtung aus der Zeit der Verbannung* concludes with the stanza:

> Ihr Deutsche, hört! Als in dem sechsten Jahr
> Des zweiten Weltkriegs jenes Ende kam,
> Wie es vorauszusehen seit langem war,
> Und neues Leben seinen Anfang nahm,
> Da sprach ein Mann: *"Im Anfang war die Scham!"*
> Von Deutschlands Wandlung sprach er, als er sprach
> Von deutscher Schande und von deutscher Schmach.[50]

Becher's reference to it is revealing: a phrase from a poem which, in its original context, stresses *German* guilt in an attempt to instil a sense of responsibility, becomes itself a denial of responsibility. The reference, whether conscious or not, is another attempt at closure in a rhetorical cliché, which contains, within a claim that his own, and the Kulturbund's, contribution to *Vergangenheitsbewältigung* has been sufficient, a jarring note which exposes the truth.

The constant tendency of language to undermine attempts to fix meanings or impose schemes which depend on polar oppositions or constant categories

---

[48] 'Grundaufgaben des Kulturbunds zur demokratischen Erneuerung Deutschlands', resolution of the Second Conference of the Kulturbund, 23–27 November 1949, in Dietrich, *Politik und Kultur*, pp. 446–48.

[49] 'Befreiung', *GW*, XVII, p. 294.

[50] 'Ein Lied von Deutschlands Wandlung', Johannes R. Becher, *GW*, V, pp. 345–49.

bedevilled the work of Marxist intellectuals in the Soviet Zone/GDR, and has distorted the analyses of many commentators since. The next chapter will discuss how these structural ambiguities informed the position of the journal *Sinn und Form*, in order to expand on my discussion of attitudes to literary discourse in the context of the Deutsche Akademie der Künste. Before this, however, I intend to discuss some of the issues arising from the Academy's documentation of its own history.

DESIRE FOR CLOSURE: THE ACADEMY DOCUMENTS ITS HISTORY

In 1993, archivists from the East Berlin Akademie der Künste published an extensive documentation of its early history as the Deutsche Akademie der Künste.[51] In accordance with the emphasis of my analysis on the development of the rhetoric of German unity and of cultural policy from the perspective of German intellectual attitudes to language, I intend to carry out a critical evaluation of the approach taken to the subject rather than to concentrate solely on a chronological account.

Walter Jens, President of the West Berlin Academy and soon-to-be President of the united Academy, expresses in his 'Vorwort' to the documentation his concern that honest critical analysis of the Academy's history may be inopportune, 'da Unwissende die gesamte DDR-Kultur, ohne Bedenken ihrer Widersprüche und Gegenläufigkeiten, als ein einziges Negativum abtun möchten'.[52] Certainly, even a passing acquaintance with the work of artists in the Soviet Zone and GDR, and with the development of critical debate in the late Forties and early Fifties, is enough to dispel the impression that 'by mid-1947' there were no 'artistic criteria [...] independent of a rapidly-narrowing Zhdanovist definition of aesthetics'.[53] Nevertheless, the selection and placement

---

[51] Petra Uhlmann and Sabine Wolf (eds), *'Die Regierung ruft die Künstler' Dokumente zur Gründung der 'Deutschen Akademie der Künste' (DDR) 1945–1953* (Berlin: Akademie der Künste, 1993). The Academy's recent document-ation of its entire history (Ulrich Dietzel and Gudrun Geißler (eds), *Zwischen Diskussion und Disziplin: Dokumente zur Geschichte der Akademie der Künste (Ost), 1945/1950 bis 1993* (Berlin: Akademie der Künste, 1997)) takes a different, thematically-based approach to the archival material, and provides a more differentiated overview, albeit in less detail. The analysis presented in the current section refers to the continuing influence of monolithic views of the GDR and 'Stalinism' on the painful process of reconciliation and recrimination after 1989.

[52] Uhlmann and Wolf, p. 7.

[53] Pike, *The Politics of Culture*, p. 63.

of documents in thecollection implies a desire to create a monument to the passing of a moment of hope, in order to facilitate a process of critical reflection and reconciliation:

Die Entwicklung zweier noch preußischer, immer Berliner, noch nicht deutscher Akademien zeigt, daß in der Tat eines Tages zusammenwachsen könnte, was trotz aller Divergenzen zusammengehört. Die Kluft, das wird deutlich, ist riesig, aber nicht unüberwindbar.[54]

Despite these declared intentions, the documentation, when placed in the broader context set out in this study, tells a somewhat different story. Underlying the interpretation which the editors have placed on the material is the bipolar model of the origins of the Cold War, which is untenable in the rigid manner in which it has been conceived.Thetakeover of the Academy by an aggressive SED faction is seen as inevitable, mirroring a view of German division which fails to take into account the recent controversies over the role of Stalin, the series of conflicts within the SED,or the tenuousness of the grip on power of the 'integrationists', represented in the Academy by figures such as Alexander Abusch.

Similarly, the understanding of the functioning of power which underlies this interpretation is based on the set of antinomies in writing about culture under so-called'totalitarian' regimes, discussed in previous chapters: that is, the dichotomy of 'Geist' and 'Macht'. The volume is an illustration of the dangers of supporting an argument almost exclusively with documentation, without either reference to broader contexts or an ability to analyse one's own position within a prevailing ideological system; the various participants in the debates are categorised as either non-conformists or *apparatchiks*, despite Jens's attempted differentiation of 'das vermeintliche Einerlei' as 'ein buntes Bild'.[55] We must, of course, contrast an ideologically-driven tendency to dismiss all GDR culture as worthless with Jens's more sensitive analysis, which corresponds in some ways to Gerd Dietrich's 'zwei Linien', but without the latter's assertion that the less dogmatic line was present within the bureaucracy itself (and which we can perhaps see in figures such as Gustav Just). The

[54] Uhlmann and Wolf, p. 8.
[55] Uhlmann and Wolf, p. 7.

interpretation which emerges in *Die Regierung ruft die Künstler* is very clear in its separation of artist and functionary (a self-image which often formed the basis of intellectuals' complicity with the regime), and thus ignores the complex of ideological issues which can serve to deepen our understanding of cultural policy in this period.

The documentation concludes in April 1953, with Becher's elevation to the post of President,thus avoiding consideration of the events leading up to 17 June. SED domination of the Academy can thus be shown to be inexorable, and the ambiguities connected with Becher's attitudes are not given the consideration which they deserve; the intentions of 'integrationists' within the SED are confused with their achievements. The resulting sense of closure gives the impression of an attempt to create a monument to a great collective trauma in the GDR artistic community, which has little relevance to contemporary Germany, aside from a regretful 'nie wieder'. However, as stated in Chapter Three of this study, a fully-contextualised analysis of the ramifications of 17 June 1953 demonstrates the immediacy and relevance for current concerns over national identity of issues of SED legitimacy and the inevitability or otherwise of German division. Doubts about the inevitability of division also call into question any sense of legitimising national identity which developed in Germany as a reaction to the defeat of Nazism.

There is an intriguing parallel here with the conclusions drawn in my analysis of attitudes to language, *Vergangenheitsbewältigung* and national identity in the GDR intellectual community: the provisional, legitimising national identity which emerged in the ambivalent complicity of left-wing intellectuals with the GDR regime stemmed from the overlap between a view of the moral certainties inherent in 'true' language and culture, stemming from German Classicism via Lukács and tested in resistance to Nazism, and a 'Leninist' promise to find a social use for the intelligentsia which would overcome the 'Geist–Macht' dichotomy while incidentally providing extensive material privileges. The contradictions in this identity, its incompatibility with the aspiration for German unity which was also fundamental to German intellectuals' view of language, are buried as language hardens into cliché, often presided over by a metaphysical 'Stalin' as an unconscious justification for the suspension of critical faculties and an escape from personal complicity in Soviet crimes. In a similar way, the legitimising language of national identity, dependant on the antinomies of the Cold War, was based on clichés (such as the 'inevitability' of division) which disguised an incomplete reckoning with the past.

In other words, there are issues at stake in any study of GDR cultural policy which require analysis, not only of the development of that policy, but also of contemporary responses. In the case under consideration, the emphasis of the interpretation in the contemporary Academy's documentation of its predecessor raises more questions than it answers. The documentation, as it is presented, gives an illusion of consistency to the policy of the SED which is belied by the limited success of the leadership's attempts to pull Party artists into line (no doubt at least in part a consequence of the continuing divisions within the leadership itself), by the confusion over the institutional position of the Academy, and by the unpredictable behaviour of Becher.

The editors of the documentation have rightly contrasted the public pronouncements about the preparations for the Academy's work with secret documents detailing its proposed role in the formalism and cosmopolitanism campaigns. The Academy was foreseen in section 21 of the *Kulturverordnung* of the Deutsche Wirtschaftskommission of 31 March 1949, so it was a matter of record that any Academy was likely to be considered principally as an economically useful instrument in the Two-Year Plan; the careful rhetoric ensured that intellectuals could feel that they were making a positive contribution to the development of the country. Paul Wandel wrote to Heinrich Mann in May 1949, putting the case for the Academy as the arbiter of artistic taste, and illustrating the flattering theory that 'high' culture had a useful social purpose:

Die Deutsche Akademie der Künste in Berlin [...] wird ein oberstes repräsentatives Gremium für alle Fragen der Kunst und Literatur sein. Sie soll die staatlichen Organe in allen diesen Fragen beraten.[56]

---

[56] Letter of 23 May 1949, Uhlmann and Wolf, p. 48.

There is a clear discrepancy between this representative role and the projected economic usefulness of the Academy; there is a space for resistance and creativity in the tension between the regime's need to suppress aggressive 'proletarian' tendencies in order to maintain a compliant intelligentsia, and the desire, as a document of the DVV detailing proposed administrative personnel for the Academy put it in February 1949, to provide 'die bis heute noch fehlende ideologische Führung der Künste'.[57] The fact is that even after October 1949, the 'integrationists' within the SED were unable to act decisively, and not simply because of the 'nicht bis ins letzte kalkulierbare[n] Künstlerschaft'.[58] On close analysis, statements which rely on an image of artists opposing faceless bureaucrats (note how easy it is to raise this opposition to an abstract 'Geist–Macht' dichotomy) can be seen to reflect a Western view of cultural affairs in the Eastern Bloc. The complexity of the functioning of power in these societies has been revealed by the gradual deconstruction of an untenable, monolithic model of 'Stalinism'; thus, it is only by creating an artificial sense of closure by excluding the ramifications of 17 June 1953 and the continuing debate on Soviet German policy, that the potentially challenging nature of this documentation can be defused.

The documentation in *Die Regierung ruft die Künstler* seems to present the Academy's development as an isolated instance, and thus avoids the questions raised by the kind of interconnections explored in this study. Similarly, issues which could position the Academy's documentation in a more meaningful context are ignored, seemingly because of a series of implied assumptions about the relationship of intellectual/artist, language and power. These assumptions underlay the vulnerability of intellectuals like Becher to the integration of the GDR into Soviet-dominated structures, and continue to form the basis of a dominant Western view of GDR culture. The common ground between the two positions, an internalised acceptance of a national identity based on the exclusion of uncomfortable aspects of history clashing with aspirations to a cultural unity which, of course, depends on its own set of exclusionary

---

[57] Uhlmann and Wolf, p. 64.
[58] Uhlmann and Wolf, p. 26.

practices, leads to the suppression of certain inconvenient and problematic issues.

The genuinely all-German activities of Academy members, such as Becher's discussion with Alfred Döblin at a PEN Club meeting in late 1950, are dismissed as a superficial side-issue intended to distract from the planned takeover by the SED (which is considered, with few exceptions, as an undifferentiated group with a unified agenda):

Ganz sicher waren die großen Namen ein unverzichtbarer Schmuck, dessen Glanz die kunstinteressierte Öffentlichkeit in Ost und West erreichen sollte. Doch wollte man die Institution von vornherein fest in das politische Machtgefüge integrieren.[59]

As a description of the political background to the Academy, this is quite inadequate: as we have seen, the high-profile membership was an absolutely essential aspect of the Academy's composition, and such a general statement about the intentions of SED cadres does no justice to the achievements of the institution in embarking upon and defending an 'all-German' orientation. A phrase like 'das politische Machtgefüge' implies a stability in GDR institutions which cannot be justified at any point before 1956. If interpretation of the documentation relies on such vague generalisations, then the juxtaposition of secret and public pronouncements takes on an entirely false emphasis.[60]

The twists and turns of the regime's rhetoric and the continued caution of its claims to hegemony can be dismissed as window-dressing, whereas in fact they represent a continuing struggle for the dominance of a tough 'integrationist' line within the SED itself, and the inability of Ulbricht's supporters to interfere in public with Stalin's approaches to the West.[61] The obverse of this process was that artists and intellectuals within the Academy, even non-Party members like Zweig, were more deeply involved in the ambiguous development of a

---

[59] Uhlmann and Wolf, p. 16.

[60] For example, the contrast between the 'Leitgedanken des Ministeriums für Volksbildung für die Tätigkeit der Akademie der Künste', published in late 1949 (Uhlmann and Wolf, pp. 108–12), and the internal SED 'Richtlinien für die Tätigkeit der Mitglieder der SED in der Akademie der Künste' (February 1950, Uhlmann and Wolf, pp. 113–15).

[61] Cf. Paul Wandel's appeal of July 1949 to the DWK to accelerate the establishment of the Academy 'als Repräsent-antin deutscher Kunst' before division becomes irrevocable (Uhlmann and Wolf, pp. 87–89).

spurious national legitimacy than it might seem if we adhere to a schematic opposition of intellectual and power.

One can detectsomething of Becher's sense of the importance of the 'all-German' orientation,and of its inseparability from issues of literary quality, in his opposition to the nomination of Erich Weinert[62] and in his objections to the formation of a 'Parteiaktiv'.[63] In the latter case, Becher's dislike of the responsibilities of Party discipline undoubtedly also played a part; he never properly tested his freedom of action, which existed because of the ambiguous status of the Academy within the overall context of Soviet German policy and the SED's problematic legitimacy. The defensive attitude revealed by his objections to the 'Parteiaktiv', and which set his personal stamp on the 'all-German' orientation of the Academy and of *Sinn und Form*, rendered him, as the most significant cultural-political figure in the GDR, ultimately incapable of exploiting his considerable freedom for manoeuvre. In this sense, he is the key figure, to a large extent responsible both for the achievements of the Academy and for its wasted potential.

The sentiments expressed in the 'Leitgedanken' are calculated to appeal to artists searchingfor a social role for their work: the Academy is to be 'die höchste Institution der Deutschen Demokratischen Republik im Bereiche der Kunst', a flattering designation for those seeking influence and recognition. The aspiration to preserve positive aspects from German cultural traditions has by now become intimately entangled with the issue of the legitimacy of the GDR, and so theterms are set for complicity with the regime. The tension between the expressed desire to work forGerman unity and the 'Verpflichtung zur Schaffung einer neuen deutschen Nationalkultur'[64] is,however, not quite a contradiction; this is the area where issues of complicity and resistance in the Academy are decided. The campaign against 'cosmopolitanism' and 'nationale Wurzel-losigkeit' is also double-edged, since it not only attracts intellectuals to a vision

---

[62] Document of SED Central Committee on composition of Academy, 23.1.1950, Uhlmann and Wolf, pp. 106–7.

[63] Cf. the critical analysis of the Academy's work by the Kulturabteilung of the SED Central Committee, June 1951, Uhlmann and Wolf, pp. 160–72, also in Dietzel and Geißler, pp. 29–38. See also Dietzel and Geißler, p. 39, 'Aus dem Protokoll einer Sitzung in der Kulturabteilung des ZK der SED von Rudolf Engel. 31. Oktober 1950', in which Becher's rejection of the idea of a 'Parteiaktiv' is criticised in similar terms.

[64] 'Leitgedanken', Uhlmann and Wolf, p. 109.

of culture which contributes to division, but also, in this specifically German context, latches onto the profound belief in German cultural unity. In this way, as we have seen, issues of complicity and resistance are more complex than the documentation in *Die Regierung ruft die Künstler* suggests.

The secret 'Richtlinien' for the work of the SED members in the Academy include requirements that the Party organise discussions on the cultural policy of the Soviet Union. The sense of German national resurgence which emerges in the rhetoric of this period is reflected in the increasing calls for the GDR to be accepted into the ranks of the People's Democracies. This seems like a simple rhetorical sleight-of-hand until one is able to apply an appropriate set of critical tools: the most ardent proponents of this resurgence were trying to create a legitimising identity for the GDR which depended to a great extent on the suppression of the past (and its projection into the demonised image of the Federal Republic). The close identification with an idealised Soviet Union not only strengthened the grip on power of the 'integrationists', but also provided a series of excuses or unconscious justifications for those who had made uncomfortable compromises with Soviet terror. Any institution which contained high-profile representatives of an 'all-German' orientation threatened to rake up uncomfortable memories and jeopardise a legitimacy based on a supposed German tradition of rationalist, radical (Nazism not being considered a 'radical' movement) and progressive culture. Further, this legitimacy was threatened not only by an obstreperous artistic community, but by the German policy of Stalin, and later Beria. Ulbricht certainly saw more clearly than his critics within the leadership that any attempted critical distance from the Soviet Union, or honest assessment of the legacy of Nazism (such as *Sinn und Form* under Peter Huchel's editorship), was under the circumstances a genuine threat to the stability of the GDR. However, the attractiveness of the temptation to seek refuge from painful memories, amounting to a retreat from responsibility in political life, was an important weapon in the hands of the 'integrationists'.

This is what Otto Grotewohl, a man whose own history of compromise, opportunism and self-delusion must have made him well aware of the deeper implications of his own words, meant in his demand for 'Parteinahme' in his inaugural speech.[65] The advantage in the battle being fought over the geographical or political interpretation of the 'two camps' theory was going the way of the 'integrationists' in the build-up to the Prague Conference where they hoped to be accepted into the community of People's Democracies. The new Five-Year Plan, announced in July 1950, was to be an important step in the development of this new legitimacy, and the arts were now considered to have a direct influence on social and economic processes. However, the members of the Academy showed little inclination to work to Party dictates or to respond to official commissions.[66]

According to Rudolf Engel, Becher had made no efforts to strengthen the ideological work of the SED members in the Academy, while declaring, 'daß er [Becher] die Partei in der Akademie vertrete'.[67] Becher's marked lack of interest in the day-to-day administrative work of the Academy is entirely consistent with his attitudes to culture: he saw the Academy both as a way of extending his personal prestige and of supporting his strongly-held belief in the unity of German culture. To this end, he persisted in cultivating contacts with Western artists, as did many other Academy members, preferring individual communication at the level of 'high' culture to involvement in bureaucratic processes. In many ways, this belief in the irreconcilable opposition of artist and bureaucrat was an important factor in the vulnerability of many Academy members, and it continues to distort interpretations up to the present day.

Becher's continuing contacts with Alfred Döblin are a case in point. These high-level communications were an important part of the Academy's work, and they were tied up with the elitist and defensive attitude to culture which Becher had developed since his hopes for an immediate post-war 'Wandlung' had receded. These contacts were generally informal, and there was little that the regime could do about them, short of demanding that the membership should spend more time discussing major issues, such as the various articles which

---

[65] 24 March 1950, Uhlmann and Wolf, pp. 125–27. Also in Dietzel and Geißler, pp. 26–28.
[66] Cf. Rudolf Engel's critical report to the Central Committee, 23 September 1950, Uhlmann and Wolf, pp. 138–40.
[67] Uhlmann and Wolf, p. 139.

appeared under the pseudonym 'N. Orlow', signalling the broadening of the Formalism campaign to include the Academy.[68]

The tendency of Academy members to ignore these articles, which were intended to produce a collective 'Stellungnahme', became a recurring theme of critical Central Committee analyses.[69] Academy members were able to keep open personal contacts with Western artists, and Becher and Zweig made a number of attempts to place these contacts onto a more institutionalised footing.[70] Alfred Döblin's response to these advances is interesting; he replies that 'die schwere und umständliche Maschinerie einer Organisation mit ihren Instanzen und Abstimmungen' would simply interfere with the most important task, which is 'sich als freie Schriftsteller irgendwo nebeneinanderzusetzen [...] und zu sprechen und zu verhandeln, was uns auf dem Herzen liegt'.[71] This fastidious objection to bureaucracy on the part of intellectuals who believed in the maintenance of 'all-German' contacts was in its own way a retreat from responsibility.

Becher'sdisillusion with the workwhich is expected of him in the Academy is traceable through the documentation in *Die Regierung ruft die Künstler*; his weakness, ill-health and unwillingness to take genuine responsibility for the effort necessary to push for the things which he believes in are major factors in the confusion of attempts by more disciplined SED members to extend their influence.[72] There are also suggestions of personal animosities between Becher, Zweig and Engel which must have soured the atmosphere considerably.[73] The important task was to strengthen 'die Zuwahl fortschrittlicher *bürgerlicher*

---

[68] Cf. N. Orlow, 'Wege und Irrwege der modernen Kunst', *Tägliche Rundschau*, 21 and 23 January 1951; cf. also a sharply-worded letter from Engel to Becher, in which Engel relays the Central Committee's disappointment with the work of the Academy, which is in danger of becoming a 'Tummelplatz zur Behandlung höchstpersönlicher Fragen' (20 December 1950, Uhlmann and Wolf, p. 149).

[69] Cf. section 5, 'Einschätzung der ideologischen Situation der Akademie', of a report by the Kulturabteilung of the Central Committee, June 1951, Uhlmann and Wolf, p. 168. Also in Dietzel and Geißler, p. 33.

[70] Cf. protocol of plenary session, 12 January 1951, at which was discussed the possibility of setting up regular exchanges with the Akademie der Künste und Wissenschaften in Mainz, Uhlmann and Wolf, pp. 151–52.

[71] Letter to Zweig and Becher, 12 February 1951, Uhlmann and Wolf, p. 154.

[72] 'Der Genosse Becher, der ständiger Sekretär dieser Sektion [Dichtkunst und Sprachpflege] ist, leitet diese Sektion nicht *beharrlich* an. Er müßte ersetzt werden, denn er ist zu überlastet.' Report of Kulturabteilung of Central Committee, June 1951, Uhlmann and Wolf, p. 169 (emphasis in original). Also in Dietzel and Geißler, p. 35.

[73] Cf. Uhlmann and Wolf., p. 172: 'Das Verhältnis zwischen dem Genossen Becher und Arnold Zweig ist zu einem arbeitsfähigen, die Arbeit der Akademie nicht hemmenden Verhältnis umzuformen.' Also in Dietzel and Geißler, p. 37. The verb 'umformen' gives an interesting insight into the utilitarian world view of certain SED cadres.

Künstler und Schriftsteller aus ganz Deutschland',[74] while tightening the ideological reins. Problems arose from the distinction that was made between
'bourgeois' artists and SED members, many of whom were just as unwilling (or
unable) to submit to ideological discipline as their non-party colleagues.

In the light of these problems, and of the fact that the 'integrationists' within
the SED were still unable to carry out openly an all-out consolidation of power
(although it seemed to Western observers that this was precisely what had
happened already), the various attempted institutional solutions to the problem
of the Academy should be read as a sign of uncertainty and weak legitimacy
rather than of strength. The setting up of the Staatliche Kommission für Kunstangelegenheiten in the summer of 1951 is another example of these ill-thought
out institutional changes, which both alienated the artistic community and,
although it had a significant influence on other aspects of cultural life, failed to
have the effect of clearing up the ambiguous status of the Academy.

The Chairman of the Kunstkommission, Helmut Holtzhauer, sent a report to
the SED Central Committee in August 1951, in which he criticised the
ideological work of the Academy and stated that most of the members regarded
it 'lediglich als eine repräsentative Körperschaft ohne Verpflichtung zur aktiven
Parteinahme in den Hauptfragen des deutschen Volkes'.[75] In the light of my
analysis of intellectuals' attitudes to cultural matters and to the question of
German cultural unity, this 'representative' function, which is often criticised in
SED reports, should be read as an expression of the 'defensive' function of the
institution, preserving with some success a policy of openness to the outside
world. It would therefore be entirely wrong to interpret the attempts to impose
Party discipline in the Academy as a consistent, step-by-step campaign; such a
high-profile institution remained relatively aloof from the campaigns against
'Formalism' until January 1951, and even after the establishment of the
Kunstkommission, the campaigns enjoyed less than complete success.

Throughout late 1951 and early 1952, Becher swung between assertions of
independence and flight from responsibility into Party discipline. However, his
ambitions for the Academy (inseparable, as with the Kulturbund, from his own

---

[74] Uhlmann and Wolf, p. 172.
[75] Uhlmann and Wolf, p. 178.

need for personal self-aggrandisement) are often close to the demands of loyalists like Engel, and yet do not coincide entirely, creating a certain amount of tension which the Party is not quite able to control. For example, at the plenary session of 26 February 1952, at which Rudolf Engel and Friedrich Wolf criticised the Academy's unwillingness to take up a unified public position on cultural-political matters, Becher replies, 'daß ein von der Akademie gefaßter Beschluß nur dann Autorität haben kann, wenn die Akademie etwas geworden ist'.[76]

In the wake of the hysterical press campaign over the Academy's Barlach exhibition in January 1952, and coming as it does shortly before Becher's nauseating public criticism of the Academy's lack of consistent 'Kulturpolitik',[77] Becher's statements in internal discussions are easily misinterpreted as simple parroting of the Party line. However,we should not overlook the consequences of his desire for self-aggrandisement. His calls for a more conspicuous public image for the Academy mirror in many ways his attempts to promote a more effective political role for the Kulturbund; his vision of public work for these bodies is inseparable from the idea of 'all-German' representation, but these calls for politicisation of the Academy's work could only function in a context which forced them to contribute to division. The reason that these considerations are important is that the institutional position of the Academy was such, that there was extra room for manoeuvre available to anybody prepared to defy the 'integrationists' in a consistent, organised way.

An important demonstration of this point is the inability of the regime to find an effective institutional way of regulating the Academy's work. The Academy lacked a set of statutes until 1955,indicating adegree of uncertainty which cannot be explained away simply as a tactical ploy. Rudolf Engel complains of this lack of consistent state support for the tasks of the 'Genossen' in the Academy:

[76] Uhlmann and Wolf, p. 190.
[77] *Tägliche Rundschau*, 2 March 1952.

Ein anderer wesentlicher Grund, der die Entwicklung der Akademie hemmt, ist die Tatsache, daß sie seit mehr als einem Jahr ohne verantwortlichen staatlichen Kontakt vegetiert; seit der Umbildung des Ministeriums für Volksbildung, in dessen Bereich die Akademie gegründet worden ist, blieb diese Frage offen, mit der bedauerlichen Auswirkung, daß weder staatliche Anleitung noch Hilfe, noch Auftragserteilung die Arbeit der jungen Akademie hätte[n] fördern können. Die dankenswerterweise durch die staatliche Kommission für Kunstangelegenheiten übernommene Weiterführung der administrativen Betreuung bis zur endgültigen Regelung kann den lebendigen Kontakt zur staatlichen Führung nicht ersetzen.[78]

In fact, even the Kunstkommission could not be an entirely effective force in controlling the Academy's work, as Engel himself had established in November 1951 that the Academy was legally answerable only to the Ministerpräsident:

Eine Unterstellung unter die Staatliche Kunstkommission könne nicht in Frage kommen, was auch die grundsätzlichen Aufgaben der Akademie beweisen, nämlich 1. gesamtdeutsche Aufgaben zu erfüllen und 2. die Qualität der künstlerischen Leistungen zu überwachen.[79]

The notion of the Academy as a bulwark against bureaucracy and as guarantor of artistic quality was widespread even among loyal 'Genossen' like Engel: in his report of March/April 1952, cited above, Engel complains about press campaigns 'mit ihrer oftmals oberflächlichen und der Begründung entbehrenden Polemik'.[80] Appeals to leading Party figures to intervene against the narrow-mindedness of certain bureaucrats are common.[81] It is easy to wonder at the naivety of some of these appeals, particularly in the cases of Becher or Brecht, who ought to have known better; however, since the Party leadership was obliged, at least until the declaration of the 'Aufbau des Sozialismus', to preserve the semblance of adherence to the 'all-German' line required by Stalin's German policy, this peculiar legal circumstance may have provided a form of limited immunity to attacks by the Kunstkommission.

Stalin's notes of March and April 1952were, as we have seen, the last gasp of his campaign for German unity, and this was an issue on which all Academy

---

[78] Rudolf Engel, 'Rückblick und Ausblick. Zwei Jahre Arbeit der Deutschen Akademie der Künste', March/April 1952, Uhlmann and Wolf, p. 194.

[79] Engel, cit. Uhlmann and Wolf, p. 27.

[80] Uhlmann and Wolf, p. 194.

[81] Cf. also Becher's proposal that the Academy should be directly answerable to Walter Ulbricht, 'um eine reibungslose Arbeit zu ermöglichen.' (Uhlmann and Wolf, p. 197)

members could agree, creating a temporaryunited front. For once, the appearance of ideological unity, which disturbed Western observers, corresponded with reality.[82] After the rejection of the March note, when the SED leadership returned from Moscow with Stalin's not quite whole-hearted approval for the 'Aufbau des Sozialismus', the 'integrationists' in the SED felt strong enough to make the kind of demands of the Academy which they had been unable to force through before. A list of 'Arbeitsaufgaben' for the Academy includes the requirement to support the militarisation of the GDR ('Unterstützung der kulturpolitischen Arbeit der Armee und Volkspolizei') and to contribute explicitly to the new sense of national legitimacy on which the triumphant 'integrationist' line relied to cement its hold on power ('Aufklärung und Erziehung der Bevölkerung zum patriotischen Denken').[83] These attempts to open up the Academy represented a real threat to the membership's commitment to the maintenance of artistic quality as a way of defending intellectuals against attack from a thoroughly utilitarian view of culture; this is where the real contradiction emerges between theories of literature which had seemed compatible to artists with the experience of Nazism behind them. Up to this point, it had been possible to reconcile the idea that literary language by its very nature conserved certain objective moral values with the theory of the social usefulness of literature, but the Party artists in the Academy were now faced with a choice. The alternative to the painful but comforting certainty of Party discipline, a life of struggle, uncertainty, ambiguity and responsibility, was unbearable for a broken figure like Becher, and his increasing reliance on Alexander Abusch is an indication of the extent of his defeat.

The vital last-minute preparations in May and June 1952 for the Second Conference of the SED were decisive in shaping the work of the SED group in the Academy. The elevation of Becher to the post of President was discussed,[84] although Engel was made responsible for 'die regelmäßigen Sitzungen des

---

[82] Cf. the 'communiqué' of the Academy's plenary session of 13 March 1952, and the manifesto in support of Stalin's notes, Uhlmann and Wolf, pp. 199–200. Also in Dietzel and Geißler, p. 39.

[83] Uhlmann and Wolf, p. 205.

[84] 'Beschlußvorschlag' of the Kulturabteilung to the Politburo, 31 May 1952, Uhlmann and Wolf, p. 208.

Präsidiums'.[85] Despite the particularly strong SED representation in the Sektion Dichtkunst und Sprachpflege (Becher, Anna Seghers, Willi Bredel, Friedrich Wolf, Hans Marchwitza and Paul Rilla), its ideological work is described as particularly weak. To counter this tendency, the Party members are instructed to consider themselves a 'Parteigruppe', in order to influence more effectively the work of the Academy, and the 'Genossen' in the Presidium (Becher, Max Lingner, Ernst Meyer and Rudolf Engel) 'sind verpflichtet, die von der Partei-gruppe oder vom ZK gegebenen Direktiven im Präsidium als Beschlüsse zu erwirken'.[86] In order to lighten Becher's workload, the posts of Vice President and Secretary of the Sektion Dichtkunst are to be separated.

The preparations for the vital elections of new Academy members (27 September 1952) were complicated by Becher's inability to apply himself to the tasks in hand. He writes in a letter to Engel: 'In einem gewissen Sinne ist es schade, daß ich gerade in dem Augenblick so schrecklich wenig Lust zur Akademie habe', and states that he feels 'ein leises Grauen angesichts der Vorstellung, unter solchen Bedingungen Initiative zu entfalten'.[87] Engel sets about persuading him of the importance of his work, and emphasises the need to create a new national identity, starting with a history of German literature ('Wie sollen sich nationales Bewußtsein und Patriotismus entwickeln ohne solche Grundlage?').[88] Certainly, Becher's mood seems to improve significantly by the Spring, as the prospect of his elevation to the post of President allows him to take refuge in discipline and work.[89]

---

[85] 'Entschließungsentwurf' for SED group in Academy, 2 May 1952, Uhlmann and Wolf, p. 212. Note that Engel, ex-ploiting his influence, takes an increasingly harsh tone with Becher: 'Da die Parteileitung unbedingt die Arbeit der Akademie auf eine wirkliche politische Plattform gestellt sehen will, bitte ich, doch zu dieser Zusammenkunft [24 June 1952] unbedingt zu erscheinen' (Uhlmann and Wolf, p. 209).

[86] Uhlmann and Wolf, p. 209.

[87] Uhlmann and Wolf, p. 215.

[88] Letter of 22 August 1952, Uhlmann and Wolf, p. 216. Also in Dietzel and Geißler, p. 40.

[89] A letter to Hans Mayer, 12 March 1953, is revealing in its picture of Becher persuading himself that his con-cerns can be simply dismissed if he submits to the right path: 'Du leistest Dir allerlei Ressentiments, Gereiztheiten und private Gefühle, die Dich von der Erfüllung Deines "gesellschaftlichen Auftrages" abhalten. Ich kann Dir das um so mehr sagen, als ich selber eine Zeitlang es nicht verstanden habe, mit meinen Ressentiments etc. nur einigermaßen fertig zu werden, aber dann habe ich es doch gelernt und bemühe mich, es immer von Neuem zu lernen, daß einzig und allein nur die Leistung überzeugt und daß durch nichts anderes als durch Arbeit, Arbeit und nochmals Arbeit der Widerstand von Dummköpfen bzw. Schädlingen und auch von Feinden überwunden werden kann' (Becher, *Briefe*, p. 449). Another feature of Becher's language here is the tendency to transform a disturbing consciousness of his complicity in the consolidation of a dictatorship into a series of personal conflicts, thus avoiding the necessity for painful self-analysis.

Despite the manoeuvring of the SED group, the elections of 27 September still did not produce convincing Party majorities in the Sektionen Musik or Darstellende Kunst, but representation in the Sektion Dichtkunst und Sprach- pflege was strengthened considerably,[90] particularly by the inclusion of Abusch, whom Becher had begun cultivating by nominating him for the GDR *National- preis*.[91] Nevertheless, the election results were still disappointing for SED loyalists, because the divisions within the Academy over aesthetic and political questions had become more, rather then less, pronounced. A report of 20 October 1952, assumed to be by Rudolf Engel, sets out in stark terms the Academy's problematic status and its uncomfortable challenge to the legitimacy of the regime:

Erschwerend kommt hinzu, daß lange Zeit und zum Teil auch noch heute sich in der Akademie die Spaltung Deutschlands in zwei sich getrennt entwickelnde Lager auswirkt. Die Meinung, zur Einheit Deutschlands beizutragen, indem man den in Westdeutschland und West-Berlin lebenden Künstlern weitgehende Konzessionen machen muß, trägt nicht dazu bei, die Verständigung innerhalb der Akademie zu erleichtern.

For this reason, and also because the artists prefer to work out their theories in practice rather than in public declarations, the report's author believes that the Academy's membership should 'vor der Öffentlichkeit mehr oder weniger stumm bleiben'.[92] An important legitimising device is to be the publication of histories of German literature, music, visual arts and theatre;[93] intellectuals who are concerned with the preservation of 'progressive' aspects of German culture can be persuaded to make a contribution to the creation of a new German national identity which directly legitimises the GDR regime. However, as subsequent events were to prove, the Academy had the potential to become a greater problem than this report implies.

---

[90] Sektion Dichtkunst: 11 SED/ 4 non-Party (Bertolt Brecht, Herbert Jhering, Arnold Zweig and Peter Huchel); Sektion Musik: 3 SED (including the newly-elected Paul Dessau)/ 6 non-Party; Sektion Bildende Kunst: 5 SED/ 3 non-Party; Sektion Darstellende Kunst: 5 SED/ 5 non-Party (including Helene Weigel); overall: 24 SED/ 18 non-Party. Cf. Uhlmann and Wolf, pp. 219–21. Also in Dietzel and Geißler, pp. 48–49.

[91] Uhlmann and Wolf, p. 215.

[92] Dietzel and Geißler, p. 50.

[93] Uhlmann and Wolf, p. 223.

The immediate task for the SED group was to replace Arnold Zweig as President, who, according to Engel, had decided that he did not want to retire at all, and that his Academy work was 'keine Last'.[94] The pressure was kept up on Zweig, and Becher took over the role of acting President from mid-December 1952, while Zweig was granted leave 'zur Fertigstellung in Vorbereitung befindlicher Arbeiten'.[95] Becher himself 'stellt die Bedingung bzw.macht den Vorschlag', that Abusch should become secretary of the Sektion Dichtkunst, if Becher was to become President;[96] despite considerable reservations about Abusch, he took up his post on 22 December.[97] Becher became Academy President on 23 April 1953.

The documentation in *Die Regierung ruft die Künstler* ends on a markedly elegiac note, with a resigned letter from Zweig to Lion Feuchtwanger,[98] as if the editors were trying to tie up all the loose ends of the story. However, the illusion of closure is only possible if the documentation ends at this point; further into 1953, with the repercussions of Stalin's death, the New Course, and 17 June, this conclusiveness becomes impossible. We have already seen in the course of this analysis how these documents, when properly contextualised, begin to unravel the story told by the editors of this volume:thecontents undermine the interpretation. One can also point to further inconsistencies which the editors have had to ignore.

For example, if Abusch is so unpopular that even prominent functionaries have their doubts about his suitability, then the SED takeover of the Academy Presidium is still far from complete. We have already seen in Chapter Three how close Ulbricht came to succumbing to the repercussions of the Slánský trial in December 1952, and so it is clear that the grip on power of the 'integrationist' line in the SED is more tenuous at this point than anyone could have suspected. Also, Becher's unpredictability is still a factor, and the personal

---

[94] Letter from Engel to Hans Lauter at the Central Committee Kulturabteilung, Uhlmann and Wolf, p. 227.

[95] Press release, 12 December 1952, Uhlmann and Wolf, p. 230.

[96] Letter from Gustav Just to Hans Lauter, 9 December 1952, Uhlmann and Wolf, p. 228. Just's unusual phrasing gives us some idea of the personal issues behind Becher's dependence on Abusch.

[97] 'Die Wahl des Genossen Abusch als Sekretär der Sektion hat manches für sich und manches gegen sich. Abusch wird sicher eine bestimmte Arbeit leisten, ob er aber versteht, alle Mitglieder der Sektion zur Arbeit heranzuziehen, ist fraglich. Bei Arnold Zweig und anderen besteht eine gewisse Abneigung.' Uhlmann and Wolf, p. 228.

[98] 24 April 1953, Uhlmann and Wolf, pp. 231–32.

prestige which he has accumulated enables him to participate in the series of surveys in early 1953 which revealed the profound disillusionment of the 'intelligentsia' with the regime; he presented recommendations based on this survey to the Politburo on 13 June.[99]

The next chapter will deal with three other 'loose ends', which, by providing differentiated views of the significance of the Academy's work and the 17 June, will reveal the inadequacy of interpretations which attempt to disguise the uncomfortable relevance of these events for our understanding of German unity.

---

[99] '12 Vorschläge zur Verbesserung der Lage der Intelligenz und unserer Intellektuellen Arbeit'. These recommend-ations were to form the basis of the Kulturbund's demands in the wake of 17 June. See Nikola Knoth, 'Loyale Intelli-genz? Vorschläge und Forderungen 1953', in Černý, pp. 149–56 (p. 151).

CHAPTER SIX

CASE STUDY NO. 1:

SINN UND FORM AND THE TREACHERY OF LANGUAGE

The problems of legitimacy experienced by the GDR regime, involving the difficulty of maintaining long-term stability as successor to the Third Reich and competitor with the Federal Republic, were brought into the open on a number of occasions in literary controversies. The apparent stability of the system between 1956 and 1989 has led to a particular kind of kremlinological literary criticism, with texts scoured for traces of oppositional or transgressive intent. The problem with this approach is that it treats the text purely as a political object from which the author's intentions can be read off by those who know the code. All too often, 'Politics' is reduced to the schematic opposition of 'Geist' and 'Macht'. Although this polarity motivated the oppositional activity of many dissidents, such a model is not a good basis for historical or literary critical discourse, since it attempts to fit the all-pervasive ambiguities into a pre-conceived scheme, and relies on a narrow definition of 'political' art.

While it is true that 'many intellectuals continued to regard cultural politicization as a way of placing art and literature at the disposal of a single party whose program they declined to consider an exclusive set of remedies for Germany's political and cultural ills', this should not lead us to dismiss as worthless all attempts by artists close to the Communist Party to come to terms with the legacy of Nazism.[1] The word 'politicisation', when used in this dismissive manner, prevents us from carrying out a differentiated analysis of various approaches to *Vergangenheitsbewältigung*. In circumstances such as prevailed in 1945, literature is *always* political; what is important is whether it takes its responsibilities seriously.

---

[1] Pike, *The Politics of Culture*, p. 176.

Several serious attempts were made to develop a responsible literary culture after 1945, and their development, successes and failures should be taken on their own merits, instead of simply trying to locate them within the East-West axis. Alfred Kantorowicz's journal *Ost und West*, which appeared between 1947 and 1949, had the subtitle 'Beiträge zukulturellen und politischen Fragen der Zeit. Herausgegeben von Alfred Kantorowicz'. The programme is explicit and the accent is on the personality of the editor, who envisages a particular role for himself, creating a 'Präzedenzfall': 'Glauben Sie nichts blindlings; lassen Sie sich nichts einreden.'[2] Kantorowicz hoped that a publication license would be granted by all four occupying powers, but in the end, only the Soviet authorities granted a license. These initial difficulties may have something to do with the problems which Kantorowicz's KPD background had caused for him in the USA; in any case, his association with, and dependence on, a single occupying power weakened his position considerably.

The high-profile presence of an editorial voice in each issue, ensuring that the overtly political stance of the journal could not be overlooked, did not leave space for the flexibility or subtlety which the absence of explicit authorial comment allowed in the case of *Sinn und Form*. Although Kantorowicz's voice could be strident,[3] it was also passionately committed to a pluralism which was simply untenable by 1949. It seems to me that Kantorowicz's conviction, 'daß es sich nicht um eine Versöhnung unvereinbarer Gegensätze handele, sondern um einen modus vivendi der Gegensätze',[4] is undermined to a certain extent by an insistence on *making explicit*. This conviction that there is an ultimate truth to be found in language led to conflict with Soviet authorities who stood by a different version of that truth.

The willingness of *Ost und West* to offer space to voices critical of extremist tendencies in the Soviet Zone was bound to lead to difficulties. Of

---

[2] Alfred Kantorowicz, 'Einführung', *Ost und West*, 1 (1947), 3–8 (6).

[3] See, for example, his essay, 'Stalin als Lehrmeister der nationalen Selbstbestimmung', *Ost und West*, 3 (1949), no. 12, 3–9.

[4] Alfred Kantorowicz, 'Abschied', *Ost und West*, 3 (1949), 94. The contrast with Becher's synthesising instincts is instructive, demonstrating the variety of individual responses to an ideological system whose effectiveness lies in its flexibility and the potency of 'Stalin' as structuring element.

particular interest is Axel Eggebrecht's condemnation of divisive voices at the First Writers' Congress, in which he criticises Wolfgang Harich's justification of political violence.[5] Kantorowicz shares many of these beliefs with Becher, but his awareness of the practical consequences of his actions prevents him from engaging in compromises to such an extent. Many of the contributions to *Ost und West* are characterised by remarkable insights into current cultural politics (a factor which naturally counted against the journal) but it is the drive to take up a position, to secure the ineradicable presence of meaning corresponding to the personality and convictions of Kantorowicz and his editor-in-chief from November 1947, Maximilian Scheer, in which we find both the journal's strength and its weakness.

These brief remarks are intended simply to illustrate something of the context for the foundation and survival of *Sinn und Form*, and provide a useful contrast with the latter's deliberately ill-defined programme. The development of *Sinn und Form*, and the attempts of an SED grouping in the Academy around Alexander Abusch to undermine Peter Huchel's editorship, have been amply documented.[6] It is beyond the scope of this study to deal in such detail with these events, although some of this material will be drawn on in the discussion of the events of June 1953 in the next chapter. I intend instead to make some comments about the attitudes to language and culture which emerge in *Sinn und Form*, in order to complement my discussion of

[5] Axel Eggebrecht, 'Kritik und Verbindlichkeit', *Ost und West*, 1 (1947), no. 4, 52–58. Note in particular his apt description of the functioning of this kind of rhetoric: 'Unser Freund Wolfgang Harich hat ausein-andergesetzt, daß die Anwendung von Gewalt unter Umständen gerechtfertigt, ja notwendig sei. Dagegen ist weder von der Logik, noch von der Ethik her etwas einzuwenden, so lange der Beweis in sich allein geschlossen dasteht, ohne Bezug auf die ganze Realität. Denken wir aber an die Wirklichkeit des Atomzeitalters, dann wird dieser Beweis für die Gewalt mit einem Male unverbindlich' (pp. 55–56).

[6] See Uwe Schoor, *Das geheime Journal der Nation* (Berlin: Peter Lang, 1992); Stephen Parker, '"Sinn und Form". Peter Huchel und der 17.Juni 1953: Bertolt Brechts Rettungsaktion', *Sinn und Form*, 45 (1994), 738–51; Stephen Parker, 'Peter Huchel und "Sinn und Form"', *Sinn und Form*, 43 (1992), no. 5, 724–38, and the accompanying documentation: 'Der Fall von Peter Huchel und "Sinn und Form"', *Sinn und Form*, 43 (1992), no. 5, 739–822. For an analysis which, it seems to me, sacrifices accuracy through the author's political stance, see Ian Hilton, 'Sinn und Form: "Ein schlimmes Kapitel ..."', in *Peter Huchel*, ed. by Axel Vieregg (Frankfurt a. M.: Suhrkamp, 1986), pp. 249–64. Other important material on *Sinn und Form* can be found in Hans Mayer, 'Erinnerungen eines Mitarbeiters von "Sinn und Form"', in *Über Peter Huchel*, ed. by Hans Mayer (Frankfurt a. M.: Suhrkamp, 1973), pp. 173–80; and in the correspondence between Huchel and Hans Henny Jahnn: Bernd Goldmann (ed.), *Peter Huchel/ Hans Henny Jahnn. Ein Briefwechsel. 1951–1959* (Mainz: Hase & Koehler, 1974). Huchel's own comments on his editorship are rare: see 'Der Fall von "Sinn und Form"', Peter Huchel, *Gesammelte Werke*, ed. by Axel Vieregg, 2 vols (Frankfurt a. M.: Suhrkamp, 1984), II, pp. 326–29.

the ideological issues arising from Becher's cultural-political work. In fact, it is only after giving serious consideration to these issues that we are able to locate *Sinn und Form* meaningfully in the context of cultural life in the Soviet Zone and GDR.

If we accept that the *Bündnispolitik* was simply a tactical manoeuvre on the part of the Soviets and their German communist allies, that the 'German road' theory was simply a temporary softening of emphasis in a consistent strategy, and that Becher was simply a consummate master of manipulative rhetoric, then it is possible to argue, with Ian Hilton, that Becher intended *Sinn und Form* to be 'Werkzeug einer unmittelbar künftigen sozialistischen Kulturrevolution'.[7] This view relies on a vision of the origins of the Cold War which still takes seriously certain aspects of the 'two camps' theory which has informed, and oversimplified, the closed system of Cold War ideological discourse. As we have seen, the 'two camps' theory, and the purposes which it was intended to fulfil are by no means as clear-cut as many commentators on cultural politics often assume; the monolithic view of SED policy and of cultural 'Zhdanovism' which this produces leads to statements to the effect that 'by 1948 the Communists hoped to use intellectuals in East *and* West to help win the cold war'.[8] It seems to me that such sweeping interpretations are entirely inadequate in the face of the evidence: Who are 'the Communists'? What could it possibly mean in 1948 to 'win the cold war'? Contemporary interpretations cannot rely on the imposition of a bipolar model which ignores the ambiguities and uncertainties which the 'integrationist' line within the SED itself failed to eradicate. The very existence of *Sinn und Form* gives the lie to such models.

Sinn und Form occupied such an anomalous institutional position, even after it was taken into the fold of the Academy in 1950, that commentators have often been unsure how to approach it, on occasion leaving it out of consideration altogether (as does David Pike). Other, more sensitive, analyses concentrate on the ability of Huchel to create spaces for himself which allowed him to pursue his own artistic agenda. Both Uwe Schoor and Gerd

---

[7] Hilton, p. 250.
[8] Pike, *The Politics of Culture*, p. 454.

Dietrich point to the links between the conception of *Sinn und Form* and the
programme ofthe Kulturbund (with Becher as the obvious linking factor):
Sinn und Form was set up 'im ursprünglichen Geist des weltoffenen
Kulturbund-Konzepts',[9]and 'läßt enge Beziehungen nicht nur zu den
"Leitsätzen", sondern zum gesamten Anliegen des Kulturbundes erkennen,
vor allem auch in bezug auf die Wiederherstellung fruchtbarer Beziehungen
zum Ausland'.[10]

There seems to meto be a problem of emphasis with these
characterisations: although they are concerned to take issue with superficial
analyses which see nothing of value in the literary life of the early GDR, they
rely on a conception of the Kulturbund which overlooks the extent to which
it was from the very outset enmeshed in the internal political processes of the
KPD, and with the direction of Stalin's *Deutschlandpolitik*. In fact, we need
to understand this much broader context if the very different institutional
positions of the Kulturbund and of *Sinn und Form* are to make sense.

Without this context, and a fuller understanding of the ideological
ambiguity of issues of complicity and resistance, analyses of *Sinn und Form*
can fall back on the schematic opposition of 'Geist' and 'Macht':
'Chefredakteur wurde Peter Huchel, der für über ein Jahrzehnt [die] Qualität
ohne ideologische Scheuklappen bewahren konnte.'[11] As a response to the
complex manoeuvring and stern insistence on high literary quality which
characterised Huchel's editorship, this description is somewhat inadequate.
I have already discussed at length the entanglement of Becher's personality
with the Kulturbund, and his flight, from political failure and the unbearable
complex of feelings connected with his experience of Soviet terror and his
involvement in a new dictatorship, into literary abstraction (which he,
perversely, thought of as 'concrete' as opposed to 'formalist'). It seems to
me, therefore, that to equate *Sinn und Form* with the Kulturbund's
'openness' is to miss the point: the emphasis on tradition, on 'objective'
standards, on the values inherent in the German language, and on

[9] Dietrich, *Politik und Kultur*, p. 188.
[10] Schoor, pp. 21–22. Before 1950, Huchel reported to the Kulturbund's literary commission on editorial policy for *Sinn und Form*.
[11] Dietrich, *Politik und Kultur*, p. 188.

communication amongst an intellectual elite in all parts of Germany, bear the unmistakable stamp of Becher's authorship.[12] The banning of the Kulturbund in the US and British Zones, and Becher's recurrent feuds with the SED leadership (for example, over the Kulturbund's initial exclusion from the Volkskongreß) had thrown Becher onto the defensive, and, as always in such situations, he retreated behind the barriers between elite and mass culture, and between free speech in the rarefied communication between intellectuals and oppressive political action.

However, as we have seen, the stress on literary quality was inseparable from a commitment to the unity of German culture; thus, *Sinn und Form* is located at a point of tension where the various exclusionary practices conflict. Hans Mayer's comments on this issue are interesting: Becher's '"subkutaner" Konservatismus' coincided after 1945 with a legitimising strategy of the 'Leute um Ulbricht' which consisted in, 'den Bereich Deutschlands, den sie zu regieren vermochten, so stark wie möglich durch bereits vorhandene und im Volk bekannte Zeichen, Chiffren und Symbole kenntlich zu machen'.[13] The word 'kenntlich' is well-chosen in the light of the SED's efforts to create a form of national self-consciousness. However, there is more to the matter than a simple attempt, prevented only by Brecht and Huchel, to create in *Sinn und Form* another cultural-political tool.

Schoor examines Becher's 'Traditionswahl',[14] an appropriate description given Becher's selective approach to the German intellectual tradition; as Schoor rightly points out, Becher's choices deliberately mirror Thomas Mann's *Maß und Wert*, both in the title and the typographic style: 'Beide Publikationen setzten ganz auf die Texte, auf den Geist der literarischen Beiträge wie auf die Fähigkeit der Leser, ihn wahrzunehmen.'[15] There was to be no editorial comment or explicit programme; the power of the literary word was considered sufficient for those who were able to follow it.

---

[12] Cf. Mayer, p. 174: 'Der Anstoß ging, wie hätte es anders sein können? von Becher aus. Der einstige Rebell, Expressionist und Dadaist erglühte seit je in geheimer Liebe zu traditionellen Ordnungen und Ritualen. Er hatte sich aus alledem eine sonderbare Synthese zur Lebens- und Kunstführung zurechtgemacht: lange vor der offiziellen Wendung sowjetischer Kulturpolitik zum Neoklassizismus.'

[13] Mayer, p. 174.

[14] Schoor, p. 20.

[15] Schoor, p. 22.

In the light of the analysis presented in this study of the attitudes of German intellectuals after 1945, such an intense preoccupation with the values inherent in language raises important questions. Schoor maintains that the extraordinary openness of *Sinn und Form* to contributors from all parts of the world demonstrates, 'daß mit dem Konzept "Sinn und Form" ein möglichst breites Bündnis für den demokratischen Wiederaufbau befördert werden sollte'.[16] It seems to me that the choice of vocabulary in this statement links *Sinn und Form* too closely with the aims of the Kulturbund. We have seen how the language of *Vergangenheitsbewältigung* and the political effectiveness of culture had begun to slip out of Becher's control; the conception of *Sinn und Form*, as well as that of the Academy, should therefore be seen as manifestations of a desire to reassert some kind of control, whether in terms of administrative influence (in the case of the Academy), of control over the meanings of words, or in terms of his own mental health, which depended to a great extent on the perceived success of his work.

As we have seen, one of these defensive strategies was to refer obsessively to great individuals, such as Goethe and Heinrich Mann, as examples of the kind of unified personality (an idealised Enlightenment humanism) to which Becher aspired. In essence, the deliberate reference to a model used by a writer whose good opinion Becher craved[17] and the appointment of Peter Huchel (who was, after all, a non-party poet who had remained in Germany between 1933 and 1945 and was therefore an outsider among the returned exiles who wielded influence in the SED) reflected a side of Becher's personality which he wanted to keep separate from the sordid business of political compromise and failure.

The problems with Becher's view of language and the continuation of an Enlightenment project of the communication of 'objective' values through the literary language have already been discussed: the questions raised by the ambivalences which emerge in a study of *Sinn und Form* show that, under

---

[16] Schoor, p. 29.

[17] Cf. letter to Thomas Mann, 11 June 1948: 'Nun haben wir doch einen Titel gefunden, der zwar in einer gewissen Weise erinnern kann an "Maß und Wert"' (Becher, *Briefe*, p. 380).

Huchel's editorship, the journal explored territory which took it far beyond Becher's intentions. The austere emphasis on the text, which is intended to reveal the truths within a language of humanism salvaged from the wreckage of Nazism, in fact increases the interpretative scope of the individual reader. This was a form of pluralism available only to a highly literate elite, but nevertheless, in the context of the GDR, an important locus of resistance against the imposition of official interpretations. By shifting the burden of judgement towards the reader, *Sinn und Form* avoids both the pitfalls of earnest explicitness (the downfall of *Ost und West*) and the problematic 'pluralism' of Becher, who, by assuming that reasoned discussion of literature would lead to a single truth and ultimate synthesis, laid himself open to manipulation by those who defined his truths for him.

The conception of the moral-political function of art which arises through *Sinn und Form* is, however, also problematic. Peter Huchel had, since 1945, made a (not entirely convincing) effort to reinvent himself as a committed left-wing artist, while leaving his relationship with the tenets of Marxism deliberately vague. The key concept which emerges in his cultural-political work is the concept of 'Verantwortung': this refers not only to the admission that the German intellectual community capitulated in the face of Nazism, but also, more specifically, to the idea that artistic and political responsibility are inseparable.[18]

We find a similar conception in many of the contributions to *Sinn und Form*, for example in Hermann Kasack's introduction to a collection of Oskar Loerke's poetry. Kasack differentiates between 'genuine' resistance writing and an inner emigration in which the poet feels obliged, 'sich in ein Reich der Schönheit flüchten zu müssen', or to confine poetic utterance to a vague humanism. In this sense, political and artistic responsibility are inseparable:

---

[18] See Peter Huchel, 'Rede zum "Tag des freien Buches"', *Gesammelte Werke* , II, pp. 261–65.

In Loerkes Gedichten seit 1933 [...] bilden die beiden Faktoren des Ewigen und Zeitlichen, der poetischen und der politischen Verantwortung eine untrennbare Einheit für das dichterische Erlebnis.[19]

This 'Polemik gegen den Ästhetizismus'[20] is a theme which links the thinking of Huchel, Becher and the contributors to *Sinn und Form*.

We have already tested Becher's conception of literary responsibility and examined its peculiar strengths and weaknesses; Huchel's publication practice in *Sinn und Form* raises a related set of questions, although the contrasts with Becher's theorising are instructive. Although the contributors to *Sinn und Form* are clear in their acknowledgement of the need to restore a sense of intellectual responsibility, the question of whether the requirement to respond to the contemporary world validates or invalidates the idea of 'eternal' (literary or moral) values pervades the journal. Thomas Mann intended *Maß und Wert* to preserve certain values against a climate of barbarism, and *Sinn und Form* places itself in this tradition, rather than making what might be called positive interventions in the reconstruction of Germany.

There are perfectly legitimate questions which could be asked of this elitism such as: Is 'bad' resistance poetry not 'true' resistance poetry? Loerke is praised as much for the quality of his verse as for his personal courage.[21] I have already discussed the consequences for Becher of the idea that 'Literature' resisted Nazism, and the first issue of *Sinn und Form*, with its contrasting voices on the social role of the writer, also occupies this ground. As we have seen, this view of literature was a double-edged sword, implying a defensive attitude to cultural values which left German intellectuals vulnerable to manipulation by those who claimed to offer a social use for the writer. Huchel avoids this dilemma by ignoring it, leaving the reader to find his/her own answers. However, on a careful reading of the early issues before

---

[19] Introduction to Oskar Loerke, 'Die Jahre des Unheils. Gedichte aus dem Nachlaß', *Sinn und Form*, 1 (1949), no. 1, 39–41 (40).

[20] Schoor, p. 53.

[21] In his editorial practice, Huchel wasted no time agonising about the ideological legitimacy of judgements on literary quality: the editor decided, and that was that. This policy continued after 1950, and although he submitted 'difficult' pieces for consideration to Becher, Brecht or Zweig, Huchel reserved the right to reject contributions from the Sektion Dichtkunst und Sprachpflege of the Academy.

the journal was taken over by the Academy, one gains the impression that *Sinn und Form* was founded more as an act of resistance to contemporary developments than as a contribution to reconstruction. This also suggests that *Sinn und Form* represents a kind of ideal *alter ego* for Becher, as a contrast with the sordidness of current politics.

Huchel's motivation seems different: the search for evidence of German resistance writing to parallel the French examples given in the first issue suggests a further step in Huchel's efforts to redefine his relationship with his past.[22] The poetry of resistance is contrasted with the self-aggrandising brilliance of Mayakovsky who represents, supposedly, the unity of the poet's social and literary responsibility.[23] However, in the light of the worsening political atmosphere in the Soviet Zone, all such contributions to *Sinn und Form* must be treated with caution, and the reader must take note of the ironies which arise from contexts unforeseen by the authors. As Schoor comments: 'Alle Texte sind, unabhängig von ihrer Enstehungszeit, in einen Gegenwartszusammenhang gerückt.'[24] The physical business of putting together the journal allows Huchel to suggest meanings which arise in the assonance or dissonance between juxtaposed texts. Even texts which appear to comment directly on current problems must be read in juxtaposition with the overall practice of the journal. For example, the hard-edged tone in Ernst Niekisch's essay, 'Zum Problem der Elite', in which he castigates bourgeois liberalism for its failure in the face of authoritarian regimes[25] (which, in the context of the journal's first issue, may *appear* to be a programmatic statement) should be contrasted with the actual *practice* of the journal, with its emphasis on quality and 'eternal values'. When we consider that this type of Marxist critique suggests a more historicist analysis of a 'bourgeois' ideology of eternal values, we can begin to make connections which should make us hesitate before equating *Sinn und Form* too closely with the positive programme of the Kulturbund. Through such attempts to engage the reader's

[22] Louis Aragon, Loys Masson, Pierre Seghers, Edith Thomas: 'Gedichte aus der Résistance', *Sinn und Form*, 1 (1949), no. 1, 98–102.

[23] Vladimir Mayakovsky, 'Ich selbst', *Sinn und Form*, 1 (1949), no. 1, 52–69.

[24] Schoor, p. 38.

[25] 'Der Ruf nach der Freiheit des Geistes war nur eine Spielart des Rufes nach der Freiheit des privaten Eigentums überhaupt', Ernst Niekisch, 'Zum Problem der Elite', *Sinn und Form*, 1 (1949), no. 1, p. 127.

critical faculties, and by relying on an established elite of writers of an older generation, Huchel resists the propagandistic versifying to which Becher was prone. The self-conscious elitism of *Sinn und Form* relies on an acceptance of irony and juxtaposition, a genuine, though not unlimited, pluralism of viewpoints, which allowed it to resist and undermine the imposition of rhetorical meanings and the narrowing definition of Realism.

Although the editorial policy of ironic juxtaposition might imply a valueless relativism, reference to contemporary events shows us that Huchel's controlling intelligence intends a more committed response on the part of the reader. For example, Werner Krauss' essay, 'Über den Standort einer Sprachbesinnung',[26] which calls for the restoration of language to a sense of responsibility in a communicative community, is commented on by Gaston Baissette's story, 'Die große Verbindungsstraße',[27] which describes in symbolic form the disrupted communication caused by war, and contrasts with a poem by Brecht which depicts the class antagonism inherent in language;[28] yet the implication in these and other items, that the potential exists to restore broken communications, is contrasted with the Enlightenment critique of Adorno and Horkheimer.[29]

In the overall context of the 'Goethe-Jahr' 1949, these comments on humanism and its successes and failures are pertinent, and *Sinn und Form*'s silence on the subject of Goethe is the most perceptive commentary on Becher's ideological acrobatics. We have seen how Becher used the figure of Goethe to justify the SED's proscription of further attempts at *Vergangenheitsbewältigung* and to suppress memories of Soviet and Nazi dictatorship; for *Sinn und Form* to begin a painstaking analysis of German responsibility in 1949 marks it out as a powerful protest against the tendency of increasing Cold War divisions to function as convenient barriers against painful memories.

---

[26] *Sinn und Form*, 1 (1949), no. 1, 104–31.

[27] *Sinn und Form*, 1 (1949), no. 5, 92–102.

[28] Bertolt Brecht, 'Aus allem etwas machen', *Sinn und Form*, 1 (1949), no. 5, 103.

[29] Cf. Max Horkheimer and Theodor W. Adorno, 'Odysseus oder Mythos und Aufklärung', *Sinn und Form*, 1 (1949), no. 4, 145–82. The platform which Huchel offered to Frankfurt School writers was an uncomfortable reminder, not only of the illegitimacy of the SED's claim to historical justification, but of the complicity of left-wing intellectuals in a series of myths which led to their compromise with the regime.

Huchel's attitude to language inevitably shares many features with Becher's, and Huchel's expressed aspirations to contribute to the *Bündnispolitik* suffer from similar elitist reflexes.[30] However, *Sinn und Form* in its first year makes no explicit claims to social effectiveness, and accepts paradox and contradiction rather than attempting any artificial synthesis. This is where we find the fundamental difference between Huchel's practice and Kantorowicz's highly politicised 'modus vivendi der Gegensätze', which overestimates the externalised effectiveness of cultural-political discourse, rather than concentrating on the provocation of the reader's critical faculties.

In terms of my analysis of the shifting and conflicting barriers which characterised the cultural life of the Soviet Zone/GDR, *Sinn und Form* accepts its distance from the 'masses' without the self-doubt and arrogance of Becher, while refusing to impose interpretations or set up artificial semantic limits to the ambiguity of language and symbol.[31] Also, as we have seen, the aspiration to German cultural unity is inseparable from the attitude to language which is Becher's legacy to *Sinn und Form*. However, in contrast to Becher, Huchel refuses to take part in the rhetoric of German national self-assertion, preferring to avoid compromise with the exclusionary practices of a political line which derives its legitimacy from conceptions of German nationhood dependent on integration of the GDR into the Soviet sphere. Huchel finds, at the cost of sacrificing a certain social effectiveness, an ingenious method of avoiding the vulnerability of German intellectuals who sought fixed meanings in language. By posing questions, rather than imposing answers, *Sinn und Form* remains enough of a threat to expose this claim to legitimacy as a sham.

---

[30] It is for this reason that, in my opinion, Schoor's analysis suffers from a tendency to overemphasise the 'openness' of *Sinn und Form* in the context of the *Bündnispolitik*: it is the unabashed elitism of the journal's practice, the kind of elitism against which committed writers like Hans Lorbeer understandably protested, which allowed Huchel to avoid the ideological minefield which leads Becher, Brecht and others into compromise with the regime.

[31] Cf. Hermann Kasack, 'Der Webstuhl', *Sinn und Form* 1 (1949), no. 1, 143–63, and Anna Seghers, 'Das Argonautenschiff', *Sinn und Form*, 1 (1949), no. 6, 38–51, for two stories characteristic of *Sinn und Form*, in which the interpretation of an ambiguous central symbol is left very much to the reader's understanding of the contemporary world.

'SPRACHROHR' OR 'GEISTIGES VISIER'?
SINN UND FORM UNDER THE WING OF THE ACADEMY

In an essay on the literary development of Johannes R. Becher, Paul Rilla
writes:

Und wenn Brechts Größe darin besteht, daß die Person des Dichters völlig hinter die
unerbittlich aussagende Sachformel zurücktritt, so besteht Bechers Größe darin, daß die Person
des Dichters nicht die Sache überlagert, vielmehr von Wandlung zu Wandlung sich in der
Sache bekennt.[32]

If we can dismiss the assessment of Brecht's work as polemical exaggeration,
there is something about the idea of the constant presence of Becher's poetic
personality in his work which rings true; the unity of work, life, thought and
political activity to which Becher aspired was an obsessive motivation.
However, we should not succumb to the temptation for literary criticism to seek
these unities of life and work, as such assumptions themselves form the
common thread which links the 'bourgeois-liberal', Marxist-avantgardist, and
Socialist Realist ideologies, elements of which coexist precariously both within
Becher's personality and in the membership of the Academy. It is the illusion of
unity, and the effort required to sustain that illusion, which is the key issue; after
the exertions of events like the First Writers' Congress and the founding of the
Academy on an 'all-German' basis, the struggle for control of *Sinn und Form*,
and Becher's final painful break with Huchel, marks the point at which the
effort becomes unsustainable.

The assured institutional and financial position which the Academy offered
Sinn und Form brought with it certain costs, although it did not become an
exclusive 'Stimme der Akademie'.[33] Those who were inclined to defend
Huchel's editorship were nevertheless obliged to define their own position
within the ideological concern for the social usefulness of art. The contrast
between, for example, the liberal-democratic view of Zweig and the more
utilitarian stance of Brecht becomes clearer in the period 1950–53, not only in

---

[32] Paul Rilla, 'Der Weg Johannes R. Bechers', *Sinn und Form*, 2 (1950), no. 4, 35–49 (p. 48).
[33] Schoor, p. 66.

their ideological position, but also in their style of resistance to the imposition of a particular form of Realism; in each case, the stand that they were required to make defined the terms for conflict and accommodation with the regime. In the case of *Sinn und Form*, the fact that the journal became, against Huchel's wishes, the carrier for many of the key debates within the Academy, for example on *Das Verhör des Lukullus*, the Barlach exhibition, or Eisler's *Johann Faustus*, forms an area of considerable tension between Huchel's editorial practice and attempts to clarify meanings and responses to works of art. In fact, Huchel generally published what the writers themselves wanted, without knowing if an SED-inspired debate would result; certainly, Brecht wanted to intervene publically in the debate over the Barlach exhibition when he was denied a platform in *Neues Deutschland*, and Eisler's publication of excerpts from his libretto was the action of a principled, and therefore naive, Marxist artist wanting to be involved in the public development of the arts in the new society. Huchel, however, had no interest in provoking such debates and the endless round of criticism and self-criticism which accompanied them.

In this respect, it seems to me that Schoor attempts to construct something of an artificial unity by overstating the correlation between the function which was demanded of *Sinn und Form* after 1950 and Huchel's artistic practice. This can at times be quite misleading. For instance, when discussing the journal's role as a showcase for defining debates within the Academy, Schoor states:

Hiermit wird eine Form des Diskurses über Literatur, Kunst überhaupt und gesellschaftliche Zustände demonstriert und gefordert, die geeignet ist, durchschaubar zu machen und Veränderung vorzubereiten. Dieser Diskurs lehrt, den Prozeß Literatur — die Annäherung an Literatur als Medium, in dem über gesellschaftliche Zustände und deren Veränderung verhandelt wird — als Prozeß der Auseinandersetzung zu begreifen, in dem Übereinstimmung gewonnen wird oder ein Verbleiben im fortzusetzenden Streit erforderlich ist.[34]

There is, though, a considerable difference between the dialectical form of debate promoted here ('Auseinander-setzen') and the process of searching for significance in the shifting relationships between the texts. The key issue is the amount of control over meaning which the arranger of the texts claims for

---

[34] Schoor, p. 67.

himself: once *Sinn und Form* is required to include contrasting contributions to a debate (as with the 'Faustus Debate'), then a potential resolution, or synthesis, is already implied in the juxtaposition. In my discussion in Chapter Four, I made it clear that I regard this tendency to think dialectically (a habit of mind which Huchel did not share) as a major factor in the vulnerability of a type of German intellectual to accommodation with the GDR regime in the years up to 1953. The requirement for *Sinn und Form* to contribute directly, rather than obliquely, to these contemporary debates, intended as exemplary set-pieces for the attention of the German intelligentsia, contrasts sharply with the journal's original conception. A debate which takes for granted that a conclusion can and will be reached within a set period is less of a threat to a cultural ideology based on the existence of an objective truth, than is a form of artistic practice in which the debate is an end in itself.

There is of course a considerable overlap between Huchel's position and, say, the liberal humanism of Arnold Zweig. Nevertheless, the tension between the two views arises from the contrasting attitude to the explicit spelling-out of meanings; in this sense, the requirement for *Sinn und Form* to take a more explicit stance on aesthetic and political matters represents a gesture of compromise with the ideological system which ensnared other left-wing intellectuals. Zweig writes:

Unsere Absicht ist es, in dieser Zeitschrift "Sinn und Form" wie bisher, nur noch geordneter um ein Ziel, das Notwendige zu gestalten, kristallinisch, blumenhaft oder im Lied, wie sich's uns aufdrängt und vorschreibt.[35]

By 'das Notwendige', Zweig means the necessity to contribute to a change in the 'Grundbau der Gesellschaft', in order to achieve 'eine gerechtere Ordnung'. His somewhat coy description of the First World War, the Weimar Republic and the Third Reich as the 'Jahrzehnte[n] seit dem Ende des Naturalismus' is an indication of the way in which intellectuals steeped in the German cultural tradition consistently overestimated the importance and social impact of literature. The periodisation of literature implied in Zweig's statement has much

---

[35] Arnold Zweig, 'Zur Übernahme der Zeitschrift durch die Deutsche Akademie der Künste', *Sinn und Form*, 2 (1950), no. 5, 5.

in common with the way in which such periodisations were used to separate a rationalist and progressive line in German culture (exemplified by Goethe) from the 'irrationalism' of figures such as Nietzsche, which supposedly culminated in Nazism. This combination of intellectual self-image and common ground with the tenets of Socialist Realism and of cultural theories intended to justify the political hegemony of the SED led individuals like Zweig to compromise, to varying extents, their sense of intellectual responsibility.

Huchel himself, despite his efforts to stay aloof, was increasingly drawn into these controversies; to use Zweig's words, the function of *Sinn und Form* as 'Sprachrohr' for the Academy's debates began to overshadow its role as 'geistiges Visier', in other words, as promoter of the kind of open-ended exchange which would contribute more to German culture than attempts to locate an 'objective truth' immanent in language. Nevertheless, Huchel managed to preserve a remarkable degree of editorial independence, refusing to print all the contributions he was offered by the Sektion Dichtkunst und Sprachpflege, and did not usually feel the need to offer an explanation (an attitude which accounts for the personal nature of the attacks on him by writers such as Friedrich Wolf). It was in fact relatively difficult for German writers to publish in *Sinn und Form* if they were not already friends or colleagues of Huchel, and contacts with foreign writers were often made simply through friendships with German writers who had lived in exile. The journal represented the 'alte Intelligenz' and made few concessions to younger writers. This younger generation was catered for by journals such as *Neue Deutsche Literatur*, which was set up by Willi Bredel in direct competition with Becher and with *Sinn und Form*, and which acted as a forum for young authors.

In exploring how Huchel positioned *Sinn und Form* in GDR cultural life, it is important to consider some of the compromises which he had to make. For example, the image of the Soviet Union which emerges from *Sinn und Form* is almost exclusively positive. There are some shameful examples of the genre of travel writing by foreign visitors to the Soviet Union, and, although these reports concentrate largely on aesthetic matters, the implication, that the healthy state of Soviet art is the sign of a healthy society, is unavoidable.[36] Works by German authors dealing with the Soviet Union are also positive.[37] Interestingly, though, contemporary Soviet literature is under-represented, particularly in comparison with the depth of critical appreciation devoted to nineteenth-century Russian literature: Huchel's stubborn insistence on high standards of quality prevents *Sinn und Form* becoming an unquestioning vehicle for Socialist Realism. As in the case of *Noviy Mir* under Alexander Tvardovsky, Huchel's policy of calculated compromise allowed him space to pursue his own ends. The demands of *Deutschlandpolitik*, that is, the coincidence of *Sinn und Form*'s internationalist stance with the tension between 'integrationist' and 'all-German' lines within the SED, and with Stalin's diplomatic efforts, gave Huchel far more leeway than Tvardovsky could have dreamed of (instructive parallels and contrasts might also be made between Tvardovsky's work at *Novy mir* and the very different circumstances of Wilhelm Girnus's editorship of *Sinn und Form*, 1964–1981). The later years of Huchel's editorship saw the publication of Soviet writers of the 'Thaw', such as Il'ya Ehrenburg, and of writers persecuted under Stalin such as Isaak Babel'.

Another interesting aspect of the response to the Soviet Union in *Sinn und Form* is the emphasis, in those contemporary Soviet works which are published, on the Soviet state as multi-national and representing a union of many traditions. Huchel is careful to include works by writers from outside the Great Russian mainstream, such as the Ukrainian Vasil Stefanik,[38] or Kimonko Dzhansi, from the tiny Udehé nation.[39] While this picture passes over in silence the forcible 'russification' of Soviet society, it does provide a voice for writers whose national identity was undervalued in their homeland. It seems to me, therefore, that Huchel's aim in presenting works from the Soviet Union is less to provide an 'objective' or 'realistic' picture of the country, but to provide a series of instructive contrasts with Germany; Soviet culture is still used as a tool for

---

[36] See, for example, Konrad Farner, 'Aus dem Reisetagebuch eines Schweizers. Gespräch mit Moskauer Künstlern', *Sinn und Form*, 3 (1952), no. 2, 138–51; Georges Sadoul, 'Ein Besuch in den Moskauer Ateliers', *Sinn und Form*, 4 (1953), no. 1, 168–71.

[37] Note, in particular, Becher's exercise in ultra-loyalism, 'Die Sowjetunion in meinem Gedicht', *Sonderheft Johannes R. Becher*, 1951.

[38] 'Zwei Erzählungen', *Sinn und Form*, 3 (1952), no. 5, 39–53.

[39] 'Wo der Sukpaj fließt ...', *Sinn und Form*, 3 (1952), no. 3, 62–72.

analysis of the German past and present, but some of the sense of freshness and open exchange has been replaced by the construction of a somewhat clichéd picture of a multicultural nation which provides a benchmark against which German culture can be judged.

By contrast, a pictureof American society emerges which is formed by authors, such as Langston Hughes and Clifford Odets, whose work was excluded from publications in the FRG. As Schoor says, this picture of US society is 'gezielt einseitig',[40] although it is consistent with Huchel's policy of publishing poetry of protest and revolution from around the world. However, the images which emerge here are signs of a change of emphasis after the journal was taken over by the Academy; the original aim of restoring German literature to its rightful place amongst the nations is still apparent, but the delicate process of literary *Vergangenheitsbewältigung* which was begun in the journal's first year is gradually overshadowed by Cold War concerns.

The Soviet Union and the USA emerge as opposing poles, between which Germany exists in a state of tension, on the threshold of a decision about its future. The development of the German nation thus depends on the exercise of political maturity in a choice between one of the two camps. This choice is not without reservations and ambiguities, but *Sinn und Form* has let itself into the struggle between the geographical and political expressions of the 'two camps' theory which was, in early 1952, dominated by those who backed the 'integrationist' line and who had fewer illusions about German unity. The emphasis is increasingly on the restoration of German nationhood in the choice between opposing clichéd images (the classic ideological operation of the Cold War) and less on the careful, drawn-out process of piecing together a sense of intellectual responsibility.

Huchel's determined stance, that the intellectual has no right to withdraw from the world, necessarily led *Sinn und Form* into the polarities of international politics in the 1950s, and explicit support for Stalin's initiatives in March and April 1952 made support for the GDR seem like the natural precondition for campaigning for German unity. The use of *Sinn und Form* for official pronouncements and commissions from the Academy, such as the 'Manifest' in

---

[40] Schoor, p. 71.

support of Stalin's March Note[41] or the special edition devoted to the 'Weltfest-spiele der Jugend' (5–19 August 1951),[42] contributed to the alignment of the journal with the GDR. However, as with the Academy, this alignment, though real, was critical and relatively open-minded rather than unquestioning; the contributions to *Sinn und Form* and the images of the outside world projected through them are selected for their relevance to acutely contemporary questions of German culture, and that meant unequivocally the whole of Germany. This is the issue over which Huchel could not compromise, and which led him to ignore all calls for the publication of reportage about the GDR.

A form of critical Marxism is being developed alongside the liberal humanism of writers like Zweig: the most important representative of this line is Ernst Bloch who, like Brecht, found that *Sinn und Form* was the only GDR publication which allowed him complete freedom of expression. Bloch's intellectual playfulness and his command of language were no doubt a threat to colleagues who justified their lesser talent with an increasing dogmatism, and contributions to *Sinn und Form* which argued, in a language familiar to the dogmatists, for a freer intellectual approach to political and aesthetic problems, were an effective intervention in the 'Realism Debate'. *Sinn und Form*'s approach is to avoid explicit definitions of Realism, but to register a protest against ever-narrowing aesthetic norms by keeping the debate open.[43]

Despite the increasingly strident nature of some of the contributions to *Sinn und Form*, and the inclusion of overtly political appeals, such as Brecht's call for freedom of expression,[44] Huchel and the writers whose interventions he published maintained the 'all-German' line of the journal. Brecht appeals for an end to division: 'Wenn [Deutsche] nicht miteinander sprechen, werden sie aufeinander schießen.' Even though it seemed possible to appeal to a significant

---

[41] As an insert in *Sinn und Form*, 3 (1952), no. 2.

[42] *Sinn und Form*, 2 (1951), no. 4.

[43] See, for example, the contrasting views in Paul Eluard's polemic against the imposition of Socialist Realist forms ('Die Gelegenheitsdichtung', *Sinn und Form*, 3 (1952), no. 4, 5–17), and, in the same issue, Becher's 'Verteidigung der Poesie' (27–61), which is essentially a plea for classical forms in literature.

[44] 'An die Künstler und Schriftsteller Deutschlands', *Sinn und Form*, 2 (1951), no. 5, 5. Similarly, Hanns Eisler's critical response to the Western music industry is intended as a means of promoting mutual understanding, as a protest against the separation of popular and avant-garde music in Western culture, and as a rejection of the simplistic *Volkstümlichkeit* demanded of GDR composers: 'Wir Komponisten müssen von den Hörern denselben Realismus verlangen, der mit Recht von uns gefordert wird' ('Brief nach Westdeutschland', *Sinn und Form*, 2 (1951), no. 6, 23).

opposition in the West to Adenauer's policy of rearmament and *Westintegration,* it should be noted,however, that this is simply a more pointed version of Becher's 'Beseitigung von Mißverständnissen', which presupposes identification with the GDR (with suitable criticism of 'bureaucratic excesses') as the embodiment of a peaceful policy. Nevertheless, we should not underestimate the good will which *Sinn und Form* could draw on in all parts of Germany, and Huchel avoided all-out polemics with the West, realising that each small step in the direction of cultural division was likely to be irrevocable. This was a delicate process, involving the cultivation of a West German readership and sympathetic voices in the press.

Huchel could count on support from colleagues in the Academy who shared his preoccupation with German cultural unity. The problem was that the maintenance of the Academy's declared 'all-German' line depended to a great extent on the good will of the membership, and since the Academy's institutional status was only vaguely defined, statements of principle had limited resonance within GDR society. As indicated previously, the tendency of artists to shrink from the minutiae of bureaucratic procedure left them unable to fully exploit their considerable room for manoeuvre. However, the Sektion Dichtkunst und Sprachpflege was able to ensure that Western writers were able to publish in *Sinn und Form*, and Becher went out of his way to try to overcome exchange rate problems so that West German writers could be paid in hard currency, or in GDR currency at three times the usual rate.[45] Similarly, the Sektion Dichtkunst passed a resolution criticising the GDR press for 'unkluge und schädliche polemische Artikel gegen westdeutsche Kulturschaffende und kulturelle Institutionen', and campaigned for the consideration of West German writers such as Hans Henny Jahnn for GDR national prizes.[46]

However, the notion of critical dialogue with the West was problematic for GDR artists who thought in terms of a dialectical *Auseinandersetzung* whose aim was to clear up misunderstandings about what they saw as the essentially peaceful policy of the SED. For example, Brecht suggested in November 1951 that *Sinn und Form*, because of the respect which it enjoyed in the FRG, should

---

[45] Protocol of 20 December 1950, cit., Schoor, pp. 129–30.
[46] Protocol of 6 November 1951, cit., Schoor, p. 129.

carry reportage about the achievements of the GDR, written by authors such as Kuba, Ludwig Renn, Michael Tschesno-Hell and Friedrich Wolf. This suggestion, which was not taken up, concerning what Schoor calls 'kulturelle Aufklärungsarbeit'[47] is a good example of the peculiar mixture of tactical astuteness and ideological naivety which characterises Brecht's interventions in GDR cultural politics. While recognising that a certain amount of compromise was necessary in order to protect *Sinn und Form* from attacks from an increasingly dominant 'integrationist' tendency in the Academy (although, as we have seen, the SED members in the Academy were far from forming a united front), Brecht's belief that the unity of Germany was an ideological necessity based on the unfolding of the dialectic blinded him to the fact that the inclusion of reportage in the journal would increase friction with the West rather than contributing to the clearing-up of misunderstandings. This seems to be the heart of the issue of the proposed changes to *Sinn und Form* in the run-up to June 1953. Huchel's original conception, based on irony, multiple viewpoints and continual open-ended dialogue as an end in itself, is defended by people who, probably without realising it, have an entirely different conception of culture; in other words, a dialectics of debate, which presupposes a final truth in line with the aims, if not necessarily the bureaucratic practice, of the SED, led to compromises with the regime which need not have been made.

For the time being, Becher was firmly in favour of this continued contact with Western artists and he defended Huchel's rejection of Friedrich Wolf's polemical article, 'Talent und Aussage', with the statement that *Sinn und Form* was 'hauptsächlich für Westdeutschland bestimmt'.[48] As we have seen, Becher's desire to cultivate dialogue with Western artists was genuine, but his words are ominous: if he is now simply concerned with the effect which the journal will have on opinion in the West, then its value as a means of promoting dialogue and intellectual responsibility inside the GDR is undermined. High-profile meetings and association with *Sinn und Form* were for Becher a useful

---

[47] Schoor, p. 133.

[48] Letter to Friedrich Wolf, 12 July 1951, Schoor, p. 127. Becher is referring to the need to prepare the ground for the meeting of the international PEN club meeting in Lausanne. Huchel's apparently curt rejection of Wolf's article was the cause of considerable bitterness: Wolf describes it as 'eine Verletzung des primitivsten Anstandes unter Schriftstellern' (letter to Becher, 10 July 1951, cit., Schoor, p. 233).

means of self-promotion, but they represented a retreat from a confrontation with the sordid realities of his involvement with the regime, and thus could be discarded in the interests of Party discipline. Becher was too weak and compromised to provide support for his pet projects after the declaration of the 'Aufbau des Sozialismus'.

The ideological consolidation which accompanied the rearmament of the GDR and the build-up to the Second Conference of the SED in July 1952 allowed the SED to tighten up Party discipline in cultural organisations, although this was by no means as simple in the Academy as it might have been in other institutions. As yet, the Party group was not strong or united enough in any of the Academy's sections to enable a direct bid for control, because internal discipline was still lacking. Nevertheless, the founding by Willi Bredel of *Neue Deutsche Literatur* during October 1952, as a forum for the development of Socialist Realism, provided a useful counter-example to use against *Sinn und Form*, which neglected the younger generation of GDR authors. Bredel's personal animus against Becher and Huchel was certainly a factor in the development of *Neue Deutsche Literatur*, souring the atmosphere in the Academy considerably. That personal rivalries could have such a profound effect on the development of GDR cultural institutions and policy is another indication of the lack of a coherent strategy on the part of the SED.

Plans to change the conception of *Sinn und Form* were already being discussed by the SED in the Autumn of 1952, although doubts among senior *Genossen* about Becher's protégé Alexander Abusch meant that the required consistency and unity of purpose was never achieved. Becher, who had always shown little inclination for organisational work, seems to have gone through a period of doubt or failing mental and physical health in mid-1952, and he cemented his recovery in a comforting return to Party discipline. The repercussions for *Sinn und Form* were serious, and Becher began to prepare to abandon Huchel, in order to secure his own career.

In November 1952, F. C. Weiskopf claimed that Becher had hinted to him that *Sinn und Form* was to undergo a change of character necessitating the replacement of Huchel, and that Weiskopf was to be considered for the editor's

position.[49] The meeting of the Academy's Presidium on 9 December 1952
marked the point at which the differences between Zweig and Becher, who
coveted the post of President, came out into the open. Becher prepares the
ground for the coming attacks on *Sinn und Form* by declaring that the journal
'mehr und mehr an literarischem Wert verliere'. Becher does not give concrete
examples to justify this criticism, presumably because it goes against his
instinctive respect for literary quality and his frequent criticisms of shallow
propagandistic poetry. He goes on to suggest that *Sinn und Form* should act as
'die ideologische Führung' for the Academy, indicating that the 'all-German'
policy and relative independence of the journal, for which Becher had himself
been largely responsible, were to be abandoned.[50]

The uneasy consensus between the leading members of the Academy's
Presidium began to unravel, reflecting the defeat of the genuine aspiration to
German unity which had formed the common ground between otherwise
irreconcilable ideological positions. The repercussions of Stalin's decisive
abandonment, at the Nineteenth Congress of the Soviet Communist Party, of
diplomatic efforts to secure German unity were filtering through the complex
causal network described in the course of this study; in ideological terms,
Stalin's new policy of integration of the GDR into Soviet security structures was
now in line with the use to which his authority had been put by Walter Ulbricht.
Since one of the reasons that the chains of command in Germany had been so
uncertain since 1945 was this friction between Stalin's ideological authority and
his actual ability to exercise power, the new alignment of forces in late 1952
provided a powerful boost to the 'integrationists' in the SED (amongst whom
we must now count Becher, in his capitulation to Party discipline).

The campaign to impose ideological conformity on the Academy took on a
new sense of purpose now that Becher was fully behind it and prepared to pull
his weight. The final case study will explore the controversies around *Sinn und
Form* and Hanns Eisler's *Faustus*, since the two issues are too interdependent to
be conveniently separated. However, the questions raised by the new

[49] Letter to Bredel, 12 November 1952, cit., Parker, '"Sinn und Form", Peter Huchel und der 17. Juni
1953', pp. 739–40.
[50] Cit., Parker, '"Sinn und Form", Peter Huchel und der 17. Juni 1953', p. 740.

constellation of forces ranged around *Sinn und Form* in the winter of 1952 are worth commenting on at this point, because they demonstrate the ways in which individuals interrelate with the ideological system.

Huchel's original conception for *Sinn und Form* had, in many ways, been compromised by its institutional association with the Academy, but this was compensated for by the measure of protection which the Academy offered for Huchel's continued (relative) independence. In terms of the journal's approach to *Vergangenheitsbewältigung*, the increasing polarisation of Cold War politics had necessitated a change of emphasis from a certain humility and a desire to avoid imposing unequivocal interpretations, a compromise with the reader over authority which was intended to demonstrate the value of open-minded critical thought as an end in itself, to a form of debate which presupposed that there was a truth towards which objective thought could proceed. That this latter, dialectical approach to literary and intellectual discourse could be at once tolerant and rigorous is clear from the case of Brecht; however, it could lead simultaneously to serious compromises with a regime which shared this predilection for imposing conformity to fixed meanings (for example, in the demand for 'Stellungnahme'). It is in the debate over *Sinn und Form* in 1953 that the irreconcilable differences between the protagonists, previously disguised by the common consensus over German unity, become obvious.

The changing conception of German nationhood which emerges in a careful reading of *Sinn und Form* was a calculated response to the SED's attempts to construct aform oflegitimacy from German cultural history, although we must be carefulnot to assume that there is an absolute opposition between the two ideas; this would be to impose an unacceptable model of 'dissidence' onto a situation which is far too ambiguous to be seen in terms of such polarities. The aspiration, expressed through *Sinn und Form*, to ease German culture back into the European mainstream by locating and developing values which were once held in common with the cultures of other countries, is played off against a critical scepticism about the ability of writer, intellectual or politician to define such values. No attempt is made on behalf of the reader to resolve this tension, which is at the heart of the vulnerability of GDR intellectuals to compromise with Party cultural policy: sometimes openly, as with Huchel's none-too-subtle digs at Becher, and sometimes with a sly, undermining irony undetectable even to Huchel and his contemporaries, *Sinn und Form* exposes the weaknesses of its own contributors.

CASE STUDY NO. 2:

BRECHT AND 'DAS VERHÖR DES LUKULLUS':

A STUDY IN REALPOLITIK?

The publication in 1993 of Joachim Lucchesi's documentation of the performance and banning of Bertolt Brecht and Paul Dessau's opera, *Das Verhör des Lukullus*,[51] was an important contribution to debate on GDR cultural policy which began to broaden with the assimilation of the mass of material which emerged after reunification. Detailed documentation and considered contextualisation of cultural-political controversies has provided an insight into the functioning of power in the GDR which calls into question many orthodox categories of debate. In this section, therefore, I intend to examine Lucchesi's documentation in the light of my analysis of the political and ideological context of the work of the Deutsche Akademie der Künste, not in order to retell the story of the controversy over Brecht and Dessau's work (which emerges with remarkable clarity in *Das Verhör in der Oper*) but to shed light on issues of intellectual accommodation with the GDR regime. It will become clear in the detail of this analysis, that the schematic 'Geist–Macht' dichotomy, which underlies the frequent categorisations of Brecht as either dissident or apologist, is untenable, and that we need to find new ways of understanding the role of German intellectuals in legitimising institutions of political authority.

Access to previously unpublished documents, particularly protocols of discussions in the Academy and the Central Committee of the SED, allows us to assess the extent of disagreement over the value of *Lukullus*, and provides an insight into the tactical uncertainty among thecultural functionaries which was all but obscured by the simplistic public rhetoric of the 'Formalism Debate'. Similarly, clashes of competence are brought to light between the Kulturabteilung of the Central Committee and the Ministerium für

---

[51] Joachim Lucchesi (ed.), *Das Verhör in der Oper. Die Debatte um die Aufführung 'Das Verhör des Lukullus' von Bertolt Brecht und Paul Dessau* (Berlin: BasisDruck Verlag, 1993). Several of the documents collected by Lucchesi also appear in abridged form in Dietzel and Geißler, pp. 105–11.

Volksbildung, and later concerning assertions of authority by the Staatliche Kommission für Kunstangelegenheiten. Most importantly, though, we gain a historically contextualised view of Brecht, allowing us to move beyond any tendency to try to impose a spurious unity onto his work, abstracted from the political considerations of his time, which can then be set in opposition to the exercise of power in the GDR. As we have seen, this model of 'dissidence' is a highly limiting view of responsibility which, in ignoring the complexities of power relations, contributed as much to the legitimisation of a 'West German' identity as to an understanding of GDR cultural policy. We should therefore take seriously Brecht's own interventions in the attempted creation of a national identity for the GDR, particularly with respect to the preservation of German cultural traditions.

The artists like Brecht and Dessau who were products of the avantgardism of the Twenties hoped to find in the GDR an atmosphere congenial to their needs; in this sense, they shared with the Neo-Classicism of Becher a hope that the new society would catch up with its artists. Less dogmatic than many of his contemporaries, Brecht refused to make an immutable principle out of this idea, hoping to avoid a fruitless polarisation of the debate between those who believed that artistic appreciation had to be learned, and those who declared that the arts 'bisher noch weit zurückgeblieben sind hinter den Forderungen des Tages'.[52] In his *Arbeitsjournal* for 25.3.1951, Brecht wrote:

Was die Absetzung des "Lukullus" angeht: es ist vorauszusehen, daß bei Umwälzungen von solchem Ausmaß die Künste selbst da in Schwierigkeiten kommen, wo sie führend mitwirken. Zusammenstoßen die Zurückgebliebenheit der Künste und die Zurückgebliebenheit des neuen Massenpublikums. Einige Künstler haben, in Protest gegen die bürgerliche Ästhetik (und den bürgerlichen Kunstbetrieb) gewisse neue Formen entwickelt; nunmehr werden sie von proletarischer Seite darauf aufmerksam gemacht, daß es nicht die Formen für die neuen Inhalte seien, dies stimmt manchmal, und manchmal stimmt es nicht. Manchmal nämlich werden die gewohnten Formen verlangt, weil die neuen Inhalte noch keineswegs allgemein

---

[52] Johannes R. Becher, 'Diskussionsbeitrag Johannes R. Bechers auf dem III. Parteitag der SED', 20. bis 24. Juli 1950, in *Dokumente zur Kunst-, Literatur-, und Kulturpolitik der SED*, ed. by Elimar Schubbe (Stuttgart: Seewald, 1972), p. 152.

bei der zur Herrschaft gelangten Klasse durchgesetzt sind und man die irrige Meinung hat, neuer Inhalt *und* neue Form sei schwerer durchzusetzen als nur eines von beiden.[53]

What emerges very clearly from Brecht's attitude here is the extent to which, for all his concern to avoid polarisation in the debate, he thinks in sociological categories which link him with the Proletkult theories which he absorbed during the Twenties.[54] Brecht felt that if one developed new forms suitable for a new age, there could be a direct meeting between 'Volk' and artist, without the mediation of functionaries: '[Gewisse Formalismus-Bekämpfer] selbst scheinen zum Volk nicht zu gehören. Dafür wissen sie genau, was das Volk will, und erkennen das Volk daran, daß es will, was sie wollen.'[55]

We come here to a central question: To what extent did Brecht idealise the 'Volk' for tactical reasons, that is, as a polemical weapon against his political opponents, and to what extent was it a sincerely held belief? It is tempting to reply that Brecht idealised the 'Volk' to exactly the same extent to which he compromised with the regime, that the ideological common ground was the source of his vulnerability. However, this would suggest consistency in ideological and administrative practice within the SED which cannot be supported by the evidence. It has become clear in the course of this study that there is no absolute distinction to be made between 'ideology' and 'real political practice' (a distinction which underlies many studies of GDR politics), so perhaps we should formulate the question in a different way: Was Brecht's favoured style of tactically combining theoretical and administrative self-defence a product of rational calculation or itself an expression of an ideologised view of the situation in which he worked? This question will underlie the analysis which follows.

Brecht and the regime were in a relationship of mutual need: each drew legitimacy from the other, and the SED's inconsistency and confusion reflect

---

[53] Bertolt Brecht, *Große kommentierte Berliner und Frankfurter Ausgabe*, ed. by Jan Knopf, Werner Hecht, Werner Mittenzwei and Klaus-Dieter Müller, 30 vols (Berlin: Aufbau and Frankfurt a. M.: Suhrkamp, 1989-1998), XXVII, p. 318. This edition hereafter referred to as *BFA*.

[54] Thus there is a certain amount of truth in Fred Oelßner's description of Brecht's adaptation of Gorky's 'Die Mutter' at the Central Committee meeting on 17 March 1951: '[...] das ist irgendwie eine Kreuzung oder Synthese von Meyer-hold und Proletkult' (cit. Lucchesi, p. 173).

[55] Brecht, *BFA*, XXVII, p. 528.

this problem. An obvious difficulty was Brecht's high international profile, which he exploited in order to protect more vulnerable colleagues. Paul Wandel summed up the leadership's dilemma succinctly during a discussion after the open rehearsal of *Lukullus* on 13 March 1951: 'Wenn wir nicht aufführen werden, wird man schreien. Wenn wir aufführen werden, wird man das, was wir im kleinen versucht haben, auch im großen versuchen.'[56] The SED leadership was genuinely feeling its way into new territory, and they were not sure how to proceed. International considerations, and the still incomplete victory of the 'integrationist' line, which needed to overcome the 'persönliche Sympathie' of Wilhelm Pieck for Brecht's work,[57] meant that a full-scale assault could not yet be made on such a well-known figure, and the prestige of the Academy provided some protection.[58]

Because of the continuing need to give public support to Stalin's campaign for German unity, there is an uncomfortable clash of principles, forming an area of tension in which a quick-witted artist like Brecht can move and create. The need to project the GDR as a society where artists can work openly, keeping the 'all-German' option open, clashes irreconcilably with the urgent necessity of creating a national identity based on the exclusion of the Federal Republic. Since the latter option was the only possible way of justifying the rule of the SED, these were difficult times. We have seen where Becher and Peter Huchel were positioned in this scheme, the former trying to pursue both aims at once, the latter retreating into an indirect, allusive, but often highly effective form of political engagement. However, Brecht is perhaps a more challenging case.

In terms of his political role in the GDR, Brecht's international profile and his relative independence of action were both an advantage and a disadvantage. They were a disadvantage in the sense that he had a tendency to misjudge the

---

[56] Cit. Lucchesi, p. 120. There are two protocols of this meeting on 13 March 1951, the first (Lucchesi, pp. 83–101) the official protocol of the Ministerium für Volksbildung, and the second taken by Käthe Rülicke of the Berliner Ensemble (pp. 101–22).

[57] Werner Mittenzwei, *Das Leben des Bertolt Brecht, oder Der Umgang mit den Welträtseln*, 2 vols (Frankfurt a. M.: Suhrkamp, 1989), II, p. 358. Ulbricht's attitude was very different, rooted in the educational aspiration of the early socialist movement. Experiments such as Brecht's, which relied on an attitude of healthy disrespect for German classical traditions, were seen as an affront to the efforts of ordinary workers to master the great works of German literature.

[58] It was in early 1952 that attacks from the Party became deadly earnest without the concession of extensive discussions with Brecht. Cf. Resolution of Abteilung Kultur of the Central Committee, 2 February 1952, demanding 'ein Exposé über die Arbeit des formalistischen Brecht-Kreises', cit. Lucchesi, p. 278.

deeper causes of problems which he felt were merely temporary manifestations of petty bureaucracy;[59] this presumably explains his constant engagement and his willingness to arrive meticulously prepared for any fight.[60] The reason for such a paradoxical combination of clear-sightedness and self-delusion is, of course, that Brecht genuinely believed in 'the cause'. There is a revealing entry in Käthe Rülicke's diary for 12 March 1951: 'Gestern Sonntag mit Brecht: Außer von Becher und sich selbst glaube er von niemandem, daß sie ehrlich für die Republik seien. Sie "machen mit".'[61] Brecht's sense of his significance as an artist depended very much on the legitimacy which the existence of the GDR gave to his experimentation and his antifascism. He therefore took great care with his public interventions, always considering the damage which overt criticism could do to the image of the GDR in the West, and his most damning statements were left unpublished. As Manfred Jäger puts it: '[...] ein Potential war da, das Bertolt-Brecht-Archiv war da: auch späte Wirkungen waren noch Wirkungen',[62] but we should be careful to distinguish between the use to which Brecht's work was put after his death and the considerations which motivated him at the time.

One of the most important of these ideological considerations was Brecht's particular interpretation of the 'deutsche Misere' theory, according to which Germany had failed to take its destiny into its own hands and follow the 'progressive' step of consolidating as a nation out of the end of feudalism, and thus had failed to bring about a bourgeois revolution in 1848. The 'progressive' classes in Germany had consequently never been able to fulfil their responsibility as historical actors, and German politics had been the province of foreign powers and the reactionary classes. The failure of the German people to overthrow Hitler was the major difficulty; the Soviet Union, in its war of

---

[59] Brecht's ideologised view of the circumstances in the GDR, and his displacement of blame for the development of the dictatorship on to the remnants of Nazi bureaucracy, is demonstrated in his 'Vorwort zu Turandot' of 1953, *BFA*, XXIV, pp. 409–10.

[60] A particularly good example is the effective self-defence which Brecht and HeleneWeigel, who was also a master of this kind of fight, carried off at the Stanislavsky Conference, 17–19 April 1953: cf. the account in Jäger, pp. 61–65.

[61] Cit. Lucchesi, p. 78. The entry continues: 'B. für die Notwendigkeit einer Übergangsdiktatur, die zwar viele Härten und Ungerechtigkeiten mit sich bringt, aber in der es um Sein oder Nichtsein geht. Ästhetische Probleme sind da zweitrangig.' Brecht was perfectly well aware of the nature of Soviet dictatorship, and yet he was still capable of considering it a lesser evil. Perhaps he imagined it was a dictatorship of people who 'mitmachen' (Käthe Rülicke was a production assistant at the Berliner Ensemble 1950–1956.)

[62] Jäger, p. 67.

liberation, had taken on the role which the German proletariat was supposed to perform. In other words, class consciousness was lagging behind the historical situation in which the population of the Soviet-occupied part of Germany found itself, and Brecht's dramatic technique was designed to help in the creation of a new consciousness. By shifting the burden of interpretation towards the spectator, Brecht's plays were designed to begin the slow process of forging a sense of historical responsibility which could not come from the action of outside parties like the Soviet Union, however beneficial their influence. His later poetry works in a similar way, and this technique is what gives his criticisms of the regime their memorable resonance.

Brecht, in his proposed solution to the 'deutsche Misere', attempts a unity of political and artistic theory and practice: responsibility lies in being able to create one's own meanings. This unity is naturally rather strained, requiring a set of theoretical acrobatics familiar in left-wing German intellectuals struggling to fit fascism into the dialectic. It also depends on a view of the GDR as embodying, at least in potential, the unity of theory and practice promised by Marxism, and in which Marxist intellectuals saw their own self-justification. Thus, in a way which contrasts fascinatingly with Becher, Brecht's theoretical stance and his self-image as an intellectual provide the context for both resistance and complicity; his aspirations to *Realpolitik* are only part of the story.

The extensive discussions over *Das Verhör des Lukullus* offer an important insight into the ways in which the theoretical principles outlined above were applied in practice. The interpretation which emerges from Lucchesi's documentation, that the early formalism campaigns were characterised by uncertainty and disunity within the SED and between Party and state institutions, and that the discussions were concerned with serious issues of legitimacy and freedom of expression as well as being part of a bid for dominance by a harder line associated with Walter Ulbricht, is supported by the evidence discussed in previous chapters. However, this interpretation suffers from a lack of contextualisation which underplays the significance of *Lukullus* for the SED's search for sources of legitimacy. What is lacking is an understanding of the fundamental reasons for moving against Brecht and

Dessau, beyond the assertion of administrative control over the 'intelligentsia' and the expression of the personal prejudices of various functionaries.

The 'integrationists' within the SED were attempting to walk a delicate ideological tightrope (a balancing act which became easier as their administrative dominance increased): a positive national identity had to be developed which could present the GDR as the continuation of progressive and rationalistic traditions in German history, which had finally found a physical expression in a separate state. Thus, any interpretation of history which shows that the German people (or a particular class: peasantry, proletariat, intelligentsia) was unable to make history in its own right, would inevitably threaten that identity, and thus the legitimacy of the SED, whose members saw themselves as the embodiment of the active and progressive historical principle. However, the only possible physical source of legitimacy was the Soviet Union, and so this feeling of national resurgence had somehow to be reconciled with a policy of absolute dependence on Soviet military power and on 'Stalin' as the ultimate source of all legitimacy. The ambivalence of the Soviet leadership towards the GDR complicated this matter considerably; the 'integrationists' were obliged to pursue a policy of increasing identification with Stalin, who was interested in detaching Germany from the immediate Soviet sphere. Walter Ulbricht gradually turned this situation to his own advantage, by creating a sense of his own legitimacy as Stalin's representative, so that Stalin was obliged to use Ulbricht as his only means of access to influence in internal German politics. However, until Stalin's concession of the remilitarisation of the GDR in early 1952, the 'integrationist' line lacked the final confirmation of the Germans' ability to make their own history.

For this reason, the accusation that the passivity of the Roman peasants in *Lukullus* and the trial in the Underworld were an admission of political powerlessness was more than just an ideological weapon designed to keep an unruly artist in line; it actually went to the very heart of the SED's problems of legitimacy:

Das Weltfriedenslager mit seinen mehr als 800 Millionen unter der Führung der Sowjetunion ist nicht nur kein 'Schattengericht', sondern es hat die reale Macht, alle Kriegsverbrecher einer sehr irdischen Gerichtsbarkeit zu unterwerfen.[63]

The tone of aggressive self-assertion which characterised the hysterical press campaign accompanying the debate is deceptive, and it would be a mistake to infer any kind of united strategy or ideological conformity from public pronouncements designed to give an impression of strength; Lucchesi's work confirms that this was a conflict, 'dessen Fronten quer durch die Lager der Diskutanten verliefen'.[64] At times, the fate of *Lukullus* seems to hang from the outcome of an administrative war of attrition, which neither side could afford to lose: the Party keeps up the pressure by concentrating on petty details, such as criticising the writer of the programme notes at the Deutsche Staatsoper[65] or requesting reserved tickets for the Ministerium für Staatssicherheit.[66] Brecht and Dessau's delaying tactics, persuading Party officials that the music should not be judged on the basis of a piano score, in order to present them with a *fait accompli* when the production was ready to be performed, met with irritation[67] but were partially successful, because the leadership realised the significance of the debate. Brecht and Dessau had achieved the desired resonance in the Federal Republic through a production in Frankfurt am Main in January and February 1952.[68]

The debate over the Berlin production of *Lukullus* was intended as a showpiece for artists in the GDR, and a proposed production in Dresden in

---

[63] Review by Heinz Lüdecke, '"Das Verhör des Lukullus": Ein mißlungenes Experiment in der Deutschen Staatsoper', *Neues Deutschland*, 22 March 1951, text in Schubbe, pp. 186–87. In the next day's edition, *Neues Deutschland* printed excerpts from Hans Lauter's speech at the vital Central Committee meeting of 15–17 March, in which *Lukullus* was condemned as 'ein Beispiel des Formalismus', thus attempting to create, entirely unconvincingly, the impression of a response to public pressure.

[64] Lucchesi, p. 19.

[65] Lucchesi, p. 52.

[66] Lucchesi, pp. 66–67.

[67] Cf. repeated requests from the Ministerium für Volksbildung, Lucchesi, pp. 57–58, and Paul Wandel's con-descending tone at the meeting on 13 March 1951, to which Brecht replies that the as yet incomplete staging will produce and entirely different effect on the audience, and that the production team should be given more time: 'Sie hören eine Musik vollkommen anders, wenn Sie dazu etwas anderes sehen. Sie ist geschrieben zu etwas, was Sie sehen sollen.' Note how, with Brecht, tactical manoeuvre and artistic principle are inseparable, reflecting Brecht's belief that the GDR embodies the *potential* to fulfil his ideological needs, and that it is just a question of clearing obstacles out of his way (Lucchesi, pp. 120–21).

[68] Cf. letter from the conductor Hermann Scherchen to Brecht, 2 February 1952: '[...] trotz der gespannten Atmo-sphäre — : 26 Vorhänge!' (Lucchesi, p. 277.)

early 1951 was banned by the Central Committee.[69] The uncertainty which this demonstrates about the effect of the production on its audiences is reflected in the decision of the Ministerium für Volksbildung in February 1951 that the Staatsoper's tickets should have slogans printed on them.[70] Once again, this nervous tinkering should by no means be seens as a sign of confidence on the part of the administration, but it reflects a fear of misinterpretations, of unpredictable audience responses forming independent meanings. Brecht's theatrical practice embodies this threat to the authority over language implied in the communist *Führungsanspruch*, although he consciously leads his audiences towards a particular interpretation. If we compare this practice with the pluralism of *Sinn und Form*, a telling contrast emerges: in both cases, the *production* of meaning on the part of the reader/spectator is what counts, but whereas with Brecht, there is an end to the process, a final synthesis at which the dialectic of his plays are aimed, *Sinn und Form* is guided by the principle that significance lies in the *absence* of a final meaning, that the process is an end in itself. Thus, although both Brecht and Peter Huchel work by the principle that political and artistic responsibility consists in allowing the reader/spectator space to construct meanings (which requires an equally serious engagement in return), only Brecht could believe that appeals to the sensibilities of Walter Ulbricht would contribute to the removal of bureaucratic obstacles.[71] Ideological preconceptions have immensely practical consequences, and cannot be considered in isolation from administrative methods.

Dessau's music presented similar ideological problems for the administration: not only was it not immediately approachable for listeners brought up on a pedantic respect for classical norms (although the responses of representatives from various mass organisations at the discussion after the open rehearsal on 13 March 1951 are by no means all negative), but, in conjunction with the text, it raised disturbing questions of meaning and interpretation. The fragmentary nature of the music, with no higher strings and an impressive array

---

[69] Resolution of Abteilung Kultur of Central Committee, 1 February 1951, Lucchesi, pp. 63–64.
[70] Lucchesi, p. 71.
[71] Cf. letter from Brecht to Ulbricht, 12 March 1951, Lucchesi, p. 81. There are echoes here of Becher's concern with 'Beseitigung von Mißverständnissen', and a similar inability to challenge ideology in the light of experience, rather than vice versa.

of percussion, is challenging, although it is by no means as tuneless as many of Dessau's accusers claim. However, Dessau's approach to melody, and his response to the text, are of a piece with avantgardistic concerns to explore cognitive responses to musical form. A melody structured with the harmonic and rhythmic balance characteristic of Classicism strives for a resolution or closure which is an end in itself. Naturally, the greatest composers exploited and undermined the listener's expectations of balance and resolution, but listeners in later ages, with different assumptions, may no longer experience this formal experimentation as shock, humour or a means of achieving psychological depth: the meaning of the musical passage, which consisted precisely in the undermining of a formal structure, is lost in the experience of closure.[72] Dessau seems to me to be trying to force a response to Brecht's text by not allowing the listener to take refuge in fulfilled expectations: perhaps a contemporary response to Beethoven's formal experi-mentation (such as his approach to word-setting in the *Missa Solemnis,* in which he exposes the contradictions, tensions and dramatic potential of the over-familiar Latin mass).

As a Party member, Dessau comes under more serious attack than Brecht; the music is an easier target for the SED, as most of its members can rally round in their dislike of it. It does not seem to embody unresolved ideological problems in the way that Brecht's text does, although Brecht is right in insisting that the two cannot be considered separately (another example of a point of principle coinciding with the tactical need to protect the more vulnerable Dessau). Dessau's experience of the pressures under which he had to work contrasts strikingly with Brecht's. Dessau responds with an affronted irony, a tone which Eisler was to adopt after the banning of his *Faustus* libretto:

[...] Ich bin angeklagt der Isolation.
Ich kann nicht sprechen und wollte gar nicht sprechen.

---

[72] Brecht makes a similar point: 'Wenn man nur alte Musik als exemplarisch hinstellt, benutzt man Musik, die konfliktlos erscheint, weil die Konflikte, die sie gestaltet, heute in der Realität gelöst sind. Wie sollen wir mit diesen Exempeln vor den Ohren die Konflikte unserer Zeit, die ungelösten, gestalten?' (cit. Lucchesi, p. 185). The dialectic is everything for Brecht, and his identification of musical form with social change is too close. However, statements like this make clear the task which Brecht and Dessau set themselves. Brecht's private assessment of the music is typically reserved: 'Ihre Schönheit ist mit verhältnismäßig wenig Studium erfaßbar' (cit. Lucchesi, p. 191).

Ich bin in keiner Isolation [...] Ich bin mit großer Freude dem Ruf der FDJ gefolgt, einen Chor zu übernehmen. Heute stehe ich im Werk Oberschönweide als Leiter eines neu aufzubauenden Chores. Ich tue das aus Liebe nicht nur zu unserer Bevölkerung, sondern aus Liebe zur Musik. Es ist nicht so, daß ich die Werktätigen hasse, aber ich hasse aus tiefstem Herzen den schlechten Geschmack der Massen. Auch das ist der Grund, daß ich morgen um 5 Uhr im Traktorenwerk Oberschönweide arbeite.

Ich bin nicht isoliert, ich bin isoliert von einer kleinen Schicht der Bevölkerung, einer kleinen Schicht. Ich fühle mich zu Hause in der Deutschen Demokratischen Republik wie in keinem Lande der Welt.[73]

By contrast, Brecht can continue to examine even the most hostile criticism for instructive lessons, and can profess to find the discussion 'erfrischend und lehrreich'.[74]

For all the attempts by various parties to turn the debate into a direct confrontation, Lucchesi is right to state, 'es ging hier nicht um pure Gegnerschaft, um unlösbare Widersprüche'.[75] There is a considerable overlap between, say, the positions of Brecht and Dessau and that of Kuba: 'Unser Volk ist unser Publikum und unser Auftraggeber.'[76] The difference lies in the willingness of one side to use administrative measures to impose a set of meanings. With his belief in a truth which the spectator will reach given the correct set of directions, Brecht belongs partially in this camp, although he, like Dessau, believes that the new type of audience, whom the GDR offers the opportunity to claim the theatre for their own, need to be educated in the understanding of art. For Brecht, this is a dialectical problem, whereas Dessau simply deplores 'bad taste'. While those in the leadership who had some sympathy for this view were able to hold their own against Ulbricht's line, the discussions could be carried out in an atmosphere that was not entirely hostile.

The Central Committee meeting of 15–17 March 1951 was a landmark in the development of the formalism campaign.[77] An example was to be made of

---

[73] Dessau at the meeting on 13 March 1951, Lucchesi, p. 113. Eva Fritzsche makes the following statement on Dessau's style: 'Ich habe den Eindruck, daß Paul Dessau den schlechten Geschmack mehr haßt, als den imperialistischen Krieg' (Lucchesi, p. 119).

[74] Letter to Berthold Viertel, June/July 1951, cit. Lucchesi, p. 243.

[75] Lucchesi, p. 21.

[76] Cit. Lucchesi, p. 95.

[77] See Lucchesi, pp. 127–77, for the protocol of the discussion on point 7 of the agenda ('Der Kampf gegen den Formalismus in der Kunst') on 17 March, with Hans Lauter's speech. The resolution, 'Der Kampf gegen den Formalismus in Kunst und Literatur, für eine fortschrittliche deutsche Kultur', is in Schubbe, pp. 178–86.

Lukullus, and the premiere was arranged for 17 March as a closed performance, so that press reaction could be coordinated with the Central Committee deliberations, and a meeting of the Sektion Musik of the Academy had produced the unedifying spectacle of senior musicians distancing themselves from Dessau.[78] Hans Lauter's speech on the motion condemning formalism in the arts forms the basis of the ideological attacks on Brecht and others, and it is notable that the definition of formalism is vague enough so that the whole leadership can agree to it; this is the semantic flexibility of Marxist-Leninist rhetoric discussed in Chapter Four, and which ultimately favours the most hard-line position.

As far as *Lukullus* is concerned, the core of the issue is the attitude to tradition and national legitimacy which emerges in Lauter's speech:

Der Kosmopolitismus, der das nationale Bewußtsein der Völker zerstören soll, ist die Wurzel des Formalismus, der nämlich das nationale Kulturerbe, der die Grundlage der nationalen Kultur in seiner Art von einer anderen Seite aus zerstört und darum von dieser Seite aus dazu beiträgt, das Nationalbewußtsein zu unterminieren, es zu schwächen und zu zerstören.[79]

Formalism casts doubt on the existence of 'progressive' currents in German culture, and thus jeopardises the legitimacy of the SED, as the embodiment of these currents, and, by extension, the legitimacy of the GDR. It is thus intimately linked with the 'deutsche Misere' theory. Brecht's questioning attitude towards the 'classics' was incompatible with the definition of Realism which emerges here, although he would claim that his methods better fulfilled the demands of a Marxist Realism, namely, to depict 'die Probleme des Volkes richtig, und was die Hauptsache ist, in ihrer Entwicklung'.[80] By exposing the ideological contradictions in artistic products of a particular period, Brecht hoped to demonstrate the direction of the dialectic concealed in social conditions, rather than projecting current conditions (suitably idealised)

---

[78] Lucchesi, pp. 124–25. The criticisms expressed here are far harsher than among the lay public of 13 March, speaking of professional jealousy and careerism. The protocol closes with members falling over each other to declare their enthusiasm for writing 'correct' music.

[79] Cit. Lucchesi, p. 137.

[80] Cit. Lucchesi, p. 135.

backwards into the past.[81] That the distinction between these two positions is subtle, to say the least, is one of the reasons for Brecht's continued willingness to go along with criticism from the Party. The central difference lies in the idea of responsibility: Brecht's insistence that the 'Volk' can be allowed to find its own way to the only possible conclusion threatens not only the *Führungsanspruch*, but also the self-image of Party intellectuals who found their justification in 'consciousness-raising'.

There is an interesting text in Lucchesi's documentation which comes to grips with this question of political and artistic responsibility in defence of *Lukullus*[82]:

[...] wer nicht des ungewohnten, aufrührenden, und *formellen* Kunstgenusses fähig ist, ist auch nicht der aktiven und sogar schöpferischen Teilnahme an der Politik fähig.
Die unmittelbare Hingabe der Werktätigen an Tschaikowsky, Mussorgsky, Lehár, Chopin, Offenbach usw. ist wesentlich derselbe Vorgang, wie das unmittelbare Mißfallen der Werktätigen an allem Krieg und an aller Staatsaktion und am Staat: es ist die Bestätigung der praktischen Machtlosigkeit und Unmenschlichkeit.[83]

The author takes direct issue with the now official SED position, that *Lukullus* reflects a form of elitism which, in claiming that the 'masses' require education before they can take over responsibility for their own governance, simply bolsters the class dominance of the 'bourgeois'. The seriousness of this debate should not be underestimated: the SED, as direct *representative* of the working class gains its legitimacy from the idea that this class has already achieved political power. Any signs of independence of thought or action on the part of individuals from the 'masses' is thus understood as a challenge to the overall dominance of the working class.

In these terms, the debate rapidly becomes polarised, so that ideas, which previously shared a remarkable amount of common ground, are simplified, and participants in the debate are forced to identify themselves with one of the

---

[81] This is the implication of the criticism of *Lukullus* in *Neues Deutschland*, cited above.

[82] May, 1951, Lucchesi, pp. 216–20. The author of these notes is unknown; they seem to be in the form of a *Diskussionsbeitrag* for a meeting.

[83] Lucchesi, p. 220. Emphasis in original. The author is referring to the accusations that *Lukullus* advocated a policy of complete pacifism.

camps. The example cited above, which expresses the intentions behind *Lukullus* in somewhat extreme terms, shows that those who wanted to defend Brecht and Dessau were finding themselves increasingly exposed. Sympathisers in the Academy, particularly in the notably obstreperous Sektion Darstellende Kunst, which consisted at this point largely of old friends of Brecht and Helene Weigel, protested about the proposed banning of the opera,[84] and there are examples of extraordinary courage on the part of people like Ernst Legal, Arnold Zweig, who defied the Central Committee on 17 March in defence of his friends,[85] and Hermann Scherchen, who dedicated himself to performances of *Lukullus* in all parts of Germany.[86] Brecht, knowing that Dessau was running a far greater risk because of his Party membership, wrote the text for the cantata *Herrnburger Bericht*, 'nicht zuletzt, um ihm [Dessau] Gelegenheit zu geben, verhältnismäßig einfache Musik beizusteuern'.[87]

Nevertheless, Brecht was obliged to agree to alterations to the text, after a meeting with Wilhelm Pieck on 24 March. Although Pieck was willing to allow further performances after suitable alterations, internal SED communications show no such awareness of the subleties of the debate: *Lukullus* is simply a 'formalistische Oper'.[88] In ideological terms, the functionaries whom Ulbricht was winning over to his line were capable of understanding the debate only where it concerned threats to their authority. The changes which were agreed by Brecht, Pieck and Dessau were a response to this tendency to fix meaning into cliché; the ideological message of the opera is to be made more explicit, so that the spectator is given less space to form interpretations independently. This is reflected in the alteration of the title to *Die Verurteilung des Lukullus*, as if to suggest that, previously, the audience could have come away from the production favourably disposed towards the figure of Lukullus.

The alterations, including the insertion of scenes suggesting that big business is behind Lukullus' wars of conquest, that the common people actively

---

[84] Cf. Lucchesi, pp. 203–4.

[85] Cf. his speech in Lucchesi, pp. 168–72.

[86] Scherchen was fired from his job as Musical Director of Radio Beromünster, Switzerland, in 1950, for his insistance on conducting behind the 'Iron Curtain'.

[87] Brecht, *Arbeitsjournal* entry, 3 July 1951, in *BFA*, XXVII, p. 322.

[88] Letter from Egon Rentzsch at the Kulturabteilung of the Central Committee to the local Party leadership, Erfurt, 27 April 1951, cit. Lucchesi, p. 213.

condemn him, and that the text is directed only against wars of aggression, not of self-defence, satisfied the Politburo sufficiently for permission to be granted for a new production in the Autumn.[89] Brecht sets about publicly justifying the changes, and the Formalism Debate, out of his concern for the international standing of the GDR:

In Wirklichkeit sind Erscheinungen wie die Formalismus-Realismus-Debatte ohne Kenntnis der großen [gesellschaftlichen] Umwälzungen nicht zu verstehen und also auch nicht zu beurteilen.
Daß die Neu-Organisation, schon durch die ökonomische und politische Umwälzung, auf dem kulturellen Gebiet ohne Irrtümer und Fehler vor sich geht, kann kein vernünftiger Mensch erwarten.[90]

Considering that the Staatliche Kommission für Kunstangelegenheiten had been working since Summer 1951, systematically obstructing the work of artists in the GDR, the veneer of Brecht's *Realpolitik* is wearing very thin. It is beginning to look as if he needs the GDR to legitimise his life's work more than the GDR needs him: after January 1952, the 'integrationists' have solved their problems of legitimacy by achieving remilitarisation, and any reminder of the 'deutsche Misere', which questions the German people's role as positive historical actor, is an obstacle.

Nevertheless, the Kunstkommission was still unable to exert its authority over the proposed new production of *Lukullus*, indicating possible conflicts of interest between state and Party institutions, and the performances went ahead in October 1951.[91] This is a moment of respite before attacks on Brecht begin

---

[89] Resolution of Politburo, 15 May 1951.

[90] Letter to Günther Strupp, 18 January 1952, cit. Lucchesi, pp. 275–76. Note that this date marks the beginning of the run-up to the declaration of the 'Aufbau des Sozialismus' with Stalin's agreement to the remilitarisation of the GDR. See also Brecht's speech at the Cultural Congress, 16–18 May 1951, 'Einige Bemerkungen über mein Fach', in *BFA*, XXIII, pp. 150–52.

[91] Cf. the series of exasperated letters in September 1951 (Lucchesi, pp. 263–65) from Kurt Bork at the Kunst-kommission to Ernst Legal, demanding to see the new score, before permission can be granted for performance: 'Wir hatten Ihnen mitgeteilt, daß eine Terminierung in der Angelegenheit "Lukullus" nur nach Genehmigung der neuen Partitur erfolgen könne. Einem Gespräch mit Ihnen entnehmen wir, daß die Aufführung des "Lukullus" bereits für den 11. Oktober 1951 angesetzt worden ist. Bei der Festsetzung des Termins stützen Sie sich auf eine Unterredung, die bei uns stattgefunden hat. Erlauben Sie uns, doch darauf hinzuweisen, daß hier ein Mißverständnis vorliegen muß' (29 September 1951, Lucchesi, p. 265). With evident relish, Lucchesi follows these letters with Legal's reply, in which he states bluntly that the performance will go ahead anyway (1 October 1951, Lucchesi, p. 266).

again in 1952, but it seems to have been enough to convince him that the GDR
has the potential to become the kind of society where his art is appreciated.

Brecht deliberately evades confrontation with the realities of cultural life in
the GDR, considering that the changes to *Lukullus* represent 'die Beseitigung
einiger möglicher Mißverständnisse'.[92] This phrase, with its echo of Becher's
self-justifications, lies at the heart of the problem: Brecht cannot help
considering problems in the light of his dedication to the practical application
of the dialectic (in this, he is much more down-to-earth than Becher). For this
reason, he searches all criticisms for the point of principle, so that he can
project a positive image of the GDR both to the West and to himself.

The changes to *Lukullus* are a case in point. Brecht's dramatic technique
consists in allowing the spectator to arrive independently at a predefined
conclusion; the compromise which he comes to with the SED is thus a natural
one. Since both sides were agreed on the nature of the conclusion, making
explicit the meaning at the end of the opera could be seen as a compromise over
methodology, rather than on principle, and Brecht could justify it in terms of
historical change:

[...] als ich vor dem Zweiten Weltkrieg 'Das Verhör des Lukullus' schrieb, schien es mir
überflüssig, die Verurteilung des Angreifers hinzuzufügen. Jetzt, nach diesem Krieg, scheint
es mir nötig, und mein Vertrauen auf die Urteilskraft der Leute kommt mir nur noch
merkwürdig vor.[93]

However, the abandonment of a committment to the inculcation of a sense of
responsibility in the German people was far more than a mere methodological
matter; it contributed directly to the legitimisation of a political line which
strove for the further integration of the GDR into the Soviet sphere (although,
as became clear in June 1953, the triumph of this line was by no means as
secure as it seemed).

Brecht's remarkable ability to combine tactical manoeuvre and principled
argument was in many ways his greatest strength, and yet his need for the
legitimacy which the GDR granted to his work drove this ability to a point

---

[92] Letter to Wilhelm Pieck, 6 April 1951, cit. Lucchesi, p. 206.
[93] Letter to Dolf Sternberger, March 1952, cit. Lucchesi, p. 278.

where he was unable himself to distinguish tactic and principle. Since the progression of his life's work would have had no goal were it not for the existence of the GDR (as a necessary synthesis emerging from the defeat of Nazism), he had to believe that this society would develop further in a positive direction. The privileges which he was granted by the regime naturally helped his thought processes along this path, and, paradoxically, his non-Party status gave him a rosier view of SED rule than might otherwise have been the case.

Thus, we can identify precisely the area in which Brecht fought out issues of resistance and complicity. He cultivated with remarkable dedication his self-image as *Realpolitiker*, making compromises with power for the sake of his work, which he hoped would contribute to the long-term improvement of the GDR. However, he could not foresee the consequences of his compromises because his understanding of the nature of SED rule was in itself highly ideologised. The GDR in which he pursued his *Realpolitik* was not the GDR in which he lived.

CASE STUDY NO. 3:

'ICH MEIN DAS GANZE: DEUTSCHLAND!'[1]

HANNS EISLER'S *FAUSTUS* AND THE PROBLEM OF NATIONAL IDENTITY

This final case study will examine the controversy within the Academy over Eisler's libretto for his planned opera, *Johann Faustus*, which was to be a model for 'die deutsche Nationaloper' in the GDR.[2] Eisler's work was seized on by the increasingly confident 'integrationist' grouping amongst the Party members in the Academy as 'das Exempel, um den Künstlern das Rückgrat zu brechen'.[3] This debate, along with the attempts to impose alterations on *Sinn und Form*, is important in several respects. First, it was intended to demonstrate the security of the SED's grip on power. Such a demonstration was vital since, despite the triumph of the 'integrationist' line at the Second Conference, the rearmament of the GDR, and the state's acceptance into the Soviet Bloc, the leadership had only just managed to prevent Ulbricht falling victim to the Slánský purge in December 1952. The problems became more acute after Stalin's death when factional conflicts within the Soviet Politburo began to have repercussions in Germany.

Second, the SED had, since the Third Party Congress in 1950, attempted to construct a new sense of national identity which would justify the Party's leading role and portray the GDR as the legitimate successor to all progressive movements in German history. This new sense of national resurgence depended on a suspension of all literary *Vergangenheitsbewältigung*, which might stir up uncomfortable questions about past KPD failures and the complicity of ordinary Germans in National Socialism. Since this concept of nationhood depended

[1] Hanns Eisler, *Johann Faustus: Oper* (Berlin: Aufbau-Verlag, 1952), act 1, scene 6, p. 32. Extracts from Eisler's libretto also appeared in *Sinn und Form*, 3 (1952), no. 6, 21–58.

[2] Ernst Fischer, 'Doktor Faustus und der deutsche Bauernkrieg', *Sinn und Form*, 3 (1952), 59–73 (73).

[3] Hans Bunge, *Die Debatte um Hanns Eislers 'Johann Faustus'. Eine Dokumentation* (Berlin: BasisDruck Verlag, 1991), p. 19.

crucially on identification with the Soviet Union as guarantor of German unity, any further independent thinking about Nazism had to be suppressed in case it led to problematic comparisons with Soviet terror or criticism (or even mention) of the Hitler-Stalin Pact. For SED functionaries who had survived the years of exile in the Soviet Union, it was particularly important that these matters should not be discussed.

The tenuousness of the SED's claim to power is clear to us with the benefit of hindsight, but the ideological arguments had a great influence on many politicians and intellectuals at the time, as they seemed to offer a justification for their efforts. Perhaps Walter Ulbricht saw the danger with greater clarity than his colleagues and rivals: he understood that the SED could only hope to retain any influence in German politics if the GDR was fully protected by Soviet military power. Any reunification of Germany or liberalisation (as Beria proposed) would expose the SED's unpopularity and end in electoral disaster. Many in the GDR only became aware of the Party's lack of legitimacy and support in June 1953.

Thus, the ideological issues were a matter of real importance in this crucial period, and anything which threatened the SED's drive to bind the intelligentsia into its camp was liable to expose the fraudulence of the new Party approach to history and national identity. The controversy over the *Faustus* libretto both reflects and intervenes in this tense political atmosphere. It is the key issue in an understanding of the relationship of the older generation of intellectuals in the GDR to the establishment of SED power, and the debate is important not only as an example of SED tactics, but also in the substance of the arguments.

'DEUTSCHE MISERE' AND 'DEUTSCHER WEG': ANTIFASCISM AND INTELLECTUAL RESPONSIBILITY

The *Bündnispolitik* of the KPD in 1945 reflected a set of political realities: the need for the Soviet Union to maintain its relations with the Allies required a definition of the origins of Nazism which excluded all but monopoly capitalists, and the heads of government and military. The broad-based conception which emerged from ambitious enterprises such as the Nationalkomitee Freies Deutschland and the Bund Deutscher Offiziere failed to produce the intended German uprising against Hitler, but formed the basis of a strategy which represented the only realistic opportunity for the KPD to exercise any kind of influence on post-war politics. For this reason, and to the disgust of many ordinary KPD members, the Party's programme of 1945 was less radical than that of the SPD, leading to considerable problems with Party discipline.[4]

Nevertheless, for all its dependence on political expediency, the antifascist-democratic concept of the KPD did provide the context for a number of serious attempts to come to terms with the significance of fascism in German history, and to extend the analysis of responsibility beyond the targets sanctioned by the leadership. One of the most important of these early Marxist analyses in the Soviet Zone is Alexander Abusch's *Irrweg einer Nation*, which represents a genuine reworking of history, with National Socialism as the key moment.[5] Whatever the shortcomings of the Marxist historical paradigm which Abusch employs, there is a certain independence of thought which comes as something of a surprise when one considers the shameful role which he was later to play in the Academy and the Ministry of Culture. In his adaptation of motifs from Friedrich Engels' *Bauernkrieg*, Abusch reaches back to an earlier stage of Marxist theory which owes little to standard Leninist views of imperialism and fascism, and the emphasis on independent Marxism and on the exceptional nature of German history clearly links *Irrweg einer Nation* with the 'German Road to Socialism' as an attempt to assert a renewed sense of political responsibility. Sigrid Meuschel calls the book 'ein veritables Werk des Antifaschismus', despite its obvious utility as 'eine politische Kampfschrift'.[6] Many examples in the course of this study have shown that, in the years 1945–1953, the coexistence of principle and expediency was absolutely characteristic of the ideological system: to attempt to separate 'rhetoric' from 'real political intentions' is to misunderstand both, particularly where Marxist

---

[4] See Stefan Creuzberger, 'Die Liquidierung antifaschistischer Organisationen in Berlin', *Deutschland Archiv*, 26 (1993), 1266–78.

[5] Alexander Abusch, *Irrweg einer Nation* (Berlin: Aufbau, 1946).

[6] Sigrid Meuschel, *Legitimation und Parteiherrschaft: Stabilität und Revolution in der DDR* (Frankfurt a.M.: Suhrkamp, 1992), p. 66.

historians are concerned, for whom historiography 'functions as an active history-making force on behalf of different classes and groups'.[7]

According to Abusch, the origins of the 'deutsche Misere' lay in the defeat of the Peasants' Revolt of 1525, and the establishment of feudal princely particularism which set back the cause of German unity and the development of capitalist production. In this conception, Martin Luther and the development of Protestantism were, in the final reckoning, historically retrograde. The final balance of Luther's work is assigned to the Counter-Reformation, because he turned against a peasantry which had taken inspiration from his ideas, and the 'kleinstaatliche Untertanentum' of Lutheranism set back the development of the humanist universalism of Renaissance Rome.[8] Not only did this stall economic development, but it also prevented the unification of Germany under an absolutist monarchy, as was occurring throughout the rest of Western Europe. In terms of historical materialism, the establishment of monarchical absolutism on the French or English model was a progressive step, in the sense that a unified national government removed many of the obstacles from the development of capitalist forms of production, thus contributing to the growth of a bourgeois class which would eventually take up the revolutionary struggle for freedom.

In Germany, however, no such developments could take place in the petty princedoms; instead, 'deutsche "Verinnerlichung" unter der Allmacht der Fürsten'[9] developed into characteristic German submissiveness and Prussian militarism, chauvinism and bureaucracy. The failure of the bourgeoisie in 1848 is ascribed to its willingness to compromise with the nobility, and the weakness and passivity of the peasantry and the developing proletariat stemmed from disunity and poor leadership. A clear line of historical development is posited from this failure to unite Germany, through the defeat of the 1848 revolutions, to nationalism and fascism. Nationalism is thus shown to be profoundly *antinational*, contributing to division and defeat, and, conversely, national division is seen as the direct cause of fascism; the German *Sonderweg* is

---

[7] Andreas Dorpalen, *German History in Marxist Perspective: The East German Approach* (Detroit: Wayne State University Press, 1985), p. 46.

[8] Abusch, *Irrweg*, p. 27.

[9] Abusch, *Irrweg*, p. 28.

conceived in terms of setting the nation back onto the path of historical progress by coming to an understanding of the causes of National Socialism: 'Um zu wissen, wohin Deutschland nun gehen soll, muß geklärt sein, woher das Deutschland Hitlers kam.'[10]

This is the theoretical justification for the ideological precept of the *Bündnispolitik*, namely, the 'Vollendung der Revolution von 1848'.[11] It is problematic because the 'Misere' concept clearly implies a far broader share of responsibility for the disaster than the politically expedient need to blame it all on the monopolists and militarists, and yet the concept was designed to encourage the cooperation of the middle classes in the construction of a 'bourgeois-democratic' republic. However, this concept contained at least the potential for a genuine reassessment of national responsibility, and, for all the weaknesses of Marxist historiography, is an attempt to analyse the social origins of Nazism for a mass audience. Many contributions to the early issues of *Aufbau* are characterised by attempts to explore and deepen the 'Misere' concept, with results which are more differentiated than the official KPD/SED line.

However, the idea that German history had been characterised by the failure of all progressive movements led the SED to move against the 'Misere' concept. Criticisms had been voiced against the theory during 1942/3, when the KPD leadership in exile required a more positive and nationalistic history for its work with the Nationalkomitee Freies Deutschland, particularly since the concentration of the 'Misere' theory on the failure of revolutionary movements might suggest that German resistance to Nazism was minimal. Indeed, the 'Misere' theory could provide a convenient explanation as to why the Soviet Union had to liberate Germany at all, but this would have clearly demonstrated the inadequacy and illegitimacy of the KPD. Thus, for the purposes of recruitment, the Party leadership expanded resistance from 'eine kleine Arbeitergarde' into 'das große Kulturvolk'.[12]

---

[10] Abusch, 'Einleitung' to *Irrweg einer Nation*, n.p.

[11] Cf. *Gründungsaufruf* of KPD, 1945.

[12] Cf. Meuschel, p. 67.

After 1945, the criticisms abated for a while, as Abusch's diagnosis that the blame for the rise of Hitler lay in the disunity of the working class was Party orthodoxy, a point which contributed a powerful emotional resonance to the campaign for the unity of KPD and SPD. As we have seen, however, the SED needed a different approach by 1950, which conflated Party with national history. Speakers at the Third Congress in 1950 took up the nationalistic theme once more, and warned against 'nihilistic' approaches to history. By the time of the Second Conference in 1952, Ulbricht could call explicitly for a 'nationale Geschichtsbetrachtung',[13] and advocate the replacement of the 'Misere' theory with a story of successful national-revolutionary struggles, with a new pantheon of heroes including military figures such as Blücher. Similarly, Kurt Hager, head of the propaganda department of the Central Committee, demanded in 1952 that GDR historians should study and master historical materialism.[14] This was to put an end to the German inferiority complex which Grotewohl had spoken of in 1950; in other words, it represented the end of any serious attempt at *Vergangenheitsbewältigung*. Other aspects of German history were also reassessed, so that the 1918 uprising could now be seen as a proletarian revolution in solidarity with the Bolsheviks, rather than as an attempt to complete the task unfinished in 1848. The 'integrationists' within the SED, whose survival depended on a nationalism which claimed all progressive ideas and historical figures and on a tie with an ambivalent Soviet Union which precluded all independent thought about the nature of dictatorship, were liable to crack down hard on anything which questioned that legitimacy.

This was the atmosphere in which Hanns Eisler chose to present his *Johann Faustus* for discussion as a principled approach to German history.

---

[13] Meuschel, pp. 67–68.
[14] Cf. Dorpalen, p. 49.

FAUST AND THE PEASANTS' REVOLT

The historiography of the Peasants' Revolt went through a series of shifts in emphasis in the GDR, depending on the current needs of the SED Politburo.[15] In the late 1940s and early 1950s, the Reformation was seen as a revolutionary situation, in which Martin Luther laid the foundations of an ideology, expressed in religious terms, which fused incoherent class struggles into a social revolution culminating in the Peasants' Revolt. Luther's teachings were seen as part of the struggle of the embryonic bourgeoisie and the peasantry against a reactionary church, and the 'treachery' of the bourgeois classes was held to have prevented the unification of Germany. Later, when prospects for the reunification of GDR and FRG had faded, the emphasis changed, and historians stressed that national unity had not been an option in the sixteenth century, and the figure of Luther was rehabilitated to a certain extent as a member of the progressive bourgeoisie, in order to prevent West German historians 'claiming' him for their cause.

This shift in interpretation of the Reformation had the consequence of contributing to the ideological reassessment of German national identity which the SED had begun to undertake since 1950. If the Peasants' Revolt had a genuinely positive effect on German history, by contributing to the development of capitalist modes of production, then the peasantry need no longer be portrayed as passive, and Thomas Müntzer's doctrines could be shown to have foreshadowed Marx, Engels, and even Lenin.[16] A positive German revolutionary tradition is discovered, which reestablishes German history in the mainstream of European development, in that it follows the same dialectical laws as other countries. GDR authors spent a considerable amount of effort trying to demonstrate that the class struggle continued after 1525, and that the peasantry was by no means passive in the face of defeat.[17]

---

[15] See the chapter, 'From Feudalism to Capitalism: The Reformation to the Thirty Years War', in Dorpalen, pp. 99–137.

[16] Cf. Dorpalen, pp. 115–16.

[17] Cf. Dorpalen, p. 128.

The 'deutsche Misere' theory needed to be discarded, because it suggested that the German people were unable to determine their own fate, and had to rely on outside parties (such as the Soviet Union) to carry out their revolutions for them. At the same time, the admission of the GDR among the People's Democracies required the rigorous refutation of any remnant of an independent German road to socialism. The squaring of this circle depended on a renewed nationalist assertiveness, which served the purpose of entrenching German division (the progressive and reactionary traditions having crystallised into the two German states), strengthening the integration of the GDR into the Soviet sphere, and avoiding a principled assessment of Nazi and Soviet dictatorship.

The figure of Faust portrayed by Eisler appears in a sixteenth-century social context which is very close to the view of history which the SED leadership was repudiating. The peasantry has been defeated by the forces of reaction, but survives unbowed in the figure of the crippled Karl. Eisler's Faust shares many characteristics with Luther, unwilling to follow through the logic of his ideology, 'die humanitas in gesellschaftliche Tat umzusetzen'.[18] By failing to provide the ideological leadership which is the task of the intellectual and by opposing a historically progressive movement which would lead to German unity, Faust shirks his historical task. Shamed by Karl's wounds, he says: 'Man hätte nicht zu den Waffen greifen sollen', and is roundly condemned.[19] In this scene with Karl, Eisler shows the consequences of the disunity of the intellectual and the masses, of 'Geist' and 'Volk': Karl's body is broken, so he cannot fulfil his social function, but his spirit is strong, whereas Faust is healthy, because he stayed out of the war, but his mind, cut off from the source of its strength (that is, Faust's peasant roots), cannot contribute to progress. Whatever his intentions, history condemns the German humanist as a renegade. In words which would come back to haunt him, Ernst Fischer calls Eisler's Faust 'eine Zentralgestalt der deutschen Misere'.[20]

---

[18] Fischer, p. 63. Fischer's article is important, in that the interpretation which he presents becomes the focus for the attacks on Eisler and *Sinn und Form*. The Austrian Marxist Fischer, writing from Vienna, was not wholly in touch with developments in East Berlin.

[19] *Faustus*, act 1, scene 2, p. 18.

[20] Fischer, p. 63.

The scenes set in a more modern era reflect a Marxist analysis of the past in terms of its development into the present; Faust's journey to Italy in the traditional puppet play is replaced by a satire on American capitalism, which show the durability of traditions of resistance through a chorus of slaves. The lord of the Underworld is a capitalist boss, who summons his agents like a Mafia don. Mephisto appears dressed as a Junker, to underline Faust's betrayal of his peasant roots. In order to escape his feelings of guilt at his own treachery, Faust commands Mephisto to make him forget the battle songs of the Junkers and the Peasants in an attempt to remain aloof from the class struggle.

Another humiliation is Mephisto's demand that Faust renounce love. Faust protests, but Mephisto shows him that there is nothing for him to love; he cannot love Germany, because it is divided geographically and along class lines. Faust despises the Germany of the Princes, is despised by the Germany of the rising bourgeoisie, and has forfeited his right to speak for the peasants. In his 'Confessio', Faust comes to an understanding that neutrality serves only the enemies of progress, but it is too late, and he is dragged back from his position in front of the curtain into the continuing action, from which he cannot escape (a dangerously formalist device).[21]

Eisler's juxtaposition of themes from the sixteenth century with scenes condemning imperialism, in order to demonstrate the historical continuity proposed by the 'Misere' theory, is ambitious. It demonstrates that Eisler was confident (as he had every right to be) that his music would act as the carrier of the message of continuity, linking the Junkers with the imperialists and the German peasants with the chorus of slaves. As was the case in the debate over *Das Verhör des Lukullus*, the idea that music and text were inseparable, and should be considered as an artistic unity, was alien to Eisler's attackers.

The literary form of the text is a clear challenge to Socialist Realist orthodoxies, although Eisler naturally considered himself a Realist, and was simply concerned with exploring broader possibilities for the genre. As an intervention in the 'Realism Debate', *Faustus*, and Fischer's article, with its

---

[21] *Faustus*, act 3, scene 5, pp. 73–77.

enthusiasm for 'das Phantastisch-Sagenhafte',[22] became a hostage to fortune for a whole group of like-minded intellectuals and artists in the GDR.

DIALECTIC WITHOUT DEVELOPMENT:
TRAPPING A GOOD COMMUNIST

What strikes the reader of the transcripts of the discussions in the Academy concerning *Faustus* and *Sinn und Form* in May and June 1953 is not only the stubbornness and bankruptcy of the arguments brought against Eisler, but also the willingness of Eisler's defenders to give ground to their opponents.[23] Naturally, the threat of coercion hung over the meetings, and one should not underestimate the atmosphere of fear and suspicion generated by accusations of ideological error. However, between 1945 and 1953, it was still possible for those who sympathised with the SED's declared aims to believe that the regime enjoyed popular legitimacy, as well as ideological justification. Eisler was concerned to make a serious statement about the function of art in the new society, and his unwise decision to present his text for discussion reflects the feeling, which we have already seen in Brecht, that reasoned debate and comradely criticism were the best way to ensure that intellectuals and artists fulfilled their social role. Similarly, Eisler's decision to take up the Faust legend seems to have something provocative about it in the light of the use to which the figure of Goethe had been put in the GDR, and the questions which his text and his audacious choice of subject brought up were urgent and uncomfortable.

Not only did the text challenge many assumptions about German history, the role of German intellectuals and their attitudes to culture, but it is also in many ways the continuation of a line in the debates on the 'kulturelles Erbe' which had caused rancour amongst German artists in exile. Brecht's influence is

---

[22] Fischer, p. 70.

[23] The selection of documents in Dietzel and Geißler gives a somewhat limited view of the 'Faustus Debate'; the interaction of the most important personalities, principally Brecht, Eisler, Becher, Abusch and Zweig, is more complex than this documentation might at first suggest. The outcome of the debate before the 17 June was not quite the unambiguous defeat for Eisler's defenders which, for example, Hans Mayer considers it to be: 'Im Falle von Hanns Eisler verzeichneten Girnus und seine Mitstreiter einen vollen Erfolg.' Hans Mayer, *Brecht* (Frankfurt a. M.: Suhrkamp, 1996), p. 70.

tangible in Eisler's writing, and Brecht's journals (25 to 30 August 1952) record that he had a hand in its composition. A Marxist-avantgardist sensibility is at work here, derived from the 1920s experimentation of Erwin Piscator, who saw past cultural artifacts as texts whose internal contradictions need to be forcibly exposed, the better to learn from them. A necessary violence is done to the text in order to show it in the light of social conditions contemporary to both the text's author and to its later adaptor, thus exposing the underlying connections and the development of the historical dialectic. The radical juxtaposition achieved by reaching back from the present to a past moment of defeat or victory, and the ambiguities of interpretation which arise from a view which sees history and culture as a text to be manipulated by the artist are of no use in justifying a regime's hold on power.

Eisler's approach to the 'Erbe' was, arguably, entirely appropriate for an artist influenced by the 'Misere' theory, and his examination of the role of the German intellectual and of the limits to the usefulness of cultural traditions in promoting a progressive ideology is powerful and pertinent. Eisler's defence ('Eine Parodierung [Goethes] ist wirklich nicht gemeint'[24]) is somewhat disingenuous, as some of the jokes at the expense of Goethe's language serve to bring the religious overtones down to earth, or to comment on the veneration in which Goethe's *Faust* has been held by later generations. As Deborah Viëtor-Engländer comments, '[Eislers] Umgang mit dem Erbe war also im höchsten Maße aktualitätsbezogen'.[25] With the prospect of the Federal Republic's entry into NATO, the pressure on German intellectuals to make a firm stand on one side or the other was growing, and Eisler's *Faustus* is a clear statement of support for the GDR. We can partly explain the vehemence of the attacks on such a loyal communist with reference to the campaign for legitimacy of a particular line within the SED, whose proponents had a clearer idea than less hard-line communists of the potential threat to the regime posed by any ambivalence on the question of German division. Avantgardist experimentation with history and culture was not only a perceived affront to the sensibilities of

[24] Protocol of 'Mittwoch-Gesellschaft', 13 May 1953, Bunge, p. 69.
[25] Deborah Viëtor-Engländer, *Faust in der DDR* (Frankfurt a. M.: Peter Lang, 1987), p. 178.

the working class (not to mention the conservative middle classes), but also left interpretation dangerously open.

Proponents of this avantgardist line had always run into trouble with the KPD, and it shows a great faith in the political processes of the GDR that Eisler felt able to offer up his libretto for public debate. As we have seen, the changing circumstances of late 1952, the ramifications of rearmament and the Slánský trial, had led the SED leadership to prepare an assault on the artistic community which they only now felt strong enough to carry through. However, because of the regime's continuing need for the legitimacy which its intellectuals, and the existence of the Academy, brought it, the appearance of open debate had to be maintained.

The preceding chapters of this study have shown how artists like Brecht and Becher could convince themselves that the discussions were generally constructive, and have commented on the ways in which an intellectual schooled in the application of the dialectic to problems of culture and history could be persuaded to compromise with a regime which exercises power over the production of meaning. This case study will examine the debates in the 'Mittwoch-Gesellschaften' in the light of this analysis of the relationship of these intellectuals to the ideological system. If we analyse the statements of the participants in the debates in terms of the dialectic, in other words, we take seriously the way in which intellectuals like Brecht and Eisler understood intellectual progress, then we begin to understand how they could have been led into compromise.

We have seen the way in which many of the members of the Academy saw the high-profile debates and pronouncements in the various Sektionen as a means for the 'Beseitigung von Mißverständnissen', and as a way of overcoming bureaucratic obstacles. However, Eisler's opponents do not give any ground at all, backed up as they are by simplistic statements in the press, and by healthy majorities, ensured by the machinations of Abusch, in the 'Mittwoch-Gesellschaften'. Thus, if one term of the dialectic does not move its ground, then the proponents of the antithesis, in this case, the side whose lack of access to administrative power leaves them unable to determine the orthodoxy, are forced to compromise their own position, and mistake this compromise for an attempt to move towards a synthesis. In this way, a process of compromise which seems inexplicable to observers outside the ideological system begins to make more sense. The attitude of Peter Huchel, for example, forms a useful contrasting case: although Huchel shared with Marxist colleagues such as Becher a number of assumptions about the value of literary discourse, he is influenced by a very different tradition, and the undialectical nature of his attitude to language (with its implication that there is no ultimate truth to be found in seemingly unequivocal statements) leads him to resist the imposition of ideological orthodoxy in a very different way from the committed communist Eisler.

FAUSTUS AND THE 'MITTWOCH-GESELLSCHAFTEN'

Seen in this light, the controversy over Eisler's *Faustus* is a key issue in our understanding of the SED's attempted consolidation of power in the months leading up to June 1953. The administrative measures were prepared in order to exploit the loyalty of SED members by leaving them exposed outside the mainstream; as in the case of Dessau, it was very hard for communist artists to defend themselves from this position, as the legitimacy of their belief system derived from the all-inclusive authority of 'Stalin'. Once exposed in this way, contradictions become visible which were hidden before, and the communist must either explore these contradictions or return chastened to the fold.

The ground for the moves against Eisler and *Sinn und Form* was prepared by the 'Drahtzieher'[26] Abusch, and Becher was back in line by January 1953, having overcome the mental and physical crises of the year before. *Sinn und Form* came in for criticism at the meeting of the Academy's Presidium on 15 January,[27] with the article by Ernst Fischer on *Faustus* seen as 'den letzten Anstoß', criticised by Wolfgang Langhoff as 'eine unseren Bemühungen entgegengesetzte Arbeit'. Becher suggested that Huchel should be replaced by

---

[26] Stephen Parker, '"Sinn und Form", Peter Huchel und der 17. Juni 1953: Bertolt Brechts Rettungsaktion', *Sinn und Form*, 45 (1994), 738–51, p. 741.

[27] Cf. excerpt from protocol in Dietzel and Geißler, pp. 141–42.

the more reliable F. C. Weiskopf, but despite the disappearance of the official sanction which Huchel had enjoyed, the continuing insecurity of the 'integrationist' line within the Academy, and within the regime itself, meant that he was not to be dislodged at the stroke of a pen.

In contrast to the hesitancy over *Das Verhör des Lukullus*, the hard-line SED members in the Academy had a clearer line of attack right from the start. They had learnt a lesson about organisation: the 'Faustus Debate' does not give the impression that the cadres are improvising without a set institutional context for their arguments. However, although the 'integrationist' line had become more secure since the Summer of 1952, incidents like the Slánský trial showed that the leadership could take nothing for granted. In fact, the ideological issues raised by Eisler's libretto had become all the more important in the light of Ulbricht's survival at the end of 1952, as the SED needed to bind the GDR, along with its intellectual community, more securely into the 'Soviet Bloc'.

The accusations that Eisler, and especially Fischer, had a dangerously distorted view of German history began at once: Friedrich Wolf attacked *Faustus* in the Sektion Dichtkunst on 21 January,[28] and the editorial staff of *Neues Deutschland* discussed the publication of a critical article.[29] While Abusch was carefully preparing a majority against Eisler for the first 'Mittwoch-Gesellschaft', he and Becher were conspiring to unseat Huchel. A vicious attack by Friedrich Wolf in the plenary session of the Sektion Dichtkunst on 26 March, in which he declared an absolute lack of confidence in Huchel and demanded that the Sektion deal with the 'Eisler/Fischer-Komplex', was followed by Becher's request that Abusch write the *Faustus* article; this final break with Huchel led the latter to declare, 'daß er die Konsequenzen daraus ziehen müsse'.[30]

---

[28] Cf. Parker, '"Sinn und Form", Peter Huchel und der 17. Juni 1953', p. 741.

[29] Cf. Viëtor-Engländer, pp. 182–83. Hans Mayer wrote to Brecht in February 1952 that he had declined to write on *Faustus* for *Neues Deutschland*, as he felt that his views would be used as an officially-sanctioned personal attack on Eisler rather than as a contribution to debate. On 5 March, Wilhelm Girnus wrote to Eisler making it clear that planned attacks on *Faustus* were agreed with the Central Committee, stating that the editorial staff of *Neues Deutschland* 'in solchen grundlegenden Fragen niemals ohne vorherige Fühlungsnahme mit dem ZK handeln', and that Girnus felt that Eisler had been influenced 'in ungünstiger Weise' by people such as Ernst Fischer. It seems that Eisler, as a GDR artist, was to be distanced from Fischer and subjected to discipline.

[30] Parker, '"Sinn und Form", Peter Huchel und der 17. Juni 1953', p. 742.

In contrast to the carefully-prepared debates on *Faustus*, Abusch ensured that the Sektion Dichtkunst did not discuss the case of *Sinn und Form* further, preferring to push for Huchel's dismissal without open debate within the Academy's Presidium. Huchel was certainly not susceptible to any form of ideological persuasion, and so different measures were called for. If we consider the differing attitudes to culture which have emerged during the course of this study, we can see that the editorial practice of *Sinn und Form* represented a conception of language which could not be brought into line with any recognisably Marxist theory. The only way to come to terms with the dangerous ambiguity, both of this conception of language, and of *Sinn und Form*'s institutional position, was by administrative measures. On the other hand, the issues of national legitimacy and loyalty in the 'Eisler/Fischer-Komplex' had to be turned into an open demonstration. By this time, Huchel was a unique figure in GDR cultural life, representing noone but himself, whereas there were many like Eisler, principled Marxist artists vulnerable to threats, the promise of progress and a fake dialectic. The attacks on Eisler and Fischer ran parallel with the campaign against *Sinn und Form*, touching at moments when the *Faustus* debate could be used to attack Huchel for refusing to take an unequivocal stand.

The regime's austerity drive was used as a pretext for threatening to cut off *Sinn und Form*'s subsidy until the journal had undergone fundamental changes. At a meeting of the Presidium on 29 April, the day before Huchel left for Moscow with a delegation of the Schriftstellerverband, it was decided that a commission, consisting of Abusch, Brecht, Bredel and Wolf would meet to discuss the changes; Huchel was to have no part in these discussions. On 13 May, the day of the first 'Mittwoch-Gesellschaft', the Presidium passed a series of resolutions concerning *Sinn und Form*, according to which Huchel was to be relieved of his post after the required period of notice. This meant that his contract would run until 30 November, and the last four editions of *Sinn und Form* under his editorship would appear as two double numbers, the first of which was to be devoted to Walter Ulbricht's 60th birthday. Ulbricht's absurd personality cult was to cement the authority of his line in the SED, and his figure, 'der deutsche Arbeitersohn', was to embody the legitimacy of the progressive line in German culture and history, a line which was put into question by aspects of the 'Misere' theory, and by any continuing efforts to maintain contacts with the West. *Sinn und Form* was required to take sides unequivocally, to *make explicit* conclusions which the reader had previously been expected to draw independently. To this end, the resolutions passed on the 13 May removed *Sinn und Form* from the Sektion Dichtkunst, making it a journal of the whole Academy, effectively under the control of Abusch, and Huchel was dismissed *in absentia*.[31]

Although the campaigns against Eisler and *Sinn und Form* are closely entwined, the differing responses of the 'integrationist' grouping within the Academy are an indication of the strengths and weaknesses of the SED's ideological legitimacy. Both *Faustus* and *Sinn und Form* depend on a form of literary discourse which locates them in a space between the polarities of the nascent Cold War. In this sense, their own political standpoints (ambivalent in the case of Huchel, and committed in the case of Eisler) are only part of the story; however much Eisler may have believed himself to be firmly on one side of the 'two camps' equation, the issues surrounding the integration of the GDR into the Soviet sphere were, as we know, more complex than he suspected. By making use of a literary form, influenced by Brecht, which left interpretation open (at least to a certain extent), Eisler's principled approach to German history genuinely, and without Eisler being wholly aware of it, questioned the legitimacy of a line which claimed to be the arbiter of all meaning. In this sense, the 'integrationists' were entirely justified in their moves against *Faustus*.

The increasing polarisation between the two German states was also currently under threat from the precipitate actions of Beria, and, perhaps, from some last-ditch diplomatic efforts by Churchill which displeased Adenauer.[32] In the GDR, this meant that any form of political or literary discourse which called into question the meanings, fixed into cliché, which legitimised the dominance of Walter Ulbricht and his line, needed to be brought into step. As we have seen when comparing the relationship of the non-Marxist Huchel and intellectuals

---

[31] Dietzel and Geißler, pp. 144–45. See also Parker, '"Sinn und Form", Peter Huchel und der 17. Juni 1953', p. 743.

[32] See Josef Foschepoth, 'Churchill, Adenauer und die Neutralisierung Deutschlands', *Deutschland Archiv*, 17 (1984), 1286–1301.

such as Brecht and Becher with the SED's attempts to claim legitimacy, the ideological system acted in different ways on each individual. Although the development of 'Marxism-Leninism', used here as an overarching term for these varying exclusionary and legitimising practices, was by no means under the control of any individual or faction certain individuals were more vulnerable to the combination of coercion and persuasion than others.

This vulnerability can be traced back to the different kinds of ambiguity which pervade their ideological outlooks. It is at this point, when the legitimacy of the SED's claim to power rests on its intellectual community taking sides unequivocally and explicitly, that the differences become clear. Artists who shared a dialectical world-view, and thus depended on the existence of the GDR as justification for their beliefs and their work, could be persuaded to compromise in this coercive, one-sided dialectic. Artists such as Brecht and Eisler, who used literary devices which grant the reader or spectator a certain interpretive freedom as a means of reaching an expected synthesis or conclusion, were vulnerable to compromise with a regime which demanded that they make their conclusions, and thus their loyalty, explicit from the beginning.

The nuances in the responses of intellectuals which this kind of analysis exposes allows us to make more satisfactory judgements about responsibility and compromise than has often been possible, not least in the fevered debates immediately following the fall of the Berlin Wall. In the terms of this study, a sign of literary responsibility even where the artist did not break with the prevailing ideological system (which would in any case have been impossible for many who had found in it a source of strength in resisting Nazism) is resistance to the administrative imposition of meaning. This resistance took on an unexpected significance in the context of the upheavals of June 1953.

FIRST 'MITTWOCH-GESELLSCHAFT': 13 MAY 1953

While Becher and Abusch were plotting to force Huchel into an act of public self-criticism, which would have removed the troublesome problem of an intellectual whose presence in the GDR would have acted as a silent question mark over the legitimacy of the regime,[33] an extensive discussion took place in the Academy in order to intimidate Eisler into repudiating his views and withdrawing his text. The first 'Mittwoch-Gesellschaft' was introduced by Abusch, who read his essay, 'Faust: Held oder Renegat in der deutschen Nationalliteratur',[34] in which Abusch tries to redeem himself for his earlier ideological errors by repositioning his *Irrweg einer Nation* as a text which supported the SED line of 1953.

The differences between the views expressed by Abusch and by Eisler and Brecht are small, but significant; Abusch's text, and the standpoint of all the official criticism, attempts to claim a direct line of legitimacy through all progressive movements in German history. As we have seen, the Reformation is a key period for Marxists, and the struggle to claim a text like Goethe's *Faust* is important because Goethe links the Peasants' War with the period after the French Revolution, and represents the 'Gipfel des Denkens [...], der für das Bürgertum geschichtlich erreichbar war'.[35] Similarly, Mephisto, as 'Geist der steten Verneinung',[36] is taken to be a sign of the development of the dialectic in bourgeois thought, and thus an important precursor of Marx and Engels. Goethe instinctively understands the development of history, 'ohne die gesell-schaftlichen Bewegungsgesetze schon wissenschaftlich zu erfassen';[37] this conclusion mirrors Becher's earlier suggestion that the contradictions in Goethe's work are resolved in the GDR. For the purposes of Abusch's argument, Goethe's Faust is seen as a purely positive figure, 'ein großer positiver Held des klassischen Nationaldramas',[38] and thus as a literary antecedent of Socialist Realism. He therefore represents the spirit of progressive striving, driven by the mephistophelian antithesis, and by his own desire for knowledge, to attain the highest level of achievement possible for a bourgeois intellectual. By contrast, Eisler's Faustus embarks on his quest for knowledge as a way of

[33] Cf. Parker, '"Sinn und Form", Peter Huchel und der 17. Juni 1953', p. 744. While her husband was in Moscow, Monica Huchel was approached by Becher, who showed her a text in which Peter Huchel confessed to ideological errors. She refused to have anything to do with it.

[34] Abusch's essay appeared in *Sonntag*, 17 May 1953, and in *Sinn und Form*, 4 (1953), no. 3+4, 179–94.

[35] Abusch, 'Faust: Held oder Renegat', p. 181.

[36] Abusch, 'Faust: Held oder Renegat', p. 186.

[37] Abusch, 'Faust: Held oder Renegat', p. 182.

[38] Abusch, 'Faust: Held oder Renegat', p. 185.

escaping from his bad conscience, and therefore the spirit of progress which he embodies is separated from the revolutionary peasantry; bourgeois intellectual and peasant revolutionary are shown to be irrevocably at odds. What is at stake here is a vision of GDR society in 1953, where the 'integrationist' line requires a long-standing tradition of progressive thinkers (not including Eisler's Faustus) in order to present the consolidation of the GDR and a new sense of national identity as the logical conclusion of historical development. It is not simply a question of justifying the SED's rule, but of legitimising the dominance of a particular line within the SED. If intellectuals and artists depart from that line, Ulbricht's hold on power is threatened, particularly at a time when Soviet leaders like Beria and Malenkov are beginning to demand liberalisation.

Abusch's essay hovers between what might pass for scholarly analysis and a form of diction which just falls short of calling Eisler an apologist for fascism; in other words, Abusch is hedging his bets by supplying ammunition for potential use, depending on how the discussion progresses. It is notable that Ernst Fischer, as a convenient scapegoat, comes in for considerably stronger condemnation than Eisler, allowing Eisler an escape route back into discipline if he so chooses. However, by linking Eisler's attempt to return to earlier sources of the Faustus story with Thomas Mann's *Doktor Faustus*, whose protagonist, the modernist composer Adrian Leverkühn, proposes the 'Zurücknahme' of Beethoven's Ninth Symphony (and thus of German humanism), Abusch manoeuvres Eisler into opposition to the progressive intelligentsia, linking him implicitly with ideological enemies such as Nietzsche. The fact that Thomas Mann himself approved of Eisler's work goes unmentioned.[39]

The discussion in the Academy revolves around whether Faustus can be seen as a truly representative figure. The fundamental difference between the parties centres on the concept of 'das Typische', that is, whether Eisler's Faustus represents the German intellectual stratum in its 'objective' role in the

---

[39] Cf. Viëtor-Engländer, pp. 176–77.

continuing historical process.[40] The official view of the intelligentsia has changed with the rejection of the 'Misere' theory: in order to reclaim figures such as Luther (who is portrayed negatively in *Faustus*), the 'typical' intellectual is no longer seen as a renegade, but as an ally of the progressive forces. If the progressive forces are weak or defeated in German history, then it might seem as if the SED owed its legitimacy purely to the presence of the Soviet military, instead of 'die real vorhandenen, seit langem kämpfenden freiheitlichen Kräfte im deutschen Volk'.[41] Similarly, the division of Germany is legitimised by the rigid identification of progressive and reactionary camps, which have now solidified into the two German states; this is another indication of the importance of the tension between the geographical and political expressions of the 'two camps' theory as a tool in our understanding of the development of the GDR.

Internal conflict within a literary figure is therefore not 'typical', and Girnus can make the connection between a failure to follow the central tenets of Socialist Realism ('Wenn [Faust] eine große dichterische Gestalt sein soll, muß er ein Typus sein') and a slander on the names of Marx, Engels, Goethe, etc. ('Eisler verdammt in dieser Gestalt die ganze deutsche Geistesgeschichte.'[42]) Each figure must embody one of the conflicting social forces in its era, so that the conflict is externalised on the stage; any ambiguity in the linguistic cliché or crack in the monolithic image is a threat, made all the more urgent by the ambivalent signals coming out of Moscow. The significance of Nazism for an understanding of German history has been suppressed, but the experience of dictatorship underlies the discussions as an unspoken question: if the German intelligentsia, working class and progressive bourgeoisie have always opposed the reactionary forces in German history, who supported Hitler? Why was there no German revolution? Uncomfortable parallels with the Soviet regime have

---

[40] Malenkov's speech at the Nineteenth Congress of the Soviet Communist Party underlies the Socialist Realist orthodoxy. They are quoted by Girnus as a sacred text: 'Nach marxistisch-leninistischer Auffassung bedeutet das Typische keineswegs irgendeinen statistischen Durchschnitt. Typisch ist, was dem Wesen der gegebenen sozialen und historischen Erscheinung entspricht, und es ist nicht einfach das am häufigsten Verbreitete, oft Wiederkehrende, Gewöhnliche' (cit. Bunge, p. 65).

[41] Abusch, 'Faust: Held oder Renegat', p. 190.

[42] Bunge, p. 67.

also to be suppressed, and so renegades have to be demonised in the manner of Arthur Koestler or Tito.

Brecht's defence, in keeping with his theoretical stance, that a negative character can have a positive effect, depends on the idea of the bourgeois intellectual as unable to demonstrate complete commitment to either side: 'Wir haben hier einen Verräter, der aber seinen Verrat nicht wirklich vollziehen kann.'[43] In his 'Confessio', Faust comes to a positive understanding of the negativity of his life, so the essential conflict of the opera takes place within this single character. However, if the character of Faustus is to be considered 'typical', then the intellectual must not be shown as a traitor. Wilhelm Girnus takes this argument the furthest: 'Daß die Geschichte des deutschen Volkes die Geschichte der Reaktion ist, ist die Konzeption der Reaktion.' According to Girnus' conception, Eisler's work is unpatriotic because it sees German history as an exception to the norm:

Es ist absolut unerfindlich, warum das deutsche Volk als einziges eine Ausnahme von den geschichtlichen Gesetzen machen sollte, die in anderen Nationen Geltung haben. Ich meine, hier kommt bei Hanns Eisler eine Fremdheit gegenüber dem deutschen Volk, gegenüber den nationalen Traditionen des deutschen Volkes, gegenüber seiner Geschichte zum Ausdruck. Er darf mir das nicht übelnehmen, das ist keinesfalls als Diffamierung gemeint, sondern als Hilfe.[44]

If German history is an exception, then the GDR forfeits its right a) to be an independent state, and b) to retain its place as a People's Democracy in the community of progressive nations. This is how the circle is squared, so that the GDR's national consciousness as a state separate from the FRG is reconciled with its integration into the Soviet Bloc.

The concerted tactics of the hostile SED faction are in stark contrast to Eisler's defenders, who put their faith in open discussion. Zweig in particular has obviously taken great care to prepare himself for the debate, but the ideas which he brings forward are the opinions of an individual, and have little effect on the other participants. Nevertheless, considering the humiliating pressure to

---

[43] Bunge, p. 62.
[44] Bunge, p. 71.

which he had been subjected over the Presidency of the Academy, he displays considerable courage in standing up for his friends. Zweig suggests that Eisler remove all references to the Faust legend by simply renaming the character, as the name Faustus brings with it 'eine Fülle von Assoziationen'.[45] His argument is quite ingenious, but it misses the point of the debate. Brecht, on the other hand, seems fully aware of the possible consequences, so his arguments are designed to relocate Eisler within the mainstream of Marxist thinking, rather than to criticise the orthodoxy itself. This is the kind of ideologized tactical compromise which was described in the *Lukullus* case study, and it results in a further shift towards the inflexible position of his opponents.

The outcome of the first meeting is still inconclusive, but the threats to Eisler are clear. An opposition has been set up between the position of Fischer, who is identified as a reactionary, an abstract point of reference sustainable because he is not present, and of the majority, who have the full authority of the Party and the Soviet Union behind them.[46] Eisler is given time to choose, and Becher ends the meeting on a conciliatory note ('Hier geht es nicht darum, Resolutionen zu fassen, sondern: das muß man wirklich nach allen Seiten hin durchdenken'), but it is very clear that there is no middle way.[47] It is important that the pretence of open discussion is maintained, as the SED still needs its intellectuals to support the regime at this delicate time, and so they must be convinced to come over of their own free will. However, free will is problematic here: if the SED is accepted as the legitimate government of Germany, then Marxist artists draw their legitimacy from that regime, and so objecting to Party orthodoxy is not simply a matter of exercising the conscious intellect, but rather involves calling into question the ideals for which the individual has fought and suffered for many years. What was not wholly clear to artists like Eisler was that the basis of this legitimacy was so fragile, and that the debate in the Academy was

---

[45] Bunge, p. 64.

[46] Deborah Viëtor-Engländer notes (p. 184): 'Fischers Aufsatz spielte in der ganzen Auseinandersetzung eine Schlüsselrolle, denn ohne seine Unterstüzung wären die Angriffe auf Eisler womöglich wesentlich milder ausgefallen.' I feel that the usefulness of Fischer's article for the opponents of Eisler consisted in Fischer's absence from the debate, enabling him to be demonised as one of the polar opposites between which Eisler had to choose. Given the political circumstances of the debate, and the fact that moves were also being made against Brecht and the Berliner Ensemble, it would be inaccurate to suppose that Fischer's article contributed to the harshness of the criticism; it was simply useful.

[47] Bunge, p. 82.

paralleled by conflicts within the leadership which were to come into the open in June 1953.

SECOND 'MITTWOCH-GESELLSCHAFT': 27 MAY 1953

While Eisler was preparing his reply to the criticisms which he had heard in the first meeting, the pressure was stepped up through a concerted press campaign, in order to further isolate Eisler from a supposedly unanimous public opinion. This campaign had the effect of making Eisler's opponents in the debate in the Academy seem conciliatory and ready to welcome the penitent and protect him from the hostility of his critics. A substantial article appeared in *Neues Deutschland* the day after the first 'Mittwoch-Gesellschaft',[48] which restated the condemnations of Ernst Fischer's article in stronger terms. The 'Misere' theory is 'eine reaktionäre und antinationale Konzeption, die objektiv dazu dient, die nationale Würde und das Nationalbewußtsein des deutschen Volkes zu zerstören'.[49] Fischer is therefore accused of ignoring the struggle of the German people ('Hunderttausende', according to the author of the article[50]) who fought against National Socialism; this, of course, is tantamount to declaring that Fischer is a Nazi. Eisler himself is subjected to the dangerous accusation of 'cosmopolitanism', because he denies the importance of the nation:

Unzweifelhaft liegt die tiefste Ursache darin, daß dem Verfasser und seinen Ratgebern die Erkenntnis von der Bedeutung des Patriotismus für die Nation und für die Entwicklung der Kunst fehlt. Eine Konzeption, der die deutsche Geschichte nichts als Misere ist und in der das Volk als schöpferische Potenz fehlt, ist nicht wahr. Mit dieser falschen Konzeption ist notgedrungen auch eine falsche Einstellung zum Realismus in den Fragen der künstlerischen Form und der Ästhetik verbunden.[51]

A form of nationalism which gains its ultimate authority from Stalin's words at the Nineteenth Congress of the Soviet Communist Party in 1952, and from the

---

[48] 'Das "Faust"-Problem und die deutsche Geschichte', *Neues Deutschland*, 14.5.1953, in Bunge, pp. 89–101.
[49] Bunge, p. 91.
[50] Bunge, p. 97.
[51] Bunge, p. 101.

Soviet campaigns against 'cosmopolitanism', is here being used to entrench the division of Germany, rather than to promote unity; the 'creative' and 'reactionary' forces in the nation have crystallised into the two German states. Since the triumph of socialism is inevitable, the 'typical' intellectual (that is, the intellectual who represents the true historical role of the intelligentsia, who 'sich zum theoretischen Verständnis der großen geschichtlichen Bewegung hindurchgearbeitet hat'[52]) joins the cause of progress. The repercussions for the GDR of Stalin's decisive intervention in the 'Economists' Debate' are felt in the author's insistence on the precept that the collapse of capitalism is inevitable and will happen soon. The context-setting and analysis in the preceding chapters leads us to an important conclusion: although it is obvious that decisions and conflicts at the highest level in the Soviet regime had a determining influence on GDR cultural policy, the chains of causality are varied and diffuse. Therefore, it is better not to assume a direct relation between the aims of the 'integrationists' and the policies of the Soviet leadership, even when they seem to coincide, but instead to try to understand to what use the sources of authority emerging from the Soviet Union were put.

The authority of the Soviet Union as a factor in every political discussion is the most significant weakness in the line of argumentation brought forward by Eisler's defenders, handicapping them in their responses. For example, Brecht is clear enough in his criticism of some of the tenets of Socialist Realism: 'Aber der neue Mensch kann nicht durch die Dichtung produziert werden, das ist ein Aberglaube. Er muß sich selbst produzieren. Die Dichtung kann ihn anregen, nicht schaffen.'[53]

The problem with this view is that Brecht believes in the creation of 'the new man' at all. The idea of the perfectibility of humanity under a socialist system has authoritarian implications which lead Brecht to support the rule of the SED, however accurate many of his criticisms of the Party may be. His beliefs are bound up with the image of the Soviet Union, whatever private doubts he might have had about Stalin, and he mentions the Slánský trial with approval,

---

[52] Bunge, p. 99.
[53] Protocol of a discussion on Eisler's *Faustus*, cit. Bunge, p. 115.

comparing Slánský's confession with the 'Confessio' of Faust.[54] His support for the principle of purges of 'renegades' weakens his ability to defend his friends, despite the leeway which such compromises grant him, and ensures that the opportunity presented by the 17 June uprising is not fully exploited.

Although Brecht himself came under considerable personal attack in the context of the second 'Mittwoch-Gesellschaft',[55] his actions showed considerable courage, particularly since the atmosphere was more openly hostile than in the first meeting (although still mild in comparison with the raging press campaign). Eisler opened the meeting with a response to his critics which is in marked contrast to the confused defensiveness of Dessau in the *Lukullus* controversy.[56] Eisler defends the complexity of the character of Faustus, pointing out that his negativity stems from his inability to put into practice his positive insights: '[...] aus ihm spricht die von ihm verratene, verkaufte Wahrheit.'[57] Eisler also stresses the ambiguity of the German intellectual tradition, and shows a more sensitive understanding of the legacy of Nazism in German thought: 'Können wir 1945 von einem *Sieg* des deutschen humanistischen Geistes sprechen?'[58] The ability of the intellectual to hover between good and evil is exposed powerfully in the text by Mephisto,[59] but this subtle conception is still seen as an affront by cultural functionaries who draw the only possible justification for their power from the idea that the German 'Geist' resisted Hitler.

Eisler's defence of his parodies of Luther in the figure of Hanswurst is similarly offensive.[60] Hanswurst sits down to eat with the words, 'Hier sitz ich, ich kann nicht anders';[61] Eisler explains this as a materialist twist on Luther's courage in defence of his theological views, and his inability to carry these views through consistently in defence of the starving peasants whom he has

---

[54] Bunge, p. 115.
[55] Cf. the attack on the Berliner Ensemble *Urfaust* in *Neues Deutschland*, 27.5.1953, in Bunge, pp. 117–26.
[56] see, Dietzel and Geißler, pp. 132–38.
[57] Bunge, p. 140, Dietzel and Geißler, p. 133.
[58] Bunge, p. 141.
[59] Faust: Wie schnell bist du?
Mephisto: Schnell wie der Übergang vom Guten zum Bösen.
    Faustus, act 1, scene 4, p. 27.
[60] Cf. Bunge, p. 142.
[61] *Faustus*, act 2, scene 7, p. 58.

inspired. This kind of creative parody, as a form of discourse treating the past as a discontinuous textual resource rather than as a continually unfolding narrative, threatens those who rely on a legitimising continuity in history, and on unassailable representative figures, reduced to ciphers whose function is to refer forward in time (who, according to Socialist Realist orthodoxy, are 'typical').

Heinz Kamnitzer's statement: 'Die Vergangenheit ist nur sozusagen das Mittel, mit dem die Gegenwart exemplifiziert und ausgebreitet werden soll',[62] demonstrates just how close these two seemingly opposed conceptions actually are. In fact, the avantgardist approach to the past, as it emerges here, implies many possible points of connection with the present and many possible narratives; the conception defended by Abusch, Girnus and the others is simply one of these possible narratives. The reason it is called Socialist Realist is because it is what was politically expedient for the Communist Party at that moment, and for this reason, selecting any other narrative is a political act.

Under these circumstances, any attempt at self-defence by an artist who shares Marxist truth-criteria with his opponents is going to be difficult. Eisler's attempt to defend his text, and his unwillingness to make any alterations, draws criticism from his pupil Ernst-Hermann Meyer, who was not present on 13 May. The younger man's *Schadenfreude* at the discomfiture of his teacher is palpable, and the atmosphere is soured considerably: 'Du mußt entschuldigen, daß ich als dein Schüler dich kritisiere.'[63] Meyer's attitude, and the use to which it is put by Eisler's opponents, is a small-scale example of the conflict between the 'new' and 'old' intelligentsia, which was being played out in the GDR; anyone with experience of direct opposition to Nazism, let alone of exile in either the Soviet Union or the West, could still be unreliable, whether in their guilty weakness, as in the case of Becher, or in their independence of mind, as with Zweig. This is a process with certain parallels to the Soviet campaign to eliminate the old Bolsheviks in the 1930s.

Certain new arguments are brought forward, which illustrate further aspects of Socialist Realist dogma. For example, Meyer takes exception to Eisler's

---

[62] Bunge, p. 176.
[63] Bunge, p. 145, Dietzel and Geißler, p. 134.

assertion that artistic beauty has been used as a weapon of the ruling classes, in
order to keep the masses in their place. A cultural conservative such as Ulbricht
would find this attitude offensive, as it devalues working-class efforts to attain
the cultural heritage which has been denied to them. Therefore, Meyer links the
concept of beauty with 'progressive' art, with humanism, 'Volksverbundenheit'
and 'Allgemeingültigkeit', and goes on to apply Zhdanov's decrees on music to
the current debate:[64]

Schön ist diejenige künstlerische Aussage, die die Menschen in ihrem Kampf um ihre
materielle und geistige Weiterentwicklung vorwärts führt und bereichert und die sie bejahen
[...] Wer die künstlerische Schönheit, ihre Funktion und ihre Bedeutung verkennt oder
verneint oder gar verspottet, muß notwendigerweise die große Kunst der Klassik vermissen.[65]

Girnus takes up this theme in his comments on Classicism, although his
argumentation is somewhat odd, confusing two entirely separate meanings of
the word 'klassisch':

Aber warum nennen wir [die klassische Epoche] klassisch? Weil sie eben Prinzipien des
Klassischen realisiert! Das heißt, wir müssen den Begriff des Klassischen auch als eine Art
normativen Begriff gebrauchen.[66]

In other words, Classical models must be followed because they present the
identity of form and content: 'Das heißt, [...] daß also die künstlerische Form in
der denkbar adäquatesten Weise einen bestimmten gesellschaftlichen und
historischen Inhalt zum Ausdruck bringt.'[67]

This kind of statement defies analysis. What is important about such theories
is that they were considered seriously by people who did not essentially agree
with them, so that an argument which was simply an administrative weapon
could be given the appearance of a serious contribution to debate. Intellectuals
like Brecht or Becher, each in his own individual way, saw the GDR as

---

[64] Note that Brecht had warned Eisler in August 1951 that there might be problems when the SED began to apply
Zhdanov's decrees in the GDR: cf. Lucchesi, p. 258. In fact, the decrees were published for the first time in Germany
in 1951: Andrej Shdanow, *Über Kunst und Wissenschaft* (Berlin: Aufbau, 1951).

[65] Bunge, p. 148.

[66] Bunge, pp. 152–53.

[67] Bunge, p. 153.

representing this potential synthesis of 'Geist' and 'Macht' after the defeat of Nazism, and it was hard to disagree with statements by Stalin or Zhdanov on the matter. Where Brecht differs from the other participants in the discussion is in his understanding of the development of artistic form, which is more consistently dialectical than that expressed by Girnus. For example, Girnus claims that the 'Erbe' ('ein geschichtliches Faktum') must be developed further, that Goethe arrived at a conclusion, expressed in the line, 'Wer immer strebend sich bemüht, den können wir erlösen', which is developed further by dialectical materialism into the idea that the proletariat can liberate itself. Brecht, on the other hand, considers that 'die Entwicklung in Form von Widersprüchen vor sich [geht]', and that Eisler's Faustus is an antithesis, 'eine kritische Weiterentwicklung'.[68] Although these are seemingly minor disagreements, they delineate a field of conflict in which Brecht exercises his opposition to the imposition of Socialist Realism; as I have shown, individuals defined these areas of resistance and complicity on their own terms, as the ideological system provided the individual with a space in which to work out individual forms of compromise. This flexibility was one of the great strengths of Marxism-Leninism.

Abusch opposes Brecht's idea that Eisler's Faustus is 'ein dunkler Zwilling'[69] of Goethe's figure on the grounds that Eisler's conception is retrograde. A truly socialist development of the Faustus legend would show, 'daß eben diese Persönlichkeit in einem sozialistischen Sinne vollendet wird, d.h., daß das Dilemma Gesellschaft und Persönlichkeit gelöst wird'.[70] Since the GDR is the place where this synthesis occurs, a negation of Goethe is an attack on the GDR.

Opposition is particularly difficult when the argument proceeds by logical steps to the conclusion that avantgarde artists lack 'die Liebe zum deutschen Volk', and that 'der Patriotismus [...] ein unlösbarer Bestandteil des Kampfes für eine höhere Gesellschaftsordnung ist'.[71] Constant reference to Stalin's

---

[68] Bunge, pp. 167–68.
[69] Brecht, 'Gegenthesen', Bunge, p. 161, Dietzel and Geißler, p. 138.
[70] Bunge, p. 172.
[71] Bunge, p. 155.

speech at the 19th Congress shows how his change of direction on the German question brought his personal political power into line with his ideological authority, possibly for the first time since 1945, and the 'integrationists' were able to use the concept of patriotism to work against German reunification. However, now that political developments were accelerating in Moscow, the 'integrationists' could no longer take such authority for granted.

It seems to me that it is for this reason that the 'integrationist' line is being propagated so energetically, even though only a few people at the top of the leadership could have known about Beria's demands. Hans Rodenberg insists that, during the construction of socialism, 'die Entscheidung im Kunstwerk getroffen werden muß, und zwar nicht nur die negative Entscheidung, sondern die positive Entscheidung'.[72] There is a sense of urgency about the attacks on Eisler, which the regime has insisted on because of the precariousness of the situation, though Rodenberg's statement, which implies that this is only a temporary phenomenon, is not to be taken seriously.

Walter Felsenstein objects to this aggressive tone and to the vocabulary of Girnus and Meyer, which contains 'Anklagen [...] die einen Autor [...] nahezu zum kulturpolitischen Verbrecher und Vaterlandsverräter machen'.[73] Felsenstein is obviously intimidated by the proceedings, and his complaints about the tone of the discussion are met with hostility from Abusch, who implies that Fischer's article was a provocation which demanded a response. The session ends with a peroration from Walter Besenbruch which cannot help but provoke comparisons with the Inquisition:

Und mit dem Kampf gegen die Zerstörung [des nationalen Erbes] kämpfen wir um denjenigen, der, zeitbedingt, unter bedingten Umständen, wie es auch immer sei, als Träger dieser Zerstörung auftritt. Wir kämpfen um ihn solange, bis er es eingesehen hat, bis er mit seiner ganzen Potenz die Wendung vollzieht.[74]

---

[72] Bunge, p. 164.
[73] Bunge, p. 157, Dietzel and Geißler, p. 135.
[74] Bunge, p. 177.

THIRD 'MITTWOCH-GESELLSCHAFT': 10 JUNE 1953

While Eisler's humiliation was continuing in the press, the dismissal of Peter Huchel was carried out through purely administrative channels. Huchel returned to Berlin on 2 June; although the manoeuvre, planned by Abusch and Becher, to trap him with a faked 'Selbstkritik', had failed, he was still obliged at the Presidium meeting of 10 June to express agreement with the action taken against him.[75] The Presidium declared that the commission which had been formed to report on alterations to the editorial policy of *Sinn und Form*, and which had never met, should have its proposals ready for 18 June. As the atmosphere in the 'Mittwoch-Gesellschaften' becomes more vituperative, we see the tensions which were unravelling in the Soviet and GDR leaderships played out on a smaller scale in the Academy: the declaration of the 'New Course' on 9 June increased the pressure on all parties, although the extent of the changes which Beria's policy could have brought was clear to few at the time.

Nevertheless, there are signs that Eisler's supporters were fighting back at the third meeting, thanks to interventions from Arnold Zweig, Hermann Duncker and Helene Weigel.[76] Abusch opens proceedings with a recapitulation of the questions which Eisler has supposedly not answered; the position of his accusers has not changed since the last session, and they have been backed up by an extensive press campaign.[77] Under the circumstances, Zweig's scholarly defence of Eisler is courageous, but it has no perceptible effect on the course of the discussion, as Zweig is working within a conceptual scheme, that of the old-fashioned liberal humanist literary critic, which leaves him isolated. In many ways, Becher is the closest to Zweig in his attitude to literature, but the contrast is instructive. Zweig's view of literature is of a piece with his 'Weltanschauung', and he is prepared to speak out when he feels that either is threatened; however, the ideological precepts which lead him to defend Eisler

---

[75] Beschluß-Protokoll der Präsidiumssitzung vom 10.Juni 1953: 'Herr Huchel erklärt sich mit unserem Schreiben vom 15.5.1953 einverstanden, daß sein Einzelvertrag mit dem 30.11.1953 abläuft und er als Chefredakteur mit diesem Zeitpunkt ausscheidet' (Dietzel and Geißler, p. 145).

[76] The protocol of the third 'Mittwoch-Gesellschaft' is reproduced in Bunge, pp. 191–246. There is a brief extract in Dietzel and Geißler, p. 139, which does not do justice to the transformed atmosphere at the meeting.

[77] Cf. readers' letters to *Neues Deutschland*, in Bunge, pp. 181–86.

actually prevent him from intervening effectively in the debate. He is simply armed with the wrong weapons.

An indication of the distance between Zweig and the other participants is his discussion of Goethe's irony, and his criticism of the tendency of Marxist critics to see everything as 'Goethescher Ernst'.[78] The concept of irony, and of the often uncomfortably protean nature of Goethe's work, exposes the intellectual poverty of this literary purge, which reduces Goethe to a legitimising cliché. As in the case of *Sinn und Form*, Goethe's work demonstrates the impossibility of pinning down a final meaning, an ideological centredness, in language. Girnus demon-strates the problem at the core of Socialist Realism as a legitimising practice by protesting that Eisler's text is 'nicht eindeutig zu fassen'.[79] As we have seen, literary ambiguity exposes the artificiality of the semantic and political barriers of the Cold War, which were constructed to try to stem the ebb and flow of political forces described in the course of this study. Of course, the implications of this attitude to language also undermine the counter-model of 'dissidence', which is in itself a form of legitimising practice based on a very strict set of truth-claims. Attempts to claim figures such as Zweig or Huchel as 'dissidents' disguise the complexity of the issue, ignoring the way in which *Sinn und Form* in particular set out to explore and criticise many notions of reconstructed German identity after 1945.

Zweig himself shares many of the humanist literary values which had motivated Becher, insisting that there is a truth to be carried in literary language, which survived the attempts of the National Socialists to destroy it. As we saw in Chapter Three of this study, the Marxist-Leninist system was vulnerable to attack from this quarter because the ideology itself was based on many of these assumptions, but it is this common ground which leaves Zweig unable to understand the nature of the developments which he opposes. He is concerned with the contemporary relevance of the discussion, and of Eisler's work, and he invokes the Academy's 'all-German' basis without seemingly realising that the only purpose of the debate is to undermine that basis:

[78] Bunge, p. 195.
[79] Bunge, p. 209.

Ich bin nämlich der Meinung, daß unsere Diskussion ausgezeichnet war und sich gedruckt sehr anständig lesen wird, daß aber keiner merken wird, daß dies im Mai und Juni 1953 gesprochen worden ist, wo die Frage der Vereinigung Deutschlands uns auf den Nägeln brennt und wir wissen, was wir alles zu tun haben, um eine gesamtdeutsche Plattform zu erhalten.[80]

Later in the discussion, Gustav Just, who a few months before had expressed doubts about the appointment of Abusch as Permanent Secretary of the Sektion Dichtkunst, took up Zweig's comments about the effect in the West, but he put an explicitly 'integrationist' slant on the issue. He declared that the West German press will be 'mächtig geärgert', because, once public corrections are made to Eisler's text, they would no longer be able to shout about, 'wie die "Kommu-nisten" mit dem nationalen Erbe umspringen und [...] wie sie sich an der angehäuften Kultur versündigen'. Just linked this somewhat convoluted argument with the idea that the German nation is being formed 'auf unserer Seite der Barrikade', presumably before the astonished eyes of Western onlookers.[81] Of course, this is a view of German nationhood formed in opposition to the West, a political community defined by what it excludes, and as such is of a piece with the 'integrationist' project. However, Just's statements are interesting, because Eisler's critics had gone out of their way at all three meetings to deny that *Faustus* had the contemporary relevance which Brecht and Zweig see in it. We can perhaps detect a certain idealism in Just's words, a feeling, shared with Zweig, that the debate actually means something other than the administrative imposition of Party discipline. Just's fall in 1956, in the show trial with Walter Janka, seems to add credence to this suspicion.

Naturally, if the debate is assessed in its proper context, it is clear that the tone of the criticisms of Eisler is so harsh, pitched at a level designed to jeopardise any 'all-German' understanding, precisely because 'die Frage der Vereinigung Deutschlands uns auf den Nägeln brennt'. The question of German unity or division underlies every statement in the protocol; we need look no further for an explanation for the ineffectiveness of Zweig's interventions and his marginalisation in the Academy.

[80] Bunge, p. 195.
[81] Bunge, p. 225.

The bulk of the discussion concerned the questions raised by Brecht's twelve 'Thesen', which were presented by Abusch at the beginning of the session. Brecht's achievement here was to be able to bring the discussion onto ground where he and Eisler could put up a more spirited defence; Brecht had ensured that the debate revolved to a certain extent round his own personal standing, which was still high, despite the press campaign against the Berliner Ensemble. That the administrative structure of the Academy obliged such views to be heard is an expression of the tenacity of its 'all-German' foundation and the emphasis which it put on individual personalities rather than on the functions of a 'mass organisation' like the Kulturbund.

Brecht's 'Thesen' provoked a discussion which was less inquisitorial than the second 'Mittwoch-Gesellschaft', which was an attempt to put into practice the principles of 'Kritik und Selbstkritik'. Girnus asks whether the figure of Faustus as he appears in Eisler's text is able to encourage 'die Arbeiterklasse, die Bauern, und natürlich auch die Intelligenz, [...] umgestaltend auf die Wirklichkeit einzuwirken'.[82] This question is based on the criticism that the revolutionary peasantry appears only as a passive, defeated force. Girnus claims that a dramatic concept in which the protagonist is 'von den Erynnien seines eigenen Gewissens verfolgt', rather than being judged by the group with an objective grasp of historical truth, is an 'antike Konzeption'.[83]

This externalisation and reduction of conflict to the clash of sociological archetypes is a key issue in the legitimisation strategy of the SED, as it involves identifying what Heinz Kamnitzer calls the 'Träger der Nation'.[84] The concept of national unity is equated with the historical function of a particular class, and thus with the representative of that class, and so the only guarantee of national unity is for the GDR to be consolidated as the state in which this line achieves its highest expression. Brecht works within this paradigm, but he subverts it in an interesting piece of sophistry when he interprets *Faustus* as an important lesson in the development of a new generation of intellectuals:

[82] Bunge, p. 202.
[83] Bunge, p. 201.
[84] Bunge, p. 214.

[Das Proletariat] müsse aus sich heraus eine Intelligenz entwickeln, die nicht diese verräterische Haltung einnimmt, wie sie Faustus einnimmt, es habe also diesen Grundfehler zu korrigieren.[85]

Brecht pursues this line aggressively against a claim by Becher, who has been fulfilling the chairman's role with an air of neutrality, that his opinion represents a restatement of the 'Misere' theory. The theory has become a weapon to be used against opponents, in a brutally simplified form far removed from the analysis which Abusch put forward in *Irrweg einer Nation*; Becher caricatures Brecht's position thus: '[...] die ganze Intelligenz ist übergelaufen, die Arbeiterschaft muß sich eine neue Intelligenz schaffen.'[86] Brecht reacts sharply to this criticism, replying that what he means is that the proletariat should work to overcome the gap between itself and the intelligentsia. Most of his interventions in the debate are aimed at making sure that his words are not misunderstood or misused, exploiting his talent for turning questions back on an accuser in order to keep himself out of the firing line. However, a decision seems to have been made that Eisler's friends, particularly Brecht, will come out more strongly in his defence.

For example, when Walter Besenbruch tries to transform the session into a ritualised tribunal, as the second session had become, Brecht protests strongly about Besenbruch's use of the phrase 'Wühlen im Dreck' to describe Eisler's text: 'Das ist immer gesagt worden, wenn irgendwo etwas Schlechtes aufgedeckt wurde. Freude am Wühlen im Dreck.'[87] Although Besenbruch makes no gesture towards retracting his remark, the atmosphere is nevertheless changed, and Eisler's critics have to proceed less aggressively. Brecht's personal standing, the 'all-German' orientation of the Academy, and, perhaps, a certain defensiveness on the part of functionaries surprised by the 'New Course', have enabled Brecht to exploit his considerable room for manoeuvre.

---

[85] Bunge, p. 202. Dietzel and Geißler, p. 139.

[86] Bunge, p. 217. A rejection of the older generation of intellectuals would also threaten Becher's position; I have already discussed this question in relation to Becher's exchange of letters with Hans Lorbeer, and to Becher's influence on the programme of the *Kulturbund*. There is a painful continuity in Becher's self-justifications, even after he has betrayed everything which he imagined he stood for.

[87] Bunge, p. 208.

Becher tries to steer a middle course by supporting Brecht in his objection to Besenbruch's remarks, and he modifies considerably some of the more personal attacks on Eisler by taking into account Eisler's fears about the treachery of German intellectuals who have declared in favour of the Federal Republic. The fact that Eisler's text is 'mißlungen' should not be held against him personally; he is not a reactionary. Becher turns on Girnus and takes issue with the idea that progressive forces have been a constant presence in German history:

[...] wie kommt es, lieber Genosse Girnus, daß diese herrliche, strahlende, 'einmalige' Kulturnation es nie zu einer Revolution gebracht hat und zweitens einen Hitler an die Macht kommen ließ und es nicht fertiggebracht hat, selbst mit Hitler Schluß zu machen?[88]

Becher stands here in opposition to the hard-line 'integrationist' position; his remarks on the failure of 'die deutsche Literatur' to become a genuine political force before 1933 would have been described as reactionary if they had been made by Eisler. Becher ends with his customary argument that 'literature' resisted Hitler, stating, '[...] die deutsche Literatur hat [...] alles das sozusagen wieder gutgemacht',[89] but he has contributed, like Brecht, to a softening of the tone of the debate, while demonstrating his ability to separate his cultural aspirations from his administrative activity. Of course, Becher's relatively conciliatory interventions also work in another direction, as it is largely through them that Eisler's supporters can be convinced that all participants in the debate are working for the same aim, that is, to prevent the division of Germany.

The end of the debate was inconclusive, largely because Brecht was able to take the fight to his opponents. However, the administrative processes were still under way, with critical articles appearing in *Neue Deutsche Literatur* and *Neues Deutschland*.[90] Although the real fightback against the 'integrationist' line, and against the dismissal of Huchel from the editorship of *Sinn und Form*, did not begin until the aftermath of the 17 June uprising, the contrast between the protocols of the second and third 'Mittwoch-Gesellschaften' seems to

---

[88] Bunge, p. 227.

[89] Bunge, p. 226.

[90] Gerhard Schulz, 'Zur Diskussion über Hanns Eislers Faustoper', *Neue Deutsche Literatur*, 3 (1953), no. 6; 'Das Faust-Problem in der sowjetischen Literatur', *Neues Deutschland*, 17.6.1953.

indicate that an attempt to reassert intellectual freedom was under way slightly earlier, perhaps encouraged by the 'New Course'. Whether this is the case or not, the aggressive disrespect with which Eisler was treated threw him into a state of depression, expressed in his letter to the Central Committee of the SED on 30 October 1953:

Nach der Faustus-Attacke merkte ich, daß mir jeder Impuls, Musik zu schreiben, abhanden gekommen war [...] Ich habe nun aber keine Hoffnung, den für mich lebenswichtigen Impuls, Musik zu schreiben, anderswo wieder zu finden, als in der Deutschen Demokratischen Republik.[91]

---

[91] Cit. Bunge, pp. 263–64, Dietzel and Geißler, pp. 139–40.

CHAPTER SEVEN

'[...] UND DA HATTEN WIR ANDERE SORGEN.'[1]

FREE SPEECH, DISCIPLINE AND REPRESSION IN THE ACADEMY IN THE WAKE OF 17 JUNE 1953

In the course of this study, it has been shown that the development of cultural policy in the Soviet Zone/GDR cannot be properly understood in isolation from a broader context of political and ideological conflicts and processes. These processes manifested themselves in terms of a complex of power relations within which the members of the East German intellectual and artistic elite struggled to construct independent spaces for the production of meaning. The domination of individuals in an ideological system such as Marxism-Leninism should not be regarded as the purely passive reception and internalisation of ideological categories and symbolic forms, particularly not in the case of intellectuals, upon whom the system relied for legitimacy and self-perpetuation, but as an active process of self-understanding in which the Marxist intellectual creates an individual accommodation with the system. Each individual experiences this process as an act of free will, unaware that the parameters of this experience are set by a series of assumptions which are absorbed and transformed in the symbolic matrix of Marxism-Leninism. In our case, as emerged in my discussion of Becher, these assumptions include attitudes drawn from German cultural history combined with a dialectical world-view based on the possibility of reconciling a supposed dichotomy of 'Geist' and 'Macht', and the psychological need to construct the Soviet Union as an idealised abstraction to set in (dialectical) opposition to Nazism. The intellectual effort required to maintain at all costs the integrity of a world-view is a fascinating feature of the individual responses of very the different individuals who came together at the founding of the Academy.

---

[1] Alexander Abusch speaking at the Plenary session of the Deutsche Akademie der Künste, 26.6.1953: 'Die Sitzung [der Kommission für *Sinn und Form*] war für den 18. Juni vorgesehen, und da hatten wir andere Sorgen' Dietzel and Geißler, p. 146.

As we have seen, studies of Marxist-Leninist ideology have often assumed a direct, vertical transmission of ideological control, a considerable oversimplification which distorts our understanding of a whole range of issues in post-war German history and culture. A close analysis of GDR cultural politics demonstrates that the 'ideological system' should by no means be identified with the regime, with the state (a troublesome concept in its own right, fought over by the 'integrationists'), with the Soviet Union or with Stalin himself. Each of these four is both a physical entity (subject to, and source of, power) and a symbolic element in the ideological system (subject to, and source of, authority and legitimacy). The symbolic value for intellectuals like Becher, Brecht and Eisler of the SED's claim to legitimacy was not entirely under the control of the Party itself, riven as it was by conflicting interpretations of that claim; this meant that the categories of Marxism and of Marxism-Leninism could be employed in strategies which created space for independent action. Conversely, the symbolic value of this legitimacy rested on a claim of totality and of the unity of disciplined Party with working-class political aspiration (now broadened into the concept of 'Volk'); Marxist intellectuals relied on this ideologised fiction of unity for the legitimacy of their artistic and political activity, in particular giving a sense of purpose to their opposition to Nazism. Thus, the nature of the spaces which they created for independent strategies was strictly defined by their ideologised understanding of GDR society and SED rule.

The conditions for action described above are the end point of my investigation of the contradictions and (seeming) paradoxes running through the German policy of the Soviet Union and the consolidation of SED rule. Stalin's policy of trying to attain German unity for the purposes of plunder opened up in Germany an ideological battle over whose terms Stalin himself had little control. In turn, this conflict was played out, in terms determined to a great extent by the pre-dispositions of several high-profile individuals, on a more intimate scale within the East German cultural elite.

In the aftermath of 17 June 1953, the various strands in this conflict were exposed as the parties manoeuvred openly for advantage. In fact, it is only by considering the tensions which emerge in cultural policy in June and July 1953 that we can come to a satisfactory understanding of the development of cultural policy in the Soviet Zone/GDR. Without an understanding of the extraordinary conflicts in, for example, the Deutsche Akademie der Künste, the contradictions in SMAD and SED cultural policy could still be dismissed as 'tactical variants' or localised conflicts of interest. The implications for analyses of German division are profound.

Bearing this in mind, we can read the sudden reversal of fortunes in the Academy in June 1953 in terms of the ideological analysis set out above. Reading the protocols of the debates in the Academy, one is struck by the reccurrence of the contradictory responses described in the case studies in Chapter Six: the assertion of freedom of expression which, however, does not go beyond a certain limit. Prominent *Genossen* like Becher seem to have liberated themselves temporarily from Party discipline, but, as we shall see, the limits to this new discourse are set by the suppression of the implications of the 17 June uprising. The 'events' are not mentioned directly, although they resonate through the discussions; an honest appraisal of the significance of the uprising for the legitimacy of communist rule in the GDR would have disrupted the ideological self-justification of Marxist intellectuals on which their work in the GDR was based.

The illegitimacy of the SED's rule, which the uprising had exposed, is reflected in the confusion over the administrative competence of the Academy. The contradictions and weaknesses within both the regime and the Academy were exposed, rather than created, in June 1953. The more coordinated assertiveness of Huchel's defenders, which had begun after the declaration of the 'New Course', becomes an all-out attack. Eisler makes the strongest defence yet of the work of *Sinn und Form*:

Ich glaube, 'Sinn und Form' war trotz all der Schwächen, die sie hatte, eine ganz hervorragende Publikation der Akademie. Ich weiß von meinen Freunden in Westdeutschland und auch in Österreich, daß es die einzige Zeitschrift aus der DDR ist, die, allerdings in sehr begrenzten Kreisen, drüben ankommt.[2]

---

[2] Dietzel and Geißler, p. 146.

Eisler maintains that Huchel should be supported in his work, but that the journal should be 'etwas aktualisiert', which would have radically changed its character. Brecht takes up this theme with a direct attack on Friedrich Wolf: the latter had taken a small number of examples to which he objected (for example, *Faustus* or the poems of Oskar Maria Graf) and had presented them as typical in order to prove Huchel's incompetence. In Brecht's view, 'drei Jahrgänge und [...] der relativ in unserer Situation enorme Erfolg dieser Zeitschrift gerade im Westen'[3] are more important than a few errors of judgement. Becher, having freed himself from the requirements of Party discipline, and stooping from the chairman's role, where he had previously feigned neutrality, declares that the Academy should avoid demanding 'daß der arme Huchel keine Fehler machen darf'.[4]

It is notable in Becher's case that the events of 17 June have allowed him to speak freely while also enabling him to maintain the illusion that he stands above the controversy, representing 'Literature'. The posture of the artist for whom administrative matters are mere trivia, a posture which disguises his helplessness, is the point of consistency which allows him to distance himself from the plot to unseat Huchel, in which he had been intimately involved. In this way, Becher is able to suppress the full consequences of the 17 June uprising, which exposed the sordid nature of his compromise with a power which had no popular legitimacy whatsoever.

Brecht's attack continues with a forceful criticism of Abusch's handling of the *Sinn und Form* affair: 'Ich bin auch dafür, daß man Huchel dabei Hilfe an-gedeihen läßt [...] aber jedenfalls nicht eine solche Hilfe, wie sie ihm im letzten Heft durch Abusch geworden ist.'[5] Brecht objects to Abusch's attempt to sway the 'Faustus Debate' by excluding Brecht's *Gegenthesen* from publication in *Sinn und Form*. Although Brecht's criticism is stinging when he condemns Abusch's 'sehr eigentümliche Art und Weise, hier Einfluß zu gewinnen', he still considers that the debate had been 'eine sehr anständige Diskussion', despite his own awareness (demonstrated in the changing dynamics of the

---

[3] Dietzel and Geißler, p. 146.
[4] Dietzel and Geißler, p. 147.
[5] Dietzel and Geißler, p. 147.

debate after the declaration of the 'New Course') that the outcome rested on political developments in the GDR. In his juxtaposition of open debate, which would have included the publication of the *Gegenthesen*, with Abusch's machinations, Brecht demonstrates the self-deceptive sleight-of-hand discussed in the case study on *Das Verhör des Lukullus*. Firstly, he downplays (presumably deliberately) his own role as tactician in the defence of Eisler, and his ability to select arguments according to the needs of the situation. Secondly, and more seriously, his attachment to the idea of open discussion among socialist artists, the dialectical 'Beseitigung von Mißverständnissen', suppresses the fact that the 17 June uprising has called into question the very basis of that discussion. It is not a case of artist versus bureaucrat, but the radical exposure of the inadequacy of Brecht's *Weltanschauung*. Nevertheless, an examination of the material relating to Brecht's role in the Academy reveals considerable courage in the defence of his colleagues Dessau, Eisler and Huchel, and in the preservation of a more open relationship with Western artists, such as the conductor Hermann Scherchen.

In replying to Brecht, Abusch attempts to justify his own conduct by claiming that he had prevented any action being taken against *Sinn und Form*, because Huchel was away: 'ich sagte [...] eine Diskussion über "Sinn und Form" kann nur stattfinden in Gegenwart von Huchel.' This is a plain lie, different in quality from the sophisticated self-deceptions of other Academy members: if things turned against Abusch, he would be a useful scapegoat, allowing Becher to claim that he knew nothing about any plot against Huchel.The attacks on Abusch by Brecht and Eisler centre on the accusation that he tried to misrepresent the 'Faustus Debate' by making sure that *Sinn und Form* contained no counter-argument against his own piece. The concession that Brecht's *Gegenthesen* should also appear is significant, in that it undermines the claim that the Academy should be the ultimate arbiter of meaning and the benchmark of ideological correctness in GDR cultural life. For the Academy to assert its authority in the manner proposed by Friedrich Wolf earlier in the discussion would entail creating the illusion of unanimity in all public pronouncements. Considered in terms of Marxist-Leninist literary theory, this lack of unanimity is serious: radically opposed opinions in the higher echelons of the GDR intelligentsia about a subject as important as the 'Misère' theory imply the possibility of differences over the ideological and social development of the state.

The failure of members of the GDR cultural elite to think the situation through to so radical a conclusion, which would have called into question their *Weltanschauung* and the purpose of their creative activity, can be read in terms of the disparate forms of intellectual and emotional accommodation with the regime discussed in the previous chapters. Thus, even after the Soviet intervention in East Berlin, Brecht is able to suggest the following improvements for *Sinn und Form*:

Wir brauchen Beiträge, die die großen historischen Errungenschaften der DDR beschreiben, so daß die Leute in Westdeutschland und in der DDR sie wirklich als sachlich aufnehmen und verstehen können. Die Fakten sind überwältigend.[6]

With these words, Brecht sets the limits of the discussion on *Sinn und Form*, the significance of the uprising and of the Soviet intervention has been swept under the carpet, and the task is now simply seen as a question of removing bureaucratic obstructionism, so that *Sinn und Form* can help the GDR fulfil its historical mission. The important concessions won for *Sinn und Form* are thus both a victory and a defeat. The commission appointed at the Plenary Session of 26 June to discuss possible 'improvements' to *Sinn und Form* met on 2 July,[7] giving Huchel an opportunity to defend himself with vigorous objections to Abusch's methods. The real success of Huchel's defenders is the stabilisation of the institutional position of *Sinn und Form*, allowing Huchel to continue at his post with full responsibility for producing the journal and selecting material for publication, despite suggestions by Wolf that the journal should become an almanach reflecting the work of all sections of the Academy. In stark contrast to

---

[6] Stephen Parker, '"Sinn und Form"', Peter Huchel und der 17. Juni 1953', p. 749, cited from the protocol of the meeting on 2 July 1953 of the commission for *Sinn und Form*. The stenographic summary of the meeting reproduced by Dietzel and Geißler (p. 149) does not hint at the extraordinary nature of the meeting, which gives us a decisive insight into the relationship of figures such as Brecht and Abusch with the exercise of power in the GDR.

[7] The commission consisted of Abusch, Dessau, Brecht, Huchel, Jhering and Wolf; also present were Eisler and Zweig.

the atmosphere of the *Mittwoch-Gesellschaften*, such suggestions are given no serious consideration, and Huchel is able to ensure that *Sinn und Form* can continue to be published as before.

The documentation discussed here, when read in the context of the continuing debate over conflicts of interest within the KPD/SED and SMAD, and in the light of Stalin's German policy, demonstrates the intimate connection between international political developments and the internal tensions within the GDR cultural elite. A full understanding of the nature of these tensions, and of the issues of resistance and complicity have explored in this study, is not possible without these interlocking contexts. However, the connections between the various levels of command are by no means direct, monolithic or mechanistically vertical, as many commentators have assumed, but are shot through with ambiguities, conflicts of interest and fundamental questions of ideology, legitimacy and artistic and political responsibility. There is a period in late June and early July 1953 when these conflicts emerge into the open, and the power relations within the GDR regime and the Academy are drastically altered. It is only by taking seriously these power struggles that we can explain the contradictions and inconsistencies in cultural policy in the Soviet Zone/GDR, and the incomplete success of the attempts of the 'integrationists' within the SED to dominate political and artistic discourse within the Academy.

At this point, in June and July 1953, the various levels which have been explored in the course of this study are connected in a moment of immense upheaval, from the arrest of Beria and Ulbricht's survival to the abrupt reversal of power relations in the Academy. Yet, for reasons which have been discussed in my exploration of the work and motivation of Becher, Brecht and others, what was achieved in the Academy fell far short of the potential for change. The full extent of this potential is clear from Abusch's despairing attempts at self-defence: 'Für "Sinn und Form" kann es, auf Grund der internationalen Entspannungen und der Aussicht auf die Einigung Deutschlands, ungeahnte Möglichkeiten geben.'[8] This extraordinary statement gives us some idea of the panic in the leadership of the SED in June and July 1953, an impression which is reinforced by the documentation of the witchhunt against Rudolf Herrnstadt,

---

[8] Parker, '"Sinn und Form"', Peter Huchel und der 17. Juni 1953', p. 749.

referred to in Chapter Three of this study. By the time of the Central Committee meeting of 24–26 July, Ulbricht and his supporters had begun to reassert themselves, and the space which had opened for a brief period, allowing a form of discourse which had been suppressed since the late 1940s, to be expressed again in political and cultural institutions, was abruptly closed. Helmut Müller-Enbergs, in his documentation of the 'Herrnstadt Case', notes the consternation among senior SED cadres after the Politburo had heard the first mention of the charges against Herrnstadt and Wilhelm Zaisser on 23 July.[9] The Party closes ranks around Ulbricht, and Becher reverts to the discipline which he had abandoned only a month before. Müller-Enbergs records Becher's condemnation of Herrnstadt on the 25 July. Becher reminds the gathered *Genossen* of a phrase which Herrnstadt had used at a Politburo meeting: 'Dein Fehler, Genosse Becher, ist der, daß Du nicht einsiehst, daß Ihr nicht genug geprügelt worden seid.' Becher then twists this sentence into a vicious condemnation of Herrnstadt's supposed inability to accept criticism, and the tenor of his remarks ('Lieber Genosse Herrnstadt, ich habe ein erstklassiges Gedächtnis.'[10]) speaks volumes about Becher's fear that he could be caught up in the approaching purge. However, it seems to me that Becher's fears at this point probably result from an exaggerated sense of his own importance and influence in the Party: he was constitutionally incapable by this point of exploiting the room for manoeuvre which the 17 June uprising had offered him.The true extent of this opportunity emerges from a detailed study of the available documentation and its contextualisation in terms of the debates over the role of Stalin in German division. Bearing in mind the ques-tions raised in studying this documentation, particularly with reference to Abusch's extra-ordinary volte-face in distancing himself from a campaign which he and Becher had initiated, but whose consequences only Becher seemed likely to survive, we can begin to resolve some of the paradoxes which have driven my discussion of GDR cultural policy.

---

[9] Herrnstadt and Zaisser approached Grotewohl to complain about the charges, but the latter refused to hear them: 'Was wollt ihr von mir? Ich bitte, mich in Ruhe zu lassen! Ich kann nichts tun! Ich lehne jede Unterhaltung ab!' (Müller-Enbergs, p. 271).
[10] Müller-Enbergs, p. 304.

The inability of a particular strand in German cultural-historical discourse, a strand which became an orthodoxy of sorts, to register the significance of the 17 June uprising in both its European and its cultural context, meant that discrepancies in the imposition of control in GDR cultural life could be dismissed as unimportant. In other words, too consistent an analysis of the reasons for the illegitimacy and precariousness of the SED's rule in East Germany would have cast uncomfortable light on different, but related, questions of West German national identity as it was being formed in the 1950s.

Interpretations which focus on the internal contradictions of 'Stalinist' power structures are still controversial, revealing unresolved issues of dominance, orthodoxy and marginalisation in post-Reunification cultural and political discourse. For this reason, the questions of German cultural unity which have been discussed in this study are still of intense relevance to current concerns. Similarly, the approach questions of ideology, conformity and resistance put forward in this study should shed some light on the reasons why the GDR intellectual community failed to understand the true extent of the opportunity which had come their way. Becher's concluding statement on the 25 July stands as a fitting summary of the intellectual and personal weaknesses which had crippled his ability to act: 'Unser höchstes Freiheitsgefühl besteht in der Parteidisziplin.'[11]

---

[11] Müller-Enbergs, p. 305.

BIBLIOGRAPHY

Abusch, Alexander, *Irrweg einer Nation: Ein Beitrag zum Verständnis der deutschen Geschichte* (Berlin: Aufbau, 1946)

Ackermann, Anton, 'Gibt es einen besonderen deutschen Weg zum Sozialismus?', *Einheit*, no.1 (February 1946), 22–32

Adorno, Theodor, *Negative Dialektik*, in *Gesammelte Schriften*, 23 vols (Frankfurt a. M.: Suhrkamp, 1973–1986), VI

Aksenov, Yurii S., 'Postwar Stalinism: The Attack on the Intelligentsia', *Russian Studies in History*, 31 (1993), no. 4, 44–66

Andert, Reinhold, and Wolfgang Herzberg, *Der Sturz: Erich Honecker im Kreuzverhör* (Berlin and Weimar: Aufbau, 1990)

Bacon, Edwin, *The Gulag at War: Stalin's Forced Labour System in the Light of the Archives* (Basingstoke: Macmillan, 1994)

Badstübner, Rolf, '"Beratungen" bei J. W. Stalin: Neue Dokumente. Dokumente aus den Jahren 1945–1948', *Utopie kreativ*, 7 (March 1991), 99–116

Badstübner, Rolf, 'Die Abkehr vom "besonderen deutschen Weg": Die Hinwendung zum sowjetischen Modell', in *Brüche–Krisen–Wendepunkte: Neubefragung von DDR-Geschichte*, ed. by Jochen Černý (Leipzig: Urania-Verlag, 1990), pp. 14–27

Badstübner, Rolf and Wilfried Loth (eds), *Wilhelm Pieck: Aufzeichnungen zur Deutschland-politik 1945–1953* (Berlin: Akademie Verlag, 1994)

Baras, Victor, 'Beria's Fall and Ulbricht's Survival', *Soviet Studies*, 27 (1975), 381–95

Baring, Arnulf, *Der 17. Juni 1953* (Cologne and Berlin: Kiepenheuer & Witsch, 1957, 3rd edn., 1966)

Barth, Bernd-Rainer, Christoph Links, Helmut Müller-Enbergs and Jan Wiegohs, *Wer war Wer in der DDR: Ein biographisches Handbuch* (Frankfurt a. M.: Fischer, 1995)

Bathrick, David, *The Powers of Speech: The Politics of Culture in the GDR*, (Lincoln and London: University of Nebraska Press, 1995)

Becher, Johannes R., *Gesammelte Werke*, ed. by Johannes-R.-Becher Archiv der Akademie der Künste zu Berlin, 18 vols (Berlin and Weimar: Aufbau, 1966–1979)

Becher, Johannes R., *Briefe 1909–1958*, ed. by Rolf Harder (Berlin and Weimar: Aufbau, 1993)

Becher, Johannes R., *Briefe an Johannes R. Becher 1909–1958*, ed. by Rolf Harder (Berlin and Weimar: Aufbau, 1993)

Bender, Klaus, *Deutschland einig Vaterland? Die Volkskongreßbewegung für deutsche Einheit und einen gerechten Frieden in der Deutschlandpolitik der Sozialistischen Einheitspartei Deutschlands* (Frankfurt a. M.: Peter Lang, 1992)

Beria, Sergo, *Moi otets: Lavrentii Beriya* (Moscow: Sovremennik, 1994)

Besymenski, Lew, '1953: Berija will die DDR beseitigen', *Die Zeit*, 15 October 1993, 81–83

Bialer, Seweryn (ed.), *Stalin and his Generals: Soviet Military Memoirs of World War II* (New York: Pegasus, 1969)

Bialer, Seweryn (ed.), *The Domestic Context of Soviet Foreign Policy* (Boulder, Colorado: Westview Press, 1981)

Bonwetsch, Bernd, 'Deutschlandpolitische Alternativen der Sowjetunion 1945–1955', *Deutsche Studien*, 24 (1986), 320–40

Borev, Yurii, *Staliniada* (Moscow: Sovetskii pisatel', 1990)

Bouvier, Beatrix W. and Horst-Peter Schultz (eds), *'... die SPD aber aufgehört hat, zu existieren.' Sozialdemokraten unter sowjetischer Besatzung* (Bonn: J. H. W. Dietz Nachf., 1991)

Brecht, Bertolt, *Große kommentierte Berliner und Weimarer Ausgabe*, ed. by Werner Hecht, Jan Knopf, Werner Mittenzwei, Klaus-Detlef Müller, 29 vols (Berlin and Weimar/Frankfurt a. M.: Suhrkamp/Aufbau, 1989–1998)

Broszat, Martin and Hermann Weber (eds), *SBZ-Handbuch: Staatliche Verwaltungen, Parteien, gesellschaftliche Organisationen und ihre Führungskräfte in der sowjetischen Besatzungszone Deutschlands 1945–1949* (Munich: Oldenbourg, 1993)

Bullock, Alan, *Hitler and Stalin: Parallel Lives* (London: HarperCollins, 1991)

Bunge, Hans, *Die Debatte um Hanns Eislers 'Johann Faustus': Eine Dokumentation* (Berlin: BasisDruck Verlag, 1991)

Bunge, Hans, *Fragen Sie mehr über Brecht: Hanns Eisler im Gespräch* (Munich and Leipzig: Rogner & Bernhard GmbH & Co./VEB Deutscher Verlag für Musik, 1975)

Buttlar, Wallrab von, *Ziele und Zielkonflikte der sowjetischen Deutschlandpolitik 1945–1947* (Stuttgart: Klett-Cotta, 1980)

Campbell, David, *Writing Security: United States Foreign Policy and the Politics of Identity* (Manchester: Manchester University Press, 1992)

Černý, Jochen (ed.), *Brüche–Krisen–Wendepunkte: Neubefragung von DDR-Geschichte* (Leipzig: Urania-Verlag, 1990)

Clark, Katerina, *The Soviet Novel: History as Ritual* (Chicago and London: University of Chicago Press, 1981)

Conquest, Robert, *Power and Policy in the USSR: The Study of Soviet Dynastics* (London: Macmillan, 1961)

Creuzberger, Stefan, 'Die Liquidierung antifaschistischer Organisationen in Berlin: Ein sowjetisches Dokument', *Deutschland Archiv*, 26 (1993), 1266–78

Davies, R. W., 'Forced Labour under Stalin: The Archive Revelations', *New Left Review*, 214 (Nov/Dec 1995), 62–80

Debus, Friedhelm, Manfred W. Hellmann and Horst Dieter Schlosser, *Sprachliche Normen und Normierungsfolgen in der DDR* (Hildesheim: Georg Olms, 1986)

Deicke, Günther, 'Über meine Jahre als NDL-Redakteur', *Sinn und Form*, 39 (1988), 330–41

Déry, Tibor, 'Zwischen Hoffnung und Argwohn: Stellungnahme im Petöfi-Kreis am 27. Juni 1956', *Sinn und Form*, 42 (1991), 625–36

Deutsches Institut für Zeitgeschichte, *Dokumente zur Deutschlandpolitik der Sowjetunion* (Berlin: 1957)

Dietrich, Gerd, 'Zwei Linien in der Kulturpolitik? Diskussionen in der SED-Führung 1947/48', in *Brüche–Krisen–Wendepunkte: Neubefragung von DDR-Geschichte*, ed. by Jochen Černý (Leipzig: Urania-Verlag, 1990), pp. 40–51

Dietrich, Gerd, *Politik und Kultur in der Sowjetischen Besatzungszone Deutschlands (SBZ) 1945–1949* (Bern: Peter Lang, 1993)

Dietzel, Ulrich and Geißler, Gudrun (eds), *Zwischen Diskussion und Disziplin: Dokumente zur Geschichte der Akademie der Künste (Ost), 1945/1950 bis 1993* (Berlin: Stiftung Archiv der Akademie der Künste, 1997)

Djilas, Milovan, *Conversations with Stalin* (London: Rupert Hart-Davis, 1962)

Dobrenko, Evgeni, 'Sumerki kul'tury: o natsional'nom samoznanii kul'tury pozdnego stalinizma', *Druzhba Narodov*, 2 (1991), 249–71

Dorpalen, Andreas, *German History in Marxist Perspective: The East German Approach* (Detroit: Wayne State University Press, 1985)

Dunham, Vera, *In Stalin's Time: Middleclass Values in Soviet Fiction* (Durham and London: Duke University Press, 1990)

Dunlop, John B., Richard Haugh and Alexis Klimoff (eds), *Aleksandr Solzhenitsyn: Critical Essays and Documentary Materials* (Belmont, Mass.: Nordland, 1973)

Eagleton, Terry, *Ideology* (London and New York: Longman, 1994)

Ebon, Martin, *Malenkov: A Biographical Study of Stalin's Successor* (London: Macmillan, 1953)

Eggebrecht, Axel, *Der halbe Weg: Zwischenbilanz einer Epoche* (Reinbek: Rowohlt, 1975)

Erler, Peter, Horst Laude and Manfred Wilke (eds), *'Nach Hitler kommen wir'. Dokumente zur Programmatik der Moskauer KPD-Führung 1944/45 für Nachkriegsdeutschland* (Berlin: Akademie Verlag, 1994)

Feuchtwanger, Lion / Arnold Zweig, *Briefwechsel 1933–1958*, 2 vols (Berlin and Weimar: Aufbau, 1984)

Filitov, A. M., *Germanskii vopros: ot raskola k ob"edineniyu* (Moscow: Mezhdunarodnye otnosheniya, 1993)

Fischer, Alexander, *Sowjetische Deutschlandpolitik im Zweiten Weltkrieg 1941–1945* (Stuttgart: Deutsche Verlagsanstalt, 1975)

Fischer, Alexander (ed.), *Studien zur Geschichte der SBZ/DDR* (Berlin: Duncker & Humblot, 1993)

Fischer, Ernst, 'Doktor Faustus und der deutsche Bauernkrieg', *Sinn und Form*, 3 (1952), 59–73

Foschepoth, Josef, 'Churchill, Adenauer und die Neutralisierung Deutschlands', *Deutschland Archiv*, 17 (1984), 1286–1301

Foucault, Michel, *Discipline and Punish: The Birth of the Prison* (Harmondsworth: Penguin, 1991)

Fuegi, John, *The Life and Lies of Bertolt Brecht* (London: HarperCollins, 1994)

Fulbrook, Mary, 'New *Historikerstreit*, Missed Opportunity, or New Beginning?', *German History*, 12 (1994), 203–7

Fulbrook, Mary, *Anatomy of a Dictatorship: Inside the GDR 1949–1989* (Oxford: Oxford University Press, 1995)

Gansel, Carsten (ed.), *Johannes R. Becher: Der gespaltene Dichter: Gedichte, Briefe, Dokumente 1945–1958* (Berlin: Aufbau Taschenbuch Verlag, 1991)

Garrard, John and Carol Garrard, *Inside the Soviet Writers' Union* (London: I. B. Tauris & Co., 1990)

Getty, J. Arch, Gábor Rittersporn and V. N. Zemkov, 'Victims of the Soviet Penal System in the Prewar Years: A First Approach on the Basis of Archival Evidence', *American Historical Review*, 98 (1993), 1017–49

Getty, J. Arch and Roberta T. Manning (eds), *Stalinist Terror: New Perspectives* (Cambridge: Cambridge University Press, 1993)

Gill, Graham, *Stalinism* (Atlantic Highlands, NJ: Humanities Press International, 1990)

Gniffke, Erich, *Jahre mit Ulbricht* (Cologne: Verlag Wissenschaft und Politik, 1966)

Goldmann, Bernd (ed.), *Peter Huchel / Hans Henny Jahnn: Ein Briefwechsel 1951–1959* (Mainz: Hase & Koehler, 1974)

Göttinger Arbeitskreis (ed.), *Die Deutschlandfrage von der staatlichen Teilung Deutschlands bis zum Tode Stalins*, Studien zur Deutschlandfrage, vol. 13 (Berlin: Duncker & Humblot, 1994)

Graml, Hermann, 'Die Legende von der verpaßten Gelegenheit', *Vierteljahrshefte für Zeitgeschichte*, 29 (1981), 307–41

Grotewohl, Otto, *Im Kampf um Deutschland: Reden und Aufsätze* (Berlin: Dietz, 1948)

Grotewohl, Otto, *Im Kampf um die einige Deutsche Demokratische Republik* (Berlin: Dietz, 1959)

Hacker, Jens, *Deutsche Irrtümer: Schönfärber und Helfershelfer der SED-Diktatur im Westen* (Frankfurt a. M. and Berlin: Ullstein, 1992)

Hahn, Werner G., *Postwar Soviet Politics: The Fall of Zhdanov and the Defeat of Moderation 1946–1953* (New York: Cornell University Press, 1982)

Harder, Rolf, 'Zum Anteil Johannes R. Bechers an der Herausbildung einer Konzeption zur politisch-moralischen Vernichtung des Faschismus', *Weimarer Beiträge*, 31 (1983), 724–33

Harding, Neil, *The State in Socialist Society* (London: Macmillan, 1984)

Hartmann, Anneli, Kubas "Gedicht vom Menschen" und die sowjetische Poemtradition', *Weimarer Beiträge*, 36 (1990), 1430–48

Hartmann, Anneli and Wolfgang Eggeling, 'Zum "Verbot" des Kulturbunds in West-Berlin 1947', *Deutschland Archiv*, 28 (1995), 1161–70

Havel, Václav, *Disturbing the Peace* (New York: Vintage, 1991)

Havemann, Robert, *Fragen antworten Fragen: Aus der Biographie eines deutschen Marxisten* (Munich: R. Piper, 1970)

Heider, Magdalena and Kerstin Thöns (eds), *SED und Intellektuelle in der DDR der fünfziger Jahre: Kulturbund-Protokolle* (Cologne: Edition Deutschland Archiv, 1990)

Heider, Magdalena, *Politik–Kultur–Kulturbund: Zur Gründungs- und Frühgeschichte des Kulturbundes zur demokratischen Erneuerung Deutschlands 1945–1954 in der SBZ/DDR* (Cologne: Bibliothek Wissenschaft und Politik, 1993)

Heitzer, Heinz, 'Für eine radikale Erneuerung der Geschichtsschreibung über die DDR', *Zeitschrift für Geschichte*, 38 (1990), 498–500

Heller, Mikhail and Alexander Nekrich, *Geschichte der Sowjetunion*, 2 vols (Frankfurt a. M.: Fischer, 1985)

Heym, Stefan, *Fünf Tage im Juni* (Frankfurt a. M.: Fischer, 1977)

Hilton, Ian, 'Sinn und Form: "Ein schlimmes Kapitel ..."', in *Peter Huchel*, ed. by Axel Vieregg (Frankfurt a. M.: Suhrkamp, 1986), pp. 249–64

Hirschman, Albert O., 'Exit, Voice and the Fate of the German Democratic Republic: An Essay in Conceptual History', *World Politics*, 45 (1993), 175–98

Holloway, David, *Stalin and the Bomb: The Soviet Union and Atomic Energy 1939–1956* (New Haven: Yale University Press, 1994)

Huchel, Peter, *Gesammelte Werke*, ed. by Axel Vieregg, 2 vols (Frankfurt a. M.: Suhrkamp, 1984)

Jäger, Manfred, 'Der Fall Peter Huchel: "Sinn und Form" dokumentiert den Hinauswurf seines ersten Chefredakteurs', *Deutschland Archiv*, 25 (1992), 1140–44

Jäger, Manfred, *Kultur und Politik in der DDR: Ein historischer Abriß* (Cologne: Edition Deutschland Archiv, 1st edn. 1982 and 2nd edn. 1995)

Jäger, Manfred, 'Ohne Gedächtnisverlust: Walter Jankas letzte Bücher', *Deutschland Archiv*, 28 (1995), 860–62

Jänicke, Martin, *Der dritte Weg: Die antistalinistische Opposition gegen Ulbricht seit 1953* (Cologne: Neuer Deutscher Verlag, 1988)

Johnson, Paul, *Intellectuals* (London: Weidenfeld & Nicolson, 1988)

Kaelbe, Hartmut, Jürgen Kocka and Hartmut Zwahr (eds), *Sozialgeschichte der DDR* (Stuttgart: Klett-Cotta, 1994)

Kantorowicz, Alfred, 'Einführung', *Ost und West*, 1 (1947), 3–8

Kantorowicz, Alfred, *Deutsches Tagebuch,* 2 vols (Munich: Kindler, 1959)

Kennedy-Pipe, Caroline, *Stalin's Cold War: Soviet Strategies in Europe 1943 to 1956* (Manchester and New York: Manchester University Press, 1995)

Kershaw, Ian, *The Nazi Dictatorship: Problems and Perspectives of Interpretation*, 3rd edn. (London: Edward Arnold, 1993)

Kessel, Martina, *Westeuropa und die deutsche Teilung: Englische und französische Deutschlandpolitik auf den Außenministerkonferenzen 1945–1947* (Munich: Oldenbourg, 1989)

Khrushchev, Nikita, *Khrushchev Remembers*, trans. by Strobe Talbot (London: Sphere, 1971)

Kiefer, Markus, 'Die Reaktion auf die "Stalin-Noten" in der zeitgenössischen deutschen Publizistik: Zur Widerlegung einer Legende', *Deutschland Archiv*, 22 (1989), 56–76

Kiefer, Markus, *Auf der Suche nach der nationalen Identität und Wegen yur deutschen Einheit: Die deutsche Frage in der überregionalen Tages- und Wochenpresse der Bundesrepublik 1949–1955* (Frankfurt a. M.: Peter Lang, 1992)

King, Janet, *Literarische Zeitschriften 1945–1970* (Stuttgart: Sammlung Metzler, 1974)

Kleinschmidt, Sebastian, 'Entretien avec Sebastien Kleinschmidt, rédacteur en chef de Sinn und Form', *La Revue des Revues*, 15 (1993), 29–41

Kleßmann, Christoph and Georg Wagner (eds), *Das gespaltene Land: Leben in Deutschland 1945 bis 1990: Texte und Dokumente* (Munich: C. H. Beck'sche Verlagsbuchhandlung, 1993)

Knight, Amy, *Beria: Stalin's First Lieutenant* (Princeton: Princeton University Press, 1993)

Knoll, Viktor and Lothar Kölm (eds), *Der Fall Berija: Protokoll einer Abrechnung: Das Plenum des ZK der KPdSU Juli 1953: Stenographischer Bericht* (Berlin: Aufbau, 1993)

Knoth, Nikola, 'Johannes R. Becher 1956/57: Eine DDR-Misere? Dokumentarischer Bericht', *Deutschland Archiv*, 24 (1991), 502–11

Knoth, Nikola, 'Loyale Intelligenz? Vorschläge und Forderungen 1953', in *Brüche–Krisen– Wendepunkte: Neubefragung von DDR-Geschichte*, ed. by Jochen Černý (Leipzig: Urania-Verlag, 1990), pp. 149–56

Kocka, Jürgen (ed.), *Historische DDR-Forschung: Aufsätze und Studien* (Berlin: Akademie Verlag, 1993)

Koestler, Arthur, *Frühe Empörung* (Vienna, Munich, Zurich: Molden, 1970)

Kondratovich, Alexei, 'Das letzte Jahr: Twardowski und "Nowy Mir" 1969', *Sinn und Form*, 42 (1991), 649–63

Kotkin, Stephen, *Magnetic Mountain: Stalinism as a Civilization* (Berkeley: University of California Press, 1995)

Kraus, Elisabeth, *Ministerien für das ganze Deutschland? Der alliierte Kontrollrat und die Frage Gesamtdeutscher Zentralverwaltungen* (Munich: Oldenbourg, 1990)

Krenzlin, Leonore, 'Theoretische Diskussionen und praktisches Bemühen um die Neu-bestimmung der Funktion der Literatur an der Wende der fünfziger Jahre', in *Literarisches Leben in der DDR 1945 bis 1960*, ed. by Ingeborg Münz-Koenen (Berlin: Akademie Verlag, 1980), pp. 152–95

Krenzlin, Leonore, 'Das "Formalismus-Plenum: Die Einführung eines kunstpolitischen Argumentationsmodells', in *Brüche–Krisen–Wendepunkte: Neubefragung von DDR-Geschichte*, ed. by Jochen Černý (Leipzig: Urania-Verlag, 1990)

Krisch, Henry, *German Politics under Soviet Occupation* (New York and London: Columbia University Press, 1974)

Kunert, Günter, 'Zu Besuch in der Vergangenheit: Wie Brecht einmal von der Volkspolizei eine Anzeige bekam', *Neue Rundschau*, 1 (1996), 140–59

Laufer, Jochen, 'Die UdSSR, die SED und die deutsche Frage', *Deutschland Archiv*, 26 (1993), 1201–04

Lemke, Michael, 'Wer demontierte das zweite Gleis? Zum Realitätsgehalt der Wiedervereinigungskonzeptionen von Bundesregierung und Führung der DDR', *asien, afrika, lateinamerika*, 19 (1991), 623–41

Lewin, Moshe, *The Making of the Soviet System: Essays in the Social History of Interwar Russia* (London: Methuen, 1985)

Lewin, Moshe, 'Byurokratiya i stalinizm', *Voprosi istorii*, 3 (1995), 16–28

Linz, Susan J., *The Impact of World War II on the Soviet Union* (Totowa, NJ: Rowman & Allanheld, 1985)

Lippmann, Heinz, *Honecker: Porträt eines Nachfolgers* (Cologne: Verlag Wissenschaft und Politik, 1971)

Loth, Wilfried, 'Die Historiker und die deutsche Frage', *Historisches Jahrbuch*, 122 (1992), 336–82

Loth, Wilfried (ed.), *Die deutsche Frage in der Nachkriegszeit* (Berlin: Akademie Verlag, 1994)

Loth, Wilfried, *Stalins ungeliebtes Kind: Warum Moskau die DDR nicht wollte* (Berlin: Rowohlt, 1994)

Loth, Wilfried, 'Stalin, die deutsche Frage und die DDR: Eine Antwort auf meine Kritiker', *Deutschland Archiv*, 28 (1995), 290–98

Loth, Wilfried, 'Kritik ohne Grundlagen: Erwiderung auf Gerhard Wettig', *Deutschland Archiv*, 28 (1995), 749–50

Lucchesi, Joachim (ed.), *Das Verhör in der Oper: Die Debatte um die Aufführung "Das Verhör des Lukullus" von Bertolt Brecht und Paul Dessau* (Berlin: BasisDruck Verlag, 1993)

Lukács, Georg, *Geschichte und Klassenbewußtsein: Studien über marxistische Dialektik* (Berlin: Malik-Verlag, 1923)

Marsh, Rosalind, *History and Literature in Contemporary Russia* (London: Macmillan, 1995)

Maslov, N. N., 'Short Course of the History of the All-Russian Communist Party (Bolshevik): An Encyclopedia of Stalin's Personality Cult', *Soviet Studies in History*, 28 (1989/1990), 41–66

Mastny, Vojtech, *Russia's Road to the Cold War: Diplomacy, Warfare and the Politics of Communism 1941–1945* (New York: Columbia University Press, 1979)

Mayer, Hans (ed.), *Über Peter Huchel* (Frankfurt a. M.: Suhrkamp, 1973)

Mayer, Hans, *Der Turm von Babel: Erinnerungen an eine Deutsche Demokratische Republik* (Frankfurt a. M.: Suhrkamp, 1991)

Mayer, Hans, *Wendezeiten: Über Deutsche und Deutschland* (Frankfurt a.M.: Suhrkamp, 1995)

Mayer, Hans, *Brecht* (Frankfurt a. M.: Suhrkamp, 1996)

McCagg, W. O. Jr., 'Domestic Politics and Soviet Foreign Policy at the Cominform Conference in 1947', *Slavic and Soviet Studies*, 12 (1977), 3–31

McCauley, Martin, *Marxism-Leninism in the German Democratic Republic* (London: Macmillan, 1979)

Meiklejohn Terry, Sarah (ed.), *Soviet Policy in Eastern Europe* (New Haven and London: Yale University Press, 1984)

Meissner, Boris (ed.), *Das Ostpakt-System* (Frankfurt a. M. and Berlin: Alfred Metzner, 1955)

Melnikov, Daniil E., 'Illusionen oder eine verpaßte Chance? Zur sowjetischen Deutschland-politik 1945–1952', *Osteuropa*, 41 (1991), 593–601

Meuschel, Sigrid, *Legitimation und Parteiherrschaft* (Frankfurt a. M.: Suhrkamp, 1992)

Meyer-Landrut, Nikolaus, *Frankreich und die deutsche Einheit: Die Haltung der französichen Regierung und der Öffentlichkeit zu den Stalin-Noten 1952* (Munich: Oldenbourg, 1988)

Mittenzwei, Werner, *Das Leben des Bertolt Brecht*, 2 vols (Frankfurt a. M.: Suhrkamp, 1989)

Mohr, Heinrich, 'Der 17. Juni als Thema der Literatur in der DDR', in *17. Juni 1953: Arbeiteraufstand in der DDR*, ed. by Ilse Spittmann and Karl-Wilhelm Fricke, 2nd edn. (Cologne: Edition Deutschland Archiv, 1988), pp. 87–111

Molotov, Vyacheslav M., *Sto sorok besed s Molotovym: Iz dnevnika F. Chueva* (Moscow: Terra, 1991)

Müller, Heiner, *Ich bin ein Neger: Diskussion mit Heiner Müller* (Darmstadt: Verlag der Georg Büchner Buchhandlung, 1986)

Müller, Heiner, 'Was wird aus dem größeren Deutschland?', *Sinn und Form*, 42 (1991), 666–69

Müller-Enbergs, Helmut, *Der Fall Rudolf Herrnstadt: Tauwetterpolitik vor dem 17. Juni* (Berlin: LinksDruck Verlag, 1991)

Münz-Koenen, Ingeborg (Leiterin des Autorenkollektivs), *Literarisches Leben in der DDR 1945 bis 1960* (Berlin: Akademie Verlag, 1980)

Naimark, Norman, Bernd Bonwetsch and Gennadii Bordyugov, *SVAG: Upravlenie propagandy (informatsii) i S. I. Tyul'panov 1945–1949: Sbornik dokumentov* (Moscow: Rossiya Molodaya, 1994)

Naimark, Norman, *The Russians in Germany: A History of the Soviet Zone of Occupation 1945–1949* (Cambridge, Mass. and London: Belknap Press of Harvard University, 1995)

Nolte, Ernst, *Deutschland und der Kalte Krieg* (Munich: R. Piper & Co., 1974)

Nove, Alec (ed.), *The Stalin Phenomenon* (London: Weidenfeld & Nicolson, 1993)

Otto, Wilfriede, 'Dokumente zur Auseinandersetzung in der SED 1953', *Beiträge zur Geschichte der Arbeiterbewegung*, 32 (1990), 655–72

Otto, Wilfriede, 'Sowjetische Deutschlandnote 1952: Stalin und die DDR: Bisher unver-öffentlichte handschriftliche Notizen Wilhelm Piecks', *Beiträge zur Geschichte der Arbeiterbewegung*, 33 (1991), 374–89

Otto, Wilfriede, 'Sowjetische Deutschlandpolitik 1952/53: Forschungs- und Wahrheitsprobleme', *Deutschland Archiv*, 26 (1993), 948–54

Parker, Stephen, 'Collected–Recollected–Uncollected: Peter Huchel's *Gesammelte Werke*', *German Life and Letters*, 40 (1986), 49–70

Parker, Stephen, 'Peter Huchel und "Sinn und Form"', *Sinn und Form*, 43 (1992), 724–38

Parker, Stephen, 'Der Fall von Peter Huchel und "Sinn und Form": Dokumente', *Sinn und Form*, 43 (1992), 739–822

Parker, Stephen, '"Sinn und Form": Peter Huchel und der 17. Juni 1953: Bertolt Brechts Rettungsaktion', *Sinn und Form*, 45 (1994), 738–51

Pike, David, *German Writers in Soviet Exile 1933–1945* (Chapel Hill: University of N. Carolina Press, 1982)

Pike, David, *Lukács and Brecht* (Tübingen: Max Niemeyer, 1986)

Pike, David, *The Politics of Culture in Soviet-Occupied Germany 1945–1949* (Stanford: Stanford University Press, 1992)

Procacci, Giuliano (ed.), *The Cominform. Minutes of the Three Conferences 1947/1948/1949* (Milan: Fondazione Giangiacomo Feltrinelli, 1994)

Protokoll des III. Parteitages der Sozialistischen Einheitspartei Deutschlands, 2 vols (Berlin: Dietz, 1951)

Ra'anan, Gavriel, *International Policy Formation in the USSR: Factional 'Debates' during the Zhdanovshchina* (Hamden, Conn.: Archon, 1983)

Raddatz, Fritz, *Traditionen und Tendenzen: Materialien zur Literatur der DDR* (Frankfurt a. M.: Suhrkamp, 1972)

Radzinsky, Edvard, *Stalin* (London: Hodder and Stoughton, 1996)

Reichman, Henry, 'Reconsidering "Stalinism"', *Theory and Society*, 17 (1988), 57–90

Reising, Russell, 'Lionel Trilling, *The Liberal Imagination*, and the Emergence of the Cultural Discourse of Anti-Stalinism', *boundary 2*, 20 (1993), 94–124

Rittersporn, Gábor, 'Rethinking Stalinism', *Russian History*, 11 (1984), 343–61

Rittersporn, Gábor, *Stalinist Simplifications and Soviet Complications: Social Tensions and Political Conflicts in the USSR 1933–1953* (Reading: Harwood, 1991)

Rohrwasser, Michael, *Der Stalinismus und die Renegaten: Die Literatur der Exkommunisten* (Stuttgart: Metzler, 1991)

Rupieper, Hermann-Josef, 'Zu den Sowjetischen Deutschlandnoten 1952: Das Gespräch Stalin–Nenni', *Vierteljahrshefte für Zeitgeschichte*, 33 (1985), 547–57

Rüther, Günther, *Kulturbetrieb und Literatur in der DDR* (Cologne: Verlag Wissenschaft und Politik, 1987)

Ryan-Hayes, Karen, *Contemporary Russian Satire: A Genre Study* (Cambridge: Cambridge University Press, 1995)

Sahl, Hans, *Memoiren eines Moralisten: Erinnerungen* (Zurich: Amman, 1983)

Scammell, Michael (ed.), *The Solzhenitsyn Files* (Chicago: edition q inc., 1995)

Schapiro, Leonard, *The Communist Party of the Soviet Union* (London: Methuen, 1970)

Schenk, Fritz, *Im Vorzimmer der Diktatur: Zwölf Jahre Pankow* (Cologne and Berlin: Kiepen-heuer & Witsch, 1962)

Scherstjanoi, Elke and Christian Stappenbeck, '"Dibelius war in Karlshorst ... wollte Mittelsmann sein zwischen SKK und Adenauer": Ein geheimes Gespräch zwischen Bischof Dibelius, Armeegeneral Tschujkow und

Politberater Semjonow im November 1951', *Deutschland Archiv*, 28 (1995), 1031–47

Scherstjanoi, Elke, '"Wollen wir den Sozialismus?" Dokumente aus der Sitzung des Polit-büros des ZK der SED am 6. Juni 1953', *Beiträge zur Geschichte der Arbeiterbewegung*, 33 (1991), 650–80

Scherstjanoi, Elke (ed.), *"Provisorium für längstens ein Jahr": Die Gründung der DDR* (Berlin: Aufbau, 1993)

Schlosser, Horst Dieter, *Die deutsche Sprache in der DDR zwischen Stalinismus und Demokratie: Historische, politische und kommunikative Bedingungen* (Cologne: Verlag Wissenschaft und Politik, 1991)

Schönhaven, Klaus and Dietrich Staritz (eds), *Sozialismus und Kommunismus im Wandel: Hermann Weber zum 65. Geburtstag* (Cologne: Bund Verlag, 1993)

Schoor, Uwe, *Das geheime Journal der Nation* (Berlin: Peter Lang, 1992)

Schubbe, Elimar, *Dokumente zur Kunst-, Literatur-, und Kulturpolitik der SED* (Stuttgart: Seewald, 1972)

Semjonow, Wladimir, *Von Stalin bis Gorbatschow: Ein halbes Jahrhundert in diplomatischer Mission 1939–1991* (Berlin: Nikolaische Verlags-buchhandlung, 1995)

Shdanow, Andrej, *Über Kunst und Wissenschaft* (Berlin: Dietz, 1951)

Shepherd, David, 'Canon Fodder? Problems in the Reading of a Soviet Production Novel', in *Discontinuous Discourses in Modern Russian Literature*, ed. by Catriona Kelly, Michael Makin and David Shepherd (London: Macmillan, 1989), pp. 39–59

Shepherd, David, *Beyond Metafiction: Self-Consciousness in Soviet Literature* (Oxford: Clarendon Press, 1992)

Solzhenitsyn, Aleksandr, *Sobranie sochinenii*, 17 vols (Paris and Vermont: YMCA Press, 1988)

Sperber, Manès, *Essays zur täglichen Weltgeschichte* (Vienna: Europa Verlag, 1981)

Spittmann, Ilse and Karl-Wilhelm Fricke (eds), *17. Juni 1953: Arbeiteraufstand in der DDR*, 2nd edn. (Cologne: Edition Deutschland Archiv, 1988)

Spriano, Paolo, *Stalin and the European Communists*, trans. by Jon Rothschild (London: Verso, 1985)

Stalin, Iosif, *Sochineniya*, 3 vols (Stanford: Stanford University Press, 1967)

Staritz, Dietrich, 'Ein "besonderer deutscher weg" zum Sozialismus?', *Aus Politik und Zeitgeschichte*, B 51–52/82 (25 December 1982), 15–31

Staritz, Dietrich, *Geschichte der DDR 1949–1985* (Frankfurt a. M.: Suhrkamp, 1985)

Staritz, Dietrich, 'Zwischen Ostintegration und nationaler Verpflichtung: Zur Ost- und Deutschlandpolitik der SED 1948 bis 1952', in *Westdeutschland 1945–1955: Unterwerfung, Kontrolle, Integration*, ed. by Ludolf Herbst (Munich: Oldenbourg, 1986), pp. 279–89

Staritz, Dietrich, *Die Gründung der DDR: Von der sowjetischen Besatzungsherrschaft zum sozialistischen Staat*, 2nd edn. (Munich: dtv, 1987)

Staritz, Dietrich, 'Auf der Suche nach der verlorenen Zeit: Die DDR-Historiographie in der "DDR" nach der "Wende"', *Beiträge zur Geschichte der Arbeiterbewegung*, 32 (1990), 759–61

Staritz, Dietrich, 'Die SED, Stalin, und der "Aufbau des Sozialismus" in der DDR: Aus den Akten des Zentralen Parteiarchivs', *Deutschland Archiv*, 24 (1991), 686–700

Staritz, Dietrich, 'Die SED, Stalin und die Gründung der DDR: Aus den Akten des Zentralen Parteiarchivs', *Aus Politik und Zeitgeschichte*, B 5/91 (25 January 1991), 3–16

Staritz, Dietrich, 'The SED, Stalin and the German Question: Interests and Decision-Making in the Light of New Sources', *German History*, 10 (1992), 274–89

Steininger, Rolf, 'Zur Geschichte der Münchener Ministerpräsidentenkonferenz 1947', *Vierteljahrshefte für Zeitgeschichte*, 23 (1975), 375–453

Steininger, Rolf, 'Wie die Teilung Deutschlands verhindert werden sollte: Der Robertson-Plan aus dem Jahre 1948', *Militärgeschichtliche Mitteilungen*, 33 (1983), 49–89

Steininger, Rolf, *Eine vertane Chance: Die Stalin-Note vom 10. März 1952 und die Wiedervereinigung* (Berlin: J. H. W. Dietz Nachf., 1986)

Steininger, Rolf, '"Dieser Vorfall bedeutet die Spaltung Deutschlands": Neue Dokumente zur Münchener Ministerpräsidentenkonferenz im Juni 1947', *Geschichte im Westen*, 7 (1992), 213–30

Stöckigt, Rolf, 'Direktiven aus Moskau: Sowjetische Einflußnahme auf DDR-Politik 1952/53', in *Brüche–Krisen–Wendepunkte: Neubefragung von DDR-Geschichte*, ed. by Jochen Černý (Leipzig: Urania-Verlag, 1990), pp. 81–88

Stöckigt, Rolf, 'Ein Dokument von großer historischer Bedeutung vom Mai 1953', *Beiträge zur Geschichte der Arbeiterbewegung*, 5 (1990), 648–50

Stulz-Herrnstadt, Nadja, *Das Herrnstadt-Dokument: Das Politbüro der SED und die Geschichte des 17. Juni 1953* (Reinbek: Rowohlt, 1990)

Thurston, Robert, *Life and Terror in Stalin's Russia 1934–1941* (New Haven: Yale University Press, 1996)

Tischler, Carola, *Flucht in die Verfolgung: Deutsche Emigranten im sowjetischen Exil 1933–1945* (Münster: LIT, 1996)

Torpey, John, *Intellectuals, Socialism and Dissent: The East German Opposition and its Legacy* (Minneapolis: University of Minnesota Press, 1995)

Tschubarjan, Alexander O., 'Auf dem Weg nach Europa—aus Moskauer Sicht', in *Der lange Weg nach Europa*, ed. by Wolfgang J. Mommsen (Berlin: Peter Lang, 1992), pp. 267–302.

Uhlmann, Petra and Sabine Wolf (eds), *'Die Regierung ruft die Künstler':
Dokumente zur Gründung der 'Deutschen Akademie der Künste'* (Berlin: Akademie der Künste, 1993)

Varga, Eugen, *Izmeneniya v kapitalisticheskoi ekonomike v itoge vtoroi mirovoi voiny* (Moscow: Gospolitizdat, 1946)

Vieregg, Axel (ed.), *Peter Huchel* (Frankfurt a. M.: Suhrkamp, 1986)

Viëtor-Engländer, Deborah, *Faust in der DDR* (Frankfurt a. M.: Peter Lang, 1987)

Vinke, Hermann (ed.), *Akteneinsicht: Christa Wolf: Zerrspiegel und Dialog: Eine Dokumentation* (Hamburg: Luchterhand, 1993)

Volkogonov, Dmitri, *Triumf i tragediya: I. V. Stalin, politicheskii portret* (Moscow: Agenstvo pechati Novosti, 1989)

Voßke, Heinz and Gerhard Nitzsche, *Wilhelm Pieck: Biographischer Abriß* (Berlin: Dietz, 1975)

Wacket, Markus, '"Wir sprechen zur Zone": Die politischen Sendungen des RIAS in der Vorgeschichte der Juni-Erhebung 1953', *Deutschland Archiv*, 26 (1993), 1035–48

Weber, Hermann, *Geschichte der DDR* (Munich: Oldenbourg, 1985)

Weber, Hermann (ed.), *DDR: Dokumente zur Geschichte der Deutschen Demokratischen Republik 1945–1986* (Munich: Oldenbourg, 1986)

Weber, Hermann, *Die DDR 1945–1986* (Munich: Oldenbourg, 1988)

Weber, Hermann, 'Die DDR-Geschichtswissenschaften im Umbruch? Die Aufgabe der Historiker bei der Bewältigung der stalinistischen Vergangenheit', *Deutschland Archiv*, 23 (1990), 1058–60

Weber, Hermann, *Aufbau und Fall einer Diktatur: Kritische Beiträge zur Geschichte der DDR* (Cologne: Bund Verlag, 1991)

Wettig, Gerhard, 'Sowjetische Wiedervereinigungsbemühungen im ausgehenden Frühjahr 1953? Neue Aufschlüsse über ein altes Problem', *Deutschland Archiv*, 25 (1992), 943–58

Wettig, Gerhard, 'Die Deutschland-Note vom 10.März auf der Basis diplomatischer Akten des russischen Außenministeriums: Die Hypothese des Wiedervereinigungsangebots', *Deutschland Archiv*, 26 (1993), 786–805

Wettig, Gerhard, 'Neue Erkenntnisse über Berijas Deutschland-Politik', *Deutschland Archiv*, 26 (1993), 1412–13

Wettig, Gerhard, 'Nochmals: Berijas Deutschland-Politik', *Deutschland Archiv*, 26 (1993), 1089–93

Wettig, Gerhard, 'Zum Stand der Forschung über Berijas Deutschland-Politik im Frühjahr 1953', *Deutschland Archiv*, 26 (1993), 674–82

Wettig, Gerhard, 'Übereinstimmung und Auseinandersetzung über die sowjetische Deutschlandpolitik im Frühjahr 1952', *Deutschland Archiv*, 26 (1993), 1205–10

Wettig, Gerhard, 'Die KPD als Instrument der sowjetischen Deutschland-Politik: Festlegungen 1949 und Implementierungen 1952', *Deutschland Archiv*, 27 (1994), 816–29

Wettig, Gerhard, 'Allzu schnell abgewehrte Kritik: Erwiderung auf Wilfried Loth', *Deutschland Archiv*, 28 (1995), 973

Wettig, Gerhard, 'Die beginnende Umorientierung der sowjetischen Deutschland-Politik im Frühjahr und Sommer 1953', *Deutschland Archiv*, 28 (1995), 495–507

Wettig, Gerhard, 'Stalin: Patriot und Demokrat für Deutschland?', *Deutschland Archiv*, 28 (1995), 743–48

Wilke, Manfred, '"Es wird zwei Deutschlands geben": Entscheidungen über die Zusammen-setzung der Kader: Eine Niederschrift Piecks über ein Treffen Stalins mit der KP-Führung', *Frankfurter Allgemeine Zeitung*, 30 March 1991

Wilson, Elisabeth, *Shostakovich: A Life Remembered* (London: Faber & Faber, 1994)

Žižek, Slavoj, *The Sublime Object of Ideology* (London: Verso, 1989)

Žižek, Slavoj (ed.), *Mapping Ideology* (London: Verso, 1994)

Zhukov, Yurii, 'Bor'ba za vlast' v rukovodstve SSSR v 1945–1952 godakh', *Voprosy istorii*, 1 (1995), 23–39

INDEX